PENGUIN BOOKS

THE PENGUIN BOOK OF LIES

Philip Kerr was born in Edinburgh in 1956 and now lives in London. As a freelance journalist he has written for a number of newspapers and magazines, including the *Sunday Times*. He is the author of the novels *March Violets*, *The Pale Criminal* and *A German Requiem* (also published by Penguin in one volume as *Berlin Noir*). He is also the author of *A Philosophical Investigation*, *Dead Meat* and *Gridiron*, and has edited *The Penguin Book of Lies* and *The Penguin Book of Fights, Feuds and Heartfelt Hatreds*.

THE PENGUIN BOOK OF LIES

EDITED BY PHILIP KERR

PENGUIN BOOKS

PENGUIN BOOKS

Published by the Penguin Group
Penguin Books Ltd, 27 Wrights Lane, London W8 5TZ, England
Penguin Books USA Inc., 375 Hudson Street, New York, New York 10014, USA
Penguin Books Australia Ltd, Ringwood, Victoria, Australia
Penguin Books Canada Ltd, 10 Alcorn Avenue, Toronto, Ontario, Canada M4V 3B2
Penguin Books (NZ) Ltd, 182–190 Wairau Road, Auckland 10, New Zealand

Penguin Books Ltd, Registered Offices: Harmondsworth, Middlesex, England

First published in Great Britain by Viking 1990
First published in the USA by Viking 1990
Published simultaneously in Canada
Published in Penguin Books 1991
5 7 9 10 8 6 4

The acknowledgements on pp. 540–43 constitute an extension of this copyright page

Printed in England by Clays Ltd, St Ives plc

Magnanimous lie! and when was truth so beautiful that it could be preferred to thee?

Tasso, *Jerusalem Delivered*

O, what a goodly outside falsehood hath!

Shakespeare, *The Merchant of Venice*

It is an art to have so much judgement as to apparel a lie well, to give it a good dressing.

Ben Jonson, *Explorata: Mali Choragi Fuere*

Contents

Introduction

The Gospel according to St John records the following exchange between Jesus and Pontius Pilate: 'Pilate therefore said unto him, Art thou a king then? Jesus answered, Thou sayest that I am a king. To this end was I born, and for this cause came I into the world, that I should bear witness unto the truth. Every one that is of the truth heareth my voice.' Francis Bacon takes up the story in his essay 'Of Truth': 'What is truth? said jesting Pilate, and would not stay for an answer.'

But can you really blame him? The trouble is that attempting to find out what truth actually amounts to is, as Bacon admits, 'a matter of difficulty and labour'. In the circumstances in which the Roman procurator – in all likelihood, a cynical imperialist – found himself, as the governor of a rather uninteresting and troublesome province of religious fanatics on the fringes of the Roman Empire, truth must have looked even more tenuous. Probably it was a hot day, and the prospect of a long philosophical debate on the nature of truth was considerably less attractive to Pilate than a cool bath.

The fact is that 'What is truth?' is simply not a very interesting way of initiating debate of a complex metaphysical question. It promises very little in the way of the intellectual satisfaction that might attend the metaphysical debating of the question that is phrased 'What is a lie?'. Truth is perceived to be something more elusive and inhuman, whereas the lie is all too human. The love of truth may indeed have its reward in heaven, but lies, as Nietzsche said, are 'necessary to life', and that they should be so is 'part and parcel of the terrible and questionable character of existence'.

If that were all it was then a lie would indeed be little more than an unfortunate necessity of life, like having to shave, and had Nietzsche been neither German nor syphilitic, unsuccessful nor finally insane, he might have realized that lying is not just one of the terrible necessities of life, but that it is also one of life's most enjoyable pleasures.

You need only imagine two dinner tables, one attended by the great men of truth such as Augustine, Knox, Wesley, Kant, Hume and Bentham, and the other attended by such liars and tellers of tall stories as Machiavelli, Casanova, Rousseau, Napoleon, Oscar Wilde and Ernest Hemingway, to appreciate just how entertaining lying can be, especially when compared with the truth.

But the fact that there exists a greater fascination with and enjoyment of the lie is more easily demonstrated, for would you honestly have purchased a book entitled 'The Penguin Book of Truth'? I think not. 'Lord, Lord,' says Falstaff, 'how this world is given to lying.' Aye, given over and bound tight, for without the lie mankind would die of boredom, a thought echoed by H. L. Mencken: 'Without the ameliorations that it offers life would become a mere syllogism, and hence too metallic to be borne.' For do we not admire the plausible lie in much the same way as we admire a great card-trick, or a well-told story – a good portion of which, according to Erasmus, 'consists in knowing how to lie'. It is part of that very same appreciation for lying that makes as many successful liars as there are, something which was recognized by Robert Browning's Mr Sludge, the Medium: 'There's a real love of a lie, Liars find ready-made for lies they make, As hand for glove, or tongue for sugar-plum.'

Oscar Wilde had no doubt of the great worth of the world's first liar, he 'who first, without having gone out to the rude chase, told the wandering cavemen at sunset how he had . . . slain the Mammoth in single combat': it was he, said Wilde, who was 'the true founder of social intercourse' and 'the very basis of civilized society'. George Steiner paints a similarly quaint anthropological picture of the origin of liars. The capacity for lying, for 'alternity', is, he says, 'the greatest of man's tools by far. With this stick he has reached out of the cage of instinct to touch the boundaries of the universe and time.' And Karl Popper has suggested that 'the moment when a man invented a story, a myth in order to excuse a mistake he had made – perhaps in giving a danger signal when there was no occasion for it; . . . the evolution of specifically human language, with its characteristic means of expressing negation – of saying that something signalled is not true – stems very largely from the discovery of systematic means to *negate* a false report, for example a false alarm, and from the closely related discovery of false stories – lies – used either as excuses or playfully'.

Popper's view of the origin of liars would seem to be strongly supported by Chomsky's belief that we are genetically pre-programmed to master the use of language. Chomsky holds that language grows in an infant's mind just as it has grown arms and legs while still in its mother's womb. Inherent in that growth of the language function must be the capacity for lying. Indeed, says Popper, lying 'has made the human language what it is: an instrument which can be used for misreporting almost as well as for reporting'.

It seems unlikely that man learned to speak *before* he learned to lie, but rather that he learned to lie *at the same time* as he learned to speak. Thus the capacity for lying is essential to the speech function. Just try imagining the man who had no capacity to lie: one might just as well say that a man was dumb and could not speak at all.

That lying is instinctive rather than learned may be perceived in the early speech of children, for whom there only ever exists the vaguest dividing line between true and false reporting. Truth is a moral concept that has to be taught.

My own early childhood memories certainly bear this out. The first lie I can remember telling was pure instinct – as much a matter of attention-seeking fantasy as it was of cruelty. At the age of five I maintained to my hated schoolteacher Miss McKendrick, who had slapped my face for the heinous offence of pencilling a full-stop that was 'as big as a football', the lie that my mother had recently given birth to my second sister. In fact this child who was named Fiona, had died in infancy several years before. For many weeks afterwards Miss McKendrick, an ageing spinster – I seem to think that I sensed a greater vulnerability there concerning the subject of babies, even other people's – regularly inquired after the health of the baby, and I answered that Fiona was doing very well; and then one day when she asked, I answered with cool negligence, 'Her? Oh, she died . . . ages ago.' I still remember the look of shock and horror that creased my teacher's features. Probably she thought I was certifiable. Doubtless I had told many lies before that – but there are none that I remember quite as vividly.

Certainly I have told a good many since – after all, there are so many lies that one can tell. As that great liar Mark Twain himself admitted, 'there are 869 different forms of lying, but only one of them has been squarely forbidden. Thou shalt not bear false witness against thy neighbor.' As a schoolboy I took this to heart, and my heroes and champions were the great dissemblers. While my friends fenced with imaginary swords and upheld the honour of the King's Musketeers, I was alone in venerating the person of the Cardinals Richelieu and Mazarin, having postcards of their portraits pinned to the inside of my desk-lid. Not only that, but from the age of eleven until I went to university Machiavelli's classic of *realpolitik*, *The Prince*, remained by my bedside.

I read Law, the only possible course of study for one who is possessed, as I was, in Sheridan's phrase, of 'a heart for falsehood framed'. Those who doubt the truth of this proposition need only look to the great number of politicians who are qualified lawyers.

Yet it was to a job in advertising that I went from university, an equivocating trade if ever there was one. Advertising is about selective truth, for no lie is so reckless as to be without some sort of proof. If I may enlist the help of W. S. Gilbert, advertising is 'merely corroborative detail intended to give artistic verisimilitude to a bald and unconvincing narrative'. So it was that I spent the next few years of my life, writing nonsense to the effect that freeze-dried coffee tastes as good as ground (it doesn't) and that a certain airline is the world's favourite (when did they ask it?). Advertising is full of people who will 'lie as fast as a dog will lick a dish', but conforming as it does to a few half-baked notions as to what may and may not fairly be said, the equivocations of this loathsome trade are really only half-way to lying, and that is its problem: to be neither wholly honest, nor completely mendacious, is to make the advertising business worthy of the condemnation of both honest men and professional liars such as myself.

Now I find myself working in another field in which many lies are told – the newspaper business. Left to its own devices by *laissez-faire* governments in both Britain and America, the press is seen to be in a pretty parlous state, and it is generally accepted that its worst excesses urgently need to be curbed. Thomas Jefferson's low opinion of the press could equally apply today: 'The man who never looks into a newspaper is better informed than he who reads them; inasmuch as he who knows nothing is nearer to the truth than he whose mind is filled with falsehood and errors.'

As well as a freelance journalist, I am also a novelist, a teller of stories and creator of fictions, which is perhaps the safest profession for a liar. There are some, however, who would even have disapproved of that. Edmund Gosse relates how, brought up in a strict Plymouth Brethren home, his mother held such a devout abhorrence of lying and such a reverence for the truth that even harmless fairy stories were forbidden him as a child. This is a terrible fate, for 'to so gentle lies, pardon is due. A lie, well told, to some taste is restoritie; besides, we poets lie by good authoritie.' As to what that authority is, I'm not sure, and here what remains in me of the lawyer would suggest that the principle of Precedent ought to be sufficient.

There will be some who will rightly remark upon the number of careers that I have pursued. To this I would answer that it is one of the identifying characteristics of the liar and fraudster to have tried his hand at many different trades, and I mention them in this introduction if only to demonstrate my temperamental qualifications for editing a book of lies.

This book is, however, more than just a few collected *fleurs du mal*. There has been so much written on 'what is a lie', by most of the world's greatest men of thought, that I felt that this could only have been properly called *The Penguin Book of Lies* if something of that writing on lying were to be included. Thus lies have been historically juxtaposed with contemporary thought on lying. It is for this reason that I have avoided defining exactly what a lie is – not to mention the fact that I should be attempting to do, in a matter of a few pages, that to which others before me have devoted whole books. But there is also a moral corollary that must attend any attempt at a proper definition, and this would surely be to colour what is after all supposed to be a type of historical record.

Over the twenty-five centuries or so that this book spans, opinions on lying have necessarily changed. For example, the question of whether every lie is a mortal sin. Augustine, writing towards the end of the fourth century after Christ, thought every lie *was* a mortal sin; Aquinas, writing some eight centuries later, thought that only malicious lies were mortal sins, and that pious frauds – or white lies as we call them now – were not; and five hundred years after Aquinas, opinion had changed again, with John Wesley holding that all lies were 'an abomination to the God of Truth'. Today, theologians of almost every denomination agree that it is perfectly acceptable to tell lies in order to prevent a greater evil.

Whatever our moral judgement of lies and lying, it does seem to be a subject that we find more fascinating now than at any other time in the history of the world. I think that this is largely due to the fact that it has never been more difficult for those that govern us to lie and remain undetected, thanks to the revolution in media: almost their every word is recorded or videotaped, and this means that it is no longer easy to claim that one has been misquoted.

A celebrated instance of governmental mendacity was not only one that was reported by television, but one in which television found itself playing a central role, with a President of the United States appearing on it before the American people and lying not once, but dozens of times. More than any other event in history, the Watergate affair proved to people everywhere, not that their government was capable of telling lies – Nixon was always distrusted, yet still managed to get himself elected – but that it was capable of *getting caught*.

Government today is even more likely to be caught lying. The difference is that people seem less inclined to do anything about it. The fact is that since Watergate there have been other instances of governmental mendacity that were every bit as criminal: for example, the Westland affair in Britain, and the Iran–Contra affair in the USA. But somehow the discovery that a President or a Prime Minister has tried to lie his or her way out of a situation seems to be less of a big deal than it was before. Perhaps people lack the will to make it so. Whereas before we expected politicians to lie, and to resign if they were caught, today we expect them to lie just as much, and then we excuse them for it because of who and what they are, and because of the great responsibility that we have heaped on to them. We seem to want to excuse them just as we would want to be excused ourselves.

Ethics, honesty and truth are no longer perceived to be of such fundamental importance in public life because they are not perceived to be of much importance in private life either. Our sensitivity to lying has decreased in inverse proportion to our greater greed and selfishness, because that's the kind of society we have. It may even be the kind that we want.

In all walks of life we are exposed to lies to a degree unparalleled in our history. Millions of people watch television shows like 'Dallas' and 'Dynasty', whose families would rival the Borgias with their lying. Our best-selling newspapers – the *Sun* and the *National Inquirer* – have made a cult not just of the tall story (this would be forgivable if it were merely lying for lying's sake), but of the lie that is intended to sell more newspapers. The proliferation of electronic media means that not only politicians, but advertisers are able to lie to more of us, more powerfully than ever before. Even in my own field, that of books, the last three decades have seen the publication of hundreds of the kind of sensationalist book that alleges the lying conspiracies of one institution or another. In a sense *The Penguin Book of Lies* is also very much a book of its time. Today lying seems to have attained, if not responsibility, then some kind of acceptability. It is clear that we don't just get the government we deserve, but the culture too. 'Mendacity is a system that we live in,' wrote Tennessee Williams. 'Liquor is one way out an' death's the other.'

I have not included the many lies that have been repeated in poetry and prose. There is enough lying in real life without having to take account of the fictitious lie as well. Even while I was writing this introduction, the government of the People's Republic of China were issuing their mendacious version of the massacre of students in Tiananmen Square, Peking. As Edmund Burke said, 'Falsehood has a perennial spring.'

In the course of putting together this book I have regularly requested 'lies' from friends and acquaintances, and I hope that they will accept my general and heartfelt thanks for their invaluable suggestions. I must, however, single out Jane Thynne for her constructive criticism and, at all times, her patience. In truth, I would have found my way darker without her.

London P.K.
August 1989

A hairy lie

THE BIBLE: GENESIS

And it came to pass, that when Isaac was old, and his eyes were dim, so that he could not see, he called Esau his eldest son, and said unto him, My son: and he said unto him, Behold, here am I.

And he said, Behold now, I am old, I know not the day of my death.

Now therefore take, I pray thee, thy weapons, thy quiver and thy bow, and go out to the field, and take me some venison;

And make me savoury meat, such as I love, and bring it to me, that I may eat; that my soul may bless thee before I die.

And Rebekah heard when Isaac spake to Esau his son. And Esau went to the field to hunt for venison, and to bring it.

And Rebekah spake unto Jacob her son, saying, Behold, I heard thy father speak unto Esau thy brother, saying,

Bring me venison, and make me savoury meat, that I may eat, and bless thee before the LORD before my death.

Now therefore, my son, obey my voice according to that which I command thee.

Go now to the flock, and fetch me from hence two good kids of the goats; and I will make them savoury meat for thy father, such as he loveth:

And thou shalt bring it to thy father, that he may eat, and that he may bless thee before his death.

And Jacob said to Rebekah his mother, Behold, Esau my brother is a hairy man, and I am a smooth man:

My father peradventure will feel me, and I shall seem to him as a deceiver; and I shall bring a curse upon me, and not a blessing.

And his mother said unto him, Upon me be thy curse, my son: only obey my voice and go fetch me them.

And he went, and fetched, and brought them to his mother: and his mother made savoury meat, such as his father loved.

And Rebekah took goodly raiment of her eldest son Esau, which were with her in the house, and put them upon Jacob her younger son:

And she put the skins of the kids of the goats upon his hands, and upon the smooth of his neck:

And she gave the savoury meat and the bread, which she had prepared, into the hand of her son Jacob.

And he came unto his father, and said, My father: and he said, Here am I; who art thou, my son?

And Jacob said unto his father, I am Esau thy first-born; I have done according as thou badest me: arise, I pray thee, sit and eat of my venison, that thy soul may bless me.

And Isaac said unto his son, How is it that thou hast found it so quickly, my son? And he said, Because the LORD thy God brought it to me.

And Isaac said unto Jacob, Come near, I pray thee, that I may feel thee, my son, whether thou be my very son Esau or not.

And Jacob went near unto Isaac his father; and he felt him, and said, The voice is Jacob's voice, but the hands are the hands of Esau.

And he discerned him not, because his hands were hairy, as his brother Esau's hands: so he blessed him.

And he said, Art thou my very son Esau? And he said, I am.

And he said, Bring it near to me, and I will eat of my son's venison, that my soul may bless thee. And he brought it near to him, and he did eat: and he brought him wine, and he drank.

And his father Isaac said unto him, Come near now, and kiss me, my son.

And he came near, and kissed him: and he smelled the smell of his raiment, and blessed him, and said, See, the smell of my son is as the smell of a field which the LORD hath blessed:

Therefore God gives thee of the dew of heaven, and the fatness of the earth, and plenty of corn and wine:

Let people serve thee, and nations bow down to thee: be lord over thy brethren, and let thy mother's sons bow down to thee: cursed be every one that curseth thee, and blessed be he that blesseth thee.

•

Samson lies to Delilah concerning the secret of his strength

THE BIBLE: JUDGES

And it came to pass afterward, that he loved a woman in the valley of Sorek, whose name was Delilah.

And the lords of the Philistines came up unto her, and said unto her, Entice him, and see wherein his great strength lieth, and by what means we may prevail against him, that we may bind him to afflict him: and we will give thee, every one of us, eleven hundred pieces of silver.

And Delilah said to Samson, Tell me, I pray thee, wherein thy great strength lieth, and wherewith thou mightest be bound to afflict thee.

And Samson said unto her, If they bind me with seven green withs that were never dried, then shall I be weak, and be as another man.

Then the lords of the Philistines brought up to her seven green withs which had not been dried, and she bound him with them.

Now there were men lying in wait, abiding with her in the chamber. And she said unto him, The Philistines be upon thee, Samson. And he brake the withs, as a thread of tow is broken when it toucheth the fire: so his strength was not known.

And Delilah said unto Samson, Behold, thou hast mocked me, and told me lies; now tell me, I pray thee, wherewith thou mightest be bound.

And he said unto her, If they bind me fast with new ropes that never were occupied, then shall I be weak, and be as another man.

Delilah took therefore new ropes, and bound him therewith, and said unto him, The Philistines be upon thee, Samson. And there were liers in wait abiding in the chamber. And he brake them off his arms like a thread.

And Delilah said unto Samson, Hitherto thou hast mocked me, and told me lies: tell me wherewith thou mightest be bound. And he said unto her, If thou weavest the seven locks of my head with the web.

And she fastened it with the pin, and said unto him, The Philistines be upon thee, Samson. And he awaked out of his sleep, and went away with the pin of the beam, and with the web.

And she said unto him, How canst thou say, I love thee, when thine heart is not with me? thou hast mocked me these three times, and hast not told me wherein thy great strength lieth.

And it came to pass, when she pressed him daily with her words, and urged him, so that his soul was vexed unto death,

That he told her all his heart, and said unto her, There hath not come a razor upon mine head; for I have been a Nazarite unto God from my mother's womb: if I be shaven, then my strength will go from me, and I shall become weak, and be like any other man.

And when Delilah saw that he had told her all his heart, she sent and called for the lords of the Philistines, saying, Come up this once, for he hath showed me all his heart. Then the lords of the Philistines came up unto her, and brought money in their hand.

And she made him sleep upon her knees; and she called for a man, and she caused him to shave off the seven locks of his head; and she began to afflict him, and his strength went from him.

And she said, The Philistines be upon thee, Samson. And he awoke out of his sleep, and said, I will go out as at other times before, and shake myself. And he wist not that the LORD was departed from him.

But the Philistines took him, and put out his eyes, and brought him down to Gaza, and bound him with fetters of brass; and he did grind in the prison house.

•

The father of lies

HERODOTUS

Herodotus has been called by Cicero 'the Father of History', and his *Histories* is almost certainly the first great prose work in European literature. Many ancient references, including Thucydides, brand him a liar, and this belief has persisted into modern times: it was Oscar Wilde who dubbed Herodotus 'the Father of Lies'. To be fair, Herodotus was often doing no more than preserving stories that were told in his times, and to that extent we ought to be grateful to him for their preservation. The story of the gold-digging ant is, however, a really tall story that is repeated as fact, and as such may be included here.

There are other Indians further north, round the city of Caspatyrus and in the country of Pactyica, who in their mode of life resemble the Bactrians. They are the most warlike of the Indian tribes, and it is they who go out to fetch the gold – for in this region there is a sandy desert. There is found in this desert a kind of ant of great size – bigger than a fox, though not as big as a dog. Some specimens, which were caught there, are kept at the palace of the Persian king. These creatures as they burrow underground throw up the sand in heaps, just as our own ants throw up the earth, and they are very like ours in shape. The sand has a rich content of gold, and this it is that the Indians are after when they make their expeditions into the desert.

•

Tissaphernes' treachery

XENOPHON

Sparta had sent an army of mercenaries to assist the young prince Cyrus, brother of Artaxerxes, King of Persia, in an attempt to take the throne for himself. But Cyrus was defeated at the battle of Cunaxa, not far from Babylon, and the Spartans – the Ten Thousand – with Cyrus dead, half their leaders arrested, and a thousand miles from home, were given the choice of submitting to the King or marching home, with all its attendant risks. They chose the latter course, and with Xenophon the Athenian in charge, succeeded in reaching home. Tissaphernes was one of the commanders of the Persian King's army, and had established a truce with Clearchus, the most prominent Spartan general. Xenophon relates how his lying treachery cost Clearchus and four other Spartan generals their lives. With each side believing that the other was about to break the truce, Clearchus met Tissaphernes and told him of his intention to keep to the truce, to which Tissaphernes made the following reply:

'I am really delighted, Clearchus, to hear your sensible speech. With the sentiments which you have, it seems to me that, if you were to contemplate doing me an injury, you would be simultaneously plotting against your own interests. But, now, you must listen in your turn so that you may be convinced that you, too, would be wrong in entertaining any lack of confidence either in the King or in me.

'If we really wanted to destroy you, do you think we are short in numbers of cavalry or infantry or in the right sort of equipment with which to be able to damage you, while incurring no risk of retaliation? Or do you think it likely that we could not find favourable ground on which to attack you? Remember all the flat country which you go through with great difficulty even when the inhabitants are friendly to you. Consider all the mountains you have to cross which we could occupy first and make impassable for you. Think of all the rivers where we could cut you into detachments and engage with as many at a time as we liked ... With all these means of making war on you at our disposal, and with none of them entailing any risk on us, how can you imagine that out of them all we should choose the one method which involves wickedness in the sight of the gods and shame in the eyes of men? It is simply and solely among people who are without means and desperate and without any other way out (and even then they must be villains) that you will find men willing to secure their ends by perjury to the gods and faithlessness to men. It is not so with us Clearchus. We are not such blockheads and simpletons.

'You may ask why, since we have the power to destroy you, we have not proceeded to do so. Let me tell you that what is responsible for this is my own desire that I should earn the confidence of Greeks and that I should, by doing good to them, return to the coast with the support of that mercenary army on which Cyrus, in his journey inland, relied only because he gave them their pay. As to the ways in which your help is useful to me, you have mentioned some of them yourself. The most important of them, though, is one that I know of. I mean, that it is for the King alone to wear the crown upright on his head; but with your help, someone who is not the King might easily, perhaps, have the crown in his heart.'

Clearchus thought that in this he was speaking sincerely. 'Those people then,' he said, 'who try by their slanders to make us enemies, when we have all these reasons for friendship, – do they not deserve the worst that can happen to them?'

'Yes,' said Tissaphernes, 'and if you are prepared, generals and captains, to come to me, I will name openly those who told me that you were in a conspiracy against me and my army.'

'I will bring them all,' said Clearchus, 'and on my side will let you know where I get my information about you.'

After this conversation Tissaphernes behaved with great affection towards Clearchus, urged him to stay with him for the time being and had him as his guest at supper.

Next day, on his return to camp, Clearchus made it clear that he considered that he was on very good terms with Tissaphernes, and that those Greeks who were proved to have been spreading slanders should be punished as traitors and disaffected to the Greek cause. It was Menon whom he suspected of spreading the slanders, as he knew that he and Ariaeus had had an interview with Tissaphernes, and also that he was secretly forming a party of opposition against him with the idea of getting the whole army on to his side and becoming a friend of Tissaphernes. Clearchus wanted to have the loyalty of the whole army himself and to have grumblers put out of his way.

Some of the soldiers opposed Clearchus, saying that all the captains and generals ought not to go, and that they ought not to trust Tissaphernes; but Clearchus insisted strongly, until in the end he succeeded in getting five generals and twenty captains to go. About two hundred of the other soldiers went with them too, as though to buy provisions.

When they arrived at the entrance of Tissaphernes' tent, the generals were invited inside. They were Proxenus the Boetian, Menon the Thessalian, Agias the Arcadian, Clearchus the Spartan and Socrates the Achaean. The captains waited at the entrance. Not long afterwards, at one and the same signal, those who were inside were seized and those who were outside were massacred. After that contingents of native cavalry rode over the plain and killed all the Greeks they could find, slaves and free-men alike. The Greeks saw with surprise these cavalry manoeuvres from their camp and were in doubt about what they were doing until Niarchus the Arcadian escaped and came there with a wound in his stomach and holding his intestines in his hands. He told them everything which had happened.

•

Can the gods lie?

PLATO

The *Republic* is the best known of all the philosophical dialogues of Plato. In this extract, Socrates discourses with Plato's brother, Adeimantus, on the unsuitability for children of most of the stories in literature. They should 'stop mothers being misled by them and scaring their children with harmful myths by telling tales about a host of gods that prowl about at night in a strange variety of shapes'. Here Socrates argues against such tales because, he says, God is changeless and incapable of deceiving us, and should never be otherwise represented.

'Then if the gods are themselves incapable of change, will they deceive us and bewitch us into thinking that they appear in all sorts of disguises?'

'They might, I suppose.'

'Come,' said I, 'can god want to disguise himself and lie to us, either in word or action?'

'I don't know,' he replied.

'But,' I asked, 'don't you know that gods and men all detest true falsehood, if I may so describe it?'

'What do you mean?'

'I mean that no man wants to be deceived in the most important part of him and about the most important things; that is when he is most terrified of falsehood.'

'I still don't understand.'

'Because you think I'm talking about something mysterious,' I answered. 'But all I'm talking about is being deceived in one's own mind about realities, and so being the victim of falsehood and ignorance; that is where men are least ready to put up with the presence of falsehood and particularly detest it.'

'Yes, I agree with that.'

'But surely when a man is deceived in his own mind we can

fairly call his ignorance of the truth "true falsehood". For a false statement is merely some kind of representation of a state of mind, an expression consequent on it, and not the original unadulterated falsehood. Don't you agree?'

'Yes.'

'So real falsehood is detested by gods and men.'

'I agree.'

'But what about spoken falsehood? Is it not sometimes and on some occasions useful, and not then detestable? We can use it, for example, as a kind of preventative medicine against our enemies, or when anyone we call our friend tries to do something wrong from madness or folly. And we can make use of it in the myths we are engaged in discussing; we don't know the truth about the past but we can invent a fiction as like it as may be.'

'That's perfectly true.'

'In which of these ways is falsehood of use to god? Does he need to make up fictions because he does not know the past?'

'It would be absurd to suppose so.'

'So god is not the author of poetic fictions.'

'No.'

'Does he tell lies because he is afraid of his enemies, then?'

'Certainly not.'

'Or because of the folly or madness of any of his friends?'

'God loves neither the foolish nor the mad,' he replied.

'God has, then no reason to tell lies.'

'So we conclude that there is no falsehood at all in the realm of the spiritual and divine?'

'Most certainly.'

'God is therefore without deceit or falsehood in action or word, he does not change himself, nor deceive others, awake or dreaming, with visions or words or special signs.'

'I agree entirely with what you say.'

•

The noble lie

PLATO

In the *Republic*, Plato argues that the weakness of man is the reason why states are formed. This society should be an image of man himself. The state, therefore, must have its rulers, its philosophers, its guardians or auxiliaries, and its craftsmen. In this famous passage, fundamental to political philosophy, Plato argues the case for 'the noble lie' – the lie that may be told to people in order to convince them of the case for class distinction, and thereby preserve social harmony.

How then may we devise one of those needful falsehoods of which we lately spoke – just one royal lie which may deceive the rulers, if that be possible, and at any rate the rest of the city?

What sort of lie? he said.

Nothing new, I replied; only an old Phoenician tale of what has often occurred before now in other places (as the poets say, and have made the world believe) though not in our time, and I do not know whether such an event could ever happen again, or could now even be made probable, if it did.

How your words seem to hesitate on your lips!

You will not wonder, I replied, at my hesitation when you have heard.

Speak, he said, and fear not.

Well, then, I will speak, although I really know not how to look you in the face, or in what words to utter the audacious fiction, which I propose to communicate gradually, first to the rulers, then to the soldiers, and lastly to the people. They are to be told that their youth was a dream, and the education and training which they received from us, an appearance only; in reality during all that time they were being formed and fed in the womb of the earth, where they themselves and their arms and appurtenances were manufactured; when they were completed, the earth, their mother, sent them up; and so, their country being their mother and also their nurse, they are bound to advise for her good, and to defend her against attacks, and her citizens they are to regard as children of the earth and their own brothers.

You had good reason, he said, to be ashamed of the lie which you were going to tell.

True, I replied, but there is more coming; I have only told you half. Citizens, we shall say to them in our tale, you are brothers, yet God has framed you differently. Some of you have the power of command, and in the composition of these he has mingled gold, wherefore also they have the greatest honour; others he has made of silver, to be auxiliaries; others again who are to be husbandmen and craftsmen he has composed of brass and iron; and the species will generally be preserved in the children. But as all are of the same original stock, a golden parent will sometimes have a silver son, or a silver parent a golden son. And God proclaims as a first principle to the rulers, and above all else, that there is nothing which they should so anxiously guard; or of which they are to be such good guardians, as of the purity of the race. They should observe what elements mingle in their offspring; for if the son of a golden or silver parent has an admixture of brass and iron, then nature orders a transposition of ranks, and the eye of the ruler must not be pitiful towards the child because he has to descend in the scale and become a husbandman or artisan, just as there may be sons of artisans who having an admixture of gold or silver in them are raised to honour, and become guardians or auxiliaries. For an oracle says that when a man of brass or iron guards the State, it will be destroyed. Such is the tale; is there any possibility of making our citizens believe in it?

Not in the present generation, he replied; there is no way of accomplishing this; but their sons may be made to believe in the tale, and their sons' sons, and posterity after them.

I see the difficulty, I replied; yet the fostering of such a belief will make them care more for the city and for one another. Enough, however, of the fiction which may now fly abroad upon the wings of rumour, while we arm our earth-born heroes, and lead them forth under the command of their rulers.

•

Social qualities concerned with truth and falsehood

ARISTOTLE

We have spoken . . . of those who cause pain and pleasure by their social relations with others. Let us now deal similarly with those who exhibit truth and falsehood in their speech and actions, i.e. in their pretensions. Well, the boaster is regarded as one who pretends to have distinguished qualities which he possesses either not at all or to a lesser degree than he pretends. The ironical man conversely is thought to disclaim qualities that he does possess, or to depreciate them; while the one who is intermediate between these two is a sort of individualist, sincere both in his daily life and in his speech, acknowledging the qualities that he possesses and neither exaggerating nor depreciating them. All these three types may perform their several actions either with or without an ulterior object; but in the latter case each of them speaks and acts and lives in accordance with his character. Falsehood is in itself bad and reprehensible, while the truth is a fine and praiseworthy thing; accordingly the sincere man, who holds the mean position, is praiseworthy, while both the deceivers are to be censured, particularly the boaster.

•

How Crassus and his army succumbed to Arab lies

PLUTARCH

Marcus Crassus (112–53 B.C.) was one of the great generals during the period of the collapse of the Roman Republic, and is chiefly remembered for his suppression of the revolt of the gladiators. Having been proclaimed second consul, Crassus took command of the Syrian army and prepared to make war on the Parthians. After crossing the Euphrates, Crassus and his officers, Octavius and Cassius, were discussing how they might attack King Hyrodes and his army when an Arab chieftain called Ariamnes put in an appearance.

This Ariamnes was a sly treacherous character; indeed he played the greatest and most decisive part in all that combination of evil which fortune had designed for the destruction of the Romans. Some of the soldiers who had served in the east with Pompey knew that he had benefited from Pompey's kindness and that he was supposed to be pro-Roman. In fact he was acting in collusion with the King's generals and was trying to worm his way into the confidence of Crassus with the idea of getting him to turn away as far as possible from the river and the foothills and to bring him down into the wide open plain where he could be surrounded. For the Parthians had not the least intention of engaging the Romans face to face in regular battle.

This native, then, who also had the gift of speaking plausibly, came to Crassus. He began by expressing his admiration for his benefactor Pompey, and by congratulating Crassus on his own army. He criticized him, however, for wasting so much time in making his preparations; what Crassus needed, he said, was not a great weight of armament but quick hands and very quick feet to catch up with an enemy who, for some time now, had been trying to get together all their most valuable property and slaves and to fly with them into the depths of Scythia or Hyrcania. 'And yet,' he said, 'if you do intend to fight, you ought to do so quickly before all the King's forces are concentrated into one place and the King gets back his courage. At the moment there are just advance guards under Surena and Sullaces put there to check your pursuit, while the King himself has simply disappeared.'

The whole of this story was untrue. In fact Hyrodes had at

once divided his army into two parts. He himself with one part was now devastating Armenia to punish Artavasdes and he had sent Surena with the other part against the Romans . . . Cassius once again strongly disapproved. Seeing that his attitude only annoyed Crassus, he gave up trying to advise him. But he took the native chieftain aside and spoke to him without mincing his words. 'What evil spirit brought you to us, you villain?' he said. 'What drugs and sorceries have you been using to persuade Crassus to pour his army into a great yawning wilderness and to follow a route that is better fitted for a captain of Arabian robbers than for a Roman imperator?' The native, however, was full of cunning. Putting on the most humble air, he tried to encourage them and begged them to endure a little longer. He would run along beside the soldiers, helping them with their tasks, laughing and making jokes. 'Do you think that you are marching through Campania?' he would say. 'Are you longing for the fountains and streams there, and the shady places, yes, and the baths and the taverns? Oh, no, you must remember that the country you are going through is the border land between Assyria and Arabia.' So the native managed the Romans as if they were children, and rode off himself before his treachery was discovered. He went with the full knowledge of Crassus. In fact he actually persuaded Crassus that he was going to work in his interests by sowing confusion in the minds of the enemy.

We rejoin the story after half the Roman army had been destroyed by the Arab general Surena, and Crassus and what remained of his command had taken refuge on a hill.

Surena now saw that his own men were becoming less eager to press their attacks home. He realized that, if night came on and the Romans succeeded in getting to the mountains, they would be entirely beyond his reach. So he resorted to deception. He set free some of his prisoners who, while in his camp, had heard deliberately framed conversations among the natives to the effect that the King had no wish to be involved in an irreconcilable struggle with the Romans and that what he wanted to do was to regain their friendship by going out of his way to treat Crassus kindly. After this the natives stopped fighting and Surena, with the chief men in his army, rode quietly up the hill. He unstrung his bow, held out his hand, and invited Crassus to come to an understanding. 'It was against the King's wishes,' he said, 'that we have been testing the courage and power of your soldiers. In reality he has no harsh feelings towards you and wants of his own accord to prove his friendship by offering you a truce if you will withdraw and by allowing you to go away in safety.'

The Roman soldiers were overjoyed at hearing these words from Surena and were eager to accept his offer. Crassus, however, was not impressed. Every defeat which he had suffered at the hands of the natives had been due to treachery, and this sudden change in their attitude did not seem to him to make sense. He therefore wished to reflect on the matter. But the soldiers kept on shouting and urging him to accept; then they began to abuse him, and say what a cowardly thing it was for him to force them to fight in battle with an enemy whom he himself was afraid to meet even for the purpose of conversation and when they had no arms in their hands. At first Crassus tried entreaties. If only, he said, they would hold out for what was left of the day, they could reach the mountains and the rough country during the night; he pointed out the way to them and begged them not to give up hope when they were so close to safety. But the soldiers were infuriated with him; they began to clash their shields together and to threaten him. Crassus was terrified and began to go towards Surena. As he went, he turned round and spoke simply these words: 'Octavius and Petronius and all you other Roman officers present, you see that I am being forced to go this way. You are eye-witnesses of the shameful and violent treatment which I have received. But if you escape and get safely home tell them all there that Crassus died because he was deceived by the enemy, not because he was handed over to the enemy by his own countrymen.'

For once Crassus was right, and he and most of what remained of his army were massacred.

•

Sharp practice and the law

CICERO

Now law and philosophy have their different methods of combating sharp practice. The law attempts its conquest by forcible coercion, the philosophers by reasoning and logic, which, they argue, make any employment of deception, pretence or trickery out of the question. Well, surely setting traps comes under the heading of deception! – even if one does not intend to start the game or drive it into the traps; for whether someone is after the animals or not they often get caught in the traps all the same. Advertising a house for sale raises just the same point. Clearly you ought to make your advertisement into a trap which you hope will catch some victim unawares.

Nevertheless, the standards demanded by public opinion are not so high as they were, and I find that nowadays actions of this sort are not normally regarded as wrong, or penalized by statute or civil law. But what forbids them is the moral law which nature itself has ordained. As I have said before – and it needs constant repetition! – there is a bond of community that links every man in the world with every other. Though this bond is universal in application, it is particularly strong as a unifying link between people of the same race: between actual compatriots the link is closer still.

The existence of this natural bond of community between all human beings explains why our ancestors chose to make a distinction between the civil law of the land and the universal law. The law of the land, it is true, ought to be capable of inclusion within the universal law, but they are not synonymous since the latter is more comprehensive.

Not that we possess any clear-cut, tangible images to show us what true, authentic Law and Justice really look like! We only have outline sketches. And the extent to which we allow ourselves to be guided even by these leaves a great deal to be desired. For at least they have the merit of derivation from the finest models – those which have been vouchsafed to us by nature and by truth. Think of the nobility of that formula: that I be not deceived and defrauded because of you and because of trust in you. And that other golden phrase: between honest men there must be honest dealing and no deception.

But that still leaves big questions unanswered: who are the honest men? and what is honest dealing?

The chief priest Quintus Mucius Scaevola attributed special importance to all arbitration cases involving the expression in good faith. He attributed the widest possible validity to this formula, applying as it does to wardships, associations, trusts, commissions, buying and selling, hiring and letting: in fact, to all the transactions which make up our daily human relationships. According to Scaevola's view the assessment of one man's obligation to another in these spheres, with all the counter-claims that are frequently involved, demands a judge of outstanding calibre.

Sharp practice, then, must go. And so must every kind of trickery masquerading as intelligence, seeing that the two things are entirely different and remote from one another. The function of intelligence is to distinguish between good and bad; whereas trickery takes sides between them, actually preferring what is bad and wrong.

Real estate is not the only field in which our civil law, basing itself on the dictates of nature, penalizes trickery and deception. In the sale of slaves, for example, all deception on the part of the seller is again forbidden. For the aediles have ruled that if a man knows that a slave he is selling is unhealthy, or a runaway, or a thief, he must (unless the slave is one he has inherited) report accordingly.

This then is the conclusion to which we come. Nature is the source of law: and it is contrary to nature for one man to prey upon another's ignorance. So trickery disguised as intelligence is life's greatest scourge, being the cause of innumerable illusions of conflict between advantage and right. For extremely few people will refrain from doing a wrong action if they have the assurance that this will be both undiscovered and unpunished!

•

Throwing sand in the judge's eyes

CICERO

Despite his denunciation of sharp practice, as a practising lawyer Cicero was no stranger to dishonest advocacy. For example, it is almost certain that at the trial of his client Cluentius he was well aware that both sides in the case had bribed the court. Moreover Cicero himself was guilty of an inordinate amount of time-wasting. He won the case, and later on was reputed to have boasted in a private letter that he had thrown sand in the eyes of the judge. Here, in this extract from his treatise 'On Duties', we may see for ourselves just how cavalier was Cicero's attitude towards the truth where it affected the interests of his own client.

But there is no need, on the other hand, to have any scruples about occasionally defending a person who is guilty – provided that he is not really a depraved or wicked character. For popular sentiment requires this; it is sanctioned by custom, and conforms with human decency. The judges' business in every trial is to discover the truth. As for counsel, however, he may on occasion have to base his advocacy on points which look like the truth, even if they do not correspond with it exactly. But I must confess I should not have the nerve to be saying such things, especially in a philosophical treatise, unless Panaetius, the most authoritative of Stoics, had spoken to the same effect. The greatest renown, the profoundest gratitude, is won by speeches defending people. These considerations particularly apply when, as sometimes happens, the defendant is evidently the victim of oppression and persecution at the hands of some powerful and formidable personage. That is the sort of case I have often taken on.

•

Peter denies he knows Jesus

THE BIBLE: LUKE

Then they took him, and led him, and brought him into the high priest's house. And Peter followed afar off.

And when they had kindled a fire in the midst of the hall, and were set down together, Peter sat down among them.

But a certain maid beheld him as he sat by the fire, and earnestly looked upon him, and said, This man was also with him.

And he denied him, saying, Woman, I know him not.

And after a little while, another saw him, and said, Thou art also of them. And Peter said, Man, I am not.

And about the space of one hour after, another confidently affirmed, saying, Of a truth this fellow also was with him: for he is a Galilean.

And Peter said, Man, I know not what thou sayest. And immediately, while he yet spake, the cock crew.

And the Lord turned, and looked upon Peter. And Peter remembered the word of the Lord, how he had said unto him, Before the cock crow, thou shalt deny me thrice.

And Peter went out, and wept bitterly.

•

Nero clears himself of any involvement in his mother's death

TACITUS

Having concluded that his mother, Agrippina, was intolerable, the Emperor Nero ordered her murder. A scheme was put forward by Anicetus, an ex-slave who commanded the fleet at Misenum, whereby a ship which was to carry her would have a section that would come loose at sea, and in this way she would drown. But the plan failed when Agrippina swam to safety. Realizing that the only way to escape from the plot was to profess ignorance of it, she sent a messenger, Agerinus, to tell Nero that she had survived a serious accident without grave injury, and that he must not worry about her. Word of Agrippina's escape preceded her messenger, however, and fearful that she might now try and kill him, the Emperor sent Anicetus to kill her in a rather more straightforward fashion – with a sword. It only remained to find a scapegoat.

It was at this point that Agrippina's messenger arrived. When Nero was told, he took the initiative and staged a fictitious incrimination. While Agerinus delivered his message, Nero dropped a sword at the man's feet and had him arrested as if caught red-handed. Then he could pretend that his mother had plotted against the Emperor's life, been detected, and – in shame – had committed suicide. When news reached Nero that Agrippina was finally dead, he set about distancing himself from any attachment of blame.

Nero's insincerity took a different form. He adopted a gloomy demeanour, as though sorry to be safe and mourning for his parent's death. But the features of the countryside are less adaptable than those of men; and Nero's gaze could not escape the dreadful view of that sea and shore. Besides, the coast echoed (it was said) with trumpet blasts from the neighbouring hills – and wails from his mother's grave. So Nero departed to Neapolis.

He wrote the senate a letter. Its gist was that Agerinus, a confidential ex-slave of Agrippina, had been caught with a sword, about to murder him, and that she, conscious of her guilt as instigator of the crime, had paid the penalty. He added older charges. 'She had wanted to be co-ruler – to receive oaths of allegiance from the Guard, and to subject senate and public to the same humiliation. Disappointed of this, she had hated all of them – army, senate and people. She had opposed gratuities to soldiers and civilians alike. She had contrived the deaths of distinguished men.' Only with the utmost difficulty, added Nero, had he prevented her from breaking into the senate-house and delivering verdicts to foreign envoys. He also indirectly attacked Claudius' regime, blaming his mother for all its scandals. Her death, he said, was providential. And he even called the shipwreck a happy accident. For even the greatest fool could not believe it accidental – or imagine that one shipwrecked woman had sent a single armed man to break through the imperial guards and fleets. Here condemnation fell not on Nero, whose monstrous conduct beggared criticism, but on Seneca who had composed his self-incriminating speech.

•

The burning of Rome

TACITUS

It is uncertain whether the most terrible and destructive fire that Rome had ever experienced was accidental or caused by a criminal act on the part of Nero. After the gods had been appeased, the search for scapegoats began.

But neither human resources, nor imperial munificence, nor appeasement of the gods, eliminated sinister suspicions that the fire had been instigated. To suppress this rumour, Nero fabricated scapegoats – and punished with every refinement the notoriously depraved Christians (as they were popularly called). Their originator, Christ, had been executed in Tiberius' reign by the governor of Judaea, Pontius Pilate. But in spite of this temporary setback the deadly superstition had broken out afresh, not only in Judaea (where the mischief had started) but even in Rome. All degraded and shameful practices collect and flourish in the capital.

•

How the orator should employ a lie

QUINTILIAN

Quintilian was a Roman writer on rhetoric, and during the reign of the Emperor Domitian he was charged with the education of the Emperor's two great-nephews. It is with their training in eloquence that Quintilian concerns himself in his *Institutio Oratoria* – the most thorough treatment of an orator's education in classical literature. Here, Quintilian deals with how the orator may make the best use of falsehood.

Sometimes, too, we get a false statement of facts; these, as far as actual pleading is concerned, fall into two classes. In the first case the statement depends on external support; Publius Clodius, for instance, relied on his witnesses when he stated that he was at Interamna on the night when he committed abominable sacrilege at Rome. The other has to be supported by the speaker's native talent, and sometimes consists simply in an assumption of modesty, which is, I imagine, the reason why it is called a gloss, while at other times it will be concerned with the question at issue. Whichever of these two forms we employ, we must take care, first that our fiction is within the bounds of possibility, secondly that it is consistent with the persons, dates, and places involved, and thirdly that it presents a character and sequence that are not beyond belief: if possible, it should be connected with something that is admittedly true and should be supported by some argument that forms part of the actual case. For if we draw our fictions entirely from circumstances lying outside the case, the liberty which we have taken in resorting to falsehood will stand revealed. Above all we must see that we do not contradict ourselves, a slip which is far from rare on the part of spinners of fiction: for some things may put a most favourable complexion on portions of our case, and yet fail to agree as a whole. Further, what we say must not be at variance with the admitted truth. Even in the schools, if we desire a gloss, we must not look for it outside the facts laid down by our theme. In either case the orator should bear clearly in mind throughout his whole speech what the fiction is to which he has committed himself, since we are apt to forget our falsehoods, and there is no doubt about the truth of the proverb that a liar should have a good memory. But whereas, if the question turns on some act of our own, we must make one statement and stick to it, if it turns on an act committed by others, we may cast suspicion on a number of different points. In certain controversial themes of the schools, however, in which it is assumed that we have put a question and received no reply, we are at liberty to enumerate all the possible answers that might have been given. But we must remember only to invent such things as cannot be checked by evidence: I refer to occasions when we make our own minds speak (and we are the only persons who are in their secret) or put words in the mouth of the dead (for what they say is not liable to contradiction) or again in the mouth of someone whose interests are identical with ours (for he will not contradict), or finally in the mouth of our opponent (for he will not be believed if he does deny).

•

The first thing we should learn

EPICTETUS

Epictetus was a Stoic, and the *Encheiridion*, from which the following extract is taken, was one of the principal manuals of Stoic philosophy.

The science of philosophy is divided into three parts: the utility and importance of the principles established; the proofs or demonstrations by which these are sustained; and the organization or arrangement of the various parts which constitute such proofs and demonstrations. The most essential part of this division, and that to which our attention should be especially directed, is the utility and importance of the principles; because it is on the knowledge and practice of these our present and future felicity depends. But, yet, what perversity marks our career! We devote almost all our attention to the last-mentioned part, that is, the technical arrangement of the constituent points of proofs and arguments; while with a reckless indifference we pass the others by. Thus it happens that, while we are ever ready with technical arguments to prove the impropriety of speaking falsehoods, our tongues never cease to usher forth misrepresentations and lies. The first thing we should learn, is not to lie: to prove that it behoveth us not to lie, is a mere auxiliary branch of knowledge.

•

Eight kinds of lie

ST AUGUSTINE

The first type of lie is a deadly one which should be avoided and shunned from afar, namely, that which is uttered in the teaching of religion, and to the telling of which no one should be led under any condition.

The second is that which injures somebody unjustly: such as a lie as helps no one and harms someone.

The third is that which is beneficial to one person while it harms another, although the harm does not produce physical defilement.

The fourth is the lie which is told solely for the pleasure of lying and deceiving, that is, the real lie.

The fifth type is that which is told from a desire to please others in smooth discourse.

When these have been avoided and rejected, a sixth kind of lie follows which harms no one and benefits some person, as, for instance, when a person, knowing that another's money is to be taken away unjustly, answers the questioner untruthfully and says that he does not know where the money is.

The seventh type is that which is harmful to no one and beneficial to some person, with the exception of the case where a judge is questioning, as happens when a person lies because he is unwilling to betray a man sought for capital punishment, that is, not only a just and innocent person but even a criminal, because it belongs to Christian discipline never to despair of the conversion of anybody and never to block the opportunity for repentance. Now, I have spoken at length concerning these last two types, which are wont to evoke considerable discussion, and I have presented my opinion, namely, that by the acceptance of sufferings which are borne honourably and courageously, these lies, too, may be avoided by strong, faithful, and truthful men and women.

The eighth is that type of lie which is harmful to no one and beneficial to the extent that it protects someone from physical defilement, at least, from that defilement which we have mentioned above. Now, the Jews considered it a defilement to eat with unwashed hands. If anyone considers that as defilement, then a lie must not be told in order to avoid it. However, we are confronted with a new problem if a lie is such that it brings injury to any person, even though it protects another person from that defilement which all men detest and abhor. Should such a lie be told if the injury resulting from it is not in the nature of the defilement of which we have been treating? The question here does not concern lying; rather it is whether harm should be done to any person, not necessarily through a lie, so that such defilement may be warded off from another person. I am definitely inclined to oppose such licence.

•

A letter to Consentius

ST AUGUSTINE

Towards the end of the fourth century, the Christian Church executed Priscillian, Bishop of Avila, as a heretic, being the first person so to die. As a result of his death, Priscillian's followers were obliged to continue their heretical practices in secret, while at the same time observing the prevailing form of Christian worship. Consentius saw himself as a follower of the true Catholic Church, and sought to infiltrate the Priscillian movement and reveal their mendacity. Despite his anti-heretical zeal to uncover the enemies of the Church, however, he had doubts as to the ethics of the deception that achieving this result would have entailed. He wrote to Augustine for his advice on whether or not it was morally justifiable to lie in unmasking those who themselves lied about their beliefs. Here is part of Augustine's reply.

I am delighted with your eloquence, with your memory of sacred Scripture, with your adroitness of mind, with your distress in stinging indifferent Catholics, with your zeal in raging against even latent heretics. But I am not persuaded that they should be drawn out of hiding by our lies. For, why do we try with so much care to track them and hunt them down? Is it not so that, when they have been caught and brought into the open, we may either teach them the truth themselves or else, by convicting them of error, keep them from harming others? Is it not, in short, so that their falsehood may be blotted out or guarded against and God's truth be increased? Therefore, how can I suitably proceed against lies by lying? Or should robbery be proceeded against by means of robbery, sacrilege by sacrilege, and adultery by adultery? 'But if through my lie the truth of God has abounded,' are we, too, going to say, 'Why should we not do evil that good may come from it?' You see how much the Apostle detests this. But what is it to say: 'Let us lie in order to bring lying heretics to the truth,' if not the same thing as saying, 'Why should we not do evil that good may come from it?' Or is lying sometimes a good, or sometimes not an evil? Why, then, has it been written: 'Thou hatest all the workers of iniquity: thou wilt destroy all that speak a lie'? He has not made exception of some or said indefinitely: 'Thou wilt destroy tellers of lies,' so as to allow that certain ones be understood, but not every one. But he has brought forth a universal proposition, saying: 'Thou wilt destroy all that speak a lie.' Or, because it has not been said: 'Thou wilt destroy all that speak any lie or that speak any lie whatsoever,' are we to think, therefore, that room has been made for a certain kind of lie and that God will not destroy those who tell a certain kind of lie, but only those who tell unjust lies, not any lie whatsoever, because there are found just lies, too, which ought actually to be matter for praise rather than reproach?

Do you not see how much this argument supports the very ones whom we are trying to catch as great quarry by our lies? That, as you yourself have shown, is precisely the opinion of the Priscillianists. To establish this opinion they produce evidence from Scripture, urging their followers to lie as if in accordance with the example of the Patriarchs, Prophets, Apostles, and angels, not hesitating to add Christ our Lord Himself, thinking that they cannot otherwise prove their falsehood to be true except by saying that the Truth is mendacious. They must be refuted, not imitated. We must not participate with the Priscillianists in that evil in which they are proved to be worse than all other heretics, for they alone, or at least they especially, in order to hide what they think is their truth, are found to give dogmatic sanction to lying. And this great evil they deem just, for they say that what is true must be kept in the heart, but that it is no sin to utter what is false with the tongue to strangers. They say that it has been written: 'He that speaketh truth in his heart,' as if that were sufficient for justice, even if one tells a lie with his tongue when a stranger and not a neighbour is listening. On this account they even think that the Apostle Paul, when he had said:

'Put away lying and speak truth,' at once added: 'each one with his neighbour, because we are members of one another,' so that it plainly might be lawful and dutiful to tell a lie to those who are not our neighbours in the community of truth and not, as it were, our co-members . . .

Because we are men and live among men, I confess that I am not yet in the number of those who are not troubled by compensatory sins. Often, in human affairs, human sympathy overcomes me and I am unable to resist when someone says to me: 'Look, here is a patient whose life is endangered by a serious illness and whose strength will not hold out any longer if he is told of the death of his dearly beloved only son. He asks you whether the boy is still alive whose life you know has ended. What will you answer when, if you say anything except "He is dead" or "He is alive" or "I don't know", the patient will believe that he is dead, because he realizes that you're afraid to say and do not want to lie? It will be the same no matter how hard you try to say nothing. Of the three convincing answers, two are false: "He is alive" and "I don't know", and you cannot utter them without lying. But, if you make the one true answer, namely that he is dead, and if the death of the anguished father follows hard upon it, people will say that he was slain by you. And who can bear to hear them exaggerate the evil of avoiding a beneficial lie and of loving homicide as truth?'

I am moved by these arguments – more powerfully than wisely! For, when I put before my mind's eye the intellectual beauty of Him from whose mouth nothing false proceeded, then, although my weakness reverberates in palpitation before the radiance of the truth shining ever more brightly, I am so inflamed by love of such great beauty that I despise all human considerations that call me back from there. It is hard for this feeling to persist so far that its effect is not lost in time of temptation. Indeed, when I am contemplating the luminous good on which there is cast no shadow of a lie, I am not moved by the fact that, when we are unwilling to lie and men die upon hearing what is true, truth is called homicide. Why, if a shameless woman expects to be defiled and then dies of her fierce love because you do not consent, will chastity also be called homicide? Or indeed, because we read: 'We are the fragrance of Christ for God, alike as regards those who are saved and those who are lost; to these an odour that leads to death, but to those an odour that leads to life,' shall we also pronounce the fragrance of Christ to be homicide? But, because we are men and because human sympathy generally overcomes or harasses us amid such questions and objections, therefore, he, too, added, And for such offices; who is sufficient?

Besides this there is the more distressing fact that, if we grant that we ought to lie about the son's life for the sake of that patient's health, little by little and bit by bit this evil will grow and by gradual accessions will slowly increase until it becomes such a mass of wicked lies that it will be utterly impossible to find any means of resisting such a plague grown to huge proportions through small additions. Hence, it has been most providentially written: 'He that contemneth small things, shall fall by little and little.' What of the fact that such lovers of this life as do not hesitate to prefer it to the truth want us not only to lie but also to perjure ourselves in order that a man may not die a little later? They would have us take the name of the Lord our God in vain in order that the vain health of man may not pass away a little sooner. And there are in these matters learned men who even make rules and set limits for when we ought and when we ought not to be perjured. O where are you, ye fountains of tears? And what shall we do? Where shall we go? Where shall we hide ourselves from the wrath of truth, if we not only disregard the avoidance of lies, but venture in addition to teach perjuries? Let the advocates and defenders of lies look to what kind or kinds of lying it pleases them to justify! Only in the worship of God may they grant that we must not lie; only from perjuries and blasphemies may they restrain themselves; only where God's name, God's testimony, God's oath is introduced, only where talk of divine religion is brought forth, may no one lie, or praise or teach or enjoin lying or say that lying is just. About other kinds of lies, let him who believes that we ought to lie choose for himself what he thinks is the mildest and most innocent kind of lying. This much I know, that even he who teaches that we ought to lie wants to appear to be teaching the truth. For, if what he teaches is false, who would want to study the false doctrine where the teacher deceives and the learner is deceived? But if, in order that he may be able to find some pupil, he declares that he is teaching the truth when he teaches that we ought to lie, how will that lie be of the truth, since John the Apostle protests that no lie is of the truth? Therefore, it is not true that sometimes we ought to lie. And what is not true we should never try to persuade anyone to believe.

•

When, according to the Talmud, a Jew may lie

LOUIS JACOBS

The Talmud is that collection of Jewish civil and religious law, religious and moral doctrine which is founded on Scripture. Completed in the fourth and fifth centuries A.D., it is the most important influence in Jewish life, after the Bible itself. Here, a leading Jewish scholar examines Talmudic law as it affects the telling of white lies.

Here is the place to consider the 'white lie': when the truth need not be told and where even a false statement is permissible. This subject is discussed in a famous passage in the Talmud. Here it is said that if a scholar claims that an article which has been found belongs to him it may be returned to him since pious scholars do not utter falsehoods. But, the Talmud goes on to say, there are three cases where even so pious a scholar is absolved from telling the truth. The three exceptions to the rule of truthfulness are given as 'tractate', 'bed' and 'hospitality'. 'Tractate' is explained by the commentaries to mean that if a scholar is asked if he is familiar with a certain portion of the Talmud he may, from modesty, untruthfully say that he is ignorant. An untruth is permitted if its aim is the avoidance of a parade of learning. 'Bed' is understood by Rashi to mean that if a scholar is asked questions concerning his marital relations he may give an untruthful answer. Other commentaries remark that it is unlikely that questions of this kind would be put to a scholar by his associates and understand 'bed' to mean that if a scholar had absented himself from the House of Study because he had not yet immersed himself in a ritual bath after marital relations (as was the custom in Talmudic times) he may give some other reason for his absence. According to both interpretations delicacy of feeling may prompt the telling of a 'white lie'. 'Hospitality' is understood to mean that a scholar who had been generously treated by his host may decide not to tell the truth about his reception if he fears that as a result the host may be embarrassed by unwelcome guests. In addition there is the general principle of the Talmud that where peace demands it a lie may be told.

The idea behind the above teaching is that though truth is important it must not be made into a fetish. Truth is a value which exists for the benefit of society and may, on occasion, be set aside if the well-being of society demands it. This idea appears to be behind the Midrashic teaching that when God was about to create man the angels formed themselves into two factions. Love said: 'Let him be created, for he will do works of love.' Truth said: 'Let him not be created, for he will practise deception.' Justice said: 'Let him be created, for he will do justice.' Peace said: 'Let him not be created, for he will be all controversy.' What did God do? He seized truth and hurled it to the earth! If absolute truth were always to prevail man could not endure, but the world cannot endure without truth. Consequently man must try to live by the truth but there are times when truth imperils man's existence and then truth must be cast to the earth.

•

Gullible Belisarius

PROCOPIUS

Procopius was a civil servant of the sixth century, who served Belisarius (first general to the Emperor Justinian), and finally the Emperor himself, as Prefect of the city of Byzantium. Here he describes how Belisarius's wife, Antonina, on one particular occasion lied brazenly to her gullible husband. Which only goes to show that liars succeed only where there are men who want to believe.

The household of Belisarius included a young Thracian of the name of Theodosius, who had been brought up in the belief called Eunomanianism.* On the eve of his voyage to Libya, Belisarius washed this youngster in the sacred bath, then lifted him out in his arms, thereby making him the adopted son of his wife and himself in accordance with the rules for adoption observed by Christians. From that moment Antonina, as was to be expected, loved Theodosius, since the sacred word had made him her son; and she watched over him with extreme care and kept him under her wing. Then a little while after she fell madly in love with him during this voyage, and surrendering herself body and soul to her passion threw off all fear and respect for the laws of God and men, and had intercourse with him, at first in secret but finally in the eyes of domestics of both sexes. For by now she was helpless against this desire and unmistakably the slave of her lust, so that she could no longer see any impediment to its indulgence. Once, in Carthage, Belisarius surprised them in the very act; yet he swallowed his wife's lying explanation open-mouthed. He had found them together in a basement room, and though he was mad with rage she did not flinch or disguise what she had done, but merely remarked, 'I came so that the young

*The heresy of Eunomius, a fourth-century bishop of Cyrus.

man could help me conceal the pick of the spoils here, in case the Emperor should get to know about them.' This of course was only an excuse, but he seemed satisfied and let the matter drop, though he saw that Theodosius had unfastened the belt holding up the trousers which covered his nakedness. For his passionate love for the woman compelled him to pretend that the evidence of his own eyes was utterly false.

•

A dissembling hypocrite

PROCOPIUS

Procopius describes the untruthful character of the Emperor Justinian, and provides an example of his dissembling hypocrisy.

He never spoke the truth himself to those he happened to be with, but in everything that he said or did there was always a dishonest purpose; yet to anyone who wanted to deceive him he was easy meat. He was by nature an extraordinary mixture of folly and wickedness inseparably blended. This perhaps was an instance of what one of the Peripatetic philosophers suggested many years ago – that exactly opposite qualities may on occasions be combined in a man's nature just as in the blending of colours. However, I must limit my description to facts of which I have been able to make sure.

Well, then, this Emperor was dissembling, crafty, hypocritical, secretive by temperament, two-faced; a clever fellow with a marvellous ability to conceal his real opinion, and able to shed tears, not from any joy or sorrow, but employing them artfully when required in accordance with the immediate need, lying all the time; not carelessly, however, but confirming his undertakings both with his signature and with the most fearsome oaths, even when dealing with his own subjects. But he promptly disregarded both agreements and solemn pledges, like the most contemptible slaves, who by fear of tortures hanging over them are driven to confess misdeeds they have denied on oath . . . I will show what a dissembling hypocrite he was. The Liberius whom I mentioned a few pages back was dismissed from the office which he held and replaced by an Egyptian, John Laxarion. When this became known to Pelagius, who was a very intimate friend of Liberius, he asked the Emperor whether the report concerning Laxarion was correct. Justinian flatly denied it, assuring him that he had done no such thing; and he handed him a letter to Liberius, instructing him to hold on to his office with might and main and in no circumstances to relinquish it: he had no intention of relieving him of it at that stage.

But John had an uncle in Byzantium called Eudaemon, who had attained the rank of consul and had made a great deal of money, becoming for a time controller of the Emperor's private property. When Eudaemon heard the story, he in turn asked the Emperor whether his nephew had been definitely appointed to the office. Justinian, denying all knowledge of the letter he had written to Liberius, wrote a letter to John instructing him to take possession of his office and to brook no interference: he himself had had no second thoughts about the matter. Taking these statements at their face value John ordered Liberius to vacate his official quarters, as he had been relieved of his post. Liberius emphatically refused to accept his orders, he too relying of course on the letter he had received from the Emperor. John then armed his followers and went for Liberius, and Liberius with his own supporters took steps to defend himself. A fight developed and many lost their lives, among them John himself, the new holder of the office.

After urgent representations from Eudaemon Liberius was instantly summoned to Byzantium, where the Senate, after making a thorough investigation of the case, acquitted him, as he had not been the aggressor but had been defending himself when this dreadful thing had happened. The Emperor, however, did not allow the matter to drop until he had secretly forced him to pay a heavy fine. Such was Justinian's notion of truth-telling and straightforwardness.

•

An Irish penitential

ANON.

If anyone utters [such] a falsehood deliberately, without doing harm, he spends three days in silence except for the appointed prayers or readings; or else he receives 700 blows of a lash on his hands and keeps a half-fast or recites the 150 psalms.

Anyone who utters a falsehood in words whereof good results, by giving a false description to a man's enemies, or by carrying pacific messages between disputants, or by anything that rescues a man from death, there is no heavy penance, provided it is done for God's sake.

•

Bumptious bishops

NOTKER THE STAMMERER

We have shown how, in his wisdom, Charlemagne exalted the humble. Let us now tell how he humbled the proud. There was a certain bishop who was vainglorious and greatly occupied with all manner of stupid things. Charlemagne was highly observant, and came to hear of this. He gave instructions to a Jewish merchant, who often visited the Holy Land and was in the habit of bringing home across the sea many rare and wonderful objects, that he was to cheat and deceive this bishop in any way he cared.

The Jew caught an ordinary house mouse. He stuffed it with various spices and then offered it for sale to the bishop, pretending that he had brought home from Judea a most costly creature never before seen by man. The bishop was overjoyed at such an opportunity and offered the Jew three pounds of silver in exchange for so remarkable a piece of merchandise. 'A fine price for such an unusual object!' exclaimed the Jew. 'I would rather throw it into the sea than let anyone acquire it at so cheap and shameful a price!' The bishop was rich, for he never gave anything to the poor and needy. He promised the Jew ten pounds, if he could have this incomparable oddity. The clever merchant pretended to lose his temper and replied: 'May the God of Abraham forbid that I should lose my labour in this way, and the cost of the transport, too!' The greedy bishop, his mouth agape with desire for the costly rarity, offered him twenty pounds. The Jew became angrier still. He wrapped the mouse in precious silk and prepared to leave. Then the bishop, deceived and indeed thoroughly open to deception, called him back and offered him a full measure of silver, if only he could have the priceless object. At long last the merchant yielded to his entreaties and gave in, although with much show of reluctance. He took the money which he had received to the Emperor and told him all that had happened.

A few days later the King called all the bishops and the chief men of that province to a council. Inevitably there was much preliminary discussion, after which he ordered all the silver to be produced and placed in the middle of his palace. He then spoke himself. 'Elders, stewards, bishops of our Church,' said he, 'it is your duty to minister to the poor, and not to waste your substance on stupid objects. Nowadays you act completely to the contrary; and even more than other mortals, you are guilty of luxury and covetousness.' Then he added: 'One of your number has given all this silver to a Jew in exchange for a painted mouse.' The bishop who had been so cruelly deceived ran forward and threw himself at the Emperor's feet, begging forgiveness for his sin. Charlemagne upbraided him as he deserved and then let him take himself off in confusion.

There was another bishop of a minute township who, while he still lived in the flesh, wanted to be worshipped with divine honour, instead of being considered merely as one who interceded with God, as were the apostles and martyrs. However, he was determined to conceal his arrogance, so that he could continue to be called a holy man of God, and not be execrated along with all the other idols worshipped by the people. Among his townfolk he had a certain retainer, not of low birth, but a man quick to act and full of energy. I will not say that this man did the bishop any particular favour, and he certainly did not fawn upon him when he spoke. In fact, he was not quite sure what to do to please his bishop, who was a harsh man. He decided that he might find favour in the bishop's eyes if he could prove that he had performed some miracle in his name. Whenever he set out from his home to visit the bishop, he led on a leash two little bitches, of the breed called *veltres* in French. In view of their speed these dogs could easily catch foxes and other small animals, and what is more they would often seize quails and other birds which flush quickly. One day, as he rode along, the man saw a fox sitting on one of the stone walls. Without a word he suddenly set his dogs after it. They rushed after the fox at full speed and came up with it in a single bow-shot. The man followed behind as fast as he could and wrested the fox alive and unharmed from the teeth and claws of the dogs. He tied the dogs in a suitable spot and hurried joyfully off to his master with his gift. He went to the bishop and said to him humbly: 'My Lord, just see what sort of gift I have been able to find for you.' The bishop laughed and asked him how he had been able to capture the fox without harming it. The man went closer to him, swore by his master's good health that he could not conceal the truth and then answered: 'My Lord, I was riding through the field back there. I saw this fox, which was quite close to me. Letting my reins fall loose, I began to ride after it. Then, when the fox was so far away that I could scarcely see it any more, I raised my hand and addressed it in these words: "In the name of my master Recho, be still and go no step farther." Lo and behold, the fox stood fast upon that spot, as if it had been chained to the ground, until I picked it up, just as if it were a lost sheep.' The bishop swelled up with empty pride and said in the hearing of all: 'Now my divinity is quite clear. Now I know who I am and now I recognize what I shall be.' From that day onwards he showed greater affection to this execrable man than to anyone else in his household.

•

An early smear campaign

WILLIAM OF MALMESBURY

Athelstan came to the English throne in A.D. 924. According to the chronicle of William of Malmesbury, Athelstan's accession was not without opposition, in the person of Elfred, who falsely accused Athelstan of being a bastard. That Elfred's accusation was false may be seen from the divine judgement which befell him.

In the year of our Lord's incarnation 924, Athelstan, the son of Edward, began to reign, and held the sovereignty sixteen years. His brother, Ethelward, dying a few days after his father, had been buried with him at Winchester. At this place, therefore, Athelstan, being elected king by the unanimous consent of the nobility, was crowned at a royal town, which is called Kingston; though one Elfred, whose death we shall hereafter relate in the words of the king, with his factious party, as sedition never wants adherents, attempted to prevent it. The ground of his opposition, as they affirm, was, that Athelstan was born of a concubine.

This place seems to require that I should relate the death of Elfred in the words of the king, for which I before pledged the faith of my narrative . . . 'Be it known to the sages of our kingdom, that I have not unjustly seized the lands aforesaid, or dedicated plunder to God; but that I have received them, as the English nobility, and even John, the pope of the church of Rome himself, have judged fitting on the death of Elfred. He was the jealous rival both of my happiness and my life, and consented to the wickedness of my enemies, who, on my father's decease, had not God in his mercy delivered me, wished to put out my eyes in the city of Winchester: wherefore, on the discovery of their infernal contrivances, he was sent to the church of Rome to defend himself by oath before pope John. This he did at the altar of St Peter; but at the very instant he had sworn he fell down before it, and was carried by his servants to the English School, where he died the third night after.

At the great assembly of Grately, King Athelstan made several new laws, not the least of which was his law against perjury: 'And he who swears a false oath, and it becomes known against him, is never afterwards to be entitled to an oath, nor is he to be buried in a consecrated cemetery when he dies, unless he has the witness of a bishop in whose diocese he is that he has done penance for it as his confessor has prescribed for him.'

•

How King Canute engineered the legality of his succession

FLORENCE OF WORCESTER

Like Edmund Ironside, the strongest enemy he had ever known, King Canute recognized that force was no real basis for governing Saxon England: that the best way was a properly observed social contract between a king and his subjects. It was a contract that Canute was determined to achieve, whatever the cost. After Edmund's death, Canute gave orders that all the nobles of the English people were to assemble at London.

When they had come before him, he, as if in ignorance, questioned shrewdly those who had been witnesses between him and Edmund when they had made the pact of friendship and the division of the kingdom between them, how he and Edmund had spoken together concerning the latter's brothers and sons; whether his brothers and sons should be allowed to reign after their father in the kingdom of the West Saxons, if Edmund were to die in Cnut's lifetime. And they said that they knew beyond doubt that King Edmund had entrusted no portion of his kingdom to his brothers, either in his life or at his death; and they said that they knew that Edmund wished Cnut to be the supporter and protector of his sons, until they were old enough to reign. In truth, God is to witness, they gave false testimony, and lied deceitfully, imagining that he would be more gracious to them because of their lying, and that they would receive a big reward from him. Some of these false witnesses were put to death not long afterward by that same king. Then after the above-mentioned inquiry, King Cnut tried to obtain from the aforesaid nobles oaths of fealty. And they swore to him that they would elect him as their king and humbly obey him, and make a payment to his army; and, accepting a pledge from his bare hand, along with oaths from the leading men of the Danes, they utterly renounced the brothers and sons of Edmund, and repudiated them as kings.

•

Byzantine lying

MICHAEL PSELLUS

Upon his becoming Emperor of the Eastern Roman or Byzantine Empire, Michael V (reigned 1041–2) – himself of low birth and formerly commander of the Empress's bodyguard – resolved to have the whole palace to himself. Thus he planned 'a foul lying story' to be rid of the dowager Empress Zoe, she who had adopted him as her own son and heir.

Certain charges were fabricated against his adopted mother, who was innocent of any plot aimed at himself, and the wretched boy condemned her as a poisoner. She, still knowing nothing of his machinations, was driven from her bedchamber – she who had been born there, driven out by a *parvenu*! She, the daughter of a most noble family, was dispossessed by a man sprung from the gutter. Witnesses were suborned to give false evidence and he proceeded to question her on matters of which she knew nothing. She was compelled to account for her actions and was then convicted of the most abominable crimes. At once she was put on board ship, together with certain persons who were given full liberty to insult her. Exiled from the palace, she was landed on one of the islands lying off Byzantium, called Prinkipo.

. . . Yet that rascal cherished even more terrible designs against her and trouble was heaped on trouble. In the end, a party was dispatched to cut off her hair – perhaps it would be more correct to say that they were sent to kill her. She was to be offered up so to speak, as a whole burnt-offering, not to please the Lord maybe, but certainly to appease the wrath of the emperor who gave this order. However, once the design was satisfactorily carried out, he left her alone. So far as he was concerned, the empress was already dead, but he gave a dramatic account of the whole affair to the Senate. It was like a scene from a play. Her so-called plots against himself were revealed, while he told them how for a long time past he had suspected her; worse than that, he had more than once caught her red-handed, but had concealed her misdoings out of respect for the Senators. After inventing such lies – sheer nonsense it was – and after winning their approval (they passed remarks suited to the occasion), he considered his defence before them was adequate, and next put his case to the people. Some of the latter were already quite prepared to dance to his tune, and to them he told his story. They gave him their verdict. There was obviously support for his policy in that quarter as well, so this second meeting was dismissed, and he, like a man who has accomplished some mighty exploit, took a rest from his great labours and gave himself up to childish delight, all but dancing and leaping from the ground in his pleasure. Yet retribution was near; the usurper's pride was to meet its downfall in the not distant future.

Michael was deposed not long afterwards. Zoe returned to the palace, and Michael's eyes were gouged from his head before he was sent to a monastery.

•

Harold Godwin swears fealty to Duke William of Normandy

E. A. FREEMAN

In the year 1064 Harold Godwin visited Normandy, probably in order to confirm King Edward the Confessor's promise of the English throne to Duke William. The historian E. A. Freeman examines the various versions of the story of the famous oath which Harold is reputed to have sworn and later broken, and judges their truthfulness.

The nature of the oath is as little certain as its time or place . . . nearly every account represents it as containing an engagement to marry one of William's daughters; some accounts seem to make that engagement and its breach the whole ground of the quarrel between the two Princes. Others add that Harold further engaged to give his sister in marriage to an unnamed Norman noble. Most accounts add also far more important political stipulations. Harold is to become the man of William; he is to receive him, on Edward's death, as his successor on the throne of England; meanwhile he is to be the guardian of William's interests in England, and to act in some sort as his lieutenant. He is at once to give up the castle of Dover, with its well, to the Duke, and to receive a Norman garrison in it; he is to build other castles at other points on English ground, where the Duke may think good, and there also he is to receive and maintain Norman garrisons. The highest place in William's favour, when he shall have attained the English Crown, honours, grants, even to the half of the Kingdom, are of course promised to Harold as the reward of faithfully carrying out all these promises.

To all this, or to some part of all this, we are told that Harold swore. He swore, it is said, after some form of more than usual solemnity, something beyond the ordinary oath of homage. He swore upon the relics of the saints. And one famous version of the tale represents this more solemn form of oath as something into which Harold was unwittingly trapped by a base trick on the part of William. It is not an English apologist of Harold, but a Norman admirer of William, who tells us how the Duke filled a chest with all the holiest relics of the saints of Normandy; how Harold swore on the chest, not knowing on what he swore; how William then drew away the covering with which the holy things had been hidden, and bade Harold see how fearful was the oath which he had taken, and how awful was the vengeance which would light on him who failed to keep it. His hand trembled and his flesh quivered when he laid his hand on the chest, while still unknowing of all that was in it; how much more frightened was he when he knew by how awful a sanction he had unwittingly bound his soul. This may be history or it may be legend; at any rate it is the honour of the Norman rather than that of the Englishman which is staked on truth or falsehood.

. . . I have told this famous tale in that one of the many shapes which it has taken which seems least widely removed from the probabilities of the case. It is at least not impossible, which is more than can be said of the other shapes. But I would not be understood as pledging myself to the accuracy of a single detail. The charge of perjury against Harold is a charge in which there is no statement for the defence, while the witnesses for the prosecution contradict one other. To my own mind, as I have said before, the strongest argument against Harold is that there is no statement for the defence. Had there been a single distinct English contradiction of the story, direct or implied, I should have cast away the whole tale as pure invention. But, while we have such contradictions on almost every other point, on this point we have none. It was clearly a weak point in Harold's case; it was a subject on which his friends shrank from entering. This to my mind proves a great deal; but we must beware of dealing with it as if it proved more than it really does. It proves that there was some groundwork for the Norman story; it proves that Harold took some engagement the breach of which could easily be represented as perjury. But it proves no more.

•

The deliverance of error

ABU HAMID MUHAMMED AL-GHAZALI

Al-Ghazali, the 'Light of Islam', has sometimes been called the greatest Muslim after the Prophet himself, and this reputation is well deserved. Much of his writing bears a remarkable resemblance to that of Descartes, to such an extent that had any translation of Al-Ghazali's work existed in the days of Descartes, people might have wondered if some plagiarism had been involved.

Keep your tongue from lying, whether in earnest or in jest. Do not accustom yourself to lying in jest, for it will lead you to lying in earnest. Lying is one of the sources of the greater sins, and, if you come to be known as a liar, your uprightness becomes worthless, your word is not accepted, and [men's] eyes scorn and despise you. If you want to know the foulness of lying for yourself, consider the lying of someone else and how you shun it and despise the man who lies and regard his communication as foul. Do the same with regard to all your own vices, for you do not realize the foulness of your vices from your own case, but from someone else's. What you hold bad in another man, others will undoubtedly hold bad in you. Do not therefore be complacent about that in yourself.

•

The king's submission

DR GILES

When King Henry II heard his bishops blame their suspension and excommunication on his Archbishop of Canterbury, Thomas à Becket, and that the Archbishop was making a circuit of the kingdom at the head of a large body of men, he asked them what to do. In Fitzstephen's chronicle we read that at length one of these bishops said: 'My Lord, while Thomas lives, you will not have peace or quiet or see another good day.' Fitzstephen goes on to record that on hearing this, 'such fury, bitterness and passion took possession of the King, as his disordered look and gesture expressed, that it was immediately understood what he wanted'. Edward Grim, in describing the scene, adds the King's words: 'I have nourished and promoted in my realm sluggish and wretched knaves who are faithless to their lord, and suffer him to be tricked thus infamously by a low clerk.' Seeing this feeling, several of Henry's knights and barons, seeking to please him, murdered Becket in Canterbury Cathedral. After Becket's death, Henry sought to clear his name before the Church legates. History has given it to us that Henry had not truly wished Becket dead, but the question has to be asked: how was anyone to know that? In those days the power of the King was absolute, and he had only to say something for it to be done, as Henry knew full well. Hence the inclusion here of Henry's own half-truthful version of the events that led up to Becket's murder.

The first meeting between our lord the king and the legates took place at Gorham on the Tuesday before Rogation; and the legates were admitted to kiss his Majesty on the cheek. The next day they came to Savigny, where the archbishop of Rouen and many bishops and nobles were assembled. After a long conference, the king refused to take the oath which they required, and left them in great anger, saying 'I shall return to Ireland, where I have many things to attend to; and you may go anywhere you please in my dominions, and exercise your legation as you think proper,' and so saying he left them.

After this the cardinals held a secret council with Lisieux, the archdeacon of Poitiers, and the archdeacon of Salisbury, and by their mediation the king and cardinals again met at Avranches on the following Friday. His Majesty then heard all the cardinals had to propose, and assented with great urbanity and kindness to all their suggestions. But he wished his son to be present, and join in the terms which should be agreed to, for which cause the meeting was again adjourned to the following Sunday, which was the Sunday before the Lord's Ascension. On that day the king, laying his hand on the Gospels, made oath that he had never commanded nor wished that the archbishop of Canterbury should be put to death, and that when he heard of it, he rather grieved than rejoiced. He added also of his own accord, that he grieved more than he did for the death of his father or mother, and swore that he would perform to the letter whatever penance or satisfaction the cardinals should require of him. For he admitted before all that he had been the occasion of the archbishop's death, which had taken place entirely through him; not that he had commanded it, but that his friends and attendants seeing the alteration in his countenance and the flashing of his eye judged how his mind was disturbed within him, and when they had heard his words of complaint about the archbishop, they prepared to revenge his wrongs, for which cause he would now do all that the legates required of him.

•

How to identify lying books

GIRALDUS CAMBRENSIS

Giraldus Cambrensis was a Norman–Welsh traveller, autobiographer and ecclesiastic whose independence of mind and strong prejudices are obvious in his writings. It is difficult to say how much of 'Geoffrey

Arthur' or Geoffrey of Monmouth's *History of the Kings of Britain* is fact and how much pure invention. But even in his day the *History* was looked upon with more than a degree of suspicion, as this historical anecdote by Cambrensis (which must itself be taken with a not inconsiderable amount of salt) demonstrates.

It is worthy of observation that there lived in the City of Legions in our time a Welshman called Melerius, who, under the following circumstances, acquired the knowledge of future and occult events. Having on a certain night, namely that of Palm Sunday, met a damsel, whom he had long loved, in a pleasant and convenient place, while he was indulging in her embraces, suddenly, instead of a beautiful girl, he found in his arms a hairy, rough, and hideous creature, the sight of which deprived him of his senses, and he became mad. After remaining for many years in this condition, he was restored to health in the Church of St David's through the merits of the saints. But having always an extraordinary familiarity with unclean spirits by seeing them, talking with them, and calling each by his proper name, he was enabled through their assistance to foretell future events. He was indeed often deceived (as they are) with respect to circumstances at a great distance of time and place, but was less mistaken in affairs which were likely to happen nearer, or within the space of a year. The spirits appeared to him usually on foot, equipped as hunters, with horns suspended from their necks, and truly as hunters not of animals, but of souls. He particularly met them near monasteries and monastic cells; for where rebellion exists, there is the greatest need of armies and strength. He knew when anyone spoke falsely in his presence, for he saw the Devil, as it were, leaping and exulting on the tongue of the liar. If he looked on a book faultily or falsely written, or containing a false passage, although wholly illiterate he would point out the place with his finger. Being questioned how he could gain such knowledge, he said he was directed by the demon's finger at the place. In the same manner, entering into the dormitory of a monastery, he indicated the bed of any monk not sincerely devoted to religion.

He said that the spirit of gluttony and surfeit was in every respect sordid; but that the spirit of luxury and lust was more beautiful than others in appearance, though in fact most foul. If the evil spirits oppressed him too much, the Gospel of St John was placed on his bosom, when, like birds, they immediately vanished; but when the book was removed, and the History of the Britons by Geoffrey Arthur was substituted in its place, they instantly reappeared in greater numbers, and remained a longer time than usual on his body and on the book.

•

The Prester John letter

ANON.

Prester John is the name of a potent Christian monarch of shadowy renown, whose dominions were placed by writers of the Middle Ages sometimes in the remote parts of Asia and sometimes in Africa, and of whom such contradictory accounts were given by travellers of those days that his very existence or that of his kingdom came to be considered doubtful. But at a time when the growing power of the Turks represented a threat to European interests in India, a letter written putatively by Prester John began to circulate in France, in which he announced his intention to liberate the holy places from the infidels and extended an invitation to all Christian rulers to join him. The letter was without doubt a forgery serving as it did the purpose of a Church intent on claiming India for Christ. In other words, any non-Christian power with ambitions in India would now have to take account of local Christian opposition. It would seem strange to us today that this rather obvious piece of mendacity should have achieved the popularity which it did; but that this should have happened is due in no small way to the letter's traditionally fantastic content, an example of which is quoted here.

There are in our country elephants and other animals called

dromedaries and also white horses and wild bulls of seven horns, white bears, and the strangest lions of red, green, black, and blue colour. We have also wild asses with two little horns, wild hares as big as sheep, and swift horses with two little horns who gallop faster than any other animal. You should also know that we have birds called griffins who can easily carry an ox or a horse into their nest to feed their young. We have still another kind of birds who rule over all other fowl in the world. They are of fiery colour, their wings are as sharp as razors, and they are called Yllerion. In the whole world there are but two of them. They live for sixty years, at the end of which they fly away to plunge into the sea. But first they hatch two or three eggs for forty days till the young ones come out. Then the old pair, father and mother, take off and go to drown themselves in the sea, as it was said before. And all the birds who meet them escort them till they are drowned. And when this has happened, the companions return and they go to the fledglings and feed them till they grow up and can fly and provide for themselves. Likewise, you should know that we have other birds called tigers who are so strong and bold that they lift and kill with ease an armoured man together with his horse.

Know that in one province of our country is a wilderness and that there live horned men who have but one eye in front and three or four in the back. There are also women who look similar . . . We have in our country also other men who have hoofed legs like horses and at the back of their heels they have four strong and sharp claws with which they fight in such a way that no armour can withstand them; and yet they are good Christians and willingly till their lands and ours and pay us annually a big tribute.

. . . Know also that in our country there grows wild pepper amidst trees and serpents. When it becomes ripe, we send our people to gather it. They put the woods on fire and everything burns, but when the fire has died out, they make great heaps of pepper and serpents and they put the pepper together and carry it later to a barn, wash it in two or three waters, and let it dry in the sun. In this way it becomes black, hard, and biting.

Near this region is a fountain and whoever drinks of its water three times on an empty stomach will have no sickness for thirty years; and when he has drunk of it, he will feel as if he has eaten the best meat and spices, for it is full of God's grace. A person who can bathe in this fountain, be he of a hundred or thousand years, will regain the age of thirty-two. Know that we were born and blessed in the womb of our mother five hundred and sixty-two years ago and since then we have bathed in the fountain six times.

•

The vilification of King John

W. L. WARREN

Ten years after the death of King John of England in 1216, a monk of St Albans called Roger of Wendover wrote a great chronicle in which he included an account of the reign. It is an account which is of a highly dubious nature, but was as nothing beside the lies and vilifications that were perpetrated not long afterwards by Matthew Paris, as the historian W. L. Warren tells us here.

The portrait that emerges from Paris is . . . even further removed from reality than that in Wendover, but it is eminently more readable. One of the new passages that Paris introduced is particularly arresting. He would have us believe that in 1213, when John was hard pressed by enemies both at home and abroad, he sought to gain a protector by offering to make England tributary to the Moslem ruler of North Africa, and to abandon Christianity, 'which he considered false', and to embrace Islam. Paris, as a born raconteur, fills out his story of the experience of John's envoys with much picturesque detail, so that even so essentially improbable a tale takes on some semblance of authenticity. When the envoys had penetrated innumerable and terrifying guards to reach the emir's presence, he says, they found him reading a copy of the epistles of St Paul in Greek. He confessed that he was profoundly impressed by St Paul, but could not stomach his desertion of the faith of his fathers. Indeed, the emir felt so strongly about apostasy that the mission was hopeless from the start. None the less he was interested to hear what the envoys had to say. Speaking to their brief, they dwelt glowingly on England's prosperity and happy condition under an illustrious monarch. They overdid it: instead of seeing England as a desirable acquisition, the emir only became incredulous that John should propose submitting it to the rule of another:

> 'The ambassadors were retiring discomfited,' writes Paris, 'when the emir became aware of the third member of the party, Robert the clergyman, who was small and swarthy with a misshapen hand (for two fingers stuck together) and a face like a Jew. He called for him to be brought back for he had noticed that while the others had done the talking Robert had remained silent and detached, and it occurred to him that so ill-favoured a person would not be sent on so delicate a mission unless he was thought to be particularly shrewd and intelligent. Moreover, he realized from the man's tonsure that he was a member of the clergy. So keeping him back and dismissing the others, the emir had a long private talk with him, which Robert afterwards related to his friends. The emir wanted to know if King John were a man of sound morals, if he were virile and bore lusty sons, adding that if Robert did not reply truthfully he would never believe a Christian again, certainly not a tonsured one. So Robert, promising on his word as a Christian to tell the truth, was obliged to admit that John was a tyrant not a king, a destroyer instead of a governor, crushing his own people and favouring aliens, a lion to his subjects but a lamb to foreigners and rebels. He had lost the duchy of Normandy and many other territories through sloth, and was actually keen to lose his kingdom of England or to ruin it. He was

an insatiable extorter of money; he invaded and destroyed his subjects' property; and he had bred no worthy children but only such as took after their father. He detested his wife and she him. She was an incestuous and depraved woman, so notoriously guilty of adultery that the king had given orders that her lovers were to be seized and throttled on her bed. He himself was envious of many of his barons and kinsfolk, and seduced their more attractive daughters and sisters. As for Christianity he was unstable and unfaithful. When the emir heard this he no longer merely despised John: he loathed him.'

•

Is every lie a mortal sin?

THOMAS AQUINAS

Thomas Aquinas (*c.* 1225–74) is perhaps the greatest of the Christian theologians. The bulk of his work consists of discussions of existing Christian teaching. Aquinas agrees with Augustine that all lies are sins, but not that they are all mortal sins. He distinguishes three kinds of lies: officious, or helpful lies; jocose lies, told in jest; and malicious lies, told to harm someone. It is only this last kind of lie, the malicious lie, that Aquinas argues must be judged as a mortal sin.

. . . lies may be divided with respect to their nature as sins, and with regard to those things that aggravate or diminish the sin of lying, on the part of the end intended. Now the sin of lying is aggravated, if by lying a person intends to injure another, and this is called a mischievous lie, while the sin of lying is diminished if it be directed to some good – either of pleasure and then it is a jocose lie, or of usefulness, and then we have the officious lie, whereby it is intended to help another person, or to save him from being injured. In this way lies are divided into the three kinds aforesaid . . .

A mortal sin is, properly speaking, one that is contrary to charity whereby the soul lives in union with God . . . Now a lie may be contrary to charity in three ways: first, in itself; secondly, in respect of the evil intended; thirdly, accidentally.

A lie may be in itself contrary to charity by reason of its false signification. For if this be about divine things, it is contrary to the charity of God, whose truth one hides or corrupts by such a lie; so that a lie of this kind is opposed not only to the virtue of charity, but also to the virtues of faith and religion: wherefore it is a most grievous and mortal sin. If, however, the false signification be about something the knowledge of which affects a man's good, for instance if it pertain to the perfection of science or to moral conduct, a lie of this description inflicts an injury on one's neighbour, since it causes him to have a false opinion, wherefore it is contrary to charity, as regards the love of our neighbour, and consequently is a mortal sin. On the other hand, if the false opinion engendered by the lie be about some matter the knowledge of which is of no consequence, then the lie in question does no harm to one's neighbour; for instance, if a person be deceived as to some contingent particulars that do not concern him. Wherefore a lie of this kind, considered in itself, is not a mortal sin.

As regards the end in view, a lie may be contrary to charity, through being told with the purpose of injuring God, and this is always a mortal sin, for it is opposed to religion; or in order to injure one's neighbour, in his person, his possessions or his good name, and this is also a mortal sin, since it is a mortal sin to injure one's neighbour, and one sins mortally if one has merely the intention of committing a mortal sin. But if the end intended be not contrary to charity, neither will the lie, considered under this aspect, be a mortal sin, as in the case of a jocose lie, where some little pleasure is intended, or in an officious lie, where the good also of one's neighbour is intended. Accidentally a lie may be contrary to charity by reason of scandal or any other injury resulting therefrom: and thus again it will be a mortal sin, for instance if a man were not deterred through scandal from lying publicly.

. . . Some say that for the perfect every lie is a mortal sin. But this assertion is unreasonable. For no circumstance causes a sin to be infinitely more grievous unless it transfers it to another species. Now a circumstance of person does not transfer a sin to another species, except perhaps by reason of something annexed to that person, for instance if it be against his vow: and this cannot apply to an officious or jocose lie. Wherefore an officious or jocose lie is not a mortal sin in perfect men, except perhaps accidentally on account of scandal. We may take in this sense the saying of Augustine that it is a precept of perfection not only not to lie at all, but not even to wish to lie: although Augustine says this not positively but dubiously, for he begins by saying: Unless perhaps it is a precept, etc. Nor does it matter that they are placed in a position to safeguard the truth: because they are bound to safeguard the truth by virtue of their office in judging or teaching, and if they lie in these matters their lie will be a mortal sin: but it does not follow that they sin mortally when they lie in other matters.

•

The greatest liar of all time

SIR JOHN MANDEVILLE

The Travels of Sir John Mandeville (*c.* 1371) has rightly been judged by history to be a work of almost complete fabrication. Sir Thomas Browne called Mandeville 'the greatest liar of all time', a verdict that has been consistently supported by many historians. Hugh Murray, writing at the beginning of the nineteenth century, found that much of Mandeville was copied from the travels of Odoric, a seventh-century friar, and was only accurate where it remained true to Odoric's own text. What Mandeville added of his own, said Murray, consisted 'quite exclusively of monstrous lies'. Nevertheless it is easy to see why Mandeville's incredible writings were so popular (even more so than Marco Polo's *Travels*). We begin this extract from Mandeville's writings with his account of a land called Natumeran (the Nicobar Islands).

It is a large and fair island, whose circuit is nearly a thousand miles. Men and women of that isle have heads like dogs, and they are called Cynocephales. These people, despite their shape, are fully reasonable and intelligent. They worship an ox as their god. Each one of them carries an ox made of gold or silver on his brow, as a token that they love their god well. They go quite naked except for a little cloth around their privy parts. They are big in stature and good warriors; they carry a large shield, which covers all their body, and a long spear in their hand, and dressed in this way they go boldly against their enemies. If they capture any man in battle, they eat him.

. . . From this isle men go south by sea to another which is called Dundeya, a big island [the Andaman Islands] . . . There are a great many different kinds of people in these isles. In one, there is a race of great stature, like giants, foul and horrible to look at; they have one eye only, in the middle of their foreheads. They eat raw flesh and raw fish. In another part, there are ugly folk without heads, who have eyes in each shoulder; their mouths are round, like a horseshoe, in the middle of their chest. In yet another part there are headless men whose eyes and mouths are on their backs. And there are in another place folk with flat faces, without noses or eyes; but they have two small holes instead of eyes, and a flat lipless mouth. In another isle there are ugly fellows whose upper lip is so big that when they sleep in the sun they cover all their faces with it. In another there are people of small stature, like dwarfs, a little bigger than pygmies. They have no mouth, but instead a little hole, and so when they must eat they suck their food through a reed or a pipe. They have no tongues, and hiss and make signs as monks do, to each other, and each of them understands what the other means. In another isle there are people whose ears are so big that they hang down to their knees. In another, people have feet like horses, and run so swiftly on them that they overtake wild beasts and kill them for their food. In another isle there are people who walk on their hands and their feet like four-footed beasts; they are hairy and climb up trees as readily as apes. There is another isle where the people are hermaphrodite, having the parts of each sex, and each has a breast on one side. When they use the male member, they beget children; and when they use the female, they bear children. There is another isle where the folk move on their knees marvellously, and it seems as if at each step they would fall; on each foot they have eight toes. There is still another isle where the people have only one foot, which is so broad that it will cover all the body and shade it from the sun. They will run so fast on this one foot that it is a marvel to see them. There is also another isle where the people live just on the smell of a kind of apple; and if they lost that smell, they would die forthwith. Many other kinds of folk there are in other isles about there, which are too numerous to relate.

•

Let God decide the right: trial by combat

JEAN FROISSART

Sir Jean de Carrouges went on an overseas expedition, leaving a young and beautiful wife at home. During his absence Jacques Le Gris, counsellor to the Count of Alençon, visited her in her home and raped her. When he had done, Le Gris told her not to mention it to anyone or she would be dishonoured. But on her husband's return, the lady told him all.

At first the knight could not believe it, but she so insisted that he came round and said: 'All right, then, my lady, if the thing happened as you say, I forgive you; but the squire shall die for it in some way to be decided by my friends and yours. And if I find that what you have told me is not true, you shall never live with me again.' The lady maintained and insisted even more strongly that it was absolutely true.

That night passed. The next day Sir Jean had a number of letters written and sent to his wife's closest friends and his own, with the result that soon after they all came to the castle of *Argenteuil* . . . He asked for their opinion and was advised to go to his lord the Count of Alençon and tell him the whole story, which he did. The Count, who was extremely fond of Jacques Le Gris, refused to believe him, and appointed a day for the two parties to appear before him. He required the lady who was accusing Jacques Le Gris to be present, in order to describe what had happened in her own words. She came, and many members of her family with her, to the Count of Alençon's court. The proceedings were long and heated, with Jacques Le Gris being accused of the crime both by the knight and by the full account which his wife gave of it. Jacques Le Gris firmly maintained his innocence, saying that there was no truth in the charge and that the lady was accusing him unjustly. He was at a loss, he said in his speech, to know why the lady hated him. He proved clearly, by the evidence of members of the Count's household, that on the day when it happened he had been seen there at four o'clock, and the Count said that at ten o'clock he was attending him in his chamber. He added that it was quite impossible in the time for him to have done what he was accused of doing and ridden the distance there and back, seventy-two miles in four and a half hours.* The Count told the lady, in order to support his squire, that she must have dreamt it, and he made a formal order for the charge to be annulled and for no further questions ever to be raised about it. The knight, who possessed great courage and believed his wife, refused to obey this ruling. He went to Paris and laid his case against Jacques Le Gris before the High Court. Jacques responded to his summons and gave securities pledging him to abide by the court's decision.

The proceedings went on for more than a year and a half. The two parties could not be reconciled because the knight believed

*Evidently leaving one and a half hours for his visit to the castle. For the distance, the original has 'twenty-four leagues'. Alençon is twenty-eight miles from Argentan by the modern road, and if the latter town was meant, the distance given by Froissart for the double journey is not too far out.

absolutely in his wife's account and because the case had become so notorious that he felt bound to pursue it to the end. The Count of Alençon was so infuriated by his obstinacy that there were many times when he could have had him killed, but for the fact that they had already gone to court.

After much deliberation and argument the court pronounced that, since the lady of Carrouges could not prove anything against Jacques Le Gris, the matter should be settled by a duel to the death. All the parties, the knight, the squire and the knight's lady, were ordered to be present in Paris on the day appointed, which was to be the first Monday of the year 1387.

The day of the combat arrived at about the beginning of the year counted as 1387 according to the custom of Rome. The lists were prepared in St Catherine's Square, behind the Temple. The King of France was there with his uncles and vast crowds of people came to watch. At one side of the lists big stands had been erected, from which the lords could see the fight between the two champions. These came on to the field and were armed from head to foot as was required of them, and seated each in his separate chair. Sir Jean de Carrouges was seconded by Count Waleran de Saint-Pol, and Jacques Le Gris by the Count of Alençon's men. Before the knight entered the lists, he went over to his wife, who was sitting clothed in black in a carriage draped entirely in black also, and said to her: 'Lady, on your evidence I am about to hazard my life in combat with Jacques Le Gris. You know if my cause is just and true.' 'My Lord,' replied the lady, 'it is so. You can fight confidently. The cause is just.' 'In God's hands be it then,' said the knight. He kissed his wife, pressed her hand, then made the sign of the cross and entered the lists.

The lady remained in the black-draped carriage, praying fervently to God and the Virgin Mary, entreating them humbly to grant her victory on that day in accordance with her right. You will understand that she was in a great anxiety and far from certain that her own life was safe, for if her husband got the worst of it, the sentence was that he should be hanged and she burnt without appeal. I do not know – for I never spoke with her – whether she had not often regretted having gone so far with the matter that she and her husband were in such grave danger – and then finally there was nothing for it but to await the outcome.

When the two champions had taken the oath, as is usual before such combats, they were placed opposite each other and told to say why they had come together. They then mounted their horses and sat them very prettily, for both were skilled in arms. The first part of the combat was a joust, in which neither of them was injured. They then dismounted and continued on foot, both fighting very courageously. The first to suffer was Sir Jean de Carrouges, who was wounded in the thigh, to the great alarm of his supporters, but he fought on so stoutly that he felled his opponent and, thrusting his sword into his body, killed him on the spot. He turned and asked whether he had done his duty and was told that he had. Jacques Le Gris's body was delivered to the executioner of Paris, who dragged it to Mountifaucon and hanged it there.

This was the last known occasion on which the Parlement of Paris ordered a trial by combat.

•

A mendacious monk

ISAAC D'ISRAELI

Annius of Viterbo (1432–1502), also known as Giovanni Nanni, was a Dominican monk and writer whose great work, *Antiquitatem Rarorium*, professed to contain the works of several authors of remote antiquity. But as Isaac D'Israeli, father of Benjamin, tells us, this was simply not the case.

. . . when literary forgeries are published by those whose character hardly admits of a suspicion that they are themselves the impostors, the difficulty of assigning a motive only increases that of forming a decision; to adopt or reject them may be equally dangerous.

In this class we must place Annius of Viterbo, who published a pretended collection of historians of the remotest antiquity, some of whose *names* had descended to us in the works of ancient writers, while their works themselves had been lost. Afterwards he subjoined commentaries to confirm their authority by passages from known authors. These at first were eagerly accepted by the learned; the blunders of the presumed editor, one of which was his mistaking the right name of the historian he forged, were gradually detected, till at length the imposture was apparent! The pretended originals were more remarkable for their number than their volume; for the whole collection docs not exceed 171 pages, which lessened the difficulty of the forgery; while the commentaries which were afterwards published must have been manufactured at the same time as the text. In favour of Annius, the high rank he occupied at the Roman Court, his irreproachable conduct, and his declaration that he had recovered some of these fragments at Mantua, and that others had come from Armenia, induced many to credit these pseudo-historians. A literary war soon kindled; Niceron has discriminated between four parties engaged in this conflict. One party decried the whole of the collection as gross forgeries; another obstinately supported their authenticity; a third decided that they were forgeries before Annius possessed them, who was only credulous; while a fourth party considered them as partly authentic, and ascribed their blunders to the interpolations of the editor, to increase their importance. Such as they were, they scattered confusion over the whole face of history. The false Besorus opens his history before the deluge, when, according to him, the Chaldeans through preceding ages had faithfully preserved their historical evidences! Annius hints, in his commentary, at the archives and public libraries of the Babylonians: the days of Noah comparatively seemed modern history with this dreaming editor. Some of the fanciful writers of Italy were duped: Sansovino, to delight the Florentine nobility, accommodated them with a new title of antiquity in their ancestor Noah, *Imperatore e monarcha delle genti, visse e mori in quelle parti.* The Spaniards complained that in forging these fabulous origins of different nations, a new series of kings from the ark of Noah had been introduced by some of their rhodomontade historians to pollute the sources of their history. Bodin's otherwise valuable works are considerably injured by Annius's suppositious discoveries. One historian died of grief, for having raised his elaborate speculations on these fabulous originals; and their credit was at length so much reduced, that Pignori and Maffei both announced to their readers that they had not referred in their works to the pretended writers of Annius! Yet, to the present hour, these presumed forgeries are not always given up. The problem remains unsolved – and the silence of the respectable Annius, in regard to the forgery, as well as what he affirmed when alive, leave us in doubt whether he really intended to laugh at the world by these fairy tales of the giants of antiquity.

•

Getting the hump

JEREMY POTTER

Like King John, Richard III has had a bad press. Most of the chroniclers of Richard's time do not do much more than repeat the slanders and rumours that circulated during the establishment of the new Tudor regime. John Rous, for example, revealed that Richard spent two years in his mother's womb and emerged with shoulder-length hair and a full set of teeth. Here the historian Jeremy Potter examines the fanciful origin of Richard's hump.

The records of the city of York contain an account of a drunken squabble in the year 1490 during which one party abused the

Earl of Northumberland for betraying King Richard at Bosworth 'with much other unfitting language concerning the said earl' and the other attacked King Richard as a hypocrite and a 'crouch-back', rightly buried in a dyke like a dog. The parties then came to blows.

This is the only recorded contemporary or near-contemporary use of the word 'crouchback' in connection with Richard's appearance. If not mere drunken abuse, it may indicate that, like many people then and now, he was round-shouldered or walked with a slight stoop. If that constitutes deformity, those similarly deformed in the twentieth century must be numbered in millions.

. . . The painting of Richard III now in Windsor Castle is the prototype of many similar portrayals of the king. Like the rather different picture once belonging to the Paston family and now to the Society of Antiquaries (dated by the tree-ring method to between 1512 and 1520 and showing no trace of physical deformity), it was painted some thirty years after his death and is not a royal icon, like earlier Plantagenet portraits and their images on coins, but the picture of a real person, copied presumably from a likeness taken during his lifetime. As X-raying has recently revealed, one shoulder was later doctored to suggest deformity, but not the face, which is that of an earnest, anxious, not ill-looking man, giving no credence or credibility to the Tudor demonology . . .

Richard's hunchback and withered arm were the figments of Thomas More's fertile imagination. They represented a distortion apposite to the burden of his homily and were perhaps not intended to be understood as historical truth. Their *raison d'être* was the common superstition of the period that a warped body signified an evil character. Deformity was a sign of the devil's own or at least the mark of God's disfavour. From More and for this reason Shakespeare developed his famous lump of foul deformity, and the tradition continued to develop under its own impetus. By 1643, in Baker's *Chronicle of the Kings of England*, Richard has become splay-footed and goggle-eyed: 'born a monster in nature . . . and just such were the qualities of his mind'.

Perkin Warbeck

JAMES GAIRDNER

The fate of Edward IV's sons has remained a mystery throughout history, and it is often popularly supposed that 'the little princes' were murdered in the Tower of London at the order of Richard III, their wicked uncle. Following his victory over Richard at the Battle of Bosworth, Henry VII was never quite free of claims by pretenders to be one of the two princes. Perhaps the most interesting of these claims was that of the Duchess of Burgundy's protégé, Perkin Warbeck. Here is an account by a nineteenth-century historian, James Gairdner, of how Perkin might have been caught out in the lie that he was the Duke of York. The plot against Henry VII, such as it existed, was unsuccessful, and unfortunately for Perkin was to cost him his life.

It was about this time that Warbeck wrote a letter to Queen Isabella, desiring the support of Spain. Margaret of Burgundy was doubtless well aware that Isabella had long ago been anxious for an alliance with the House of York, and she probably thought her protégé would gain more from an application to her than to her consort, Ferdinand of Aragon. In this letter Perkin declares that he had already been countenanced by the King of France, the Duchess of Burgundy, the King of the Romans, and his son the Archduke of Austria, the Duke of Saxony, and the Kings of Denmark and Scotland. He also gives an account of his adventures, in the course of which he says he was nearly nine years old when his brother, Edward V, was murdered; and that the man appointed to do the same for him had had compassion on him, and sent him abroad, after exacting from him a solemn oath not to reveal his name or lineage for a certain number of years. He adds that he had led a miserable, wandering life for about eight years; that he had been in Portugal and in Ireland; and that in the latter country he had been joyfully received by his 'cousins', the

Earls of Desmond and Kildare; and he promises the Spanish sovereigns that if ever restored to his kingdom he will continue in closer alliance with them than ever King Edward did.

This letter was endorsed by the Spanish Secretary Almazan, as 'from Richard who calls himself King of England'. It clearly had very little effect upon the Spanish sovereigns, and surely if it could have influenced them at all it was not by inducing them to believe in the truth of the adventurer's story. There was one flaw, indeed, in his statements which Ferdinand and Isabella may not have been able to detect – the Pretender made himself nearly nine years old, instead of eleven at the time that his brother Edward V was murdered; but they must have clearly seen the gross improbability of the whole story, and the manifestly strained effort to account for the concealment of an heir to the crown for fully eight long years. That was in itself rather a considerable period of time for a person of so much consequence to lie hid; but when at last the concealed Prince thought he might safely throw off his cloak of darkness, what need could there have been for further mystery about the person who preserved him and the two jailers to whose custody he had been committed? The tale involved a great many circumstances which clearly would not bear the light of inquiry; and Warbeck could hardly have deceived anyone who did not wish to be deceived.

•

The two log books of Christopher Columbus

WASHINGTON IRVING

Early in the morning of 6 September 1492, Christopher Columbus set sail from the island of Gomera, taking leave of the Old World in search of the New. Gradually, the last of the Canary Islands faded from the horizon.

On losing sight of this last trace of land, the hearts of the crew failed them. They seemed literally to have taken leave of the world. Behind them was every thing dear to the heart of man; country, family, friends, life itself; before them everything was chaos, mystery, and peril. In the perturbation of the moment, they despaired of ever more seeing their homes. Many of the rugged seamen shed tears, and some broke into loud lamentations. The admiral [Columbus] tried in every way to soothe their distress, and to inspire them with his own glorious anticipations. He described to them the magnificent countries to which he was about to conduct them: the islands of the Indian seas teeming with gold and precious stones; the regions of Mangi and Cathay, with their cities of unrivalled wealth and splendour. He promised them land and riches, and every thing that could arouse their cupidity or inflame their imaginations, nor were these promises made for purposes of mere deception; he certainly believed that he should realize them all.

He now issued orders to the commanders of the other vessels, that, in the event of separation by any accident, they should continue directly westward; but that after sailing seven hundred leagues, they should lay by from midnight until daylight, as at about that distance he confidently expected to find land. In the mean time, as he thought it possible he might not discover land within the distance thus assigned, and as he foresaw that the vague terrors already awakened among the seamen would increase with the space which intervened between them and their homes, he commenced a stratagem which he continued throughout the voyage. He kept two reckonings; one correct, in which the true way of the ship was noted, and which was retained in secret for his own government; in the other, which was open to general inspection, a number of leagues was daily subtracted from the sailing of the ship, so that the crews were kept in ignorance of the real distance they had advanced.

•

How Amerigo Vespucci discovered South America

WASHINGTON IRVING

Amerigo Vespucci is considered by many to have been the first discoverer of South America. But by a singular quirk of fate (or so it would seem) his name has been given to the whole of the New World. Of this, Ralph Waldo Emerson wrote that Vespucci 'managed in this lying world to suppress Columbus and baptize half the world with his own dishonest name'. Here Emerson was alluding to the accusation that Vespucci deliberately falsified a voyage to Paria and the Brazils one year before Columbus landed there in 1498. It is not disputed that Vespucci did visit the continent on the 1499 voyage commanded by Ojeda, and on several subsequent voyages. But in 1504, shortly after Vespucci's return from his last expedition to the Brazils, he wrote a letter to the Duke of Lorraine which contained a summary account of all his voyages, including a voyage to the Brazils which supposedly took place in 1497. This is the point of the controversy, for it was, and still is, strenuously asserted that no such voyage took place, and that Vespucci's account of a voyage made by him in 1497 was a lie told for the purpose of claiming the discovery of the southern continent.

The credibility of this voyage was tested in a suit instituted in 1508 against the Crown of Spain by the heir of Columbus. It was the object of the Crown to disprove the discovery of the coast of Paria by Columbus, as it was maintained that unless he discovered it, the claim of his heir with respect to a share in the profits would be invalid. Despite the evidence of many persuasive witnesses to support this claim, and in spite of the fact that neither Vespucci or any of his co-mariners were called to the court, the claim was resisted. Here, the nineteenth-century historian Washington Irving examines the case against Amerigo Vespucci.

It has been the endeavour of the author to examine this question dispassionately; and after considering the statements and arguments advanced on either side, he cannot resist a conviction, that the voyage stated to have been made in 1497 did not take place, and that Vespucci has no title to the first discovery of the coast of Paria.

The question is extremely perplexing from the difficulty of assigning sufficient motives for so gross a deception. When Vespucci wrote his letters there was no doubt entertained but that Columbus had discovered the mainland in his first voyage; Cuba being always considered the extremity of Asia, until circumnavigated in 1508. Vespucci may have supposed Brazil, Paria, and the rest of the coast, part of a distinct continent, and have been anxious to arrogate to himself the fame of its discovery. It has been asserted that, on his return from his voyage to the Brazils, he prepared a maritime chart, in which he gave his name to that part of the mainland; but this assertion does not appear to be well substantiated. It would rather seem that his name was given to that part of the continent by others, as a tribute paid to his supposed merit, in consequence of having read his own account of his voyages.

It is singular that Fernando, the son of Columbus, in his biography of his father, should bring no charge against Vespucci of endeavouring to supplant the admiral in this discovery. Herrera has been cited as the first to bring the accusation, in his history of the Indies, first published in 1601, and has been much criticized in consequence, by the advocates of Vespucci, as making the charge of his mere assertion. But, in fact, Herrera did but copy what he found written by Las Casas, who had the proceedings of the fiscal court lying before him, and was moved to indignation against Vespucci, by what he considered proofs of great imposture.

It has been suggested that Vespucci was instigated to this deception at the time when he was seeking employment in the colonial service of Spain; and that he did it to conciliate the Bishop of Fonseca, who was desirous of anything that might injure the interests of Columbus. In corroboration of this opinion, the patronage is cited, which was ever shown by Fonseca to

Vespucci and his family. This is not, however, a satisfactory reason, since it does not appear that the bishop ever made any use of the fabrication. Perhaps some other means might be found of accounting for this spurious narration, without implicating the veracity of Vespucci. It may have been the blunder of some editor, or the interpolation of some book-maker, eager, as in the case of Trivigiani with the manuscript of Peter Martyr, to gather together disjointed materials, and fabricate a work to gratify the prevalent passion of the day.

In the various editions of the letters of Vespucci, the grossest variations and inconsistencies in dates will be found, evidently the errors of hasty and careless publishers. Several of these have been corrected by the modern authors who have inserted these letters in their works. The same disregard to exactness which led to these blunders may have produced the interpolation of this voyage, garbled out of the letters of Vespucci and the accounts of other voyagers. This is merely suggested as a possible mode of accounting for what appears so decidedly to be a fabrication, yet which we are loath to attribute to a man of the good sense, the character, and the reputed merit of Vespucci.

Irving's want of alacrity at accusing Vespucci of mendacity is to his credit. In view of the poor treatment and monumental ingratitude which Columbus had already received from the King of Spain, it seems not unreasonable to accuse the Crown itself of having perpetrated this lie in order to deny the heirs of Columbus a share in the profits. Kings were ever greedy.

•

Lucretia Borgia regains her virginity

FERDINAND GREGORIUS

The house of Sforza having lost all its influence, Pope Alexander VI (1492–1503) decided that his daughter's marriage to Giovanni Sforza of

Pesaro promised him nothing more, and so he set about the manufacture of a more profitable match. A request for a divorce was made. There was, however, one difficulty, which necessitated the most public and laughable of lies.

Alexander had appointed a commission under the direction of two cardinals for the purpose of divorcing Lucretia from Giovanni Sforza. These judges showed that Sforza had never consummated the marriage, and that his spouse was still a virgin, which, according to her contemporary Matarazzo of Perugia, set all Italy to laughing. Lucretia herself stated that she was willing to swear to this.

During these proceedings her spouse was in Pesaro. Thence he subsequently went in disguise to Milan to ask the protection of Duke Ludovico and to get him to use his influence to have his wife, who had been taken away, restored to him. This was in June. He protested against the decision which had been pronounced in Rome, and which had been purchased, and Ludovico il Moro made the naive suggestion that he subject himself to a test of his capacity in the presence of trustworthy witnesses, and of the papal legate in Milan, which, however, Sforza declined to do. Ludovico and his brother Ascanio finally induced their kinsman to yield, and Sforza, intimidated, declared in writing that he had never consummated his marriage with Lucretia.

The formal divorce, therefore, took place December 20, 1497, and Sforza surrendered his wife's dowry of thirty-one thousand ducats.

Although we may assume that Alexander compelled his daughter to consent to this separation, it does not render our opinion of Lucretia's part in the scandalous proceedings any less severe; she shows herself to have had as little will as she had character, and she also perjured herself. Her punishment was not long delayed, for the divorce proceedings made her notorious and started terrible rumours regarding her private life . . .

Even before Lucretia's new betrothal was settled upon it was rumoured in Rome that her former affianced, Don Gasparo, was again pressing his suit and that there was a prospect of his being accepted. Although the young Spaniard failed to accomplish his purpose, Alexander now recognized the fact that Lucretia's betrothal to him had been dissolved illegally.

In a brief dated June 10, 1498, he speaks of the way his daughter was treated – without special dispensation for breaking the engagement, in order that she might marry Giovanni of Pesaro, which was a great mistake – as illegal. He says in the same letter that Gasparo of Procida, Count of Almenara, had subsequently married and had children, but not until 1498 did Lucretia petition to have her betrothal to him formally declared null and void. The Pope, therefore, absolved her of the perjury she had committed by marrying Giovanni Sforza in spite of her engagement to Don Gasparo, and while he now, for the first time, declared her formal betrothal to the Count of Procida to have been dissolved, he gave her permission to marry any man whom she might select. Thus did a pope play fast and loose with one of the holiest of the sacraments of the Church.

•

How princes should honour their word

NICCOLÒ MACHIAVELLI

Everyone realizes how praiseworthy it is for a prince to honour his word and to be straightforward rather than crafty in his dealings; none the less contemporary experience shows that princes who have achieved great things have been those who have given their word lightly, who have known how to trick men with their cunning, and who, in the end, have overcome those abiding by honest principles.

You should understand, therefore, that there are two ways of fighting: by law or by force. The first way is natural to men, and the second to beasts. But as the first way often proves inadequate one must needs have recourse to the second. So a prince must understand how to make a nice use of the beast and the man. The ancient writers taught princes about this by an allegory, when they described how Achilles and many other princes of the ancient world were sent to be brought up by Chiron, the centaur, so that he might train them his way. All the allegory means, in making the teacher half beast and half man, is that a prince must know how to act according to the nature of both, and that he cannot survive otherwise.

So, as a prince is forced to know how to act like a beast, he should learn from the fox and the lion; because the lion is defenceless against wolves, therefore one must be a fox in order to recognize traps, and a lion to frighten off wolves. Those who simply act like lions are stupid. So it follows that a prudent ruler cannot, and should not, honour his word when it places him at a disadvantage and when the reasons for which he made his promise no longer exist. If all men were good, this precept would not be good; but because men are wretched creatures who would not keep their word to you, you need not keep your word to them. And a prince will never lack good excuses to colour his bad faith. One could give innumerable modern instances of this, showing how many pacts and promises have been made null and void by the bad faith of princes: those who have known best how to imitate the fox have come off best. But one must know how to colour one's actions and to be a great liar and deceiver. Men are so simple, and so much creatures of circumstance, that the deceiver will always find someone ready to be deceived.

There is one fresh example I do not want to omit. Alexander VI was always, and he thought only of, deceiving people; and he always found victims for his deceptions. There never was a man capable of such convincing asseverations, or so ready to swear to the truth of something, who would honour his word less. None the less his deceptions always had the result he intended, because he was a past master in the art.

•

Calumnies

NICCOLÒ MACHIAVELLI

For reasons that are about to become obvious, Machiavelli is often accused of inconsistency, specifically that *The Prince* (from which the previous extract was taken) is inconsistent with *Discourses* (the source of this extract). As Machiavelli himself tells us in the first chapter of *The Prince*, 'all the states, all the dominions under whose authority men have lived in the past and live now have been and are either republics or principalities'. Thus in *The Prince*, he devotes himself to the subject of the principality, hereditary or new, and in the *Discourses*, he writes about the political republic, to which idea he was fundamentally attached. This apparent dichotomy results from Machiavelli's hope that in *The Prince* he might curry favour with Lorenzo de Medici and thereby obtain some public office for himself. And as translator George Bull writes, 'if Machiavelli in one place writes from the viewpoint of a republican and in another from that of an autocrat, he is not advocating now liberty and now tyranny. Least of all must we let any anachronistic notions of opposition between democracy and totalitarianism confuse our interpretation of his motives. The Florentine Republicans hated the Medici, but the Medici were no more totalitarians than the Republicans were advocates of universal suffrage.'

Although the virtue of Furius Camillus, who had freed Rome from the yoke of the Gauls, had caused all the citizens of Rome to give him precedence without its appearing to them that, by so doing, they were diminishing their own repute or rank, none the less Manlius Capitolinus could not bear that so much honour and glory should be ascribed to Camillus, since it seemed to him that his own merits were as great as those of Camillus, since it was he who had saved the Capitol, nor was he inferior to Camillus in other praiseworthy military exploits. Consequently, so fraught was he with envy, that he could not remain tranquil while

Camillus had such glory, but, realizing that he could not sow discord among the patricians, he turned to the plebs and disseminated among them divers sinister rumours. Among other things, he said that the treasure which had been collected to give to the Gauls, had not been given to them, but had been appropriated by private citizens, and that, if it could be recovered, it might be used to the advantage of the public either in lessening the taxation of the plebs or in the discharge of certain private debts. This speech had a considerable effect on the plebs, who began to hold meetings and to raise numerous tumults in the city as it pleased them. This displeased the senate, to whom it appeared to be a serious matter and dangerous. So they appointed a dictator who should take cognizance of the situation and restrain the impetuosity of Manlius. The dictator accordingly cited Manlius to appear in public, where they confronted one another, the dictator surrounded by the nobles and Manlius surrounded by plebeians. Manlius was asked to state in whose hands the treasure was of which he had spoken, for the senate was as desirous to be informed of this as were the plebs. In his reply Manlius gave no details, but evaded the issue, saying that it was unnecessary to tell them what they already knew. So the dictator sent him to prison.

It is clear from this incident in what detestation calumnies should be held in free cities and in all other forms of society, and how with a view to checking them no institution which serves this end should be neglected. Nor for their prevention can there be anything better than an institution which provides adequate facilities for charges to be brought, because indictments are as helpful to republics as calumnies are harmful. The difference between them is this. There is no need of witnesses or of any other corroboration of the facts to set calumnies going, so that anybody can be calumniated by anybody else. But one cannot in this way be indicted, for indictments must be corroborated and circumstances be induced to prove the truth of the indictment. Indictments are made before magistrates, before the people, and before the courts. Calumnies are circulated in the squares and in the arcades. Calumnies are more prevalent in cities in which less use is made of public accusations, and in which less provision has been made for receiving them. He, therefore, who constitutes a republic should do it in such a way that charges may be brought against any citizen without fear of any kind and without respect to persons. Where provision for this has been made, and due recourse is had to it, calumniators should be severely punished. Nor can they complain of such punishment, since they had an opportunity to make charges openly against those whom they calumniated in private. But where adequate provision for this has not been made, there invariably ensue considerable disorders. For calumnies do not castigate citizens, they do but exasperate them; and, since hate is more quickly aroused than is fear, they think, when exasperated, how to get their own back for what has been said against them.

This eventuality, as has been said, was adequately provided for in Rome, but was ever badly provided for in our city of Florence. And, as in Rome such provision did much good, the lack of it in Florence did much harm. Anyone who reads the history of that city will notice how at all times calumnies have been spread against such of its citizens as were employed in important public affairs. Of one they said that he had embezzled the public funds; of another that he had failed in some undertaking because he had been bribed; of yet another that through ambition he had caused such and such an inconvenience. It thus came about that hatred arose on all sides; whence came divisions; from divisions factions, and from factions ruin. Whereas, if in Florence provision had been made for the accusing of citizens and for the punishment of calumniators, there would not have ensued the innumerable scandals that did ensue. For citizens, whether condemned or acquitted, would not have been able to harm the city, and there would have been fewer people indicted than there were calumniated, since, as I have said, it is not possible to bring an indictment against anyone as it is to calumniate anyone.

Calumnies, too, are among the various things of which citizens have availed themselves in order to acquire greatness, and are very effective when employed against powerful citizens who stand in the way of one's plans, because by playing up to the populace and confirming the poor view it takes of such men, one can make it one's friend. Of this it would be possible to adduce numerous examples, but I propose to confine myself to just one. The Florentine army was encamped about Lucca, under the command of Messer Giovanni Guicciardini, its commissary. Owing either to mismanagement or to misfortune, the taking of that city did not come about. Anyhow, whichever was the case, Messer Giovanni took the blame for it, since it was said that he had been suborned by the Lucchese. This calumny, fostered by his enemies, almost drove Messer Giovanni to despair. For, although, to justify himself, he offered to place himself in the hands of the 'Captain' [of Florence], he none the less was unable ever to justify himself, since in that republic there were no means of doing so. This gave rise to considerable indignation alike among Messer Giovanni's friends, who comprised most people of standing, and among those who desired to introduce innovations in Florence. The affair, for this reason and others like it, grew to such dimensions that it led to the downfall of that republic.

Manlius Capitolinus, then, was a calumniator, not an accuser; and the Romans have shown us in his case precisely how calumniators should be punished. They should be made to bring a formal charge, and, when the charge is borne out by the facts, should be rewarded or at any rate not punished; but, when it is not borne out by the facts, they should be punished, as Manlius was.

•

Rules for thinking in the church

IGNATIUS LOYOLA

Loyola was the founder of the Society of Jesus, whose members became known as Jesuits. The aim of the Society was to combat the

Reformation. Discipline, organization and secrecy were the three cornerstones of Jesuit power. Owing to the casuistical principles maintained by many of the Jesuit leaders, the name Jesuit acquired a derogatory connotation, and is sometimes taken to be synonymous with being a deceiver. Illustrative of the mendacious mental discipline that perhaps contributed to this opprobrium is this precept, number 13 in Loyola's *Spiritual Exercises* (1548), which has a real ring of Stalinism about it.

13. That we may be altogether of the same mind and in conformity with the Church herself, if she shall have defined anything to be black which to our eyes appears to be white, we ought in like manner to pronounce it to be black. For we must undoubtedly believe that the Spirit of our Lord Jesus Christ, and the Spirit of the Orthodox Church His Spouse, by which Spirit we are governed and directed to Salvation, is the same.

•

Dealing with rebels

HENRY VIII

The Pilgrimage of Grace of 1536–7 was a popular rising which took place against the policies of King Henry VIII – in particular, enclosures and the dissolution of the monasteries. Led by Robert Aske, the pilgrims – who included members of the gentry – presented a serious threat to Henry, and it was only after a truce was effected by the Duke of Norfolk, based on promises which Henry had no intention of keeping, that the rebels were persuaded to disperse. Henry's letter to Norfolk, instructing him in how to lie to the pilgrims, is a classic piece of Machiavellianism. Upon the army being dispersed, Henry was able to execute some 200 rebels.

And if so be that the heads and captains of the rebels shall, upon this declaration, which we desire you with all dexterity to set forth unto them, condescend and agree, as well to dissolve again their forces and garrisons, as to meet with you in a peaceable sort and out of arms; then our pleasure is, you shall keep the day of meeting appointed, or such other day as shall be agreed upon between you and them. And at your coming together, you shall first engrieve their attemptates sithens the appointment* taken at Doncaster; dilating as well therein their new assembly made at this time, the taking of Ralph Evers and Edward Waters, with our ship, munitions, and money, and the sending of Robert Bowes to take our Cousin of Cumberland; as all other their innovations mentioned in our former instructions given to you, our Cousin of Norfolk, and our Admiral, at your departure from us. And thereupon, moving them first by all the good means you can devise to repair and redub their attemptates, you shall then declare unto them, how that, of our most inestimable clemency and goodness, we have not only made answer to such petitions as they have exhibited unto us, but also granted their suit and desire for their pardon, in such a liberal and free sort as they may have good cause, both to receive it most humbly, and to devise, by their lowly submission and fidelity, to be showed hereafter towards us, to show themselves so true and faithful subjects, as, with their present repentance for this offence, and their good continuance after, they may repair and redub that which hath been, in this part transgressed and offended; which pardon you shall, by all the ways and means to you possible, induce them humbly to desire, and so to receive, in such form, as in your former instructions is prescribed. And if they shall, nevertheless, refuse to accept the said pardon, unless it were general and without exception, and either make desire for a Parliament, or for the granting of any other articles, which percase in speciality they shall express unto you; you shall thereunto make answer that your commission extendeth not to the granting of any of those things; nevertheless, such is your love and zeal to those parties, and such is your desire to do that thing

*'frustrate their endeavours subsequent to the appointment . . .', etc.

that might avoid the extremity of mischief from them which seek by this their folly, that in case they will frankly signify unto you what they would have, what they do desire, and what they have resolved upon, you will adventure to take an abstinence; and not only advertise us thereof, but also join with them as humble suitors and petitioners unto us, if their requests, petitions, and desires shall be such as subjects may, in any case, offer to their Prince and Sovereign Lord, and as the same may again grant unto them with his honour. And if they shall, upon this general overture, declare unto you that they desire only the said free pardon and Parliament, you shall promise them, as is aforesaid, to be suitors with them; so as they will set their hands to the articles thereof, and, with the same, promise no further to molest us with other particular or public matters, ne to administer unto us any further occasions that might provoke our indignation against them, but to use themselves in all things like good and faithful subjects. And having once concluded upon the same and received their writing thereof, you shall take an abstinence for 6 or 7 days, as though you should send hither unto us, specially, for that purpose; and when that time shall be expired, at the day to be prefixed, declare unto them that with great suit you have obtained their petitions; and so present unto them the general pardon, which at this time we send unto you by our servant, Sir John Russell, whom we have specially commanded not to deliver them out of his hands to any person, until such time as they shall determine to receive the same, in such sort as we have prescribed; having first advised them to apply themselves to receive it with such humility as shall appertain to subjects, not only in the receiving of the oath, but also into the withdrawing of all their violent misdemeanours, and the peaceable yielding of themselves to their labours: and semblably you shall grant them a Parliament, to begin at such place as we shall appoint for the same.

•

Advantages from an inventory of relics

JOHN CALVIN

. . . as evil leads on to evil, another unhappy consequence was, that vile objects, out of number, and altogether devoid of sense and beauty, were received as relics of Christ and the Saints. So blind was the world, that, under whatever name the vain toys were presented, they were at once received without examination and selection as genuine. In this way, men made no difficulty in hugging any ass's or dog's bones which any trifler chose to bring forward as the bones of martyrs. The same thing, as we will afterwards show, happened in other cases, and, I doubt not, by just punishment from God. For when the world, inflamed, as it were, with a kind of rage, longed after relics, that they might pervert them to superstition, it might have been anticipated that God would permit lie to follow upon lie. For in this way is He wont to avenge insult offered to his name, when the glory due only to Himself is transferred to others. Wherefore, the true explanation of the fact, that so many spurious relics exist, is just that when men were delighting in lies, God permitted them to fall into a double error.

The duty of Christians was, to leave the bodies of saints in their tombs in obedience to the universal sentence by which it is declared, that man is dust, and to dust will return; not to raise them up in sumptuousness and splendour, as if they were fabricating a premature resurrection. This duty, however, was not at all understood; but on the contrary, against the decree of God, the bodies of the faithful were dug up and exalted in splendour, when they ought to have rested in the grave as in a bed till the last day. They were sought after and confided in, and even worshipped; in short, every mark of reverence was paid to them. And what was the result? The devil perceiving the infatuation, thought it not enough to deceive men in one way, but added also the imposture of inscribing the names of relics on things altogether profane; while God, in just vengeance, deprived them of all thought and discernment, so that, without any investigation, whether the thing was white or black, they received indiscriminately whatever was offered to them.

At present, indeed, it is not my design to show what abomination there is in abusing the relics both of Christ and the Saints, in the way in which it has hitherto been done, and is common even in the present day in the greater part of Christendom, for the subject would require a volume to itself. But as it is clear that a great majority of the relics that are exhibited are spurious, being brought forward by certain deceivers, who have impudently imposed on the meanest of people, it has occurred to me to mention some things which may furnish men of sense with an occasion of thought and reflection. For often, when preoccupied by error or opinion, we approve inconsiderately, without taking time to examine and form a right judgement, and in this way our thoughtlessness deceives us. But, when put on our guard, we begin to attend, our wonder is, how we could have been so giddy and easy in believing what had no appearance of truth. This is exactly what has happened in the present case. For men not being at all on their guard, but being preoccupied by a false opinion, when it is said, 'there is the body of such a saint, there are his shoes, there his sandals,' easily persuade themselves that it is so. But when I shall have called attention to frauds which cannot be now denied, every man, of even the least prudence, will open his eyes, and employ his mind in considering what had never occurred to himself.

But in this short treatise, I am not able to accomplish what I particularly desire, for it would be necessary to obtain catalogues from all quarters, that it might be known what relics are said to exist in every separate place, so that they might be compared with each other. In this way it would be made manifest that every Apostle has more than four bodies, and every Saint two or three. The same thing would appear in other instances; in short, when the whole heap was collected, there is no man who would not be amazed at seeing how ridiculously the whole world had been blinded. The way in which I considered the matter with myself was this: – Since there is no catholic church so small as not to have an infinity of bones and such like frivolities, what would it be if we were to pile up the whole multitude contained in three or four thousand dioceses, in twenty or thirty thousand abbacies, forty thousand monasteries, nay more, in the whole multitude of parishes and chapels? Still the best thing would be to see the things, and not merely to give their names, for, indeed, they are not all known by name. It was said, that in this city there was an arm of St Anthony. While enclosed in its case, all kissed and worshipped it, but when brought forward into view it proved to be a nameless part of a stag. On a certain great altar lay part of the brain of St Peter. So long as it was in its case no man doubted, – for it would have been blasphemy not to credit the name, – but when the nest was shaken up, and observed more accurately, it turned out to be a pumice-stone. I might give many similar examples, but these will suffice to show what rubbish would be brought to light, if all the relics throughout Europe were carefully visited, provided it were done with prudence and discrimination.

. . . Let us begin then with Christ. As his natural body could not be possessed . . . instead of it they have collected six hundred frivolities to compensate for its absence. They have not even allowed the body of Christ to escape entirely, but have managed to retain a portion. For, besides teeth and hair, the monks of Charrox give out that they have the prepuce, that is, the pellicle cut off in his circumcision. And how, pray, did this pellicle come to them? The Evangelist Luke relates that the Lord was circumcised, but it is nowhere said that the skin was preserved for relics. All ancient histories are silent respecting it, and for the space of five hundred years this subject was not once broached in the Christian Church. Where was it lying hid all the time, and how did it so suddenly burst into notice? Moreover, how came it to travel so far as Charrox? But as a proof of its genuineness, they say that some drops of blood fell from it. They, indeed, say this, but they should prove it. It is plainly a mere absurdity. But were we to grant that this pellicle was preserved, and so might be there or elsewhere, what shall we say of the prepuce which is shown at Rome, in the church of Joannes Lateranensis? As it is certain there was only one, it cannot possibly be both at Rome and Charrox. Thus the falsehood becomes manifest.

. . . Next come certain things which were in contact with the body of our Lord, or, at least, things which could be collected, and in the absence of his body be converted into relics, so as to keep it in remembrance. First, there is shown at Rome, in the church of the elder Mary, the manger in which he was laid at his birth, and in the church of St Paul, the linen in which he was swaddled, although some portion of it is said to be in the church of St Salvator in Spain. There is also shown his cradle, together with the shirt which his mother, Mary, put upon him. Likewise at Rome, in the church of St James, is the altar on which he was placed on his being presented in the temple – as if various altars had then existed, as under the Papacy, where they are erected at pleasure. In this matter, the lie appears without disguise.

•

Judas the liar

MARTIN LUTHER

A liar is far worse, and does greater mischief, than a murderer on the highway; for a liar and false teacher deceives people, seduces souls, and destroys them under the colour of God's Word; such a liar and murderer was Judas, like his father the devil. It was a marvel how Judas should sit at the table with Christ, and not blush for shame, when Christ said: 'One of you shall betray me,' &c. The other disciples had not the least thought that Judas would betray Christ; each was rather afraid of himself, thinking that Christ meant him; for Christ trusted Judas with the purse, and the whole management of the house-keeping, whence he was held in great repute by the apostles.

Cellini deceives the Duke

BENVENUTO CELLINI

Benvenuto Cellini (1500 – 1571) was the most celebrated goldsmith of the Late Renaissance, although he is perhaps best known for his *Autobiography*. In this extract Cellini tells us how he was obliged to lie to his patron, the great Duke Cosimo de Medici of Florence.

. . . the Duchess had sent to see what his Excellency was doing, and her page reported to her that he was talking and laughing with Benvenuto, and was in a very good mood. On hearing this the Duchess immediately came into the wardrobe and, on finding the Duke absent, sat down next to us. She watched us work for a while, and then very graciously turned to me and showed me a string of large and really very rare pearls. When she asked me for my opinion I said that it was very beautiful. At this her Most Illustrious Excellency said to me:

'I want the Duke to buy it for me, so, my dear Benvenuto, praise it to the Duke as highly as you are capable of doing.'

When I heard what she wanted, as respectfully as I could I spoke my mind to the Duchess.

'My lady,' I said, 'I was under the impression that this pearl necklace belonged to your Excellency, and so it would not have been right for me to say what now, knowing that it doesn't belong to you, I am bound to say. I must confess, your Excellency, that from my intimate knowledge of these things I can perceive very many defects in these pearls, and for that reason I would never advise your Excellency to buy them.'

At this she said: 'The merchant is offering them to me for six thousand crowns, and if it weren't for those little defects they'd be worth more than twelve thousand.'

In answer to this I said that even if the necklace were absolutely flawless I would never advise anyone to pay as much as five thousand crowns; for pearls were not jewels, they were fishes' bones, and they suffered with time, but diamonds and rubies and emeralds did not grow old, any more than sapphires: all those were jewels, I said, and it was advisable to buy them.

The Duchess was somewhat annoyed at this, and she went on: 'But I want these pearls, and so I beg you to take them to the Duke and praise them as highly as you possibly can, and although you may have to tell one or two little lies, do so for me and it will be well worth your while.'

I have always been a lover of truth and a hater of lies, which were now being forced on me, but I was unwilling to lose the favour of so great a princess and so very miserably I took those damned pearls and went with them into the other apartment where the Duke had retired. As soon as he saw me he said: 'Ah, Benvenuto, what are you up to?'

I uncovered the pearls and said: 'My lord, I've come to show you a very beautiful string of pearls, they're very rare, and really very worthy of your Excellency: there are eighty of them, and I don't believe that as many as that number could be found to make a better necklace. So do buy them, my lord, because the necklace really is a miracle.'

At once the Duke replied: 'I haven't any intention of buying them; they're not the pearls you claim them to be nor are they as excellent as you say. I've seen them already, and they don't please me.'

'Pardon me, my lord,' I said, 'these pearls are infinitely finer than any pearls ever assembled on a necklace before.'

The Duchess, meanwhile, had got up and was standing behind the door, hearing all that I was saying. And then, after I had said a thousand things more than I am writing here, the Duke looked at me with a benevolent expression and remarked:

'My dear Benvenuto, I know that you know all about these things, and if these pearls possessed that rare excellence you attribute to them I wouldn't hesitate to buy them, whether to please the Duchess or merely to possess them: in fact I need such things, not so much for the Duchess as in connection with my arrangements for my sons and daughters.'

Then having begun to tell lies I followed them up with others, even more boldly, and made them as plausible as I could to make the Duke believe me, relying on the Duchess to come to my help when I needed her. If the bargain were concluded more than two hundred crowns would fall to me – the Duchess had said as much – but, if only for safety's sake, I had made up my mind and was fully determined not to touch a single crown, so that the Duke would never imagine that I had done it from greed. The Duke – very graciously – began to address me again, saying:

'I know that you're an expert on these matters, and so if you're the honest man I've always taken you for tell me the truth now.'

So then, blushing and with my eyes rather moist from tears, I said:

'My lord, if I tell your Excellency the truth the Duchess will become my deadliest enemy; and as a result I'll be forced to move away from Florence and my enemies will at once attack me on the score of my Perseus, which I've promised to your Excellency's noble school of artists: so I beg your Excellency to protect me.'

After the Duke had learnt that all I had been saying I had as it were been compelled to, he said to me:

'If you trust in me there's no need to worry about anything in the world.'

Again I said to him: 'But look, my lord, what can possibly stop the Duchess from finding out?'

Then, as a pledge of good faith, the Duke raised his hand and said: 'Everything you say will be kept under lock and key.'

At these noble words I immediately told him the truth as to my opinion concerning the pearls and I said that they were not worth much more than two thousand crowns. The Duchess thought we had finished because as far as possible we were talking softly, and so she came forward and said:

'My lord, I hope your Excellency will be kind enough to buy me that string of pearls, because I am very anxious to have them, and your Benvenuto says that he has never seen any more beautiful.'

Then the Duke said: 'I don't want to buy them.'

'But, my lord, why does your Excellency not want to please me by buying the necklace?'

'Because it does not please me to throw money away.'

The Duchess insisted: 'But oh, what do you mean by "throw money away", when your Benvenuto, who so much deserves the trust you put in him, has told me it would be a good bargain even if it cost more than three thousand crowns?'

At this the Duke said: 'Madam, my Benvenuto has told me that I would be throwing my money away if I bought it, since the pearls are neither round nor even, and many of them are old. And to prove it, look at this one, and that, and look here and here . . . No, they're not for me.'

As he said this, the Duchess shot a malevolent look at me, and with a menacing nod of her head left us to ourselves. My immediate impulse was to run away and be rid of Italy; but as my Perseus was all but finished I was reluctant to go without having displayed it. But you can understand what a serious plight I found myself in.

The Duchess subsequently employed a villainous good-for-nothing broker to persuade the Duke to buy the pearls. He was so persistent that the Duke gave in and bought them. Cellini bitterly records how fortune favoured a villainous man above an honest one:

Now here one can see the way ill-fortune rages against a poor man and the shameless way in which a villain is favoured. I completely lost the favour of the Duchess, and as a result nearly lost the Duke's, and he won a fat commission and their regard. So it is not enough merely to be an honest virtuous man.

•

A liar should have a good memory

MICHEL DE MONTAIGNE

This essay by the French philosopher Montaigne is based on an old saying which occurs in the *Proverbs* of Erasmus; it can be traced to St Jerome in the fourth century, and beyond, to the *Institutio Oratoria* of the rhetorician Quintilian.

Not without reason is it said that no one who is not conscious of having a sound memory should set up to be a liar. I know quite well that grammarians make a distinction between telling an untruth and lying. They say that to tell an untruth is to say something that is false, but that we suppose to be true, and that the meaning of the Latin 'mentiri', from which our French word for lying derives, is to go against one's conscience, and that consequently it applies only to those who say the opposite of what they know; and it is of them I am speaking.

Now liars either invent the whole thing, or they disguise and alter an actual fact. If they disguise and alter, it is hard for them not to get mixed up when they refer to the same story again and again because, the real facts having been the first to lodge in the memory and impress themselves upon it by way of consciousness and knowledge, they will hardly fail to spring into the mind and dislodge the false version, which cannot have as firm and assured a foothold. The circumstances, as they were first learned, will always rush back into the thoughts, driving out the memory of the false or modified details that have been added.

If liars make a complete invention, they apparently have much less reason to be afraid of tripping up, in as much as there is no contrary impression to clash with their fiction. But even this, being an empty thing that offers no hold, readily escapes from the memory unless it is a very reliable one. I have often had amusing proof of this, at the expense of those who profess to suit their speech only to the advantage of the business in hand, and to please the great men to whom they are speaking. The circumstances to which it is their wish to subordinate their faith and their conscience being subject to various changes, their language has also to change from time to time; and so they call the same thing grey one moment and yellow the next, say one thing to one man, and another to another. Then, if these listeners happen to bring all this contrary information together as a common booty, what becomes of all their fine art? Besides they trip up so often when they are off their guard. For what memory could be strong enough to retain all the different shapes they have invented for the same subject? I have seen many in my time who have desired a reputation for this subtle kind of discretion, not seeing that the reputation and the end in view are incompatible.

Lying is indeed an accursed vice. We are men, and we have relations with one another only by speech. If we recognized the horror and gravity of an untruth, we should more justifiably punish it with fire than any other crime. I commonly find people taking the most ill-advised pains to correct their children for their harmless faults, and worrying them about heedless acts which leave no trace and have no consequences. Lying – and in a lesser degree obstinacy – are, in my opinion, the only faults whose birth and progress we should consistently oppose. They grow with a child's growth, and once the tongue has got the knack of lying, it is difficult to imagine how impossible it is to correct it. Whence it happens that we find some otherwise excellent men subject to this fault and enslaved by it. I have a decent lad as my tailor, whom I have never heard to utter a single truth, even when it would have been to his advantage.

If, like the truth, falsehood had only one face, we should know better where we are, for we should then take the opposite of what a liar said to be the truth. But the opposite of a truth has a hundred thousand shapes and a limitless field.

The Pythagoreans regard good as certain and finite, and evil as boundless and uncertain. There are a thousand ways of missing the bull's eye, only one of hitting it. I am by no means sure that I could induce myself to tell a brazen and deliberate lie even to protect myself from the most obvious and extreme danger. An ancient father [St Augustine] says that we are better in the company of a dog we know than in that of a man whose language we do not understand. Therefore those of different nations do not regard one another as men, and how much less friendly is false speech than silence!

King Francis the First boasted of having by this means drawn circles round Francesco Taverna, ambassador of Francesco Sforza, Duke of Milan – a man of great reputation in the art of speechmaking. Taverna had been sent to make his master's excuses to His Majesty in a matter of great importance, which was this: the King wished to have constant channels of information in Italy, from which he had recently been expelled, and especially in the Duchy of Milan. He had decided, therefore, to keep a gentleman of his own at the Duke's court, an ambassador in effect, but in appearance a private individual ostensibly there on his own personal business. For the Duke very much depended on the Emperor – especially at that moment when he was negotiating a marriage with his niece, the King of Denmark's daughter, now the Dowager Duchess of Lorraine – and he could not establish open relations or intercourse with us without great prejudice to himself. A Milanese gentleman named Merveille, one of the King's equerries, was chosen for this office, and was despatched with secret credentials and instructions as ambassador, also with letters of recommendation to the Duke in the matter of his own private affairs as a mask and a show. However, he was at Court so long that the Emperor began to grow suspicious; and it was this, we believe, that gave rise to the subsequent events, which were that one fine night the Duke had Merveille's head cut off on a false charge of murder, his whole trial having been hurried through in a couple of days!

Francesco Taverna had come with a long falsified account of the affair – for the King had addressed himself to all the princes in Christendom, as well as to the Duke, demanding satisfaction – and he was received in audience one morning. In support of his case he advanced several plausible justifications for the deed, carefully prepared for the purpose. He pleaded that his master had never taken our man for anything but a private gentleman and a subject of his own, who had come to Milan on his own business and resided there in no other character. He denied all knowledge that Merveille was a member of the King's household or was even known to the King, much less that he was his ambassador. King Francis, in his turn, pressed objections and questions upon him, attacking him from all sides and cornering him at last on the point of the execution, carried out at night and apparently in secret. To which the poor embarrassed man replied, as if to put an honest face on the matter, that out of respect for His Majesty the Duke would have been sorry to let the execution take place in daylight. You can guess how quickly he was caught out in this clumsy self-contradiction, made in the presence of such a nose as King Francis had.

•

The handbook of lies

BARTHOLOMAEUS INGANNEVOLE

In the late sixteenth century, the Catholic Church, under Pope Sixtus V, sought to control the publication of all written matter in an attempt to suppress that which it deemed to be unsuitable for the faithful. 'Libraries and printing offices, wherever they are, must be visited; if in Rome, by the Master of the Sacred Palace, but in other places by the Bishops or other superior clergy, and by the Inquisitors, or, at least by such persons as they deputize . . . Let no books be offered for sale unless a list of them is made out and signed by the authorities aforesaid; nor may any other books than those marked in the list be offered for sale under such penalties as those authorities may please to fix.' This strict control even extended to books that were left in the wills of the deceased: 'the heirs and executors of last wills must not use the books left by the deceased, nor give them to others to be used, nor let them go out of their hands on any account whatever before they have had a list made by persons authorized, and have obtained a licence from the same'. One book that was expressly forbidden to the faithful was the *Enchiridion Mendacii* – the Handbook, or Manual of Lies by one Bartholomaeus Ingannevole. 'Let all men know that the Handbook of Lies by the heretic Bartholomaeus Ingannevole, is a book interdicted from the faithful. Neither Jews nor infidels, nor other such people dwelling or being in Christian provinces or places may have it, read it, buy it, sell it, or carry it away. And let all men know that it is not lawful for anyone to tear it or burn it by his own authority, but it must be delivered to the Master of the Sacred Palace at Rome, or, in other places to the chief clergyman and the Inquisitor whose duty it will be to make diligent inquiry of the person who delivers it. But where an office of the Holy Inquisition is not established and there is a University, the Bishop and the Dean must do all this.

'And whoever shall offend in this matter shall be punished by the aforesaid according to the gravity of this offence. And, moreover, the Handbook of Lies is also prohibited into whatsoever language it may be translated.' It seems almost certain that both book and author were consigned to the flames, and this introduction is sadly all that remains of the first book of lies.

The pursuit of Truth is a chimera. That is why there are none who can say what Truth amounts to, and none who can demonstrate its permanency, and all those who pursue Absolute Truth are themselves deceived. He who recognizes that all men are born liars, best knows all the Truth that need concern him, for he will then know himself and have an advantage over others. For will not he who believes in Absolute Truth admit nothing of its opposite? But a Lie may exist being alloyed with a little Truth. Search the world and you will find that everywhere it is men who allow Truth to become extreme that are dangerous. Whereas men who lie know convenience, and therein lies happiness in this life. Truly, never to lie admits of no imagining which is all that God did give man to distinguish him from the beasts of the field. Know therefore that the happiness of men may not be found in Truth, nor in Falsehood, but, like iron mixed with fire, in the strength of their alloy. There is at least Truth in this. Yet even the basest fellow may see that the sun shines and speak it truly, and it takes a man of wit to know best how to dissimulate. That there is an art to lying well, and truly, could only be denied were it to say that dishonest men are never hanged. But a man who speaks Truth will strangle just as easily, and the advantage of dissimulation will be truly seen if one considers the great number of honest men who are hanged by those dishonest men who rule over them.

Know then that in this handbook may be learned methods for the dissimulation of wealth before a tax-collector, wrongdoing before the Justice, adultery before a wife, impiety before a cleric, idleness before a master, lust before a maiden, and treason before a Prince, as well as other stratagems and scenarios for the practising of various deceits, lies, falsehoods and mendacities upon the generality, including the counterfeiting of virginity, the simulation and dissimulation of pregnancy, the crafty means for the bedding of a shy maid, and divers means for avoidance of the providing of gentlemanly satisfaction in a quarrel without seeming cowardly. Herein also may be read the lies of the world's most accomplished liars, including Herodotus, Alexander the Great, Homer, Julius Caesar, Cicero, Suetonius, Tacitus, Pliny, Procopius, Psellus, Marco Polo, Machiavelli, Sanchez de las Brozas, as well as Chroniclers, Lawyers, Princes, Churchmen, and so-called Saints, for the instruction of those who would become expert in the principles of trickery and fraud. All without hazard to a man's immortal soul.

•

Of truth

FRANCIS BACON

What is truth? said jesting Pilate, and would not stay for an answer. Certainly there be them that delight in giddiness, and count it a bondage to fix a belief; affecting free-will in thinking as well as in acting. And though the sects of the philosophers of that kind be gone, yet there remain certain discoursing wits which are of the same veins, though there be not so much blood in them as was in those of the ancients. But it is not only the difficulty and labour which men take in finding out the truth, nor again that when it is found it imposeth upon men's thoughts, that doth bring lies in favour; but a natural though corrupt love of the lie itself. One of the later school of the Grecians examineth the matter, and is at a stand to think what should be in it, that men should love lies; where neither they make for pleasure, as with poets; nor for advantage, as with the merchant; but the lie for the lie's sake. But I cannot tell: this same truth is a naked and open day-light, that doth not shew the masques and mummeries and triumphs of the world, half so stately and daintily as candle-lights. Truth may perhaps come to the price of a pearl, that sheweth best by day; but it will not rise to the price of a diamond or a carbuncle, that sheweth best in varied lights. A mixture of a lie doth ever add pleasure. Doth any man doubt, that if there were taken out of men's minds vain opinions, flattering hopes, false valuations, imaginations as one would, and the like, but it would leave the minds of a number of men poor shrunken things, full of melancholy and indisposition and unpleasing to themselves? One of the fathers, in great severity, called poesy 'vinum daemonum', because it filleth the imagination, and yet it is but with the shadow of a lie. But it is not the lie that passeth through the mind, but the lie that sinketh in and settleth in it, that doth the hurt, such as we spake of before. But howsoever these things are thus in men's depraved judgements and affections, yet truth, which only doth judge itself, teacheth that the inquiry of truth, which is the love-making or wooing of it, the knowledge of truth, which is the presence of it, and the belief of truth, which is the enjoying of it, is the sovereign good of human nature. The first creature of God, in the works of the days, was the light of the sense; the last was the light of reason; and his sabbath work, ever since, is the illumination of his Spirit. First he breathed light upon the face of matter or chaos; then he breathed light into the face of man; and still he breatheth and inspireth light into the face of his chosen. The poet that beautified the sect that was otherwise inferior to the rest, saith yet excellently well: 'It is a pleasure to stand upon the shore, and to see ships tost upon the sea: a pleasure to stand in the window of a castle, and to see a battle and the adventures thereof below: but no pleasure is comparable to the standing upon the vantage ground of truth'(a hill not to be commanded, and where the air is always clear and serene), 'and to see the errors, and wanderings, and mists, and tempest, in the vale below': so always that this prospect be with pity, and not with swelling or pride. Certainly, it is heaven upon earth, to have a man's mind move in charity, rest in providence, and turn upon the poles of truth.

To pass from theological and philosophical truth, to the truth of civil business: it will be acknowledged, even by those that practise it not, that clear and round dealing is the honour of man's nature; and that mixture of falsehood is like alloy in coin of gold and silver; which may make the metal work the better, but it embaseth it. For these winding and crooked courses are the goings of the serpent; which goeth basely upon the belly, and not upon the feet. There is no vice that doth so cover a man with shame as to be found false and perfidious. And therefore Mountaigny [Montaigne] saith prettily, when he inquired the reason, why the word of the lie should be such a disgrace and such an odious charge? saith he, 'If it be well weighed, to say that a man lieth, is as much to say that he is brave towards God and a coward towards men.' For a lie faces God, and shrinks from man. Surely the wickedness of falsehood and breach of faith cannot possibly be so highly expressed, as in that it shall be the last peal to call the judgements of God upon the generations of men; it being foretold, that when Christ cometh, he shall not find faith upon the earth.

•

The second day's triumph

THOMAS DEKKER

How quickly after the art of Lying was once publicly professed, were false weights and false measures invented! And they have since done as much hurt to the inhabitants of cities as the invention of guns hath done to their walls. For though a lie has but short legs (like a dwarf's) yet it goes far in a little time, *et crescit eundo*, and at last proves a tall fellow. The reason is, that truth had ever but one father, but lies are a thousand men's bastards, and are begotten everywhere.

Look up then (thou thy country's darling), and behold what a devilish inmate thou hast entertained. The genealogy of truth is well known, for she was born in heaven, and dwells in heaven. Falsehood then and lying must of necessity come out of that hot country of hell, from the line of devils: for those two are as opposite, as day and darkness. What an ungracious generation wilt thou mingle with thine, if thou draw not this from thee: what a number of unhappy and cursed children will be left upon thy hand? For lying is father to falsehood, and grandfather to perjury: fraud (with two faces) is his daughter, a very monster: treason (with hairs like snakes) is his kinsman; a very fury! How art thou enclosed with danger? The lie first deceives thee, and to shoot the deceit off cleanly, an oath (like an arrow) is drawn to the head, and that hits the mark. If a lie, after it is moulded, be not smooth enough, there is no instrument to burnish it, but an oath. Swearing gives it colour, and a bright complexion. So that oaths are crutches, upon which lies (like lame soldiers) go, and need no other passport. Little oaths are able to bear great lies: but great lies are able to beat down great families. For oaths are wounds that a man stabs into himself, yea, they are burning words that consume those who kindle them.

What fools then are buyers and sellers to be abused by such

hell-hounds? Swearing and forswearing puts into their hands perhaps the gains of a little silver, but those pieces which Judas received, they are their destruction. Wealth so gotten, is like a tree set in the depth of winter, it prospers not.

But is it possible (thou leader of so great a Kingdom) that heretofore so many bonfires of men's bodies should be made before thee in the good quarrel of truth? And that now thou shouldst take part with her enemy? Have so many triple-pointed darts of treason been shot at the heads of thy princes, because they would not take truth out of thy temples, and art thou now in league with false witches who would kill thee? Thou art no traveller; the habit of lying therefore will not become thee, cast it off.

He that gives a soldier the lie, looks to receive the stab: but what danger does he run open that gives a whole city the lie? Yet must I venture to give it to thee. Let me tell thee then, that thou dost lie with pride, and though thou art not so gaudy, yet art thou more costly in attiring thyself than the court: because pride is the queen of sins, thou hast chosen her to be thy concubine, and hast begotten many base sons and daughters upon her body, as vainglory, curiosity, disobedience, opinion, disdain, etc. Pride by thy lying with her, is grown impudent. She is now a common harlot, and every one hath use of her body. The tailor calls her his Lemman [illicit lover], he hath often got her great with child of fantasticality and fashions, who no sooner came into the world, but the fairest wives of thy tenants snatch them up into their arms, laid them in their laps and to their breasts, and after they had played with them their pleasure, into the country were those two children [of the tailor's] sent to be nursed up, so that they lie sometimes there, but ever anon with thee.

Thou dost likewise lie with usury: how often hast thou been found in bed with her! How often hath she been openly disgraced at the cross for a strumpet! Yet still dost thou keep her company, and art not ashamed of it, because you commit sin together, even in those houses that have painted posts standing at the gates. What ungodly brats and kindred hath she brought thee? For upon usury hast thou begotten extortion (a strong but an unmannerly child), hardness of heart, a very murderer, and bad conscience, who is so unruly, that he seems to be sent unto thee, to be thy everlasting pain. Then hath she sons in law, and they are all scriveners [clerks]: those scriveners have base sons, and they are all common brokers; those brokers likewise send a number into the world, and they are all common thieves.

All of these may easily give arms: for they fetch their descent from hell, where are as many gentlemen as in any one place, in any kingdom.

Thou dost lie with sundry others, and committest strange whoredoms, which by use and boldness grown so common, that they seem to be no whoredoms at all, yet thine own abominations would not appear so vilely, but that thou makest thy buildings a brothel to others: for thou sufferest religion to lie with hypocrisy: charity to lie with ostentation: friendship to lie with hollow-heartedness: the churl to lie with simony: justice to lie with bribery, and last of all, conscience to lie with everyone. So that now she is full of diseases. But thou knowest the medicine for all these feavers that shake thee: be therefore to thy self thine own physician, and by strong pills purge away this second infection that is breeding upon thee, before it strikes to the heart.

Falsehood and lying thus have had their day, and like almanacks of the last year, are now gone out: let us follow them a step or two further to see how they ride, and then (if we can) leave them, for I perceive it grows late, because candle-light (who is next to enter upon the stage) is making himself ready to act his comical scenes. The chariot then that lying is drawn in, is made all of whetstones; wantons and evil custom are his horses; a fool is the coachman that drives them: a couple of swearing fencers sometimes lead the horses by the reins, and sometimes flourish before them to make room. Worshipfully is this Lord of Limbo attended, for knights themselves follow close at his heels; Marry they are not post and poyre-knights, but one of the post. Amongst whose train is shuffled in a company of scambling ignorant pettifoggers, lean knaves and hungry, for they live upon nothing but the scraps of the law, and here and there (like a prune in white-broth) is stuck a spruce but a mere prating unpractised lawyer's clerk all in black. At the tail of all (when this goodly pageant is passed by) follow a crowd of every trade some amongst whom lest we be smothered, and be taken to be of the same list, let us strike down my way.

•

A linguistic gaffe

IZAAK WALTON

Izaak Walton records this anecdote concerning King James I's ambassador to Italy, Sir Henry Wotton.

At his first going ambassador into Italy, as he passed through Germany, he stayed some days at Augusta: where having been in his former travels well known by many of the best note for learning and ingeniousness (those that are esteemed the virtuosi of that nation), with whom he passed an evening in merriments, was requested by Christopher Flecamore to write some sentence in his albo (a book of white paper which, for that purpose, many of the German gentry usually carry about them), and Sir Henry Wotton consenting to the motion, took an occasion from some accidental discourse of the present company to write a pleasant definition of an ambassador, in these very words:

> Legatus est vir bonus peregre missus ad mentiendum Reipublicae causa.

Which Sir Henry Wotton could have been content should thus have been Englished:

> An ambassador is an honest man sent to lie abroad for the good of his country.

But the word for 'lie' being the hinge upon which the conceit was to turn was not so expressed in Latin as would admit (in the hands of an enemy especially) so fair a construction as Sir Henry thought in English. Yet as it was, it slept quietly among other sentences in this albo almost eight years, till by accident it fell into the hands of Jasper Scioppius, a Romanist, a man of a restless spirit and a malicious pen, who with books against King James prints this as a principle of that religion professed by the King and his ambassador, Sir Henry Wotton, then at Venice; and in Venice it was presently after written in several glass windows, and spitefully declared to be Sir Henry Wotton's.

This coming to the knowledge of King James, he apprehended it to be such an oversight, such a weakness or worse in Sir Henry Wotton, as caused the King to express much wrath against him; and this caused Sir Henry Wotton to write two apologies, one to Velserus (one of the chiefs of Augusta) in the universal language, which he caused to be printed and given and scattered in the most remarkable places both in Germany and Italy, as an antidote against the venomous books of Scioppius; and another apology to King James, which were both so ingenious, so clear, and so choicely eloquent, that his Majesty (who was a pure judge of it) could not forbear at the receipt thereof to declare publicly that Sir Henry Wotton had commuted sufficiently for a greater offence.

•

The character of falsehood

HUGO GROTIUS

XI. THE CHARACTER OF FALSEHOOD, IN SO FAR AS IT IS PERMISSIBLE, CONSISTS IN ITS CONFLICT WITH THE RIGHT OF ANOTHER; THIS IS EXPLAINED.

1. In order to exemplify the general idea of falsehood, it is necessary that what is spoken, or written, or indicated by signs or gestures, cannot be understood otherwise than in a sense which differs from the thought of him who uses the means of expression.

Upon this broader signification, however, a stricter meaning of falsehood must be imposed, carrying some characteristic distinction. This distinction, if we regard the matter aright, at least according to the common view of nations, can be described, we think, as nothing else than a conflict with the existing and continuing right of him to whom the speech or sign is addressed; for it is sufficiently clear that no one lies to himself, however false his statement may be.

By right in this connexion I do not mean every right without relation to the matter in question, but that which is peculiar to it and connected with it. Now that right is nothing else than the liberty of judgement which, as if by some tacit agreement, men who speak are understood to owe to those with whom they converse. For this is merely that mutual obligation which men had willed to introduce at the time when they determined to make use of speech and similar signs; for without such an obligation the invention of speech would have been void of result.

2. We require, moreover, that this right be valid and continuing at the time the statement is made; for it may happen that the right has indeed existed, but has been taken away, or will be annulled by another right which supervenes, just as a debt is cancelled by an acceptance or by the cessation of the condition. Then, further, it is required that the right which is infringed belong to him with whom we converse, and not to another, just as in the case of contracts also injustice arises only from the infringement of a right of the contracting parties.

Perhaps you would do well to recall here that Plato, following Simonides, refers truth-speaking to justice; that falsehood, at least the type of falsehood which is forbidden, is often described in Holy Writ as bearing false witness or speaking against one's neighbour; and that Augustine himself in determining the nature of falsehood regards the will to deceive as essential. Cicero, too, wishes that inquiry in regard to speaking the truth be referred to the fundamental principles of justice.

3. Moreover, the right of which we have spoken may be abrogated by the express consent of him with whom we are dealing, as when one says that he will speak falsely and the other permits it. In like manner it may be cancelled by tacit consent, or consent assumed on reasonable grounds, or by the opposition of another right which, in the common judgement of all men, is much more cogent.

The right understanding of these points will supply to us many inferences, which will be of no small help in reconciling the differences in the views which have been cited above . . .

XIII. IT IS PERMISSIBLE TO SAY WHAT IS FALSE WHEN HE TO WHOM THE CONVERSATION IS NOT ADDRESSED IS DECEIVED, AND WHEN IT WOULD BE PERMISSIBLE TO DECEIVE HIM IF NOT SHARING IN IT.

1. The second inference is that, so long as the person to whom the talk is addressed is not deceived, if a third party draws a false impression therefrom there is no falsehood.

There is no falsehood in relation to him to whom the utterance is directed because his liberty remains unimpaired. His case is like that of persons to whom a fable is told when they are aware of its character, or those to whom figurative language is used in 'irony', or in 'hyperbole', a figure which, as Seneca says, reaches the truth by means of falsehood, while Quintilian calls it a lying exaggeration. There is no falsehood, again, in respect to him who chances to hear what is said; the conversation is not being held with him, consequently there is no obligation toward him. Indeed if he forms for himself an opinion from what is said not to him, but to another, he has something which he can credit to himself, not to another. In fine, if, so far as he is concerned, we wish to form a correct judgement, the conversation is not a conversation, but something that may mean anything at all.

2. Cato the censor therefore committed no wrong in falsely promising aid to his allies, nor did Flaccus, who said to others that a city of the enemy had been stormed by Aemilius, although in both cases the enemy was deceived. A similar ruse is told of Agesilaus by Plutarch. Nothing in fact was said to the enemy; the harm, moreover, which followed was something foreign to the statement, and of itself not unpermissible to desire or accomplish.

To this category Chrysostom and Jerome refer Paul's speech, in which at Antioch he rebuked Peter for being too zealous a Jew. They think that Peter was well aware that this was not done in earnest; at the same time the weakness of those present was humoured.

XIV. IT IS PERMISSIBLE TO SAY WHAT IS FALSE WHEN THE CONVERSATION IS DIRECTED TO HIM WHO WISHES TO BE DECEIVED IN THIS WAY.

1. The third inference is that, whenever it is certain that he to whom the conversation is addressed will not be annoyed at the infringement of his liberty in judging, or rather will be grateful therefore, because of some advantage which will follow, in this case also a falsehood in the strict sense, that is a harmful falsehood, is not perpetrated; just so a man does not commit theft who with the presumed consent of the owner uses up some trifling thing in order that he may thereby secure for the owner a great advantage.

In this great matters which are so certain, a presumed wish is taken as one that is expressed. Besides, in such cases it is evident that no wrong is done to one who desires it. It seems, therefore, that he does no wrong who comforts a sick friend by persuading him of what is not true, as Arria did by saying what was not true to Paetus after the death of their son; the story is told in the letters of Pliny. Similar is the case of the man who brings courage by a false report to one who is wavering in battle, so that, encouraged thereby, he wins victory and safety for himself, and is thus 'beguiled but not betrayed', as Lucretius says.

2. Democritus says: 'We must speak the truth, wherever that is the better course.' Xenophon writes: 'It is right to deceive our friends, if it is for their own good.' Clement of Alexandria concedes 'the use of lying as a curative measure'. Maximus of Tyre says: 'A physician deceives a sick man, a general deceives his army, and a pilot the sailors; and in such deception there is no wrong.' The reason is given by Proclus in commenting on Plato: 'For that which is good is better than the truth.'

To this class of untruths belongs the statement reported by Xenophon, that the allies would presently arrive; that of Tullus Hostilius, that the army from Alba was making a flank movement by his order; what histories term the 'salutary lie' of the consul Quinctius, that the enemy were in flight on the other wing; and similar incidents found in abundance in the writings of the historians. However, it is to be observed that in this sort of falsehood the infringement upon the judgement is of less account because it is usually confined to the moment, and the truth is revealed a little later.

XV. IT IS PERMISSIBLE TO SAY WHATEVER IS FALSE WHEN THE SPEAKER MAKES USE OF A SUPERIOR RIGHT OVER ONE SUBJECT TO HIMSELF.

1. A fourth inference, akin to the foregoing, applies to the case when one who has a right that is superior to all the rights of another makes use of this right either for his own or for the public good. This especially Plato seems to have had in mind when he conceded the right of saying what is false to those having authority. Since the same author seems now to grant this privilege to physicians, and again to deny it to them, apparently we ought to make the distinction that in the former passage he means physicians publicly appointed to this responsibility, and in the latter those who privately claim it for themselves. Yet Plato also rightly recognizes that falsehood is not becoming to deity, although deity has a supreme right over men, because it is a mark of weakness to take refuge in such devices.

2. An instance of blameless mendacity, of which even Plato approves, may perhaps be found in Joseph, who, when ruling in the king's stead, accused his brothers first of being spies, and then of being thieves, pretending, but not really believing, that they were such. Another instance is that of Solomon, who gave an example of wisdom inspired by God, when to the women who were disputing over the child he uttered the words which indicated his purpose to slay it, although his real intent was the furthest possible from such a course, and his desire was to assign to the true mother her own offspring.

•

The devils of Loudun

ALDOUS HUXLEY

The events which led to the trial of Urbain Grandier for witchcraft began as a practical joke. Some neurotic Ursuline nuns had accused him of causing their possession by devils. Unfortunately for Grandier, he had earlier opposed the will of Cardinal Richelieu, who saw these events as a way of being rid of a rather troublesome parish priest. Despite terrible tortures Grandier refused to confess; nevertheless, he was finally burned at the stake. Here Huxley recounts the evidentiary problems that were encountered by Richelieu's man, the Baron de Laubardemont, and the exorcists who sought Grandier's indictment.

During the spring and summer of 1634 the main purpose of the exorcisms was not the deliverance of the nuns, but the indictment of Grandier. The aim was to prove, out of the mouth of Satan himself, that the parson was a magician and had bewitched the nuns. But Satan is, by definition, the Father of Lies, and his evidence is therefore worthless. To this argument Laubardemont, his exorcists and the Bishop of Poitiers replied by affirming that, when duly constrained by a priest of the Roman Church, devils are bound to tell the truth. In other words, anything to which a hysterical nun was ready, at the instigation of her exorcist, to affirm on oath, was for all practical purposes a divine revelation. For inquisitors, this doctrine was a real convenience. But it had one grave defect; it was manifestly unorthodox. In the year 1610 a committee of learned theologians had discussed the admissibility of diabolic evidence and issued the following authoritative decision. 'We, the undersigned Doctors of the Faculty of Paris, touching certain questions which have been proposed to us, are of the opinion that one must never admit the accusation of demons, still less must one exploit exorcisms for the purpose of discovering a man's faults or for determining if he is a magician; and we are further of the opinion that, even if the said exorcisms should have been applied in the presence of the Holy Sacrament, with the devil forced to swear an oath (which is a ceremony of which we do not at all approve), one must not for all that give any credit to his words, the devil being always a liar and the Father of Lies.' Furthermore, the devil is man's sworn enemy, and is therefore ready to endure all the torments of exorcism for the sake of doing harm to a single soul. If the devil's evidence were admitted, the most virtuous people would be in the greatest danger; for it is precisely against these that Satan rages most violently. 'Wherefore St Thomas (Book 22, Question 9, Article 22) maintains with the authority of St Chrysostom, DAEMONI, ETIAM VERA DICENTI, NON EST CREDENDUM. (The devil must not be believed, even when he tells the truth.)' We must follow the example of Christ, who imposed silence on the demons even when they spoke truth, by calling Him, the Son of God. 'Whence it appears that, in the absence of other proofs, one must never proceed against those who are accused by devils. And we note that this is well observed in France, where judges do not recognize these depositions.' Twenty-four years later, Laubardemont and his colleagues recognized nothing else. For the humanity and good sense of the orthodox view the exorcists had substituted, and the Cardinal's agents had eagerly accepted, a heresy that was both monstrously silly and dangerous in the extreme. Ismael Boulliau, the astronomer-priest who had served under Grandier as one of the vicars of Saint-Pierre-du-Marche, qualified the new doctrine as 'impious, erroneous, execrable, and abominable – a doctrine which turns Christians into idolators, undermines the very foundations of the Christian religion, opens the door to calumny and will make it possible for the devil to immolate human victims in the name, not of Moloch, but of a fiendish and infernal dogma'. That the fiendish and infernal dogma was fully approved by Richelieu is certain. The fact is recorded by Laubardemont himself and by the author of the *Démonomanie de Loudun*, Pillet de la Mesnardière, the Cardinal's personal physician.

Licensed, sometimes even suggested, and always respectfully listened to, the diabolic depositions came pouring in just as fast as Laubardemont needed them. Thus he found it desirable that Grandier should not be merely a magician, but also a high priest in the Old Religion. The word went round, and immediately one of the lay demoniacs obliged by confessing (through the mouth of a devil who had been duly constrained by one of the Carmelite exorcists) that she had prostituted herself to the parson, and that the parson had expressed his appreciation by offering to take her to the Sabbath and make her princess at the devil's court. Grandier affirmed that he had never so much as laid eyes on the girl. But Satan himself had spoken and to doubt his word would be sacrilege.

•

A conscientious dispensation from keeping one's word

BLAISE PASCAL

Pascal was an ally of the Jansenists, a sect of Christians whose doctrine resembled Calvinism in many respects, and whose teachings were formulated by Cornelius Jansen, Bishop of Ypres. Jansenism was condemned by Pope Innocent IV in 1654, and the Jesuits, who were at that time high in favour and intoxicated with power, pursued with slander and persecution all those who inclined to Jansenism. While he was not a member of the sect, nevertheless Pascal was a sympathizer, and he was prevailed upon to lend his support to the cause. The result was the publication (at no small risk to himself) of his *Provincial Letters* (1656–7), the principal target of which was Jesuit casuistry. This extract exhibits the unsuspecting interpreter of the Casuist in communication with an ostensible disciple, who, partly by ingenious suggestions and partly by assumed docility, elicits the indiscreet zeal of a well-meaning but simple Jesuit father on the subject of telling lies.

'One of the greatest difficulties people experience, is to avoid telling lies, especially when it is wished to convey the belief in something that is untrue. This purpose is admirably served by our doctrine of equivocation; by which "it is allowed to make use of ambiguous expressions, to be understood in a sense different from that in which we use them", as is stated by Sanchez.'

'I am aware of that,' I said.

'Of course, we have circulated this doctrine so much that everyone must be acquainted with it. But do you know what ought to be done when you cannot find equivocal words?'

'I can't say that I do.'

'I thought so,' he replied. 'This point is new: it is the doctrine of "mental reservation". Sanchez says that "we may swear that we have not done a certain thing, although we have actually done it, provided that we fix it secretly in our own minds that it was not done on a given day, or before we were born, or any similar circumstance. This is convenient in many situations, and is most especially justifiable for the preservation of health, honour or property."'

'What, father! But isn't this just a lie or a perjury just the same?'

'No,' he replied. 'Sanchez demonstrates it in the same passage, and Père Filiutius also, that it is the intention that regulates the quality of the action. He gives another method of avoiding lies which is that after saying aloud "I swear that I did not do such and such a thing," one should add in a low tone "today"; or after saying aloud "I swear," to whisper, "that I say", and then to continue aloud, "that I did not do such and such a thing." You see clearly that this is telling the truth.'

'I certainly do,' I replied, 'or at least that is saying the truth "in a whisper", and a lie "aloud". But isn't it possible that everyone might have sufficient presence of mind to avail themselves of these methods?'

'Our Fathers,' he said, 'have provided for such cases in that it is enough to avoid a lie to say simply, "they have not done" that which they have really done, provided that they have a general intention of using the words in a sense which more expert persons would give them.'

'And now confess,' continued the Father, 'that you have often been in situations of great difficulty from not knowing all of this.'

'Occasionally,' I replied.

'And don't you think that it would be highly convenient to have such a conscientious dispensation from keeping your word?'

'The greatest convenience in the world.'

•

The calumnies of the Jesuits

BLAISE PASCAL

In this extract from the fifteenth of his *Provincial Letters*, which he writes to the Jesuits, Pascal addresses himself to the fact of their having withdrawn calumny from the catalogue of crimes, and of how they did not scruple to avail themselves of its aid. For all Pascal's efforts to defend Jansenism against the assaults of the Jesuits, the sect was finally put down by Pope Clement XI in 1713.

I do not mean to confine my remarks to proofs that your writings are filled with calumnies: I have a higher aim than this. It is very possible to say that which is false, while we believe it to be true: but the essence of falsehood includes the intention to lie. It shall be my endeavour, then, Reverend Sirs, to show that your intention is falsehood and calumny; and that it is with forethought and purpose, that you impute to your adversaries crimes, of which you know they are innocent; inasmuch as you have brought yourselves to believe it possible to do this without incurring the danger of falling from a state of grace. And although you are as well acquainted as myself with this doctrine of your school, I do not the more omit, in the most unequivocal terms, to hold it up to your view; my object being to sustain the assertion to your own face, and to deprive you of all possibility of denial. So common, in fact, is this tenet amongst your Society, that it is circulated not only in your writings, but also in your public theses; as (among others) those of Louvain, in the year 1645, in the following terms: 'Is it anything more than venial to calumniate, and impute false crimes; in order to impeach the credibility of those who speak ill of ourselves? . . .' And this doctrine is so universal among you, that any one daring to oppose it is regarded by you as presumptuous and ignorant.

This was not long since, the treatment experienced by Père Quiroga, a German Capuchin, on his venturing to controvert these views. Your own Père Dicastillus at once entered the field against him, and expressed himself on the question in these terms . . . 'A certain grave Friar, bare-footed and hooded . . . whom I do not name, has had the audacity to denounce this opinion amongst females and ignorant persons; and to assert that it is injurious and scandalous, contrary to sound morality, opposed to the welfare of the state and society; and, finally, at variance, not only with the opinion of the highest Catholic authorities, but also with those of all who hold Catholic sentiments. But I have contended, and do still contend, that calumny, where employed against a calumniator (even though it amount to falsehood) is no mortal sin, nor is an offence against justice or charity. And to prove this, I have furnished him with a multitude of authorities from our Fathers, and their entire Colleges, whom I have consulted . . .'

You see from this, my fathers, that there are few opinions which your Society have taken such pains to establish as this; for indeed there are few of which you stand in so much need. And it is because you have given so fully your authorization to it, that the Casuists avail themselves of it as an indubitable principle. 'It is clearly,' says Caramuel . . . 'a "probable" opinion that it is not a mortal offence to disseminate falsehoods against character, in defence of our own reputation. This has been maintained by above twenty learned doctors . . . so that if this doctrine is not to be regarded as a probable one, scarcely any can be regarded as such throughout the whole system of theology.'

Oh most flagrant and corrupted theology! according to whose tenets, if it could not be established to be allowable, with safety of conscience, to deal out mendacious calumnies in defence of our reputation, scarcely any of its decisions could be established! Can it be doubted, Sirs, that those who hold abstractedly such a principle, will find no difficulty in carrying it into practice? Our corrupt propensities so naturally incline us to this offence, that when once the restraint of conscience is removed, it will break out with irresistible force. Do you ask for an example? Caramuel will furnish you with one: 'This maxim,' said he, 'of the Jesuit Dicastillus respecting slander, having been taught by a German countess to the Empress's daughters, the belief that they would commit no more than a venial offence in uttering slanders, induced them, in a few days, to set afloat so many false and calumnious reports, that the whole court was thrown into commotion. It is easy to imagine the use to which they turned this licence; so that to allay the tumult it was found necessary to call in a worthy Capuchin, of exemplary life, named Père Quiroga (and this it was which caused Père Dicastillus so much chagrin); who forthwith expressed his opinion that the maxim in question was highly pernicious, especially among females, and he was most urgent that the Empress should immediately interdict the practice.'

No one can be surprised at the ill effects which ensued from this doctrine; on the contrary, the wonder would have been had it been otherwise. Our self-love easily persuades us that we are unjustly accused; and most especially is this the case with you, my Fathers, whose vanity so greatly blinds you, that you give out in all your writings that the Church is wounded when a member of your Society is attacked. It would have been strange, therefore, had you not put such a maxim as this into practice. No longer can it be said of you, as it might have been by those who do not know you, 'How is it possible that these worthy Fathers should calumniate their enemies, when in doing so they would endanger their salvation?' On the contrary, it may be said, 'How is it likely that these good Fathers should forgo the advantage of falsehood and slander, since they find they can use them without danger to their souls?' Let us no longer be surprised to find the Jesuits turned calumniators. Their consciences are safe; what is there to prevent them? By their credit with the world they can disseminate their slanders without fear of man's resentment; and by the latitude they have given to the conscience, they have brought themselves to believe that they have nothing to fear from the justice of God!

Here then, Reverend Father, is the fruitful source of your numerous and malignant impostures. This it was that prompted such libels on the part of your own Père Brisacier, as to bring down upon him the censure of the late pious Archbishop of Paris. This it was that led the Père D'Anjou to denounce publicly from the pulpit in the church of St Benedict, Paris, on the 8th March 1655, those persons of rank who received the contributions for the poor in Picardy and Champagne, to which they had given so liberally themselves; and to affirm, with such malignity of falsehood – as if for the very purpose of quenching the charity of any who had yielded credit to the slander – 'that he knew, for a certainty, that those persons had misappropriated the money, to employ it in purposes hostile to the Church and State'. What was the consequence? The curate of the parish, a doctor of the Sorbonne, was obliged the next day, to ascend the pulpit, and publicly contradict the calumny.

It was on the same principle that your Père Crasset, in his preaching at Orleans, uttered such gross calumnies that the Bishop of Orleans was obliged, in his Charge of 9th last September, to denounce him as a public impostor, declaring 'that he forbids Brother John Crasset, Priest of the Society of Jesus, to preach in his diocese, and to all his people to attend him, under pain of an act of mortal disobedience; inasmuch as he had learnt that the said Crasset had delivered from the pulpit a discourse filled with falsehood and calumnies, against the ecclesiastics of this city; charging them falsely with maintaining the proposition, "That the keeping the commandments of God is impossible; that internal grace is irresistible; and that Christ did not die for all men;" with other similar sentiments, condemned by Innocent X.' For here, Reverend Sirs, is your ordinary method of misrepresentation and the first species of reproach that you are wont to cast against those whom you seek to denounce. And although you may know it to be impossible to prove the charge, as in the case of your Père Crasset and the Orleans ecclesiastics, your conscience is at ease; for you believe that this method of calumniating your opponents is so clearly allowable, that you hesitate not to circulate your slanders in the most public and extensive manner.

•

Wartime lies

JEREMY TAYLOR

The seventeenth-century theologian Jeremy Taylor considers the question of whether or not it is wrong to lie to an enemy.

In a just war it is lawful to deceive the unjust enemy, but not to lie; that is, by stratagems and semblances of motions, by amusements and intrigues of action, by ambushes and wit, by simulation or dissimulation, 'by force or craft, openly or secretly', any way that you can, unless you promise the contrary: for it is in open war, if the war be just, lawful to do justice upon the enemy all the ways we can; craft is but the facilitation of the force; and when it is a state of war, there is nothing else to be looked for. But if there be a treaty or a contract, a promise or an agreement in any thing, that is a state of peace so far, and introduces a law; and then to tell a lie or to falsify does destroy peace and justice, and by breaking the law reduces things to the state of war again.

'It is lawful to do anything to destroy your enemy;' that is, so long as you profess hostility: and therefore if you tell a false tale to him to deceive him when you are fighting against him, he is a fool if he believes you, for then you intend to destroy him; but you are not unjust, you are in a state of war with him, and have no obligation upon you towards him. Thus Elisha told a lie to the Syrian army which came to apprehend him, 'This is not the city and this is not the way:' and this is approved and allowed by Plato and Xenophon, Homer and Pindar, Polybius and Thucydides, Plutarch and Lucian amongst the Greeks, Philo amongst the Jews; and S. Chrysostom amongst the Christians says, 'If you examine all the bravest generals, you shall find their bravest trophies to be the production of fraud and craft . . . and that they were more commended than such who did their work by fine force.' Thus the causing of false rumours to be spread amongst the enemies is an allowed stratagem in war, neither ignoble nor unjust. Flaccus told that Aemilius had taken the enemies' town, to dishearten the party he fought against: and Quinctius the consul caused to be spread abroad that the enemies on the right wing were fled. By such arts it is very usual to bring consternation to the hostile party: and he whom you may lawfully kill, you may as well deceive him into it as force him into it; you being no more obliged to tell him truth than to spare his life: for certainly of itself killing is as bad as lying; but when you have no obligation or law to the contrary, and have not bound yourself to the contrary, you may do either. But this is at no hand to be done in matters of treaty or promise, either explicit or implicit, as in parties and truces; and therefore it was a foul stain upon Hannibal, that he professing open war against the Romans did also profess it against faith and justice, keeping no word or promise if it was for his advantage to break it; and the Trojans were troubled in conscience at their fallacious conducting of their wars, not by stratagem, but by breaking their oaths and covenants, – 'We fight with lying and breaking promises,' which is unlawful to do. For concerning this thing, that even in war we are bound to keep faith and promise made to our enemies, it is certain and affirmed by almost all wise and good men of the world . . .

But deceiving the enemy by the stratagem of actions or words is not properly lying; for this supposes a conversation of law or peace, trust or promise explicit or implicit. A lie is the deceiving of a trust or confidence, but in fighting there is none of that; it is like wrestling and fencing, a design to make that part unarmed where he may strike the surer: and of this S. Clemens of Alexandria affirms expressly concerning stratagems in war: 'all these things it is lawful to bring to pass by persuasion or by force, by doing injury or harm there where we are to do revenge, by doing that which is just, or by telling that which is true, or by lying, or by doing any one or more of these together', '. . . when the Greeks received all these things from Moses, and how they were to use any one and every one of these, they received no small advantage.'

In this case all the prejudice which the question is like to have, is in the meaning and evil sound of the word lying; which because it is so hateful to God and man, casts a cloud upon any thing that it comes near: but lying (which S. Basil calls 'the extremity of malice') is indeed an enemy; but in war so it should be; only in peace and contracts, and civil conversation, it is intolerable. In war it is no lie, but an engine of war, against which the enemy is to stand upon his guard: and if a man may falsify a blow, much more may he falsify a word; and no justice, no promise, no charity, no law restrains the stratagems in a just war; they which may be destroyed may be deceived, and they may be deceived by false actions, by false words, if there be no collateral obligation or law to the contrary. 'A just man,' saith S. Austin, 'is to take care of nothing but that his war be just;' that is, by a just authority and for a just reason . . . 'but if it be a just war, it matters not as to the question of justice, whether he be overcome by force or by deceit.' 'Craft against a thief or enemy is good,' said Ulpian, but not perfidiousness. 'To bring war to a happy end, you may use force or wit,' said Ammianus Marcellinus, but at no hand break a promise, or be treacherous.

•

How Egyptian princes were reminded not to lie

JEREMY TAYLOR

Princes may not lie for the interests and advantages of government. Not in contracts, treaties, bargains, embassies and all the entercourses of peace and civil negotiation. For besides it is an argument of fear and infirmity to take sanctuary in the little subterfuges of craft when they are beaten from their own proper strengths, it is also a perfect destruction of government and the great bands of society and civil entercourse; and if they be used to fail, no man can be confident of that affirmative which ought to be venerable and sacred up the height of religion; and therefore the Egyptian law pressed this affair well, 'Let all that break their word and oaths die for it; because they are loaden with a double iniquity, . . . they destroy piety and reverence towards God, and faith amongst men, which is the greatest ligature of society.' And if princes do falsify their word and lie, their neighbours can have no entercourse with them but by violence and war, and their subjects none but fear and chance. For princes to lie is the greatest undecency in the world: and therefore Diodorus Siculus tells that the Egyptian princes used to wear a golden chain mixed and distinguished with curious stones, and they call it Truth; meaning that nothing was a greater ornament to a prince, nothing ought to be more sacred, or more remembered.

Holy liars

JOHN MILTON

Falsehood is commonly defined to be a violation of the truth either in word or deed, with the purpose of deceiving. Since however not only the dissimulation or concealment of truth, but even direct untruth with the intention of deceiving, may in many instances be beneficial to our neighbour, it will be necessary to define a falsehood somewhat more precisely; for I see no reason why the same rule should not apply to this subject which holds good with regard to homicide, and other cases hereafter to be mentioned, our judgement of which is formed not so much from the actions themselves, as from the intention in which they originated. No rational person will deny that there are certain individuals whom we are fully justified in deceiving. Who would scruple to dissemble with a child, with a madman, with a sick person, with one in a state of intoxication, with an enemy, with one who has himself a design of deceiving us, with a robber? unless indeed we dispute the trite maxim, CUI NULLUM EST JUST, EI NULLA FIT INJURIA. Yet, according to the above definition, it is not allowed to deceive either by word or deed in any of the cases stated. If I am under no obligation to restore to a madman a sword, or any other deposit, committed to me while in a sound mind, why should I be required to render the truth to one from whom I never received it, who is not entitled to demand it, and who will in all probability make a bad use of it? If every answer given to every interrogator with the intent of deceiving is to be counted a falsehood, it must be allowed that nothing was more common even among prophets and holiest of men.

Hence falsehood may perhaps be defined as follows: FALSEHOOD is incurred when ANY ONE, FROM A DISHONEST MOTIVE, EITHER PERVERTS THE

TRUTH, OR UTTERS WHAT IS FALSE TO ONE TO WHOM IT IS HIS DUTY TO SPEAK THE TRUTH.

. . . It follows from this definition, first, that parables, hyperboles, apologies and ironical modes of speech are not falsehoods, inasmuch as their object is not deception, but instruction . . . Secondly, that in the proper sense of the word deceit, no one can be deceived without being at the same time injured. When therefore, instead of injuring a person by a false statement, we either confer on him a positive benefit, or prevent him from inflicting or suffering injury, we are so far from being guilty of deceit towards him, however often the fiction may be repeated, that we ought rather to be considered as doing him a service against his will. Thirdly, it is universally admitted that feints and stratagems in war, when unaccompanied by perjury or breach of faith, do not fall under the description of falsehood. Now this admission is evidently fatal to the vulgar definition; inasmuch as it is scarcely possible to execute any of the artifices of war, without openly uttering the greatest untruths with the indisputable intention of deceiving; by which, according to the definition, the sin of falsehood is incurred. It is better therefore to say that stratagems, though coupled with falsehood, are lawful for the cause above assigned, namely that where we are not under an obligation to speak the truth, there can be no reason why we should not, when occasion requires it, utter even what is false; nor do I perceive why this should be more allowable in war than in peace, especially in cases where, by honest and beneficial kind of falsehood, we may be enabled to avert injury or danger from ourselves or our neighbour.

The denunciations against falsehood, therefore, which are cited from Scripture, are to be understood only of such violations of truth as are derogatory to the glory of God, or injurious to ourselves or our neighbour. Of this class . . . are the following texts: Lev. xix.11, 'ye shall not deal falsely, neither lie to one another.' Psal. ci.7, 'he that worketh deceit shall not tarry within my house; he that telleth lies shall not tarry in my sight.' Prov. vi.16, 17, 'yea, seven are an abomination unto him; a proud look, a lying tongue –.' Jer. ix.5, 'they will deceive every man his neighbour, and will not speak the truth.' In these and similar passages we are undoubtedly commanded to speak the truth; but to whom? not to an enemy, not to a madman, not to an oppressor, not to an assassin, but to our neighbour, to one with whom we are connected by the bonds of peace and social fellowship. If then it is to our neighbour only that we are commanded to speak the truth, it is evident that we are not forbidden to utter what is false, if requisite, to such as do not deserve of that name. Should any one be of a contrary opinion, I would ask him, by which of the commandments falsehood is prohibited? He will answer, doubtless by the ninth. Let him only repeat the words of that commandment, and he will be a convert to my opinion; for nothing is there prohibited but what is injurious to our neighbour; it follows, therefore, that a falsehood productive of no evil to him, if prohibited at all, is not prohibited by the commandments in question.

Hence we are justified in acquitting all those holy men who, according to the common judgement of divines, must be convicted of falsehood: Abraham for example, Gen. xxii.5, when he told his young men, for the purpose of deceiving them and quieting their suspicions, that he would return with the lad: although he must at the same time have been persuaded in his own mind that his son would be offered up as a sacrifice and left on the mount; for had he expected otherwise, his faith would have been put to no severe trial. His wisdom therefore taught him, that as his servants were in no way interested in knowing what was to happen, so it was expedient for himself that it should be for a time concealed from them. So also Rebecca and Jacob, Gen. xxvii, when by subtlety and proper caution they opened a way to that birthright which Esau had sold cheap, a birthright already belonging to Jacob by prophecy, as well as by right of purchase. It is objected that in so doing he deceived his father. Say rather that he interposed at the proper time to correct his father's error, who had been led by an unreasonable fondness to prefer Esau. So Joseph, Gen. xlii.7, &c. who according to the common definition must have been guilty of habitual falsehood, inasmuch as he deviated from the truth in numberless instances, with the express purpose of deceiving his brethren; not however to their injury, but to their exceeding advantage. The Hebrew midwives, Exod. i.19, &c. whose conduct received the approbation of God himself; for in deceiving Pharoah, they were so far from doing him an injury, that they preserved him from the commission of a crime. Moses, Exod. iii, who by the express command of God asked permission for the Israelites to go three days' journey into the wilderness under the pretext of sacrificing to the Lord; his purpose being to impose on Pharoah by alleging a false reason for their departure, or at least by substituting a secondary for the principal motive. The whole Israelitish people, who by divine command likewise, borrowed from the Egyptians jewels of gold and silver and raiment, doubtless under a promise of restoring them, though with the secret purpose of deception; for by what obligation were they bound to keep faith with the enemies of God, the transgressors of the laws of hospitality, and the usurpers, for so long a period, of the property of those who now despoiled them? Rahab, whose magnanimous falsehood recorded Josh. ii.4, 5 was no breach of duty, inasmuch as she only deceived those whom God willed to be deceived, though her own countrymen and magistrates, and preserved those whom God willed to be preserved; rightly preferring religious to civil obligations. Ehud, who deceived Eglon in two several instances, Judges iii.19, 20, and that justifiably, considering that he was dealing with an enemy, and that he acted under the command of God himself. Jael, by whose enticements Sisera perished, Judges iv.18, 19, although he was less her personal enemy than the enemy of God. Junius, indeed, considers this a pious fraud, not as a falsehood; which is a distinction without a difference. Jonathan, who was prevailed upon to assign a fictitious reason for the absence of David, 1 Sam. xx.6, 28, thinking it better to preserve the life of the innocent than to abet his father in an act of cruelty; and considering that the duties of charity were better fulfilled by favouring the escape of a friend under wrongful accusation, though at the expense of veracity, than by disclosing the truth unnecessarily, in obedience to the commands of a parent, for the purpose of aiding in the commission of a crime. All these, with numberless other saints, by a more careful inquiry into the nature of truth are rescued, as it were, from the new *limbus patrum* [the Paradise of Fools] to which the vulgar definition had consigned them.

•

A transmutation of metal

HELVETIUS

As well as being the physician to the Prince of Orange, Johann Schweitzer, also known as Helvetius, was an alchemist, and author of a book entitled *Brief of the Golden Calf*, from which the following account of a transmutation of lead into gold is taken. (There seems to be no room for any mistake or illusion; Helvetius is quite categorical, and must, therefore, be judged to be a liar.)

The 27th day of December, 1666, came a stranger to my house at the Hague, in a plebeick habit, of honest gravity and serious authority, of a mean stature, and a little, long face, black hair not at all curled, a beardless chin, and about forty-four years of age, and born in North Holland. After salutation, he beseeched me, with great reverence, to pardon his rude access, for he was a lover of the pyrotechnian art, and having read my treatises against the sympathetic powder of Sir Kenelm Digby, and observed my doubt about the philosophic mystery, induced him to ask me if I really was a disbeliever as to the existence of a universal medicine, which would cure all diseases, unless the principal parts were perished, or the predestinated time of death come. I replied, I never met with an adept, or saw such a medicine, though I had fervently prayed for it. Then I said, 'Surely, you are a learned physician.' 'No,' said he, 'I am a brass founder, and a lover of chemistry.' He then took from his bosom-pouch a neat ivory box, and out of it three ponderous lumps of stone, each about the bigness of a walnut. I greedily saw and handled this most noble substance, the value of which might be somewhere about twenty tons of gold; and having drawn from the owner many rare secrets of its admirable effects, I returned him this treasure of treasures with a most sorrowful mind, humbly beseeching him to bestow a fragment of it upon me, in perpetual memory of him, though but the size of a coriander seed. 'No, no,' said he, 'that is not lawful, though thou wouldest give me as many golden ducats as would fill this room; for it would have particular consequences, and if fire could be burned of fire, I would at this instant rather cast it into the fiercest flames.' He then asked if I had a private chamber, whose prospect was from the public street; so I presently conducted him to my best furnished room backwards, which he entered, without wiping his shoes, which were full of snow and dirt. I now expected he would bestow some great secret upon me, but in vain. He asked for a gold piece, and opening his doublet, showed me five pieces of that precious metal, which he wore upon a green riband, and which very much excelled mine in flexibility and colour, each being the size of a small trencher. I now earnestly again craved a crumb of the stone, and at last, out of his philosophical commiseration, he gave me a morsel as large as a rape seed, but I said, 'This scanty portion will scarcely transmute four grains of lead.' 'Then,' said he, 'deliver it me back;' which I did, in hopes of a greater parcel; but he cutting off half with his nail, said, 'Even this is sufficient for thee.' 'Sir,' said I, with a dejected countenance, 'what means this?' And he said, 'Even that will transmute half an ounce of lead.' So I gave him great thanks, and said, 'I would try it, and reveal it to no one.' He then took his leave, and said he would call again the next morning at nine. I then confessed, that while the mass of his medicine was in my hand the day before, I had secretly scraped off a bit with my nail, which I projected in lead, but it caused no transmutation, for the whole flew away in fumes. 'Friend,' said he, 'thou art more dexterous in committing theft, than in applying medicine. Hads't thou wrapped up thy stolen prey in yellow wax, it would have penetrated, and transmuted the lead into gold.' I then asked, if the philosophic work cost much, or required long time, for philosophers say, that nine or ten months are required for it. He answered, 'Their writings are only to be understood by the adepts, without whom no student can prepare this magistery. Fling not away, therefore, thy money and goods in hunting out this art, for thou shalt never find it.' To which I replied, 'As thy master showed it thee, so mayest thou, perchance, discover something thereof to me, who know the rudiments, and therefore it may be easier to add to a foundation than begin anew.' 'In this art,' said he, 'it is quite otherwise; for, unless thou knowest the thing from head to heel, thou canst not break open the glassy seal of Hermes. But enough: tomorrow, at the ninth hour, I will show thee the manner of projection.' But Elias never came again; so my wife, who was curious in the art whereof the worthy man had discovered, teazed me to make the experiment with the little spark of bounty the artist had left. So I melted half an ounce of lead upon which, my wife put in the said medicine; it hissed and bubbled, and in quarter of an hour the mass of lead was transmuted into fine gold, at which we were exceedingly amazed. I took it to the goldsmith, who judged it most excellent, and willingly offered fifty florins for each ounce.

•

An embassy from Persia

PHINEAS T. BARNUM

Barnum, who was no stranger to fraud himself, also took considerable pleasure in stories of other great liars, and this one is taken from his book *The Humbugs of the World* (1866). In 1667, says Barnum, something occurred that made the pampered court of Louis XIV stare – the arrival of a Persian embassy.

It was announced formally, one morning, to Louis XIV, that His Most Serene Excellency, Riza Bey, with an interminable tail of titles, hangers-on and equipages, had reached the port of Marseilles, having journeyed by way of Trebizond and Constantinople, to lay before the great 'King of the Franks' brotherly congratulations and gorgeous presents from his own illustrious master, the Shah of Persia.

. . . the Ambassador and his suite were lodged in sumptuous apartments in the Tuileries, under the care and guidance of King Louis' own assistant majordomo and a guard of courtiers and regiments of Royal Swiss. Banqueting and music filled up the first evening; and upon the ensuing day His Majesty, who thus did his visitors especial honour, sent the Duc de Richelieu to announce that he would graciously receive them on the third evening at Versailles.

Meanwhile the most extensive preparations were made for the grand audience thus accorded; and when the appointed occasion had arrived, the entire Gallery of Mirrors, with all the adjacent spaces and corridors, were crowded with the beauty, the chivalry, the wit, taste, and intellect of France at that dazzling period. Louis the Great himself never appeared to finer advantage. His truly royal countenance was lighted up with pride and satisfaction as the Envoy of the haughty Oriental king approached the splendid throne on which he sat, and as he descended a step to meet him and stood there in his magnificent robes of state, the Persian envoy bent the knee, and with uncovered head presented the credentials of his mission.

A grand ball and supper concluded this night of splendour, and Riza Bey was fairly launched at the French court; every member of which, to please the King, tried to outvie his compeers in the assiduity of his attentions, and the value of the books, pictures, gems, equipages, arms &c., which they heaped upon the illustrious Persian. The latter gentleman very quietly smoked his pipe and lounged on his divan before company, and diligently packed up the goods when he and his jolly companions were left alone. The presents of the Shah had not yet arrived, but were daily expected via Marseilles, and from time to time the olive-coloured suite was diminished by the departure of one of the number with his chest on a special mission to England, Austria, Portugal, Spain, and other European powers.

In the meantime, the Bey was feted in all directions, with every species of entertainment, and it was whispered that the fair ones of that dissolute court were, from the first, eager in the bestowal of their favours. The King favoured his Persian pet with numerous personal interviews, at which, in broken French, the Envoy unfolded the most imposing of schemes of Oriental conquest and commerce that his master was cordially willing to share with his great brother of France. At one of these chatty tête-à-têtes, the magnificent Riza Bey, upon whom the King had already conferred his own portrait set in diamonds, and other gifts worth several millions of francs, placed in the Royal hand several fragments of opal and turquoise said to have been found in a district of country bordering on the Caspian sea, which teemed with limitless treasures of the same kind, and which the Shah of Persia proposed to divide with France for the honour of her alliance. The King was enchanted.

Thus the great King-fish was fairly hooked, and Riza Bey could take his time. The golden tide that flowed in to him did not slacken, and his own expenses were all provided for at the Tuileries. The only thing remaining to be done was a grand foray on the tradesmen of Paris, and this was splendidly executed. The most exquisite wares of all descriptions were gathered in, without mention of payment; and one by one the Persian phalanx distributed itself through Europe until only two or three were left with the Ambassador.

At length, word was sent to Versailles that the gifts from the Shah had come, and a day was appointed for their presentation. The day arrived, and the Hall of Audience was again thrown open. All was jubilee; the King and the court waited, but no Persian – no Riza Bey – no presents from the Shah!

That morning three men, without either caftans or robes, but very much resembling the blacklegs of the day in their attire and deportment, had left the Tuileries at daylight with a bag and a bundle, and returned no more. They were Riza Bey and his last bodyguard; the bag and the bundle were the smallest in bulk but the most precious in value of a month's successful plunder. The turquoises and opals left with the King turned out, upon close inspection, to be a new and very ingenious variety of coloured glass.

Of course, a hue and cry was raised in all directions, but totally in vain. It was afterward believed that a noted barber and suspected bandit at Leghorn, who had once really travelled in Persia, and there picked up the knowledge and the ready money that served his turn, was the perpetrator of this pretty joke and speculation, as he disappeared from his native city about this time.

•

Lying to the wife

SAMUEL PEPYS

On 25 October 1668 Pepys records that one night, after having his hair combed by Deb, the maid, he had put his hand up her skirt, and it was thus 'with my main in her cunny', that his wife came upon the two of them locked in their embrace. Later Pepys admitted to having hugged the girl but denied kissing her, and so there ensued a week of hell for Pepys, which culminated in the entries for 9–10 November which appear here.

9. Up, and I did, by a little note which I flung to Deb, advise her that I did continue to deny that I ever kissed her, and so she might govern herself. The truth [is], that I did adventure upon God's pardoning me this lie, knowing how heavy a thing it would be for me to be the ruin of the poor girl; and next, knowing that if my wife should know all, it were impossible ever for her to be at peace with me again – and so our whole lives would be uncomfortable. The girl read, and as I bid her, returned me the note, flinging it to me in passing by. And so I abroad by [coach] to Whitehall, and there to the Duke of Yorke's to wait on him.

10. Up, and my wife still every day as ill as she is all night; will rise to see me out of doors, telling me plainly that she dares not let me see the girl; and so I out to the office, where all the morning; and so home to dinner, where I find my wife mightily troubled again, more than ever, and she tells me that it is from her of all, even to the very tocando su thing with my hand – which doth mightily trouble me, as not being able to foresee the consequences of it as to our future peace together. So my wife would not go down to dinner, but I would dine in my chamber with her; and there, after mollifying her as much as I could, we were pretty quiet and eat; and by and by comes Mr Hollier, and dines there by himself after we had dined. And he being gone, we to talk again, and she to be troubled, reproaching me with my unkindness and perjury, I having denied my ever kissing her – as also with all her old kindnesses to me, and my ill-using of her from the beginning, and the many temptations she hath refused out of faithfulness to me; whereof several she was particular in, and especially from my Lord Sandwich by the solicitation of Capt. Ferrer; and then afterward, the courtship of my Lord Hinchingbrooke, even to the trouble of his Lady. All which I did acknowledge and was troubled for, and wept; and at last pretty good friends again, and so I to my office and there late, and so home to supper with her; and so to bed, where after half-an-hour's slumber, she wakes me and cries out that she should never sleep more, and so kept raving till past midnight, that made me cry and weep heartily all the while for her, and troubled for what she reproached me with as before; and at last, with new vows, and particularly that I would myself bid the girl be gone and show my dislike to her – which I shall endeavour to perform, but with much trouble. And so, this appeasing her, we to sleep as well as we could till morning.

•

The lies in Rochester's libels

GILBERT BURNET

The Earl of Rochester was a notorious figure of the English Restoration, but he is chiefly known to us today as the author of poems of well-written obscenity. In a portrait of Rochester, his contemporary, Gilbert Burnet, describes the Earl's attitude to the lies that appeared in his poems.

He would often go into the country, and be for some months wholly employed in study, or the sallies of his wit, which he came to direct chiefly to satire. And this he often defended to me, by saying there were some people that could not be kept in order, or admonished but in this way. I replied, that it might be granted that a grave way of satire was sometimes no improfitable way of reproof. Yet they who used it only out of spite, and mixed lies with truth, sparing nothing that might adorn their poems, or gratify their revenge, could not excuse that way of reproach, by which the innocent often suffer: since the most malicious things, if wittily expressed, might stick to and blemish the best men in the world, and the malice of a libel could hardly consist with the charity of an admonition. To this he answered, a man could not write with life, unless he were heated by revenge: for to make a satire without resentments, upon the cold notions of philosophy, was as if a man would in cold blood, cut men's throats who had never offended him. And he said, the lies in these libels came often in as ornaments that could not be spared without spoiling the beauty of the poem.

•

Titus Oates and the Popish Plot

JOHN POLLOCK

The Popish Plot of 1678 was the invention of Titus Oates, who suggested there was a Jesuit plot against the Crown and people of England. When Charles II met Oates, having heard the allegations, he pronounced him to be 'a lying knave'. Nevertheless, an anti-Catholic panic ensued which cost the lives of many prominent Catholics. The historian John Pollock provides a short profile of Oates, and an account of his allegations. Oates was eventually whipped, pilloried and imprisoned by King James II.

Titus Oates has justly been considered one of the world's great impostors. By birth he was an Anabaptist, by prudence a clergyman, by profession a perjurer. From an obscure and beggarly existence he raised himself to opulence and an influence more than episcopal, and, when he fell, it was with the fame of having survived the finest flogging ever inflicted. De Quincey considered the murder of Godfrey to be the most artistic performance of the seventeenth century. It was far surpassed by the products of Oates' roving imagination. To the connoisseur of murder the mystery of Godfrey's death may be more exhilarating, but in the field of broad humour Oates bears the palm. There is, after all, something laughable about the rascal. His gross personality had in it a comic strain. He could not only invent but, when unexpected events occurred, adapt them on the instant to his own end. His coarse tongue was not without a kind of wit. Whenever he appears on the scene, as has been said of Jeffreys, we may be sure of good sport. Yet to his victims he was an emblem of tragic injustice. Very serious were his lies to the fifteen men whom he brought to death. The world was greedy of horrors, and Oates sounded the alarm at the crucial moment. In the game he went on to play the masterstrokes were his. Those who would reduce him to a subordinate of his associate Dr Tonge, the hare-brained parson whose quarterly denunciations of Rome failed to arouse the interest of Protestant London, have strangely misunderstood his character. Tonge was a necessary go-between, but Oates the supreme mover of diabolical purpose . . .

. . . For Oates had brought back from beyond seas a prodigious tale, calculated to set the most practical alarmist in action. The scope of the disclosure was vast. Written at length and with the promise of more to come, Oates' TRUE AND EXACT NARRATIVE OF THE HORRID PLOT AND CONSPIRACY OF THE POPISH PARTY AGAINST THE LIFE OF HIS SACRED MAJESTY, THE GOVERNMENT, AND THE PROTESTANT RELIGION filled a folio pamphlet of sixty-eight pages. The Pope, said Oates, had declared himself lord of the kingdoms of England and Ireland. To the work of their reduction and government the Jesuits were commissioned by papal briefs and instructed by orders from the general of the society. Jesuit agents were at work fomenting rebellion in Scotland and Ireland. Money had been raised and arms collected. The hour had only to strike for an Irish port to be opened to a French force in aid of the great scheme. The Papists had burned down London once and tried to burn it again. A third attempt would be no less successful than the first. Chief of all, a 'consult' of the English Jesuits had been held on April 24th, 1678 at the White Horse tavern in the Strand, to concert means for the king's assassination. Charles was a bastard and an excommunicated heretic. He deserved death, and the deed was necessary for the Catholic cause. Want of variety in the instruments chosen should not save him. He was to be poisoned by the queen's physician. He was to be shot with silver bullets in St James' Park. Four Irish ruffians were hired to dispatch him at Windsor. A Jesuit named Coniers had consecrated a knife a foot in length to stab him. Great sums of money were promised by French and Spanish Jesuits and by the Benedictine prior to whoever should do the work. If the Duke of York did not consent to the king's death, the same fate lay in store for him. In all this Oates had been a confidential messenger and an active agent. It was only due to the fact that he had been appointed for the task of killing Dr Tonge that the scheme thus carefully prepared was not put to the test; for Tonge had moved him to exchange the trade of murderer and incendiary for that of informer. Thus the great plot was divulged, together with the names of ninety-nine persons concerned, as well as those nominated for offices under the prospective Jesuit government, of whom the most prominent were the Lords Arundel of Wardour, Powis, Petre, Stafford, Bellasis, Sir William Godolphin, Sir George Wakeham, and Mr Edward Coleman. The falsehood of all this had been conclusively demonstrated. Not only did Oates bear all the marks of the liar and never produce the slightest evidence for what he announced, but much of his story is contradicted by the actual conditions of politics at the time. The fact of his conviction for perjury is widely known and its justice unquestioned. To rebut his accusations singly would be fruitless, because unnecessary. Their general untruth has long been known. Much time was occupied by Oates and Tonge in reducing their bulk to the shape, first of forty-three, then of eighty-one articles. Oates took a lodging in Vauxhall, near Sir Richard Barker's house, where Tonge dwelt. Together they drafted and copied until all was prepared. Nothing lacked but a proper flourish for the introduction of so grand an event.

For this a pretty little comedy was arranged. Oates was to keep behind the scenes while Tonge rang up the curtain. Nor did Tonge wish to expose himself too soon to vulgar light. He procured an acquaintance, Mr Christopher Kirkby, to act as prologue. Kirkby was a poor gentleman of good family, interested in chemistry, and holding some small appointment in the royal laboratory. Their common taste for science probably accounted for his relation with Tonge; and since he was known to the king, he could now do the doctor good service. On August 11th, 1678 Oates thrust a copy of the precious manuscript under the wainscot of a gallery in Sir Richard Barker's house. There Tonge found it, and on the following day read it to Kirkby, who declared in horror at the contents that the king should be informed. He would take this part upon himself, he said. Accordingly on August 13th, as Charles was starting for his accustomed walk in St James' Park, Kirkby slipped a note into his hand begging for a short audience on a matter of vital importance. The king read it and called Kirkby to ask what he meant. 'Sire,' returned the other, 'your enemies have a design against your life. Keep within the company, for I know not but you may be in danger in this very walk.' 'How may that be?' asked the king. 'By being shot at,' answered Kirkby, and desired to give fuller information in some more private spot. Charles bade him wait in his closet, and finished his stroll with composure.

•

The horrid tale of the bloody Colonel Kirk

ISAAC D'ISRAELI

In putting down the rebellions against King James II, Colonel Percy Kirk stands out in his cruelty. But for all his undoubted brutality, he was the subject of a 'pious fraud of the Whig party', here described by Isaac D'Israeli.

The horrid tale of the bloody Colonel Kirk has been worked up by Hume with all his eloquence and pathos; and, from its interest, no suspicion has arisen of its truth. Yet, so far as it concerns Kirk, or the reign of James the Second, or even English history, it is, as Ritson too honestly expresses it, 'an impudent and a bare-faced lie'! The simple fact is told by Kennet in a few words: he probably was aware of the nature of this political fiction. Hume was not, indeed, himself the fabricator of the tale; but he had not any historical authority. The origin of this fable was probably a pious fraud of the Whig party, to whom Kirk had rendered himself odious; at that moment stories still more terrifying were greedily swallowed, which, Ritson insinuates, have become a part of the history of England. The original story, related more circumstantially, though not more affectingly, nor perhaps more truly, may be found in Wanley's *Wonders of the Little World*, which I give, relieving it from the tediousness of old Wanley.

A governor of New Zealand, under the bold Duke of Burgundy, had in vain sought to reduce the affections of the beautiful wife of a citizen. The governor imprisoned the husband on an accusation of treason; and when the wife appeared as the suppliant, the governor, after no brief eloquence, succeeded as a lover, on the plea that her husband's life could only be spared by her compliance. The woman, in tears and in aversion, and not without a hope of vengeance only delayed, lost her honour! Pointing to the prison, the governor told her, 'If you seek your husband, enter there, and take him along with you!' The wife, in the bitterness of her thoughts, yet not without the consolation that she had snatched her husband from the grave, passed into the prison; there in a cell, to her astonishment and horror, she beheld the corpse of her husband laid out in a coffin, ready for burial! Mourning over it, she at length returned to the governor, fiercely exclaiming, 'You have kept your word! you have restored to me my husband! and be assured the favour shall be repaid!' The inhuman villain, terrified in the presence of his intrepid victim, attempted to appease her vengeance, and more, to win her to his wishes. Returning home, she assembled her friends, revealed her whole story, and under their protection she appealed to Charles the Bold, a strict lover of justice, and who now awarded a singular but exemplary catastrophe. The duke first commanded that the criminal governor should instantly marry the woman whom he had made a widow, and at the same time sign his will, with a clause importing that should he die before his lady he constituted her his heiress. All this was concealed from both sides, rather to satisfy the duke than the parties themselves. This done, the unhappy woman was dismissed alone! The governor was conducted to the prison to suffer the same death he had inflicted on the husband of his wife; and when the lady was desired once more to enter the prison, she beheld her second husband headless in his coffin as she had her first! Such extraordinary incidents in so short a period overpowered the feeble frame of the sufferer; she died – leaving a son, who inherited the rich accession of fortune so fatally obtained by his injured and suffering mother.

Such is the tale of which the party story of Kirk appeared to Ritson to have been a *rifacimento*; but it is rather the foundation than the superstructure. This critic was right in the general, but not in the particular. It was not necessary to point out the present source, when so many others of a parallel nature exist. This tale, universally told, Mr Douce considers as the origin of *Measure for Measure* and was probably some traditional event; for it appears sometimes with a change of names and places, without any of incident. It always turns on a soldier, a brother or a husband, executed; and a wife, a sister, a deceived victim, to save them from death. It was, therefore, easily transferred to Kirk, and Pomfret's poem of 'Cruelty and Lust' long made the story popular. It could only have been in this form that it reached the historian, who, it must be observed, introduces it as a 'story *commonly* told of him'; but popular tragic romances should not enter into the dusty documents of a history of England, and much less be particularly specified in the index! Belleforest, in his old version of the tale, has even the circumstances of the 'captain, who having seduced the wife under the promise to save her husband's life, exhibited him soon afterwards *through the window of her apartment suspended on a gibbet*'. This forms the horrid incident in the history of 'the bloody Colonel', and served the purpose of a party, who wished to bury him in odium. Kirk was a soldier of fortune, and a loose liver, and a great blusterer, who would sometimes threaten to decimate his own regiment, but is said to have forgotten the menace the next day. Hateful as such military men will always be, in thc present instance Colonel Kirk has been shamefully calumniated by poets and historians, who suffer themselves to be duped by the forgeries of political parties!

•

The lying Campbells

LORD MACAULAY

Following the defeat of the Jacobite army in Scotland under Viscount Dundee, there was peace north of the Border and the cause seemed dead. A free pardon was offered to all Highlanders who had borne arms against King William, provided they took an oath of allegiance before 1 January 1692. The Highlanders complied. But the King still wished to make an example of some of these rebels, and the powerful Campbells conspired to ensure that it should be their hereditary enemies, the MacDonalds of Glencoe, who would suffer. The two great Earls of Campbell, Macallum More of Argyll, and Breadalbane, having concealed from the Master of Stair (who was to execute their design) the fact that MacIan, the chief of the MacDonalds, had taken the oath, the way was now clear for the regiment named after Argyll (which included many by the name of Campbell), commanded by Lieutenant-Colonel Hamilton, to carry out the plan. But the massacre was not to be done openly, but with treachery and lies.

Had Hamilton marched openly against the Glencoe men and put them to the edge of the sword, the act would probably not have wanted apologists, and most certainly would not have wanted precedents. But the Master of Stair had strongly recommended a different mode of proceeding. If the least alarm were given, the nest of robbers would be found empty; and to hunt them down in so wild a region would, even with all the help that Breadalbane and Argyll could give, be a long and difficult business. 'Better,' he wrote, 'not meddle with them than meddle to no purpose. When the thing is resolved, let it be secret and sudden.' He was obeyed; and it was determined that the Glencoe men should perish, not by military execution, but by the most dastardly and perfidious form of assassination.

On the first of February a hundred and twenty soldiers of

Argyll's regiment, commanded by a man named Campbell and a lieutenant named Lindsay, marched to Glencoe. Captain Campbell was commonly called in Scotland Glenlyon, from the pass in which his property lay. He had every qualification for the service on which he was employed, an unblushing forehead, a smooth lying tongue, and a heart of adamant. He was also one of the few Campbells who were likely to be trusted and welcomed by the MacDonalds: for his niece was married to Alexander, the second son of MacIan.

The sight of the redcoats approaching caused some anxiety among the population of the valley. John, the eldest son of the Chief, came, accompanied by twenty clansmen, to meet the strangers, and asked what this visit meant. Lieutenant Lindsay answered that the soldiers came as friends, and wanted nothing but quarters. They were kindly received, and were lodged under the thatched roofs of the little community . . . for in hospitality, as in thievery, the Gaelic marauders rivalled the Bedouin. During twelve days the soldiers lived familiarly with the people of the glen. Old MacIan, who had before felt many misgivings as to the relation in which he stood to the government, seems to have been pleased with the visit. The officers passed much of their time with him and his family.

. . . Hamilton fixed five o'clock in the morning of the thirteenth of February for the deed. He hoped that, before that time, he should reach Glencoe with four hundred men, and should have stopped all the earths in which the old fox and his two cubs – so MacIan and his sons were nicknamed by the murderers – could take refuge. But, at five precisely, whether Hamilton had arrived or not, Glenlyon was to fall on, and to slay, every MacDonald under seventy.

The night was rough. Hamilton and his troops made slow progress, and were long after their time. While they were contending with the wind and the snow, Glenlyon was supping and playing cards with those whom he meant to butcher before daybreak. He and Lieutenant Lindsay had engaged themselves to dine with the old Chief on the morrow.

Late in the evening a vague suspicion that some evil was intended crossed the mind of the Chief's eldest son. The soldiers were evidently in a restless state; and some of them uttered strange cries. Two men it is said were overheard whispering. 'I do not like this job,' one of them muttered; 'I should be glad to fight the Macdonalds. But to kill men in their beds –' 'We must do as we are bid,' answered another voice. 'If there is any thing wrong, our officers must answer for it.' John MacDonald was so uneasy that, soon after midnight, he went to Glenlyon's quarters. Glenlyon and his men were all up, and seemed to be getting their arms ready for action. John, much alarmed, asked what these preparations meant. Glenlyon was profuse of friendly assurances. 'Some of Glengarry's people have been harrying the country. We are getting ready to march against them. You are quite safe. Do you think that, if you were in any danger, I should not have given a hint to your brother Sandy and his wife?' John's suspicions were quieted. He returned to his house, and lay down to rest.

The massacre was carried out, but bungled in that many of the MacDonalds escaped to tell the tale; however, as Macaulay says,

. . . the world was long incredulous. The habitual mendacity of the Jacobite libellers had brought on them an appropriate punishment. Now, when, for the first time, they told the truth, they were supposed to be romancing. They complained bitterly that the story, though perfectly authentic, was regarded by the public as a factious lie.

•

The man who invented Formosa

J. A. FARRAR

Remarkable from the first to the last was George Psalmanazar, still of unknown birth and origin, who made his first appearance in London early in the eighteenth century.

When Dr Johnson knew him Psalmanazar was about eighty; a man who earned a livelihood from his work for the booksellers, but a man who enjoyed a somewhat wide notoriety for the earnestness of his piety and the regularity of his devotions.

Yet George Psalmanazar is connected with one of the most astonishing frauds in the history of literature. Coming to England from the Continent under the auspices of the Reverend W. Innes, an army chaplain, he at once interested the religious world in his favour, by claiming to be a native of Formosa, who had been converted from an appalling heathenism to the truths and practices of Christianity. No one ever guessed rightly of what country he was a native, but there was nothing Oriental about his skin or hair. This, however, stood very little in his way.

. . . Psalmanazar's story was that he had left Formosa six years earlier, when he was nineteen. This would have made him twenty-five at the time of his coming to London, but he added some years to his real age in order to make his story more credible. For a youth of twenty he had some right to be regarded as a marvel. He had more than a smattering of six languages, and wrote and spoke Latin fluently. It was in Latin that he conversed with Archbishop Tenison, Innes acting as interpreter, and it was in Latin that he originally wrote his *Description of Formosa.*

The book was a reproduction of the many marvellous things about Formosa he had propounded in conversation, but not of everything. Asked, for instance, about longevity in the island, he replied that 120 was accounted a common age, and 100 a very moderate one; his own grandfather had lived to 117, and was then as fresh and vigorous as a young man, owing to his habit of sucking the blood of a viper warm every morning! There seems to have been no limit to British credulity in the early years of Queen Anne. Good people subscribed for the support of this marvellous proselyte, and the Bishop of London had him sent to study at Christ Church, Oxford, in the pious hope that he would in return instruct in Formosan some future missionaries to that promising island.

An exceeding curious book is the *Historical and Geographical*

Description of Formosa, an Island subject to the Emperor of Japan, published in 1704, and dedicated to the Bishop of London.

According to Psalmanazar, the emperor of Japan conquered Formosa in a strange manner. Under the pretext of religion, of offering sacrifices in Formosa to the God of Formosa, he sent a great army into the country. Thirty or forty soldiers were placed in large litters, drawn by two elephants, and at the windows of these litters were placed the heads of oxen or rams, which removed all suspicions from the minds of natives. Then the soldiers jumped out, and by threatening death to the natives secured their acceptance of the yoke of Japan without bloodshed or difficulty.

The Formosans were represented as having worshipped the heavenly bodies till two philosophers appeared, who bade them turn from this worship to that of one Supreme God. To Him they were bidden to raise a temple, and on an altar therein to burn the hearts of 18,000 boys under the age of nine . . .

. . . To overcome the difficulty of the depopulation consequent on such a system of religion the author made the Formosans polygamous, and the eldest son exempt from liability to sacrifice. Psalmanazar . . . cared nothing for existing authentic accounts of Formosa; for why should a real Formosan adjust his narrative to that of a Dutch missionary like George Candidius? . . . The Dutch writer had said that there was no regular government in the island, but that at most each village was governed by twelve men of the same age, not under forty; Psalmanazar declared for an elaborate hierarchy of ministers, of whose very dress he described and depicted the minutest details. Candidius had described the laws as so lenient as to be almost non-existent; robbery was barely punished at all, and a present of a few hogs was ample compensation for murder or adultery. According to Psalmanazar, robbers and murderers were hanged head downwards and shot to death with arrows, whilst other offences entailed burning alive, the cutting off of legs and arms, tearing in pieces by dogs, or the boring of the tongue with a hot iron.

Candidius also had denied the existence of gold or silver mines in the country; Psalmanazar made 'the great quantity of gold and silver' the Formosans' chief source of profit, and located three gold and three silver mines in the several islands. Nor was this enough for British consumption, for 'their temples and houses were often covered with gold, both in cities and villages'.

... From the first Psalmanazar had certain sceptics to deal with. Father Fontenay pointed out that Formosa was a dependency of China, not of Japan, as Psalmanazar declared; whilst Dr Halley, the astronomer, asked the writer some unanswerable questions. Still the book had so large a sale that a second edition was published the year following, in 1705. In the preface to this edition Psalmanazar boldly replies to twenty-five objections 'of the first magnitude' which had been raised by various critics. On no point would he give way. At most he would say about the annual sacrifice of the 18,000 boys that such was the number laid down by the law; in practice the law might be evaded. As for the 'forgeries' of Candidius, why should they be believed against the word of a native? And as to his differences from Candidius, what could more completely prove his own veracity? For surely a forger would have taken more care that his statements should conform to those of previous writers.

The secret of Psalmanazar's success lay in the fact that he not only tickled that love for the marvellous in the British people but also pandered to the strong feeling against the Jesuits then prevalent in England. He concluded his amazing *Description* with a sketch of the history of the Jesuits' mission to Japan, which he made the vehicle of a strong attack upon that society, whose pupil he had been in earlier years.

This made it difficult for Psalmanazar to clear himself of the imposture, when he came to entertain a genuine wish to set himself right with the public. But a serious illness in 1728 vanquished his irresolution, and he at once began the composition of his Memoirs. He took his leisure over it, for it seems to have occupied him for twenty-five years. It was finished before 1752, when he made his first will with directions for its posthumous publication, but it did not reach the public until 1765. But long before that there had been a semi-public recantation. To Bowen's *Complete System of Geography*, published in 1747 in two large folio volumes, Psalmanazar contributed the chapters on China and Japan, giving an account avowedly from Candidius, with whose account some forty years before he had deliberately made his own to clash!

Psalmanazar's repentance for his fraud amounted to remorse, and his self-humiliation bordered on the abject. Henceforth he would pay by voluntary self-effacement and obscurity for his earlier wicked love for notoriety.

•

On sustaining deceit

SIR RICHARD STEELE

Truth is always consistent with itself, and needs nothing to help it out; it is always near at hand, and sits upon our lips, and is ready to drop out before we are aware; whereas a lie is troublesome, and sets a man's invention upon the rack, and one trick needs a great many more to make it good. It is like building upon a false foundation, which continually stands in need of props to shore it up, and proves at last more chargeable, than to have raised a substantial building at first upon a true and solid foundation; for sincerity is firm and substantial, and there is nothing hollow and unsound in it, and because it is plain and open, fears no discovery; of which the crafty man is always in danger; and when he thinks he walks in the dark, all his pretences are so transparent, that he that runs may read them; he is the last man that finds himself to be found out, and whilst he takes it for granted that he makes fools of others, he renders himself ridiculous.

Add to all this, that sincerity is the most compendious wisdom, and an excellent instrument for the speedy dispatch of business; it creates confidence in those we have to deal with, saves the labour of many inquiries, and brings a man sooner to his journey's end than by-ways, in which men often lose themselves. In a word, whatsoever conveniences may be thought to be in falsehood and dissimulation, it is soon over; but the inconvenience of it is perpetual, because it brings a man under an everlasting jealousy and suspicion, so that he is not believed when he speaks truth, nor trusted perhaps when he means honestly. When a man has once forfeited the reputation of his integrity, he is set fast; and nothing will then serve his turn, neither truth nor falsehood.

And I have often thought, that God hath in his great wisdom hid from men of false and dishonest minds, the wonderful advantages of truth and integrity to the prosperity even of our worldly affairs: these men are so blinded by their covetousness and ambition that they cannot look beyond a present advantage, nor forbear to seize upon it, though by way never so indirect: they cannot see so far as to the remotest consequence of a steady integrity, and the vast benefit and advantages which it will bring a man at last. Were but this sort of men wise and clear-sighted enough to discern this, they would be honest out of very knavery, not out of any love to honesty and virtue, but with a crafty design to promote and advance more effectually their own interests; and therefore the justice of the Divine Providence hath hid this truest point of wisdom from their eyes, that bad men might not be upon equal terms with the just and upright, and serve their own wicked designs by honest and lawful means.

Indeed, if a man were only to deal in the world for a day, and should never have occasion to converse more with mankind, never more need their good opinion or good word, it were then no great matter (speaking as to the concernments of this world) if a man spent his reputation all at once, and ventured it at one throw: but if he be to continue in the world, and would have the advantage of conversation whilst he is in it, let him make use of truth and sincerity in all his words and actions; for nothing but this will last and hold out to the end: all other arts will fail, but truth and integrity will carry a man through, and bear him out to the last.

•

The art of political lying

JONATHAN SWIFT

We are told the devil is the father of lies, and was a liar from the beginning; so that, beyond contradiction, the invention is old: and, which is more, his first essay of it was purely political, employed in undermining the authority of the prince, and seducing a third part of the subjects from their obedience: for which he was driven down from heaven, where (as Milton expresses it) he had been viceroy of a great western province; and forced to exercise his talent in inferior regions among other fallen spirits, poor or deluded men, whom he still daily tempts to his own sin, and will ever do so, till he be chained in the bottomless pit.

But although the devil be the father of lies, he seems, like other great inventors, to have lost much of his reputation by the continual improvements that have been made upon him.

Who first reduced lying into an art, and adapted it to politics, is not clear from history, although I have made some diligent inquiries. I shall therefore consider it only according to the modern system, as it has been cultivated these twenty years in the southern part of our own island.

The poets tell us that, after the giants were overthrown by the gods, the earth in revenge produced her last offspring, which was Fame. And the fable is thus interpreted: that when tumults and seditions are quieted, rumours and false reports are plentifully spread through a nation. So that, by this account, lying is the last relief of a routed, earth-born, rebellious party in a state. But here the moderns have made great additions, applying this art to the gaining of power and preserving it, as well as revenging themselves after they have lost it; as the same instruments are made use of by animals to feed themselves when they are hungry, and to bite those that tread upon them.

But the same genealogy cannot always be admitted for political lying; I shall therefore desire to refine upon it, by adding some circumstances of its birth and parents. A political lie is sometimes born out of a discarded statesman's head, and thence delivered to be nursed and dandled by the rabble. Sometimes it is produced a monster, and licked into shape: at other times it comes into the world completely formed, and is spoiled in the licking. It is often born an infant in the regular way, and requires time to mature it; and often it sees the light in its full growth, but dwindles away by degrees. Sometimes it is of noble birth, and sometimes the spawn of a stock-jobber. Here it screams aloud at the opening of the womb, and there it is delivered with a whisper. I know a lie that now disturbs half the kingdom with its noise, [of] which, although too proud and great at present to own its parents, I can remember its whisperhood. To conclude the nativity of this monster; when it comes into the world without a sting it is still-born; and whenever it loses its sting it dies.

No wonder if an infant so miraculous in its birth should be destined for great adventures; and accordingly we see it has been the guardian spirit of a prevailing party for almost twenty years. It can conquer kingdoms without fighting, and sometimes with the loss of a battle. It gives and resumes employments; can sink a mountain to a molehill, and raise a molehill to a mountain; has presided for many years at committees of elections; can wash a blackamoor white; make a saint of an atheist, and a patriot of a profligate; can furnish foreign ministers with intelligence, and raise or let fall the credit of the nation. This goddess flies with a huge looking-glass in her hands, to dazzle the crowd, and make them see, according as she turns it, their ruin in their interest, and their interest in their ruin. In this glass you will behold your best friends, clad in coats powdered with fleurs-de-lis and triple crowns; their girdles hung round with chains, and beads, and wooden shoes; and your worst enemies adorned with the ensigns of liberty, property, indulgence, moderation, and a cornucopia in their hands. Her large wings, like those of a flying-fish, are of no use but while they are moist; she therefore dips them in mud, and, soaring aloft, scatters it in the eyes of the multitude, flying with great swiftness; but at every turn is forced to stoop in dirty ways for new supplies.

I have been sometimes thinking, if a man had the art of the second sight for seeing lies, as they have in Scotland for seeing spirits, how admirably he might entertain himself in this town, by observing the different shapes, sizes, and colours of those swarms of lies which buzz about the heads of some people, like flies about a horse's ears in summer; or those legions hovering every afternoon in Exchange-alley, enough to darken the air; or over a club of discontented grandees, and thence sent down in cargoes to be scattered at elections.

There is one essential point wherein a political liar differs from others of the faculty, that he ought to have but a short memory, which is necessary according to the various occasions he meets with every hour of differing from himself and swearing to both sides of a contradiction, as he finds the persons disposed with whom he has to deal. In describing the virtues and vices of mankind, it is convenient, upon every article, to have some eminent person in our eye, from whom we copy our description. I have strictly observed this rule, and my imagination this minute represents before me a certain great man famous for this talent, to the constant practice of which he owes his twenty years' reputation of the most skilful head in England for the management of nice affairs. The superiority of his genius consists in nothing else but an inexhaustible fund of political lies, which he plentifully distributes every minute he speaks, and by an unparalleled generosity forgets, and consequently contradicts, the next half-hour. He never yet considered whether any proposition were true or false, but whether it were convenient for the present minute or company to affirm or deny it; so that, if you think fit to refine upon him by interpreting everything he says, as we do dreams, by the contrary, you are still to seek, and will find yourself equally deceived whether you believe or not: the only remedy is to suppose that you have heard some inarticulate sounds, without any meaning at all; and besides, that will take off the horror you might be apt to conceive at the oaths wherewith he perpetually tags both ends of every proposition; although, at the same time, I think he cannot with any justice be taxed with perjury when he invokes God and Christ, because he has often fairly given public notice to the world that he believes in neither.

Some people may think that such an accomplishment as this can be of no great use to the owner, or his party, after it has been often practised and is become notorious; but they are widely mistaken. Few lies carry the inventor's mark, and the most prostitute enemy to truth may spread a thousand without being known the author: besides, as the vilest writer has his readers, so the greatest liar has his believers; and it often happens that, if a lie be believed for only an hour, it has done its work, and there is no further occasion for it. Falsehood flies, and truth comes limping after it, so that when men come to be undeceived it is too late; the jest is over, and the tale has had its effect: like a man who has thought of a good repartee when the discourse is changed or the company parted; or like a physician who has found out an infallible medicine after the patient is dead.

Considering that natural disposition in many men to lie, and in multitudes to believe, I have been perplexed what to do with that maxim so frequent in everybody's mouth, that truth will at last prevail. Here has this island of ours, for the greatest part of twenty years, lain under the influence of such counsels and persons, whose principle and interest it was to corrupt our manners, blind our understanding, drain our wealth, and in time destroy our constitution both in church and state, and we at last were brought to the very brink of ruin; yet, by the means of perpetual misrepresentations, have never been able to distinguish between our enemies and friends. We have seen a great part of the nation's money got into the hands of those who, by their birth, education, and merit, could pretend no higher than to wear our liveries; while others, who, by their credit, quality, and fortune, were only able to give reputation and success to the Revolution, were not only laid aside as dangerous and useless, but loaded with the scandal of Jacobites, men of arbitrary principles, and pensioners to France; while truth, who is said to lie in a well, seemed now to be buried there under a heap of stones. But I remember it was a usual complaint among the Whigs, that the bulk of the landed men was not in their interests, which some of the wisest looked on as an ill omen; and we saw it was with the utmost difficulty that they could preserve a majority, while the court and ministry were on their side, till they had learned those admirable expedients for deciding elections and influencing distant boroughs by powerful motives from the city. But all this was mere force and constraint, however upheld by the most dexterous artifice and management, until the people began to apprehend their properties, their religion, and the monarchy itself in danger; when we saw them greedily laying hold on the first occasion to interpose. But of this mighty change in the dispositions of the people I shall discourse more at large in some following paper: wherein I shall endeavour to undeceive or discover those deluded or deluding persons who hope or pretend it is only a short madness in the vulgar, from which they may soon recover; whereas, I believe it will appear to be very different in its causes, its symptoms, and its consequences; and prove a great example to illustrate the maxim I lately mentioned, that truth (however sometimes late) will at last prevail.

•

Rabbit breeding

ANON.

Towards the close of the year 1726, one of the most extraordinary and impudent impostures on record was carried into execution by a woman named Mary Tofts, the wife of a poor journeyman cloth-worker at Godalming, in Surrey. She is described as having been of 'a healthy strong constitution, small size, fair complexion, a very stupid and sullen temper, and unable to write or read'. Stupid as she was supposed to be, she had, however, art enough to keep up for a considerable time the credit of her fraud. She pretended to bring forth rabbits; and she accounted for this monstrous deviation from the laws of nature, by saying, that 'as she was weeding in a field, she saw a rabbit spring up near her, after which she ran, with another woman that was at work just by her; this set her longing for rabbits, being then, as she thought, five weeks gone with child; the other woman perceiving that she was uneasy, charged her with longing for the rabbit they could not catch, but she denied it. Soon after, another rabbit sprung up near the same place, which she endeavoured likewise to catch. The same night she dreamt that she was in a field with those two rabbits in her lap, and awaked with a sick fit, which lasted till morning; from that time, for above three months, she had a constant and strong desire to eat rabbits, but being very poor and indigent could not procure any.'

At first sight, it would seem that so gross an imposition, as that which was attempted by Mary Tofts, must have been universally scouted. But this was by no means the case. So well did she manage, and so ready are some people to be deceived, that she actually deluded her medical attendant, Mr Howard, a man of probity, who had practised for thirty years. There can be no doubt of his belief that, in the course of about a month, he had aided her to bring forth nearly twenty rabbits.

The news of these marvellous births spread far and wide and soon found numerous believers. It attracted the attention of even George the First, who sent down to Godalming his house surgeon, Mr Ahlers, to inquire into the fact. Ahlers went back to London fully convinced that he had obtained ocular and tangible proof of the truth of the story; so much so, indeed, that he promised to procure for Mary a pension. Mr St Andre, the king's surgeon and anatomist, was despatched in the course of a day or two, to make a further examination. He also returned to the metropolis a firm believer. The rabbits, which he and Ahlers carried with them, as testimonies, had the honour of being dissected before his majesty. An elaborate report of all the circumstances relative to their production and dissection, and to his visit to Godalming, was published by St Andre, and the public mind consequently began to be agitated in an extraordinary manner. A furious controversy arose between the credulous and the incredulous, in which Whiston is said to have borne a part, by writing a pamphlet, to show that the miracle was the exact completion of a prophecy in Esdras. On the other hand, the caricaturists of the incredulous faction exerted themselves to cast ridicule on their opponents. Among these was Hogarth, who published an engraving called Cunicularii, or, the Wise Men of Godliman.

Though the report, by St Andre, contained many circumstances which were palpably calculated to excite a suspicion of fraud, the multitude was as blind to them as he had been. The delusion continued to spread, and even the king himself was enrolled among the believers. The rent of rabbit warrens, it is affirmed, sunk to nothing, as no one would assume to eat a rabbit. The trick was, however, on the point of being found out. To Queen Caroline, then Princess of Wales, is ascribed the merit of having been active in promoting measures to undeceive the people.

The miraculous Mary Tofts was now brought to a town, where she could be more closely watched than at Godalming, and prevented from obtaining the means of carrying on her imposture. Among those who took part on this occasion, the most conspicuous was Sir Richard Manningham, an eminent physician and Fellow of the Royal Society; and he had at length the satisfaction of detecting her. She held out, however, till her courage was shaken by a threat to perform a dangerous operation upon her, which threat was backed by another from a magistrate, that she should be sent to prison. She then confessed, that the fraud had been suggested to her by a woman, who told her, that she could put her into a way of getting a good livelihood, without being obliged to work for it as formerly, and promised continually to supply her with rabbits, for which she was to receive part of the gain. The farce terminated by the Godalming miracle-worker being committed to Tothill Fields' Bridewell.

A theft

JEAN JACQUES ROUSSEAU

In the *Confessions*, Rousseau (1712–78) confesses to a crime which he committed as a young man while he was still a servant with a family in Geneva – a crime which occasioned a lie which would haunt him all his life.

It is almost inevitable that the breaking up of an establishment should cause some confusion in the house, and that various things should be mislaid. But so honest were the servants and so vigilant were M. and Mme Lorenzi that nothing was found missing when the inventory was taken. Only Mlle Pontal lost a little pink and silver ribbon, which was quite old. Plenty of better things were within my reach, but this ribbon alone tempted me. I stole it, and as I hardly troubled to conceal it it was soon found. They inquired how I had got hold of it. I grew confused, stammered, and finally said with a blush that it was Marion who had given it to me. Marion was a young girl from the Maurienne whom Mme de Vercellis had taken as her cook when she had ceased to give dinners and had discharged her chef, since she had more need of good soup than of fine stews. Marion was not only pretty. She had that fresh complexion that one never finds except in the mountains, and such a sweet and modest air that one only had to see her to love her. What is more she was a good girl, sensible and absolutely trustworthy. They were extremely surprised when I mentioned her name. But they had no less confidence in me than in her, and decided that it was important to find which of us was a thief. She was sent for, to face a considerable number of people, including the Comte de la Roque himself. When she came she was shown the ribbon. I boldly accused her. She was confused, did not utter a word, and threw me a glance that would have disarmed the devil, but my cruel heart resisted.

In the end she firmly denied the theft. But she did not get indignant. She merely turned to me, and begged me to remember myself and not disgrace an innocent girl who had never done me any harm. But, with infernal impudence, I repeated my accusation, and declared to her face that she had given me the ribbon. The poor girl started to cry, but all she said to me was, 'Oh, Rousseau, I thought you were a good fellow. You make me very sad, but I should not like to be in your place.' That is all. She continued to defend herself with equal firmness and sincerity, but never allowed herself any reproaches against me. This moderation contrasted with my decided tone, prejudiced her case. It did not seem natural to suppose such diabolical audacity on one side and such angelic sweetness on the other. They seemed unable to come to a definite decision, but they were prepossessed in my favour. In the confusion of the moment they had not time to get to the bottom of the business; and the Comte de la Roque, in dismissing us both, contented himself with saying that the guilty one's conscience would amply revenge the innocent. His prediction was not wide of the mark. Not a day passes on which it is not fulfilled.

•

The magical lies of Casanova

CASANOVA

Casanova has often been accused of lying in his prodigious *Memoirs*, not least about his skill in seducing women. More recent historians, however, have perceived him to be a reliable source, and he is usually quite frank as to when he was acting mendaciously and when he was not. In the events preceding those contained in this extract, Casanova had witnessed an accident and had sent for a physician to attend the victim. Perceiving that the patient was a member of the Venetian Senate, and therefore rich, and that the physician's treatment was in danger of killing him, Casanova overruled the doctor and decided to treat the man himself. The patient whose name was de Bragadin, subsequently recovered, whereupon his friends declared that Casanova was a most skilled physician and that de Bragadin owed his life to him. Casanova takes up the story.

The worthy nobleman considered me as his oracle, and his two friends listened to me with the deepest attention. Their infatuation encouraging me, I spoke like a learned physician, I dogmatized, I quoted authors who I had never read.

M. de Bragadin, who had the weakness to believe in the occult sciences, told me one day that, for a young man of my age, he thought my learning too extensive, and that he was certain I was the possessor of some supernatural endowment. He entreated me to tell him the truth.

What extraordinary things will sometimes occur from mere chance, or from the force of circumstances! Unwilling to hurt his vanity by telling him that he was mistaken, I took the wild resolution of informing him, in the presence of his two friends, that I possessed a certain numeral calculus which gave answers (also in numbers), to any questions I liked to put.

M. de Bragadin said that it was Solomon's key, vulgarly called cabalistic science, and he asked me from whom I learnt it.

'From an old hermit,' I answered, 'who lives on the Carpegna Mountain, and whose acquaintance I made quite by chance when I was a prisoner in the Spanish army.'

'The hermit,' remarked the senator, 'has without informing you of it, linked an invisible spirit to the calculus he has taught you, for simple numbers cannot have the power of reason. You possess a real treasure, and you may derive great advantages from it.'

'I do not know,' I said, 'in what way I could make my science useful, because the answers given by the numerical figures are often so obscure that I have felt discouraged, and I very seldom tried to make any use of my calculus. Yet, it is very true that, if I had not formed my pyramid, I never should have had the happiness of knowing your excellency.'

'How so?'

'On the second day, during the festivities at the Soranzo Palace, I inquired of my oracle whether I would meet at the ball anyone whom I should not care to see. The answer I obtained was this: "Leave the ball-room precisely at four o'clock." I obeyed implicitly, and met your excellency.'

The three friends were astounded. M. Dandolo asked me whether I would answer a question he would ask, the interpretation of which would belong only to him, as he was the only person acquainted with the subject of the question.

I declared myself quite willing, for it was necessary to brazen it out, after having ventured as far as I had done. He wrote the question, and gave it to me; I read it, I could not understand either the subject or the meaning of the words, but it did not matter, I had to give an answer. If the question was so obscure that I could not make out the sense of it, it was natural that I should not understand the answer. I therefore answered, in ordinary figures, four lines of which he alone could be the interpreter, not caring much, at least in appearance, how they could be understood. M. Dandolo read them twice over, seemed astonished, said that it was all very plain to him; it was Divine, it was unique, it was a gift from Heaven, the numbers being only the vehicle, but the answer emanating evidently from an immortal spirit.

. . . After they had assured themselves of the reality of my cabalistic science by questions respecting the past, they decided to turn it to some use by consulting it upon the present and upon the future. I had no difficulty in shewing myself a good guesser, because I always gave answers with a double meaning, one of the meanings being carefully arranged by me, so as not to be understood until after the event; in that manner, my cabalistic science, like the oracle of Delphi, could never be found in fault. I saw how easy it must have been for the ancient heathen priests to impose upon ignorant, and therefore credulous mankind. I saw how easy it will always be for impostors to find dupes, and I realized, even better than the Roman orator, why two augurs could never look at each other without laughing; it was because they had both an equal interest in giving importance to the deceit they perpetrated, and from which they derived such immense profits. But what I could not, and probably never shall, understand, was the reason for which the Fathers, who were not so simple or so ignorant as our Evangelists, did not feel able to deny the divinity of oracles, and, in order to get out of the difficulty, ascribed them to the devil. They never would have entertained such a strange idea if they had been acquainted with cabalistic science. My three worthy friends were like the Holy Fathers; they had intelligence and wit, but they were superstitious, and no philosophers. But, although believing fully in my oracles, they were too kind-hearted to think them the work of the devil, and it suited their natural goodness better to believe my answers inspired by some heavenly spirit.

. . . I completed the conquest of their friendship by relating to them the whole of my life, only with proper reserve, so as not to lead them into any capital sins. I confess candidly that I deceived them, as the Papa Deldimopulo used to deceive the Greeks who applied to him for the Oracles of the Virgin. I certainly did not act towards them with a true sense of honesty, but if the reader to whom I confess myself is acquainted with the world and with the spirit of society, I entreat him to think before judging me, and perhaps I may meet with some indulgence at his hands.

I might be told that if I had wished to follow the rules of pure morality I ought either to have declined intimate intercourse with them or to have undeceived them. I cannot deny these premises, but I will answer that I was only twenty years of age, I was intelligent, talented, and had just been a poor fiddler.

. . . I took, at least it seems to me so, the best, the most natural, and the noblest decision, if we consider the disposition of their mind, when I decided upon the plan of conduct which insured me the necessaries of life: and of those necessaries who could be a better judge than your very humble servant?

. . . Such is the history of my metamorphosis, and of the lucky stroke which, taking me from the vile profession of a fiddler, raised me to the rank of a grandee.

The lie of vanity

SAMUEL JOHNSON

When Aristotle was once asked, what a man could gain by uttering falsehoods? he replied, 'Not to be credited when he shall tell the truth.'

The character of a liar is at once so hateful and contemptible, that even of those who have lost their virtue it might be expected that from the violation of truth they should be restrained by their pride. Almost every other vice that disgraces human nature, may be kept in countenance by applause and association: the corrupter of virgin innocence sees himself envied by the men, and at least not detested by the women; the drunkard may easily unite with beings, devoted like himself to noisy merriments or silent insensibility, who will celebrate his victories over the novices of intemperance, boast themselves the companions of his prowess, and tell with rapture of the multitudes whom unsuccessful emulation has hurried to the grave; even the robber and the cut-throat have their followers, who admire their address and intrepidity, their stratagems of rapine, and their fidelity to the gang.

The liar, and only the liar, is invariably and universally despised, abandoned, and disowned: he has no domestic consolations, which he can oppose to the censure of mankind; he can retire to no fraternity, where his crimes may stand in the place of virtues; but is given up to the hisses of the multitude, without friend and without apologist. It is the peculiar condition of falsehood, to be equally detested by the good and bad: 'The devils,' says Sir Thomas Browne, 'do not tell lies to one another; for truth is necessary to all societies: nor can the society of hell subsist without it.'

It is natural to expect, that a crime thus generally detested should be generally avoided; at least, that none should expose himself to unabated infamy, without an adequate temptation; and that to guilt so easily detected, and so severely punished, an adequate temptation would not readily be found.

Yet so it is, that in defiance of censure and contempt, truth is frequently violated; and scarcely the most vigilant and unremitted circumspection will secure him that mixes with mankind, from being hourly deceived by men of whom it can scarcely be imagined, that they mean any injury to him or profit to themselves: even where the subject of conversation could not have been expected to put the passions in motion, or to have excited either hope or fear, or zeal or malignity, sufficient to induce in any man to put his reputation in hazard, however little he might value it, or to overpower the love of truth, however weak might be its influence.

The casuists have very diligently distinguished lies into several classes, according to their various degrees of malignity: but they have, I think, generally omitted that which is most common, and perhaps, not least mischievous; which, since the moralists have not given it a name, I shall distinguish as the lie of vanity.

To vanity may justly be imputed most of the falsehoods which every man perceives hourly playing upon his ear, and, perhaps, most of those that are propagated with success. To the lie of commerce, and the lie of malice, the motive is so apparent, that they are seldom negligently or implicitly received; suspicion is always watchful over the practices of interest; and whatever the hope of gain, or desire of mischief, can prompt one man to assert, another is by reasons equally cogent incited to refute. But vanity pleases herself with such slight gratifications, and looks forward to pleasure so remotely consequential, that her practices raise no alarm, and her stratagems are not easily discovered.

Vanity is, indeed, often suffered to pass unpursued by suspicion, because he that would watch her motions, can never be at rest: fraud and malice are bounded in their influence; some opportunity of time and place is necessary to their agency; but scarce any man is abstracted one moment from his vanity; and he, to whom truth affords no gratifications, is generally inclined to seek them in falsehoods.

It is remarked by Sir Kenelm Digby, 'that every man has a desire to appear superior to others, though it were only in having seen what they have not seen'. Such an accidental disadvantage, since it neither implies merit, nor confers dignity, one would think should not be desired so much as to be counterfeited: yet even this vanity, trifling as it is, produces innumerable narratives, all equally false; but more or less credible in proportion to the skill or confidence of the relater. How many may a man of diffusive conversation count among his acquaintances, whose lives have been signalized by numberless escapes; who never cross the river but in a storm, or take a journey into the country without more adventures than befell the knights-errant of ancient times in pathless forests or enchanted castles! How many must he know, to whom portents and prodigies are of daily occurrence; and for whom nature is hourly working wonders invisible to every other eye, only to supply them with subjects of conversation.

Others there are that amuse themselves with the dissemination of falsehood, at greater hazard of detection and disgrace; men marked out by some lucky planet for universal confidence and friendship, who have been consulted in every difficulty, intrusted with every secret, and summoned to every transaction: it is the supreme felicity of these men, to stun all companies with noisy information; to still doubt, and overbear opposition, with certain knowledge or authentic intelligence. A liar of this kind, with a strong memory or brisk imagination, is often the oracle of an obscure club, and, till time discovers his impostures, dictates to his hearers with uncontrolled authority; for if a public question be started, he was present at the debate; if a new fashion be mentioned, he was at court the first day of its appearance; if a new performance of literature draws the attention of the public, he has patronized the author, and seen his work in manuscript; if a criminal of eminence be condemned to die, he often predicted his fate, and endeavoured his reformation: and who that lives at a distance from the scene of the action, will dare to contradict a man, who reports from his own eyes and ears, and to whom all persons and affairs are thus intimately known?

This kind of falsehood is generally successful for a time, because it is practised at first with timidity and caution: but the prosperity of the liar is of short duration; the reception of one story is always an incitement to the forgery of another less probable; and he goes on to triumph over tacit credulity, till pride or reason rises up against him, and his companions will no longer endure to see him wiser than themselves.

It is apparent, that the inventors of all these fictions intend some exaltation of themselves, and are led off by the pursuit of honour from their attendance upon truth: their narratives always imply some consequence in favour of their courage, their sagacity, or their activity, their familiarity with the learned, or their reception among the great; they are always bribed by the present pleasure of seeing themselves superior to those that surround them, and receiving the homage of silent attention and envious admiration.

But vanity is sometimes excited to fiction by less visible gratifications: the present age abounds with a race of liars who are content with the consciousness of falsehood, and whose pride is to deceive others without any gain or glory to themselves. Of this tribe it is the supreme pleasure to remark a lady in the playhouse or the park, and to publish, under the character of a man suddenly enamoured, an advertisement in the news of the next day, containing a minute description of her person and her dress. From this artifice, however, no other effect can be expected, than perturbations which the writer can never see, and conjectures of which he never can be informed; some mischief, however, he hopes he has done; and to have done mischief, is of some importance. He sets his invention to work again, and produces a narrative of a robbery or a murder, with all the circumstances of time and place accurately adjusted. This is a jest of greater effect and longer duration: if he fixes his scene at a proper distance, he may for several days keep a wife in terror for her husband, or a mother for her son; and please himself with reflecting, that by his abilities and address some addition is made to the miseries of life.

There is, I think, an ancient law of Scotland, by which leasing-making was capitally punished. I am, indeed, far from desiring to increase in this kingdom the number of executions; yet I cannot but think, that they who destroy the confidence of society, weaken the credit of intelligence, and interrupt the security of life; harass the delicate with shame, and perplex the timorous with alarms; might very properly be awakened to a sense of their crimes, by denunciations of a whipping-post or a pillory: since many are so insensible of right and wrong, that they have no standard of action but the law; nor feel guilt, but as they dread punishment.

•

The inhabitants of the moon

EMANUEL SWEDENBORG

Swedenborg (1688–1772) was a Swedish scientist and mystic who claimed that he was in contact with the spiritual world and wrote books about his experiences. Many religious documents or revelations claim to impart that which is true, and an intention to mislead, the legal *mens rea*, is an essential factor in deciding whether or not something can be classed as a lie. Yet many of Swedenborg's own contemporaries, including John Wesley, regarded him as a liar, a kind of religious Baron Munchausen, and from this extract it is easy to see why.

Certain spirits appeared over my head, and thence were heard voices like thunder, for the thunder of their voices exactly resembled the sound of thunder from the clouds after lightning: I at first conjectured, that it was owing to a great multitude of spirits, who had the art of uttering voices attended with so loud a noise. The more simple spirits, who were with me, smiled on the occasion, at which I was much surprised; but the cause of their smiling was presently discovered to be this, that the spirits, who thundered, were not many, but few, and were also as little as children; and that on former occasions they had terrified by such noises, and yet were unable to do them any hurt. In order that I might know their nature and quality, some of them descended from on high where they were thundering, and what surprised me, one carried another on his back, and thus two of them approached me: their faces appeared not unhandsome, but longer than the faces of other spirits; in regard to stature, they appeared like children of seven years old, but more robust; thus they were dwarfs (Homunciones). It was told me by angels, that they were from the Moon. He who was carried on the other's back, on coming to me, applied himself to my left side under the elbow, and thence discoursed with me, saying, that whenever they utter their voices they thus thunder; and that thereby they terrify the spirits who are inclined to do them mischief, and put some to flight, and that thus they go with security whithersoever they are disposed. To convince me that the noise they make was of such a sort, he retired from me to some other spirits, but not entirely out of sight, and thundered in like manner. They shewed moreover, that the voice being uttered from the abdomen, like an eructation, made this thundering sound. It was perceived that this was owing to this particular circumstance, that the inhabitants of the Moon do not speak from the lungs, like the inhabitants of Earth, but from the abdomen, and thus from a certain quantity of air there collected, by reason that the Moon is not encompassed with an atmosphere like that of other Earths. I was instructed, that the spirits of the Moon, in the Grand Man, have relation to the ensiform cartilage or xiphoides, to which the ribs in front are joined, and from which descends the fascia alba, which is the fulcrum of the abdominal muscles.

That there are inhabitants in the Moon, is well known to spirits and angels, and in like manner that there are inhabitants in the moons or satellites which revolve around Jupiter and Saturn. They who have not seen and discoursed with spirits coming from those moons, still entertain no doubt but there are men inhabiting them, because they are Earths alike with the planets, and wherever an Earth is, there are men inhabitants; for Man is the end for which every Earth was created, and nothing was made by the Great Creator without an end: that the human race, as constituent of heaven, is the end of creation, may appear to every one who thinks from a rational principle at all enlightened.

•

Should pious frauds be practised on the people?

VOLTAIRE

This philosophical and anti-clerical essay in the form of a dialogue is taken from Voltaire's *Philosophical Dictionary* (1764), a deliberately revolutionary work which was denounced by the public prosecutor of Geneva, Jean Robert Tronchin, as 'a deplorable monument of the extent to which intelligence and erudition can be abused'.

One day the fakir Bambabef met one of the disciples of Confutzee, whom we call Confucius; and this disciple's name was Wang; and Bambabef maintained that the people need to be deceived, and Wang claimed that we should never deceive anybody; and here is an abstract of their debate.

BAMBABEF: We must imitate the supreme being, who does not show us things as they are. He makes the sun appear to us as if it has a diameter of two or three feet, although this star is a million times bigger than the earth. He makes us see the moon and the stars attached to one and the same blue background, whereas they are at different distances. He wants a square tower to look round at a distance. He wants fire to seem hot to us although it is neither hot nor cold. In short, he surrounds us with errors appropriate to our nature.

WANG: What you call an error isn't one. The sun placed as it is millions of millions of lis (a li has 124 paces, Volt.) beyond our globe, is not the one we see. We really perceive, and we can only perceive, the sun that is painted on our retina at a fixed angle. Our eyes were not given to us to know dimensions and distances: other aids and other operations are needed to know them.

Bambabef appeared to be very surprised by this remark. Wang, who was very patient, explained to him the theory of optics; and Bambabef, who was no fool, yielded to the demonstrations of Confucius's disciple. Then he resumed the debate in these terms:

BAMBABEF: If god does not deceive us by means of our senses, as I believed, you must at least admit that doctors always deceive children for their good: they tell them that they are giving them sugar, and really give them rhubarb. So I, a fakir, may deceive people, who are as ignorant as children.
WANG: I have two sons, whom I have never deceived. When they were ill I told them: 'Here is a very bitter medicine, you must have the courage to take it. It would harm you if it were sweet.' I have never allowed their governesses and their tutors to make them afraid of spirits, ghosts, goblins, sorcerers: in this way I have made them brave and wise young citizens.
BAMBABEF: The people are not born in such happy circumstances as your family.
WANG: All men resemble each other. They are born with the same dispositions. It is the fakirs who corrupt the nature of men.
BAMBABEF: I admit that we teach them errors, but it is for their own good. We make them believe that if they don't buy our consecrated nails, if they don't expiate their sins by giving us money, they'll become post-horses, dogs or lizards in another life; that frightens them and they become well-behaved.
WANG: Don't you see that you pervert these poor people? Among them are many more rational beings than is realized, who laugh at your nails, your miracles, your superstitions, who know perfectly well that they aren't going to be changed into lizards or post-horses. What happens? They have sense enough to see that you are preaching them an impertinent religion, but they don't have enough to raise themselves to a pure religion free from superstition, like ours. Their passions make them

believe that there is no religion because the only one they are taught is ridiculous. You become guilty of all the vices into which they plunge.

BAMBABEF: Not at all, for we teach them only good morals.

WANG: You'd be stoned by the people if you taught them impure morals. Men are so made that they are quite willing to do evil, but they don't want it to be preached to them. A wise morality should simply not be mingled with absurd fables, because your impostures, with which you could dispense, weaken the morality you're obliged to teach.

BAMBABEF: Come! you believe that the people can be taught the truth without sustaining it with fables?

WANG: I believe it firmly. The educated people are of the same stuff as our tailors, our weavers and our labourers. They adore a god who is creator, remunerator and avenger. They sully their worship neither by absurd systems nor by extravagant ceremonies; and there are far fewer crimes amid the literate than among the people. Why not deign to instruct our workers as we instruct our educated people?

BAMBABEF: You'd be committing a great folly. You might as well wish them to be equally polite, or to be legal experts: it's neither possible nor decent. There must be white bread for the masters and wholemeal bread for servants.

WANG: I admit that all men should not be equally educated, but there are things that all must be. It's necessary for everybody to be just, and the surest way to instil justice in all men is to instil them with religion without superstition.

BAMBABEF: That's a fine project, but it's impracticable. Do you think that it's enough for me to believe in a god who punishes and rewards? You told me that it often happens that the cleverest among the people rise up against my fables. They'll rise up also against your truth. They'll say: 'Who will guarantee that god punishes and rewards? Where's the proof? What's your mission? What miracle have you performed that I should believe you?' They'll laugh at you much more than at me.

WANG: That's where you're wrong. You imagine that men will shake off the yoke of an idea that is honest, convincing, useful to everybody, an idea that is in harmony with human reason, because they reject things that are dishonest, absurd, useless, dangerous, that make good sense shudder. The people are quite disposed to believe their magistrates: when their magistrates offer them only a reasonable belief, they willingly embrace it. We need no prodigies to believe in a just god who reads the heart of man. This idea is too natural to be opposed. It's not necessary to explain exactly how god will punish and reward. It's enough to believe in his justice. I assure you that I've seen entire cities which had practically no other dogmas, and they were those in which I saw the most virtue.

BAMBABEF: Take care, you will find in those cities philosophers who will deny both punishments and rewards.

WANG: You must admit that these philosophers will deny your inventions even more strongly: so that won't be any benefit to you. Should there be any philosophers who don't agree with my principles, they will be good men none the less. They will none the less cultivate virtue, which should be embraced for love, and not out of fear. Moreover I'll maintain that no philosopher will ever be sure that providence doesn't reserve punishments for the wicked and rewards for those who are good. For if they ask me who told me that god punishes, I'll ask them who told them that god doesn't punish. In a word I'll maintain that the philosophers, far from contradicting me, will help me. Do you want to be a philosopher?

BAMBABEF: Willingly; but don't tell the fakirs.

•

The Walpole letters

THOMAS CHATTERTON

Thomas Chatterton (1752–70) is chiefly remembered for his fabrications of historical poems ostensibly written during the fifteenth century, putatively by one Thomas Rowley. Having forged both poems and provenance, Chatterton set about finding himself a patron. Horace Walpole was a publisher as well as an author. The odes of his friend Thomas Gray were his first production from his famous house at Strawberry Hill. As Chatterton's biographer, E. H. W. Meyerstein, has pointed out, Walpole was a man who avowed himself none too critical, 'and whose chief eagerness appeared to be to please and divert mankind'. In other words, he must have appeared to Chatterton to be what a confidence trickster today might call 'a good mark'. Accordingly Chatterton wrote to him first on 25 March 1769:

> Sir,
>
> Being versed a little in antiquitys, I have met with several Curious Manuscripts among which the following may be of Service to you, in any future edition of your truly entertaining Anecdotes of Painting – In correcting the mistakes (if any) in the Notes you will greatly oblige
>
> Your most humble servant,
> Thomas Chatterton.

Walpole wrote back actually volunteering to print Rowley, and desired Chatterton to send him more of Rowley's work, which was more than Chatterton had ever hoped for; a further selection of Thomas Rowley's poetry was sent. Meanwhile Walpole contracted Gray, amongst others, who detected some of his own style in Thomas Rowley and pronounced the works to be forgeries. Walpole then informed Chatterton that the game was up, and that he would be best advised to return to his legal studies. Chatterton wrote back:

> Sir,
>
> I am not able to dispute with a person of your literary character. I have transcribed Rowley's poems, &c &c. from a transcript in the possession of a gentleman who is assured of their authenticity . . . The MSS. have long been in the hands of the present possessor, which is all I know of

them. – Though I am but sixteen years of age, I have lived long enough to see that poverty attends literature. I am obliged to you sir, for your advice, and will go a little beyond it, by destroying all my useless lumber of literature, and never using my pen again but in the law.

I am,

Your most humble servant,
Thomas Chatterton.

Six days later he wrote again, demanding the return of the Rowley papers for the last time. However, a longer and more controversial letter had been intended, but was never sent. Both are printed here.

Sir,

Being fully convinced of the papers of Rowley being genuine, I should be obliged to you to return the copy I sent you, having no other. Mr Barrett, a very able antiquary, who is now writing the history of Bristol, has desired it of me; and I should be sorry to deprive him, or the world indeed, of a valuable curiousity, which I know to be an authentic piece of antiquity.

Your very humble servant,
Thomas Chatterton.

Sir,

As I am now fully convinced that Rowley's Papers are genuine: should be obliged to you, if you'd send Copys of them to the Town & Country Magazine; or return them to me for that Purpose: – as it wd. be the greatest Injustice, to deprive the World of so valuable a Curiousity –

I have seen the original from whence the Extracts first sent you were first Copyed –

The Harmony is not so extraordinary: – as Joseph Iscan is altogether Harmonious –

The Stanza Rowley wrote in, instead of being introduc'd by Spencer was in use 300 Years before [words missing] by Rowley – tho' I have seen some Poetry of that Age – exceeding Alliterations without Rhyme –

I shall not defend Rowley's Pastoral: its merit can stand its own defence –

Rowley was employed by Canynge to go to the Principal Monasterys in the Kingdom to Collect drawings, Paintings & all MSS. relating to Architecture – is it then so very extraordinary he should meet with the few remains of Saxon Learning – 'Tis allow'd by evry Historian of Credit, that the Normans destroy'd all the Saxon MSS., Paintings &c that fell in their Way; endeavoring to suppress the very Language – the want of knowing what they were, is all the Foundation you can have for stiling them a barbarous Nation. If you are not satisfied with these conspicuous Truths [part of letter missing] the Honor to be of my opinion

I am, Sr

Yr very hble & obt Servt
T. Chatterton.

Walpole finally returned the manuscripts. He heard no more about them until 1771, when Oliver Goldsmith informed him of the publication of some ancient poems lately discovered at Bristol, but added that their 'discoverer' had killed himself. Sadly, this was indeed the case.

•

Officious lies

JOHN WESLEY

On 12 November 1775, John Wesley delivered a sermon to the people of Bethnal Green. This was fairly wide-ranging, but he did address himself in particular to the issue of officious lies, as originally defined by Thomas Aquinas: lies told for some useful, harmless purpose, for the well-being and convenience of another person. Aquinas thought that such lies were not a mortal sin. Five hundred years after Aquinas, Wesley disagreed, and this partly explains why Methodism was considered such a dismal alternative to the prevailing Protestantism of the day.

If any, in fact, do this: either teach men to do evil that good may come or do so themselves, their damnation is just. This is particularly applicable to those who tell lies in order to do good thereby. It follows, that officious lies, as well as others, are an abomination to the God of Truth. Therefore there is no absurdity, however strange it may sound, in that saying of the ancient Father, 'I would not tell a wilful lie to save the souls of the whole world.'

•

True confessions

JEAN JACQUES ROUSSEAU

Towards the end of his life, Rousseau composed a series of Reveries, in which are combined philosophical argument with illustrative anecdotes from his own experience. In the following extract he has decided to devote himself to a self-examination on the subject of falsehood, and returns to the subject of the ribbon (see page 158).

When I set out the next day to put this resolution into practice, my first thought on beginning to reflect was of a terrible lie I had told in my early youth, a lie the memory of which has troubled me all my life and even now, in my old age, adds sorrow to a heart already suffering in so many other ways. This lie, which was a great crime in itself, was undoubtedly still more evil in its effects; these have remained unknown to me, but remorse has painted them to me in the cruellest possible colours. Yet, if one were to consider only my state of mind at the time, this lie was simply the product of false shame, and far from its being the result of a desire to harm the girl who was its victim, I can swear to Heaven that at the very moment when this invincible shame dragged it from me, I would joyfully have given my life's blood to deflect the blow on to myself alone. It was a moment of irresponsible folly which I can only explain by saying what I feel to be true, that all the wishes of my heart were conquered by my innate timidity.

The memory of this deplorable act and the undying remorse it left in me, instilled in me a horror of falsehood that ought to have preserved my heart from this vice for the rest of my life. When I adopted my motto, I felt that I had a right to it, and I had no doubt that I was worthy of it when I began on Abbé Rozier's prompting to examine myself more seriously.

However, on going over my life more carefully, I was very surprised by the number of things of my own invention which I remembered presenting as true at the very time when my heart was proud of my love of truth and I was sacrificing my security, my best interests and my own person to this love of truth with a disinterestedness for which I know no parallel among men.

What surprised me most was that when I recalled these fabrications I felt no real repentance. I, whose horror of falsehood outweighs all my other feelings, who would willingly face torture rather than tell a lie, by what strange inconsistency could I lie so cheerfully without compulsion or profit, and by what incredible contradiction could I do so without the slightest twinge of regret, when remorse for a lie has continually tormented me these fifty years? I have never hardened myself against my faults; my moral sense has always been a faithful guide to me, my conscience has retained its original integrity, and even if it might be corrupted and swayed by personal interests, how could I explain that, remaining firm and unmoved on those occasions when a man can at least excuse himself by his weakness in the face of passion, it loses its integrity precisely over those unimportant matters where vice has no excuse? I realized that the solution to this problem would determine how correctly I judged my behaviour in this respect, and after careful consideration I reached the following conclusions.

I remember reading in some philosophical work that to lie is to conceal a truth which one ought to make known. It follows of course from this definition that to conceal a truth which one is not obliged to divulge is not lying. But if in such circumstances a man not only fails to speak the truth, but speaks the opposite of truth, is he or is he not lying? According to the definition he cannot be said to be lying. For if he gives counterfeit coin to someone to whom he owes nothing, he may indeed be a deceiver, but he is not a thief.

There are indeed two questions to be looked at here, both of them equally important. Firstly, when and how should one tell the truth to others, since one is not always obliged to tell it? Secondly, are there cases when one can deceive people blamelessly? Of course everyone knows how to answer the second question – negatively in books, where the most austere morals cost the author nothing; affirmatively in life, where the morals of books are seen as idle and impracticable chatter. So, disregarding these conflicting authorities, let me seek by my own principles to find my answers to these question.

. . . In all ethical questions as difficult as this I have always found it best to be guided by the voice of conscience rather than the light of reason. My moral instinct has never deceived me. It has always remained sufficiently pure within me for me to put my trust in it, and if in my conduct it is sometimes swayed by my passions, it has no difficulty in regaining its authority in my recollections. Then it is that I judge myself as severely perhaps I shall be judged after death by the Supreme Judge.

To judge men's words by the effects they produce is often to misjudge them. Apart from the fact that these effects are not always clear or easily ascertained, they are as infinitely varied as the circumstances in which the words are spoken. But their degree of goodness or malice can only be gauged and determined by the intention that produced them. Untruthful talk is only falsehood when deception is intended, and even the intent to deceive, far from being invariably linked to the desire to injure, is often produced by exactly the opposite motive. But for falsehood to be innocent, it is not enough that there be no deliberate harmful intent, we must also be certain that the error into which we are leading our fellow-men can harm neither them nor anyone else in any way whatsoever. It is only very rarely that we can attain this certainty; consequently it is only very rarely that a lie is completely innocent. To lie to one's own advantage is an imposture, to lie to the advantage of others is a fraud, and to lie to the detriment of others is a slander – this is the worst kind of lie. To lie without advantage or disadvantage to oneself or others is not to lie; it is not falsehood but fiction.

Fictions which have a moral end in view are called parables or fables, and since their aim is or should be to present useful truths in a form which is pleasing to the senses, there is hardly any attempt in such cases to conceal the factual untruth, which is merely the disguise of truth, and the person who tells a fable simply as a fable is not in any sense a liar.

There are also quite empty kinds of fiction, such as the majority of stories and novels, which contain no real instruction and have no object other than entertainment. Such tales, being without any moral value, can only be judged by the intention of the teller, and when he tells them as if they were actually true, it can hardly be doubted that they are in fact lies. Even so, who has ever greatly troubled his conscience over lies of this sort, and who has ever seriously reproached anyone for telling them? For instance, if there is some moral lesson in 'The Temple of Gnidus' [a story by Montesquieu], this intention is badly flawed and obscured by the licentious details and lascivious images of the book. What did the author do to spread a cloak of modesty over his work? He pretended that it was the translation of a Greek manuscript and described the discovery of this manuscript in the manner most calculated to persuade his readers of the truth of his account. If that is not positively a lie, I should like to know what the word means. Yet who has ever dreamed of holding it against the author as a crime and treating him as an impostor on account of it?

It is fruitless to argue that this was merely a joke, that even if the author did make this claim he had no intention of persuading anybody, and that the public never doubted for a moment that he himself was the author of the supposedly Greek work which he claimed to be translating. To this I should reply that a pointless joke of this kind would have been nothing but a foolish piece of childishness, that a liar is no less a liar when he fails to persuade us, and that we must distinguish between the educated public and the many simple and credulous readers who have been genuinely deceived by this manuscript story told in apparent good faith by a serious author and who have unsuspectingly drunk from what appeared to be an ancient goblet the poison of which they would at least have been wary if it had been presented to them in a modern cup.

Whether or not these distinctions are to be found in books, they are inescapable for everyone who is honest with himself and will permit himself nothing which his conscience could condemn. For it is not less of a lie to say something untrue in one's own interest than to say it to the detriment of someone else, even though the falsehood is less reprehensible. To give an advantage to someone who does not deserve it is to pervert the order of justice; falsely to attribute to oneself or to another an act which can be praised or blamed, declared innocent or guilty, is to act unjustly; and everything which by being opposed to the truth offends justice in any way is a lie. That is the line which must not be crossed, but everything which although opposed to truth does not affect justice in any way is no more than a fiction, and I confess that anyone who holds a mere fiction against himself as a lie has a more tender conscience than I have.

The lies we call white lies are real lies, because to act deceitfully in one's own interest or that of others is no less unjust than to act deceitfully against the interests of others. Whoever praises or blames untruthfully is telling a lie, if the person in question is a real person. If it is an imaginary being, he can say whatever he likes without lying, unless he makes false judgements about the morality of facts which he has invented, since in this case, even if he is not lying about facts he is betraying moral truth, which is infinitely superior to factual truth.

. . . Such were my rules of conscience concerning truth and falsehood. My heart followed these rules automatically before they had been adopted by my reason, and my moral instinct alone showed me how to apply them. The criminal lie of which poor Marion was the victim left me with eternal remorse and this has been preserved the rest of my life not only from all lies of this kind, but from all those which might in any way damage the interests or the reputations of others. By imposing on myself a general prohibition of this sort I have been able to avoid having to weigh up the rights and wrongs of particular cases so as to draw a precise line between harmful lies and white lies; regarding both as reprehensible, I have shunned them both equally.

In this as in all other matters my natural disposition has had a great influence on my principles, or rather on my habits, for I have hardly ever acted according to rules – or have hardly ever followed any other rules than the promptings of my nature. Never has a premeditated lie approached my mind, never have I lied to my own advantage; but I have often lied out of shame, to avoid embarrassment in trivial affairs or affairs that concerned only me, as when in order to keep a conversation going I have been forced by the slowness of my ideas and my lack of small talk to have recourse to fiction for something to say. When I am obliged to talk and interesting truths do not spring to mind readily enough, I invent stories rather than keep quiet, but in making up these stories I am careful as far as possible to avoid lies which would go against justice and the truth we owe to others, and to keep fictions which are a matter of equal indifference to myself and everyone else. In doing so I should naturally prefer to put a moral truth in the place of factual truth, in other words to give a true picture of the natural affections of the human heart, and to draw some useful lesson from my stories, making them like moral tales or parables; but it would call for greater presence of mind and a readier tongue than mine to be able to make such instructive use of idle chatter. The talk runs on more quickly than my ideas and forces me to speak before thinking, so that I have often been led into foolish and inept statements which my reason had condemned and my heart disowned before I had finished speaking, but which had forestalled my judgement and thus escaped its censure.

It is also because of this irresistible instinctive reaction that when I am suddenly taken by surprise, shame and timidity often impel me to tell lies which are independent of my will but in a manner of speaking anticipate it, under the pressure of the need to give an immediate answer. The profound impression made on me by the memory of poor Marion may be capable of preventing any lies which might harm other people, but not the lies which can help me to save face when I alone am involved; yet these are just as much against my conscience and my principles as those which can have an influence on other people's lives.

I swear to Heaven that if I could instantly retract the lie which exonerates me and tell the truth which incriminates me without blackening myself still further by this recantation, I should do so with all my heart, but the shame of thus being caught in the act is a further obstacle to honesty and I feel genuine repentance without daring to make amends.

. . . I have never felt my natural aversion to falsehood so clearly as when I was writing my Confessions, for this is where I often should have been sorely tempted to lie if I had been so inclined. But far from having concealed or disguised anything which was to my disadvantage, by some strange quirk which I can hardly understand and which is perhaps due to my distaste for all forms of imitation, I felt more inclined to err on the opposite side, condemning myself too severely rather than excusing myself too indulgently, and my conscience assures me that one day I shall be judged less severely than I have judged myself. Yes, I can declare with a proud consciousness of my achievement, that in this work I carried good faith, truthfulness and frankness as far, further even, or so I believe, than any other mortal; feeling that the good outweighed the evil, it was in my interest to tell the whole truth, and that is what I did.

I never said less than the truth; sometimes I went beyond it, not in the facts but in the circumstances surrounding them, and this kind of lie was the effect of a wild imagination rather than an act of will. I am wrong to speak of lies, since none of these embellishments was really a lie. When I wrote my Confessions I was already old and disillusioned with the vain pleasures of life, all of which I had tasted and felt their emptiness in my heart. I was writing from memory; my memory often failed me or only provided me with an incomplete picture, and I filled the gaps with details which I dreamed up to complete my memories, but which never contradicted them. I took pleasure in dwelling on my moments of happiness and sometimes I embellished them with adornments suggested to me by my fond regrets. I described things I had forgotten as I thought they must have been, as they perhaps really had been, but never in contradiction to my actual memories. Sometimes I decorated truth with new beauties, but I never used lies to extenuate my vices or lay claims to virtue.

•

Falsehoods which are not lies

WILLIAM PALEY

A lie is a breach of promise: for whoever seriously addresses his discourse to another, tacitly promises to speak the truth, because he knows that the truth is expected.

Or the obligation of veracity may be made out from the direct ill consequences of lying to social happiness; which consequences consist, either in some specific injury to particular individuals, or in the destruction of that confidence which is essential to the intercourse of human life; for which latter reason, a lie may be pernicious in its general tendency, and therefore criminal, though it produce no particular or visible mischief to any one.

There are falsehoods which are not lies; that is, which are not criminal: as, –

1. Where no one is deceived; which is the case in parables, fables, novels, jests, tales to create mirth, ludicrous embellishments of a story, where the declared design of the speaker is not to inform, but to divert; compliments in the subscription of a letter, a servant's denying his master, a prisoner's pleading not guilty, an advocate asserting the justice, or his belief of the justice, of his client's cause. In such instances, no confidence is destroyed, because none was reposed; no promise to speak the truth is violated, because none was given, or understood to be given.

2. Where the person to whom you speak has no right to know the truth, or, more properly, where little or no inconvenience results from the want of confidence in such cases; as where you tell a falsehood to a madman, for his own advantage; to a robber, to conceal your property; to an assassin, to defeat or divert him from his purpose. The particular consequence is by the supposition beneficial; and, as to the general consequence, the worst that can happen is, that the madman, the robber, the assassin, will not trust you again; which (beside that the first is incapable of reducing regular conclusions from having been once deceived, and the last two not likely to come a second time in your way) is sufficiently compensated by the immediate benefit which you propose by the falsehood.

It is upon this principle, that, by the laws of war, it is allowed to deceive an enemy by feints, false colours,* spies, false intelligence, and the like; but by no means in treaties, truces, signals of capitulation or surrender: and the difference is, that the former suppose hostilities to continue, the latter are calculated to terminate or suspend them. In the *conduct* of war, and whilst the war

*There have been two or three instances of late, of English ships decoying an enemy into their power, by counterfeiting signals of distress; an artifice which ought to be reprobated by the common indignation of mankind! for, a few examples of captures effected by this stratagem, would put an end to that promptitude in affording assistance to ships in distress, which is the best virtue in a seafaring character, and by which the perils of navigation are diminished to all. – A.D. 1775.

continues, there is no use, or rather no place, for confidence betwixt the contending parties; but in whatever relates to the *termination* of war, the most religious fidelity is expected, because without it wars could not cease, nor the victors be secure, but by the entire destruction of the vanquished.

Many people indulge, in serious discourse, a habit of fiction and exaggeration, in the accounts they give of themselves, of their acquaintance, or of the extraordinary things which they have seen or heard: and so long as the facts they relate are indifferent, and their narratives, though false, are inoffensive, it may seem a superstitious regard to truth to censure them merely for truth's sake.

In the first place, it is almost impossible to pronounce beforehand, with certainty, concerning any lie, that it is offensive. *Volat irrevocabile*, and collects sometimes accretions in its flight, which entirely change its nature. It may owe possibly its mischief to the officiousness or misrepresentation of those who circulate it; but the mischief is, nevertheless, in some degree, chargeable upon the original editor.

In the next place, this liberty in conversation defeats its own end. Much of the pleasure, and all the benefit, of conversation, depends upon our good opinion of the speaker's veracity: for which this rule leaves no foundation. The faith indeed of a hearer must be extremely perplexed, who considers the speaker, or believes that the speaker considers himself, as under no obligation to adhere to truth, but according to the particular importance of what he relates.

But beside and above both these reasons, *white* lies always introduce others of darker complexion. I have seldom known any one who deserted truth in trifles, that could be trusted in matters of importance. Nice distinctions are out of the question, upon occasions which, like those of speech, return every hour. The habit, therefore, of lying, when once formed, is easily extended, to serve the designs of malice or interest; – like all habits, it spreads indeed of itself.

Pious frauds, as they are improperly enough called, pretended inspirations, forged books, counterfeit miracles, are impositions of a more serious nature. It is possible that they may sometimes, though seldom, have been set up and encouraged, with a design to do good: but the good they aim at requires that the belief of them should be perpetual, which is hardly possible; and the detection of the fraud is sure to disparage the credit of all pretensions of the same nature. Christianity has suffered more injury from this cause than from all other causes put together.

As there may be falsehoods which are not lies, so there may be lies without literal or direct falsehood. An opening is always left for this species of prevarication, when the literal and grammatical signification of a sentence is different from the popular and customary meaning. It is the wilful deceit that makes the lie; and we wilfully deceive, when our expressions are not true in the sense in which we believe the hearer to apprehend them: besides that it is absurd to contend for any sense of words, in opposition to usage; for all senses of all words are founded upon usage, and upon nothing else.

Or a man may *act* a lie; as by pointing his finger in a wrong direction, when a traveller inquires of him his road; or when a tradesman shuts up his windows, to induce his creditors to believe that he is abroad: for, to all moral purposes, and therefore as to veracity, speech and action are the same; speech being only a mode of action.

Or, lastly, there may be lies of *omission*. A writer of English history, who, in his account of the reign of Charles the First, should wilfully suppress any evidence of that prince's despotic measures and designs, might be said to lie; for, by entitling his book a *History of England*, he engages to relate the whole truth of the history, or, at least, all that he knows of it.

•

The absolutist view

IMMANUEL KANT

Kant takes the Old Testament view that there is no possible excuse for a lie, and if anything he is even more absolutist in this debate than Augustine. To tell the truth, he says, is a duty which nothing can abrogate. The only virtue attaching to Kant's rigorous viewpoint is its crystal clarity in that it admits of absolutely no exceptions.

In the journal *France*, for 1797, Part VI, No. 1, page 123, in an article entitled 'On Political Reactions' by Benjamin Constant, there appears the following passage:

> The moral principle, 'It is a duty to tell the truth', would make any society impossible if it were taken singly and unconditionally. We have proof of this in the very direct consequences which a German philosopher has drawn from this principle. This philosopher goes so far as to assert that it would be a crime to lie to a murderer who has asked whether our friend who is pursued by him had taken refuge in our house.

The French philosopher on page 124 refutes this principle in the following manner:

> It is a duty to tell the truth. The concept of duty is inseparable from the concept of right. A duty is that which in no one being corresponds to the rights of another. Where there are no rights, there are no duties. To tell the truth is thus a duty: but it is a duty only in respect to one who has a right to tell the truth. But no one has a right to a truth which injures others.

The πρῶτον ψευδος in this argument lies in the sentence: 'To tell the truth is a duty, but it is a duty only toward one who has a right to the truth.'

It must first be noted that the expression, 'to have a right to truth' is without meaning. One must rather say, 'Man has a right to his own truthfulness (*veracitas*),' i.e., to the subjective truth in his own person. For to have objectively a right to truth would mean that it is a question of one's will (as in questions of what belongs to individuals generally) whether a given sentence is to be true or false. This would certainly produce an extraordinary logic.

Now the first question is: Does a man, in cases where he cannot avoid answering 'Yes' or 'No', have a right to be untruthful. The second question is: Is he not in fact bound to tell an untruth, when he is unjustly compelled to make a statement, in order to protect himself or another from a threatened misdeed?

Truthfulness in statements which cannot be avoided is the formal duty of an individual to everyone, however great may be the disadvantage accruing to himself or to another. If, by telling an untruth, I do not wrong him who unjustly compels me to make a statement, nevertheless by this falsification, which must be called a lie (though not in a legal sense), I commit a wrong against duty generally in a most essential point. That is, so far as in my lies I cause that declarations should in general find no credence, and hence that all rights based on contracts should be void and lose their force, and this is a wrong done to mankind generally.

Thus the definition of a lie as merely an intentional untruthful declaration to another person does not require the additional condition that it must harm another, as jurists think proper in their definition (*mendacium est falsiloquium in praeiudicium alterius*). For a lie always harms another; if not some other particular man, still it harms mankind generally, for it vitiates the source of law itself.

This benevolent lie, however, can become punishable under civil law through an accident (*casus*), and that which escapes liability to punishment only by accident can also be condemned as wrong even by external laws. For instance, if by telling a lie you have prevented a murder, you have made yourself legally responsible for all the consequences; but if you have held rigorously to the truth, public justice can lay no hand on you, whatever the unforeseen consequences may be. After you have honestly answered the murderer's question as to whether his intended victim is at home, it may be that he has slipped out so that he does not come in the way of the murderer, and thus that the murder may not be committed. But if you had lied and said that he was not at home when he had really gone out without your knowing it, and if the murderer had then met him as he went away and murdered him, you might justly be accused as the cause of his death. For if you had told the truth as far as you knew it, perhaps the murderer might have been apprehended by the neighbours while he searched the house and thus the deed might have been prevented. Therefore, whoever tells a lie, however well intentioned he might be, must answer for the consequences, however unforeseeable they were, and pay the penalty for them even in a civil tribunal. This is because truthfulness is a duty which must be regarded as the ground of all duties based on contract, and the laws of these duties would be rendered uncertain and useless if even the least exception to them were admitted.

To be honest in all declarations, therefore, is a sacred and absolutely commanding decree of reason, limited by no expediency.

•

When a story may be credible

JOHN PINKERTON

The following anecdote is told of one James Bruce, the author of a five-volume book entitled *Travels to Discover the Source of the Nile.*

Bruce's book is both dull and dear. We join in clubs of five, each pays a guinea, draws lots who shall have it first, and the last to keep it for his patience.

Bruce's overbearing manner has raised enmity and prejudices; and he did wrong in retailing the most wonderful parts of his book in companies. A story may be credible when attended with circumstances, which seems false if detached.

I was present in a large company at dinner, when Bruce was talking away. Someone asked him what musical instruments were used in Abyssinia. Bruce hesitated, not being prepared for the question; and at last said, 'I think I saw one lyre there.' George Selwyn whispered to his next man, 'Yes; and there is one less since he left the country.'

•

False political reports

ISAAC D'ISRAELI

'A false report, if believed during three days, may be of great service to a government.' This political maxim has been ascribed to Catherine de Medici, an adept in *coups d'état*, the *aracana imperii*! Between solid lying and disguised truth there is a difference known to writers skilled in 'the art of governing mankind by deceiving them'; as politics, ill-understood, have been defined, and as, indeed, all party-politics are. These forgers prefer to use the truth disguised to the gross fiction. When the real truth can no longer be concealed, then they can confidently refer to it; for they can still explain and obscure, while they secure on their side the party whose cause they have advocated. A curious reader of history may discover the temporary and sometimes the lasting advantages of spreading rumours designed to disguise, or to counteract the real state of things. Such reports, set a-going, serve to break down the sharp and fatal point of a panic, which might instantly occur; in this way the public is saved from the horrors of consternation, and the stupefaction of despair. These rumours give a breathing time to prepare for the disaster, which is doled out cautiously; and, as might be shown, in some cases these first reports have left an event in so ambiguous a state, that a doubt may still arise whether these reports were really destitute of truth! Such reports, once printed, enter into history, and sadly perplex the honest historian. Of a battle fought in a remote situation, both parties for a long time, at home, may dispute the victory after the event, and the pen may prolong what the sword had long decided. This has been no unusual circumstance; of several of the most important battles on which the fate of Europe has hung, were we to rely on some reports of the time, we might still doubt of the manner of the transaction. A skirmish has been often raised into an *arranged* battle, and a defeat concealed in an account of the killed and wounded, while victory has been claimed by both parties! Villeroy, in all his encounters with Marlborough, always sent home despatches by which no one could be suspected that he was discomfited. Pompey, after his fatal battle with Caesar, sent letters to all the provinces and cities of the Romans, describing with greater courage than he had fought, so that a report generally prevailed that Caesar had lost the battle: Plutarch informs us that three hundred writers had described the battle of Marathon. Many doubtless had copied their predecessors; but it would perhaps have surprised us to have observed how materially some differed in their narratives.

. . . we may observe the artifice of party writers in disguising or suppressing the real fact [with] the famous battle of the Boyne. The French catholic party long reported that Count Lauzun had won the battle, and that King William the Third was killed. Bussy Rabutin in some memoirs, in which he appears to have registered public events without scrutinizing their truth, says, 'I chronicled this account according as the first reports gave out; when at length the real fact reached them, the party did not like to lose their pretended victory.' Père Londel, who published a register of the times, which is favourably noticed in the *Nouvelle de la Republique des Lettres*, for 1699, has recorded the event in this deceptive manner: 'The Battle of the Boyne in Ireland; Schomberg is killed there at the head of the English.' This is 'an equivocator'! The writer resolved to conceal the defeat of James's party, and cautiously suppresses any mention of a victory, but very carefully gives a real fact, by which his readers would hardly doubt of the defeat of the English! We are so accustomed to this traffic of false reports, that we are scarcely aware that many important events recorded in history were in their day strangely disguised by such mystifying accounts. This we can only discover by reading private letters written at the moment. Bayle has collected several remarkable absurdities of this kind, which were spread abroad to answer a temporary purpose, but which had never been known to us had these contemporary letters not been published. A report was prevalent in Holland in 1580, that the kings of France and Spain and the Duke of Alva were dead; a felicity which for a time sustained the exhausted spirits of the revolutionists. At the invasion of the Spanish Armada, Burleigh spread reports of the thumb-screws, and other instruments of torture, which the Spaniards had brought with them, and thus inflamed the hatred of the nation. The horrid story of the bloody Colonel Kirk [see page 140] is considered as one of these political forgeries to serve the purpose of blackening a zealous partisan.

False reports are sometimes stratagems of war. When the chiefs of the League had lost the battle at Ivry, with an army broken and discomfited they still kept possession of Paris merely by imposing on the inhabitants all sorts of false reports, such as the death of the king of Navarre at the fortunate moment when victory, undetermined on which side to incline, turned for the Leaguers; and they gave out false reports of a number of victories they had elsewhere obtained. Such tales, distributed in pamphlets and ballads among a people agitated by doubts and fears, are gladly believed; flattering their wishes or soothing their alarms, they contribute to their ease, and are too agreeable to allow time for reflection.

The history of a report creating a panic may be traced in the Irish insurrection, in the curious memoirs of James the Second. A forged proclamation of the Prince of Orange was set forth by one Speke, and a rumour spread that the Irish troops were killing and burning in all parts of the kingdom! A magic-like panic instantly ran through the people, so that in one quarter of the town of Drogheda they imagined that the other was filled with blood and ruin. During this panic pregnant women miscarried, aged persons died with terror, while the truth was, that the Irish themselves were disarmed and dispersed, in utter want of a meal or a lodging!

In the unhappy times of our civil wars under Charles the First, the newspapers and the private letters afford specimens of this political contrivance of false reports of every species. No extravagance of invention to spread a terror against a party was too gross, and the city of London was one day alarmed that the royalists were occupied by a plan of blowing up the river Thames, by an immense quantity of powder warehoused at the river-side; and that there existed an organized though invisible brotherhood of many thousands with *consecrated knives*; and those who hesitated to give credit to such rumours were branded as malignants, who took not the danger of the parliament to heart. Forged conspiracies and reports of great but distant victories were inventions to keep up the spirit of a party, but oftener prognosticated some intended change in the government. When they were desirous of augmenting the army, or introducing new garrisons, or using an extreme measure with the city, or the royalists, there was always a new conspiracy set afloat; or when any great affair was to be carried in parliament, letters of great victories were published to dishearten the opposition, and infuse additional boldness in their own party. If the report only lasted a few days, it obtained its purpose, and verified the observation of Catherine de Medici. Those politicians who raise such false reports obtain their end: like the architect who, in building an arch, supports it with circular props and pieces of timber, or any temporary rubbish, till he closes the arch; and when it can support itself, he throws away the props! There is no class of political lying which can want for illustration if we consult the records of our civil wars; there we may trace the whole art in all the nice management of its shades, its qualities, and its more complicated parts, from invective to puff, and from innuendo to prevarication! we may admire the scrupulous correction of a lie which they had told, by another which they are telling! and triple lying to overreach their opponents. Royalists and Parliamentarians were alike; for to tell one great truth, 'the father of lies' is of no party.

•

Discovering Shakespeare

ANON.

There have been many forgeries of Shakespeare, but perhaps none as audacious as that of William Henry Ireland; not content with forging autographs, and manuscripts of Shakespearean plays in the bard's own hand, Ireland set about the composition of some new, 'undiscovered' plays. That the mendacity of Ireland was exposed at all was chiefly due to the scrutiny of a Shakespeare scholar by the name of Malone, for, as the story reveals, Ireland had succeeded in convincing literary figures as grand as Boswell and Sheridan.

Mr Malone, in the preface to his edition of Shakespeare, had shown that Shakespeare died at the age of fifty-two in April 1616, leaving his daughter, and her husband Dr J. Hall, executors. The will demonstrates, that he died possessed of 'baubles, gewgaws, and toys to mock apes, &c.'. Dr Hall died in 1635, leaving a will, and bequeathing his library and manuscripts to J. Nash. 'Here,' says Mr Malone, 'is a proof that the executor of Shakespeare's will left a library and manuscripts behind him.' In a satisfactory manner did Mr Malone trace down, from the public records, the legal descendants to a recent period, from which he inferred, that, amongst the present generation of them, fragments might be found, if curiosity would prompt diligence to search the repositories of concealment. The search proved successful, and from the appearance of the manuscripts of Shakespeare in 1790, every moment was expectancy of more arrivals; in fact discovery succeeded discovery so fast, that Mr Malone obtained documents enough to fill a folio. A painting of Shakespeare was also found, the very painting that enabled Droeshout to engrave the effigies of Shakespeare which were prefixed to the folio edition of his dramas, and of which Ben Jonson affirmed that 'The Graver had a strife, With nature, to outdo the life'; and everything concurred to evince the genuineness of this ancient painting.

A new discovery of Shakespearean papers was announced for exhibition in Norfolk-street, in 1794, and curiosity was again aroused.

Mr Malone, from some private reasons, seemed indifferent about these papers in Norfolk-street; and he was urged by his scepticism to contradict that probability which he had taught the imaginative world to entertain in favour of the discovery of Shakespearean fragments. Many other learned persons being, however, convinced by examination of the authenticity of these miscellaneous papers, the publication of them was undertaken by subscription, and *four guineas* a copy were freely paid by the subscribers.

When the book came out, and not till then, did Mr Malone condescend to look at it, and examine its pretensions; and he quickly decided it to be a palpable and bold forgery. This he demonstrated by a learned and critical examination of each particular paper; his inquiry was drawn up in the form of a letter, and addressed to the Right Honourable James, Earl of Charlemont, in the year 1796.

The editor of them, Mr Ireland, in his preface, had assured the public, that all men of taste who had viewed them previous to publication unanimously testified in favour of their authenticity, and declared that there was on their side a mass of irrefragable evidence, external and internal; that it was impossible, amid such various sources of detection, for the art of imitation to have hazarded itself without being betrayed; and, consequently, that these papers could be no other than the production of William Shakespeare himself.

The editor in continuation, said, that these papers came into his hands from his son, Samuel William Henry Ireland, a young man nineteen years of age, by whom the discovery was accidentally made, at the house of a gentleman of considerable property, amongst a heterogeneous collection of family papers.

The legal contracts between Shakespeare and others were, it

was said, first found by the junior Ireland, and soon afterwards, the deed of gift to William Henry Ireland, described as the friend of Shakespeare, in consequence of his having saved the dramatist's life. In pursuing this research, he was so fortunate as to meet with some deeds very material to the interests of the gentlemen at whose house he was staying, and such as established, beyond all doubt, his title to considerable property, of which he was as ignorant as he was of possessing these interesting manuscripts of Shakespeare.

Fully satisfied with the honour and liberality shown to him, the finder of these treasures did not feel justified in importuning or requesting a gentleman, to whom he was known by obligation alone, to subject himself to the impertinence and licentiousness of literary curiosity and cavil, unless he should voluntarily come forward. He had applied to the original possessor of them for his permission to print them, and only obtained it under the strongest injunctions of secrecy.

'It is to be observed,' says Malone, 'that we are not told where the deed was first discovered; it is said in a mansion house, but where situated is not stated. Another very remarkable incident is mentioned: the discoverer met the possessor, to whom he was unknown, at a coffee-house, or some public-place, and the conversation turned on old autographs, of which the discoverer was a collector; the country gentleman said to him, "If you are for autographs, I am your man; come to my chambers, any morning, and rummage my old deeds, and you will find enough of them." Accordingly the discoverer goes, and taking down a parcel, in a few minutes lighted on the name of Shakespeare. The discovery of the title to a considerable estate was so fortunate and beneficial a circumstance to this unknown gentleman, that we cannot wonder at his liberality in giving up all his right to these valuable literary curiosities; but one naturally wishes to know in what country this estate lies, or whether any suit has been instituted within the last year or two, in consequence of such a discovery of title-deeds so little dreamt of.'

According to Mr Malone, the great objections, critically speaking, to be brought against the manuscripts are, firstly, the orthography; this is not only not the orthography of Elizabeth or her time, but for the most part of no age whatever. The spelling of the copulative *and*, and the preposition *for*, ande – forre, is unprecedented. 'I have,' says Mr Malone, 'perused some thousands of deeds and manuscripts, and never once found such a spelling of them; the absurd way in which almost every word is overladen with both vowels and consonants, will strike every reader who has any knowledge on the subject.

. . . 'Secondly, the phraseology is equally faulty, particularly in the letter, supposed to be written and directed by Queen Elizabeth to William Shakespeare. The letter, in particular, it is very easy to prove a forgery; as, by an anachronism, it is directed to William Shakespeare, at the Globe by the Thames. Now the Globe was a theatre which did not open till the year 1594; yet, in the same letter, mention is made of the expected presence of Leicester, who died in September 1588, when this theatre did not exist.'

The deeds and miscellaneous papers were exhibited in Norfolk-street, long before their publication, and they were submitted to the critical examination of any one willing to question them; nor, from their appearance of venerable antiquity, was a doubt of their genuine authenticity allowed to be entertained. When the elder Mr Ireland afterwards published his 'Vindication', he showed how readily the most discerning persons yielded their faith to this imposture. Mr Boaden, he says, thus wrote to G. Stevens after having seen the manuscripts. 'In some instances credulity is no disgrace, strong enthusiasm is always eager to believe; I confess that, for some time after I had seen them, I continued to think they might be genuine; they bore the character of the poet's writing, the paper appeared of sufficient age, the water marks were earnestly displayed, and the matter diligently applauded; I remember that I beheld the papers with the tremor of utmost delight, touched the invaluable relics with reverential respect, and deemed even existence dearer as it gave me so refined a satisfaction.'

Similar and even stronger impressions were made on James Boswell, one of those literary characters who, in company with Dr Parr, signed a certificate expressing their belief of the authenticity of the papers. Previous to signing his name, Boswell fell on his knees, and, in a tone of enthusiasm and exultation, thanked God that he had lived to witness their discovery, and that he could now die in peace. In proportion to this strong belief, therefore, was the public indignation excited against the inventors of that monstrous, – and to the subscribers expensive forgery, which the critical acumen of Mr Malone had so clearly exposed. The blame of the transaction was imputed as much to Mr Ireland, the father, as to William Henry, the son, who was in reality sole contriver of this imposture. In an exculpatory pamphlet, he says, 'In justice to the memory of my father, I think it necessary to give a true account of the publication of these manuscripts. After dinner my father would read different accounts of Shakespeare and remark how wonderful it was that no vestige of his signature remains, except that at Doctor's Commons. Curiosity led me to look at the signature, in Stevens' edition of his plays, and it occurred to me, that if some old writing could be produced, and passed off for Shakespeare's, it might occasion a little mirth, and show how far credulity would go in search of antiquities. I first tried an experiment by writing a letter, as from the author of an old book in my possession, in dedication of it to Queen Elizabeth: I showed it to my father, who thought it genuine. This encouraged me to proceed till the whole work was completed, and published with the following title page: "Miscellaneous papers and legal instruments under the hand and seal of William Shakespeare, including the tragedy of King Lear, and a fragment of Hamlet, folio, London, 1796." And subsequently, "Free reflections on the miscellaneous papers, &c., in the possession of S. Ireland, to which are added extracts from the Virgin Queen, a play."'

The story of the country gentleman was told to silence the numerous inquiries as to where they came from. In conclusion, Mr S. Ireland says, 'I most sincerely regret any offence I may have given the world, or particular individuals, trusting at the same time, that they will deem the whole the work of a boy, without any evil or bad intent, but hurried on, thoughtless of any danger that awaited to ensnare him.'

The drama of Vortigern, which formed one portion of the forgery, was brought out at Drury-lane theatre, and was unanimously damned.

•

Napoleon's dispatches

BOURIENNE

Napoleon wasn't the first general to send home false dispatches from the battlefield, but according to Carlyle, the phrase 'false bulletins' became almost proverbial in Napoleon's campaigns. 'He makes what excuse he could for it: that it was necessary to mislead the enemy, to keep up his own men's courage, and so forth. On the whole, there are no excuses. A man in no case has liberty to tell lies. It had been, in the long-run, *better* for Napoleon too if he had not told any. In fact, if a man have any purpose reaching beyond the hour and day, meant to be found extant *next* day, what good can it ever be to promulgate lies? The lies are found out; ruinous penalty is exacted for them. No man will believe the liar next time even when he speaks the truth, when it is of the last importance that he be believed. The old cry of wolf! – A Lie is *no*-thing; you cannot of nothing make something; you make *nothing* at last, and lose your labour into the bargain.' And Emerson went even further in condemning Napoleon's false reporting: 'He is a boundless liar. The official papers, his *Moniteurs*, and all his bulletins, are proverbs for saying what he wished to be believed; and worse – he sat in his premature old age, in his lonely island, coldly falsifying facts, and dates and characters and giving to history a theatrical éclat.' In these two extracts Napoleon's private secretary and biographer, Monsieur de Bourienne, explains something of the first consul's military mendacity.

The siege of St Jean d'Acre was raised on the 20th May. It cost us a loss of nearly three thousand men, in killed, deaths by the plague, or wounds. A great number were wounded mortally. In those veracious documents, the bulletins, the French loss was made five hundred killed, and one thousand wounded, and the enemy's losses more than fifteen thousand.

Our bulletins may form curious materials for history; but their value certainly will not depend on the credit due to their details. Bonaparte attached the greatest importance to those documents, generally drawing them up himself, or correcting them, when written by another hand, if the composition did not please him . . .

The historian of these times ought to put no faith in the bulletins, despatches, notes, and proclamations, which have emanated from Bonaparte, or passed through his hands. For my part, I believe that the proverb, 'As great a liar as a bulletin', has much truth in it as the axiom, two and two make four.

The bulletins always announced what Bonaparte wished to be believed true; but to form a proper judgement on any fact, counter bulletins must be sought for and consulted. It is well known, too, that Bonaparte attached great importance to the place whence he dated his bulletins; thus, he dated his decrees respecting the theatres and Hamburg beef, at Moscow.

The official documents were almost always incorrect. There was falsity in the exaggerated descriptions of his victories, and falsity again in the suppression or palliation of his reverses and losses. A writer, if he took his materials from the bulletins and the official correspondence of the time, would compose a romance rather than a true history. Of this many proofs have been given in the present work.

Another thing, which always appeared to me very remarkable, was, that Bonaparte, notwithstanding his incontestable superiority, studied to depreciate the reputations of his military commanders, and to throw on their shoulders faults which he had committed himself. It is notorious, that complaints and remonstrances, as energetic as they were well founded, were frequently addressed to General Bonaparte, on the subject of his unjust and partial bulletins; which often attributed the success of a day to some one who had very little to do with it, and made no mention of the officer who actually had the command. The complaints made by the officers and soldiers stationed in Damietta, compelled General Lanusse, the commander, to remonstrate against the alteration of a bulletin, by which an engagement with a body of Arabs was represented as an insignificant affair, and the loss trifling; though the general had stated the action to be one of importance, and the loss considerable. The misstatement, in consequence of his spirited and energetic remonstrances, was corrected.

Bonaparte took Malta, as is well known, in forty-eight hours. The empire of the Mediterranean, secured to the English by the battle of Aboukir, and their numerous cruising vessels, gave them the means of starving the garrison, and of thus forcing General Vaubois, the commandant of Malta, who was cut off from all communication with France, to capitulate. Accordingly, on the 4th of September, 1800, he yielded up the Gibraltar of the Mediterranean, after a noble defence of two years. These facts require to be stated, in order the better to understand what follows.

On the 22nd February, 1802, a person of the name of Doublet, who was the commissary of the French government at Malta, when we possessed that island, called upon me at the Tuileries. He complained bitterly, that the letter which he had written from Malta to the first consul, on the 2nd Ventose, year VIII* [9 February 1800] had been altered in the *Moniteur*. 'I congratulated him,' said M. Doublet, 'on the 18th Brumaire, and informed him of the state of Malta, which was very alarming. Quite the contrary was printed in the *Moniteur*, and that is what I complain of. It placed me in a very disagreeable situation at Malta, where I was accused of having concealed the real situation of the island, in which I was discharging a public function, that gave weight to my words.' I observed to him, that as I was not editor of the

*The calendar of the French Republic.

Moniteur, it was of no use to apply to me; but I told him to give me a copy of the letter, and I would mention the subject to the first consul,* and communicate the answer to him. Doublet searched his pocket for the letter, but could not find it. He said he would send a copy, and begged me to discover how the error originated. On the same day he sent me the copy of the letter, in which, after congratulating Bonaparte on his return, the following passage occurs: 'Hasten to save Malta with men and provisions: no time is to be lost.' For this passage these words were substituted in the *Moniteur*: 'His name inspires the brave defenders of Malta with fresh courage; we have men and provisions.'

Ignorant of the motives of so strange a perversion, I showed this letter to the first consul. He shrugged his shoulders, and said, laughing, 'Take no notice of him: he is a fool; give yourself no further trouble about it.'

It was clear to me that there was nothing more to be done. It was, however, in despite of me that M. Doublet was played this ill turn. I represented to the first consul the inconveniences which M. Doublet might experience from this affair. But I very rarely saw letters or reports published as they were received. I can easily understand how particular motives might be alleged in order to justify such falsifications; for when the path of candour and good faith is departed from, any pretext is put forward to excuse bad conduct. What sort of history would he write, who should consult only the pages of the *Moniteur*?

•

Puffing

WILLIAM HAZLITT

A lady was complaining to a friend of mine of the credulity of people in attending to quack advertisements, and wondering

*Bonaparte.

who could be taken in by them – 'for that she had never bought but one half-guinea bottle of Dr —'s Elixir of Life, and it had done her no sort of good'! This anecdote seemed to explain pretty well what made it worth the doctor's while to advertise his wares in every newspaper in the kingdom. He would no doubt be satisfied if every delicate, sceptical invalid, in his majesty's dominions, gave his Elixir one trial, merely to show the absurdity of the thing. We affect to laugh at the folly of those who put faith in nostrums, but are willing to see ourselves whether there is any truth in them.

There is a strong tendency in the human mind to flatter itself with secret hopes, with some lucky reservation in our own favour, though reason may point out the grossness of the trick in general; and, besides, there is a wonderful power in words, formed into regular propositions, and printed in capital letters, to draw the assent after them, till we have proof of their fallacy. The ignorant and idle believe what they read, as Scotch philosophers demonstrate the existence of their senses. The ocular proof is all that is wanting in either case. As hypocrisy is said to be the highest compliment to virtue, the art of lying is the strongest acknowledgement of the force of truth. We can hardly believe a thing to be a lie, though we know it to be so. The 'puff direct', even as it stands in the columns of *The Times* newspaper, branded with the title of Advertisement before it, claims some sort of attention and respect for the merits that it discloses, though we think the candidate for public favour and support has hit upon (perhaps) an injudicious way of laying them before the world. Still there may be something in them; and even the outrageous improbability and extravagance of the statement on the very face of it, stagger us, leave a hankering to inquire farther into it, because we think the advertiser would hardly have the impudence to hazard such barefaced absurdities without some foundation. Such is the strength of the association between words and things in the mind – so much oftener must our credulity have been justified by the event than imposed upon. If every second story we heard was an invention, we should lose our mechanical disposition to trust to the meaning of sounds, just as when we have met a number of counterfeit pieces of coin, we suspect good ones; but our implicit assent to what we hear is a proof how much more sincerity and good faith there is in the sum of our dealings with one another, than artifice and imposture.

•

Judicial fictions

JEREMY BENTHAM

Jeremy Bentham (1748–1832) was a jurist and legal theorist – a practical if eccentric reformer who based his jurisprudence on a utilitarian model. Here he deals with the corrupt mendacity that was the legal fiction.

Uttered by men at large, wilful falsehood is termed wilful falsehood: uttered by a judge as such, it is termed fiction: understand *judicial fiction*.

Poetical fiction is one thing: judicial fiction, another. Poetical fiction has for its purpose delectation: producing, in an appropriate shape, pleasure: the purpose here a good one, or no other is so. To a bad purpose it is indeed capable of being applied, as discourse in every shape is. But in its general nature, when given for what it is, it is innoxious, and in proportion to the pleasure it affords, beneficent: no deception does it produce, or aim at producing. So much for poetical fiction, now for judicial.

In every instance, it had and has for its purpose, pillage: object, the gaining power; means, deception. It is a portion of wilful falsehood, uttered by a judge, for the purpose of producing deception; and, by that deception, acquiescence or exercise given by him to power not belonging to him by law.

If, by a lie, be understood a wilful falsehood, uttered for an evil purpose, to what species of discourse could it be applied with more indisputable propriety, than to the discourse of a judge, uttered for an evil purpose?

How much to be regretted, that for the designation of the sweet and innocent on the one hand, the caustic and poisonous on the other, the same appellation should be continually in use; it is as if the two substances, sugar and arsenic, were neither of them known by any other name than *sugar*! But the abuse made of this recommendatory word is itself a *device*: an introductory one, stuck upon the principal one.

So much for the delusion; now for the criminality.

Obtaining money by false pretences is a crime: a crime which, except where licensed by public functionaries, or uttered by them, to and for the benefit of one another, is punished with infamous punishment. Power, in so far as obtained by fiction, is power obtained by some false pretence: and what judicial fiction, that was ever uttered, was uttered for any other purpose? What judicial fiction, by which its purpose has been answered, has failed of being productive of this effect?

If obtaining money by false pretences is an immoral practice, can obtaining power by false pretences be anything less so? If silver and gold are to be had the one for the other, so can power and money; if then either has value, has not the other likewise?

If obtaining, or endeavouring to obtain money by false pretences is an act presenting a well-grounded demand for legal punishment, so in its origin, at any rate, was not the act of obtaining, or endeavouring to obtain, by those same means, power? power, whether in its own shape, or in this, or that other shape?

As to the period – the time at which this device had its commencement in practice can scarcely have been so early as the original period so often mentioned: lies are the instruments rather of weakness, than of strength; they who had all power in their hands, had little need of lies for the obtaining of it.

On every occasion, on which any one of these lies was for the first time uttered and applied to use, persons of two or three distinguishable classes may be seen, to whom, in different shapes, wrong was thus done: the functionary or functionaries, whose power was, by and in proportion to the power thus gained, invaded and diminished: and the people at large, in so far as they became sufferers by the use made of it: which is what, in almost every instance, upon examination, they would be seen to be.

In the present instance, functionaries, or say authorities, of two classes are discernible. The authority, from which the power was thus filched, was either that of the sovereign, their common superordinate – or the co-ordinate authority, viz. that of some judge or judges, co-ordinate with that of the stealers. In a certain way, by the deception thus put upon him, the sovereign was a party wronged, in so far as power was taken away from any judge to whom it had by him been given. But this was a wrong little if at all felt: the only wrong felt certainly and in any considerable degree, was that done to another judge or set of judges.

Say *stealing*, or what is equivalent, as being shorter than to say obtaining under false pretences. In each instance, if deception, and by means of it power-stealing, was not the object of the lie, object it had none; it was an effect without a cause.

By a man in a high situation, a lie told for the purpose of getting what he had already, or could get without difficulty without a lie – such conduct is not in human nature.

As to sufferings, nominal only, as above observed, were they on the part of the supreme and omnipotent functionary; here, supposing them real, no sooner had they been felt, than they would have been made to cease, and no memorial of them would have reached us.

Not so in the case of learned brethren: stealing power from them, was stealing fees. Accordingly, when, towards the close of the seventeenth century, a theft in this shape had been committed, war broke out in Westminster-hall, and fictions, money-snatching lies, were the weapons. But of this under the head of *Jurisdiction-splitting*.

There, all the while on his throne sat the king: that king, Charles II. But, to a Charles II, not to speak of a king in the abstract, war between judge and judge for fees, was war between dog and dog for a bone.

Now come the real sufferers – the people. Subjection to arbitrary power is an evil, or nothing is; an evil, and that an all-comprehensive one.

Now, every power thus acquired is in its essence arbitrary; for, if to the purpose of obtaining anything valuable – call it money, call it power – allowance is given to a man, on any occasion, at pleasure, to come out with a lie; which done, the power becomes his, what is it he cannot do? For where is the occasion on which a lie cannot be told? And, in particular, on the whole expanse of the field of law, no limits being assigned, where is the lie which, if, in his conception, any purpose of his, whatever it be, will be answered by it, may not be told?

Accordingly, wilful falsehoods, more palpably repugnant to truth, were never uttered, than may, by all who choose to see it, be seen to have been uttered, and for the purpose of obtaining power, by English judges.

Take, for example, the common recovery fiction; a tissue of lies, such, that to convey to a non-lawyer any comprehensive conception of it, would require an indefinite multitude of pages, after the reading of which it would be conceived confusedly or not at all. But what belongs to the present purpose will be as intelligible as it is undeniable.

Descriptions of persons stolen from, three: 1. Children, in whose favour a mass of property had been intended to be made secure against alienation; eventual subject-matter of this property, no less than the soil of all England: 2. Landowners, by whom, by payment of the fees exacted from them, was purchased by the judges of the court in question – the Common Pleas – that power of alienation which they ought to have gratis, or not at all: 3. Professional men – conveyancers (the whole fraternity of them) – despoiled in this way of a share of such their business, by the intrusion of these judges.

Now for the falsehood – the artful and shameless predatory falsehood – by which all these exploits were performed.

Officiating at all times in the court in which these judges were sitting, was a functionary, styled *the crier of the court*; his function, calling individuals, in proportion as their attendance was required, into the presence of the judges. Sole source and means of his subsistence, fees; in magnitude, the aggregate of them correspondent to the nature of his function. Behold now the fiction. A quantity of parchment having been soiled by a compound of absurdities and falsehoods, prepared for the purpose, and fees in proportion received for the same, a decision was by these same judges pronounced, declaring the restriction taken off, and the proprietors so far free to alienate: to the parties respectively despoiled, a pretended equivalent being given, of which presently. Persons whom it was wanted for – (not to speak of persons not yet in *esse*, and in whose instance accordingly disappointment might be prevented from taking place) young persons in existence in indefinite multitudes, from whom, on the several occasions in question, their property, though as yet in expectancy, was thus taken – taken by these same judges, whose duty it was to secure it to them. Now for the equivalent. To all persons thus circumstanced, it was thought meet to administer satisfaction: it was by a speech to the following effect, that the healing balm was applied: – 'Children, we take your estate from you, but for the loss of it you will not be worse. Here is Mr *Moreland*,' (that was always the gentleman's name:) 'he happens to have an estate of exactly the same value: this we will take from him, and it shall be yours.'

Exactly in this way, on one and the same day, were estates in any number disposed of at the appointed price by these supposed, and by suitors intitled, ministers of justice. Such was the proceeding then: and such it continues to this day.

•

Calumny, and how to avoid it

SAMUEL JOHNSON

The following extract is taken from a sermon attributed to Dr Johnson, and left for posthumous publication by Dr John Taylor. Johnson takes as his text the ninth commandment, 'Thou shalt not bear false witness against thy neighbour', and preaches on the different senses in which a man may be said to bear false witness, the enormity of the sin, and lastly – with which we are here concerned – how best to avoid it.

Calumny differs from most other injuries in this dreadful respect. He who commits it, never can repair it. A false report may spread where a recantation never reaches; and an accusation must certainly fly faster than a defence, while the greater part of mankind are base and wicked. The effects of a false report cannot be determined, or circumscribed. It may check a hero in his attempts for the promotion of the happiness of his country, or a saint in his endeavours for the propagation of truth.

Since therefore this sin is so destructive to mankind, and, by consequence, so detestable in the sight of God, it is necessary that we inquire . . . what reflections may best enable us to avoid it.

The way to avoid effects is to avoid the causes. Whoever therefore would not be tempted *to bear false witness*, must endeavour to suppress those passions which may incite him to it. Let the envious man consider, that by detracting from the character of others, he in reality adds nothing to his own; and the malicious man, that nothing is more inconsistent with every law of God, and institution of men, than implacability and revenge.

If men would spend more time in examining their own lives,

and inspecting their own characters, they would have less leisure, and less inclination, to remark with severity upon others. They would easily discover, that it will not be for their advantage to exasperate their neighbour, and that a scandalous falsehood may be easily revenged by a reproachful truth.

It was determined by our blessed Saviour, in a case of open and uncontested guilt, that *he who was without fault* should *cast the first stone*. This seems intended to teach us compassion even to the failings of bad men; and certainly that religion which extends so much indulgence to the bad, as to restrain us from the utmost rigour of punishment, cannot be doubted to require that the good should be excepted from calumny and reproach.

Let it be always remembered, that charity is the height of religious excellence; and that it is one of the chief characteristics of this virtue, that *it thinketh no ill of others*!

•

Fire in stubble

SAMUEL TAYLOR COLERIDGE

The pre-eminence of truth over falsehood, even when occasioned by that truth, is as a gentle fountain breathing from forth its air – let into the snow piled over and around it, which it turns into its own substance, and flows with greater murmur; and though it be again arrested, still it is but for a time; – it awaits only the change of the wind, to awake and roll onwards its ever increasing stream . . .

. . . But falsehood is fire in stubble; – it likewise turns all the light stuff around it into its own substance for a moment, one crackling blazing moment, – and then dies; and all its converts are scattered in the wind, without place or evidence of their existence, as viewless as the wind which scatters them.

•

The great romancer

E. J. TRELAWNY

Edward John Trelawny (1792–1881), adventurer, pirate, friend of Shelley and Byron, was also an inveterate romancer, which is another way of saying he was a confounded liar. Byron said of him: 'Trelawny could not tell the truth to save his life.' Nevertheless English society thought him a very entertaining fellow. His autobiography, *Adventures of a Younger Son* (1831), is an eloquent and improbable demonstration of Trelawny's obsessive self-aggrandisement. We find the Great Romancer as a young man, recently entered into the Royal Navy.

Before this, I had gained respect in the ship by a reckless daring. My indifference and neglect of all the ordinary duties were in some degree tolerated, owing to my unwearied diligence and anxiety in every case of difficulty, danger, or sudden squalls. In the Indian seas a squall is not to be trifled with; when the masts are being like fishing-rods, the light sails fluttering in ribands, the sailors swinging to and fro on the bow, bent yards, the ship thrown on her beam ends, the wild roar of the sea and wind, and no other light than the red and rapid lightning. Then I used to rouse myself from dozing on the carronade-slide, springing aloft ere my eyes were half open, when the only reply to Aston's trumpet was my voice. I felt at home amidst the conflict of the elements. It was a kind of war; and harmonized with my feelings. The more furious the storm, the greater my delight. My contempt of the danger insured my safety; while the solemn and methodical disciplinarians, who prided themselves on the exact performance of their separate duties at their respective stations, beheld with astonishment the youngster, whom they were always abusing for neglect of duty, voluntarily thrusting himself into every arduous and perilous undertaking, ere they could decide on the possibility or prudence of its being attempted. The sailors liked me for this, and prognosticated I should yet turn out a thorough sailor. Even the officers, who had hitherto looked on me as a useless idler, viewed my conduct with gaping wonder, and entertained better hopes of me.

But these hopes died away with the bustling scenes in which they were begotten; and, during the fine and calm weather, I lost the reputation I had acquired in storms and battles. Among my messmates I was decidedly a favourite. What I principally prided myself in was protecting the weak from the strong; and was of so unyielding a disposition, that in my struggles with those, who were not much more than my equals in strength, though above me in years, I wore them out with pertinacity. My rashness and impetuosity bore down all before them. None liked to contend with me; for I never acknowledged when I was beaten, but renewed the quarrel, without respect to time or place. Yet what my messmates chiefly lauded and respected, was the fearless independence with which I treated those above me.

The utmost of their power had been wreaked against me; yet, had the rack been added, they could not have intimidated me. Indeed, from very wantonness, I went beyond their inflictions. For instance, the common punishment was sending us to the mast-head for four or five hours. Immediately I was ordered thither, I used to lie along the cross-trees, as if perfectly at my ease, and either feign to sleep, or, if it was hot, really go to sleep. They were alarmed at the chance of my falling from so hazardous a perch; and to prevent, as it was thought, the possibility of my sleeping, the Scotchman one day during a heavy sea with little wind, ordered me, in his anger, to go to the extreme end of the top-sail yard-arm, and remain there for four hours. I murmured, but, obliged to comply, up I went; and walking along the yard on the dizzy height, got hold of the top-sail lift, laid myself down between the yard and the studding-sail-boom, and pretended to sleep as usual. The lieutenant frequently hailed me, bidding me to keep awake, or I should fall overboard. This repeated caution suggested to me the means of putting an end to this sort of annoyance, by antedating his fears, and falling overboard; – not, however, with the idea of drowning, as few in the ship could swim so well as myself. I had seen a man jump from the lower yard in sport, and had determined to try the experiment. Besides, the roll of the ship was in my favour; so, watching my opportunity, when the officers and crew were at their quarters at sunset, I took advantage of a heavy roll of the ship, and dropped on the crest of a monstrous wave. I sunk deep into its bosom, and the agony of suppressed respiration, after the fall, was horrible. Had I not taken the precaution of keeping my poise, by keeping my hands over my head, preserving an erect posture in my descent, and moving my limbs in the air, I should inevitably have lost my life. As it was, I was insensible to everything but a swelling sensation in my chest, to bursting; and the frightful conviction of going downwards with the rapidity of a thunderbolt, notwithstanding my convulsive struggles to rise, was torture such as it is vain to describe. A deathlike torpidness came over me; then I heard a din of voices, and a noise on the sea, and within it, like a hurricane; my head and breast seemed to be splitting. After which I thought I saw a confused crowd of faces bent over me; and I felt a loathsome sickness. A cold shivering shook my limbs, and I gnashed my teeth, imagining myself still struggling in the last efforts at escape from drowning. This impression must have continued for a long time. The first circumstance I can distinctly remember was Aston's voice saying 'How are you now?' I tried to speak, but in vain; my lips moved without a word. He told me, I was now safe on board. I looked round; but a sensation of water rushing in my mouth, ears, and nostrils, still made me think I was amidst the waves. For eight and forty hours I suffered in inexpressible pain; a thousand times greater in my restoration to life, than before I lost my recollection.

But what signifies what I endured? – I gained my point. The Scotch lieutenant was severely reprimanded for his unjustifiable conduct in sending me to so dangerous a place for punishment. The captain's heart was moved to order a fowl to be killed for soup; and he sent me a bottle of wine. I had the one grilled, and the other mulled, holding an antipathy to every thing insipid. I was never sent to the mast-head again; nor could anyone suspect even me of such a mad freak as to run a hazard of drowning, to rid myself of a trifling annoyance, which others bore unrepiningly.

•

The rolling spheres of falsehood

OLIVER WENDELL HOLMES

Oliver Wendell Holmes (1809–94) was Professor of Anatomy and Physiology at Harvard University. As well as writing several novels, he contributed a series of erudite and witty essays to the *Atlantic Monthly*. These take the form of discourses over the breakfast table in a Massachusetts boarding-house to the other guests, such as the schoolmistress who appears here.

When we are as yet small children, long before the time when those two grown ladies offer us the choice of Hercules, there comes up to us a youthful angel, holding in his right hand cubes like dice, and in his left spheres like marbles. The cubes are of stainless ivory, and on each is written in letters of gold – TRUTH. The spheres are veined and streaked and spotted beneath, with a dark crimson flush above, where the light falls on them, and in a certain aspect you can make out upon every one of them the three letters L, I, E. The child to whom they are offered very probably clutches at both. The spheres are the most convenient things in the world; they roll with the least possible impulse just where the child would have them. The cubes will not roll at all; they have a great talent for standing still, and always keep right side up. But very soon the young philosopher finds that things which roll so easily are very apt to roll into the wrong corner, and to get out of his way when he most wants them, while he always knows where to find the others, which stay where they are left. Thus he learns – thus we learn – to drop the streaked and speckled globes of falsehood and to hold fast the white angular blocks of truth. But then comes Timidity, and after her Good-nature, and last of all Polite-behavior, all insisting that truth must roll, or nobody can do anything with it; and so the first with her coarse rasp, the second with her broad file, and the third with her silken sleeve, do so round off and smooth and polish the snow-white cubes of truth, that, when they have got a little dingy by use, it becomes hard to tell them from the rolling spheres of falsehood.

The schoolmistress was polite enough to say that she was pleased with this, and that she would read it to her little flock the next day. But she should tell the children, she said, that there were better reasons for truth than could be found in mere experience of its convenience and the inconvenience of lying.

Yes, – I said, – but education always begins through the senses, and works up to the idea of absolute right and wrong. The first thing the child has to learn about this matter is, that lying is unprofitable, – afterwards that it is against the peace and dignity of the universe.

– Do I think that the particular form of lying often seen in newspapers, under the title, 'From our Foreign Correspondents', does any harm? – Why, no, – I don't know that it does. I suppose it doesn't really deceive people any more than the *Arabian Nights* or *Gulliver's Travels* do. Sometimes the writers compile too carelessly, though, and mix up facts out of geographies, and stories out of the penny papers, so as to mislead those who are desirous of information.

•

The king of liars

THOMAS CARLYLE

Cagliostro was a Sicilian magician who devoted himself to an Egyptian masonic sect, and became extremely rich and successful so doing. Following a scandal involving Marie Antoinette and a diamond necklace, Cagliostro was obliged to flee from France, where he had been living. He eventually reached Rome and was promptly arrested by the

Inquisition, in whose custody he finally died. During his life he was treated as a charlatan by many, and opinions varied as to his powers. But Carlyle had no doubt in assessing the worth of this forerunner of Rasputin. Nevertheless, in arriving at his view Carlyle relied on a biography of Cagliostro written by an Inquisition hireling, the accuracy of which, by Carlyle's own admission, must be judged to be suspect. Here is the introduction to the first of two essays he wrote about Cagliostro.

We are here about to give some critical account of what Herr Sauerteig would call a 'flesh and blood Poem of the purest Pasquil* sort'; in plain words, to examine the biography of the most perfect scoundrel that in these latter ages has marked the world's history. Pasquils too, says Sauerteig, 'are at times worth reading'. Or quitting that mystic dialect of his, may we not assert in our own way, that the history of an Original Man is always worth knowing? So magnificent a thing is Will incarnated in a creature of like fashion with ourselves, we run to witness all manifestations thereof: what man soever has marked out a peculiar path of life for himself let it lead this way or that way, and successfully travelled the same, of him we specially inquire, How he travelled; What befell him on his journey? Though the man were a knave of the first water, this hinders not the question, How he managed his knavery? Nay it rather encourages such a question; for nothing properly is wholly despicable, at once detestable and forgettable, but your half-knave, he who is neither true nor false; who never in his existence once spoke or did any true thing (for indeed his mind lives in twilight, with cat-vision, incapable of discerning truth); and yet had not the manfulness to speak or act any decided lie; but spent his whole life in plastering together the True and the False, and therefrom manufacturing the plausible. Such a one our Transcendentals have defined as a moral hybrid and chimera; therefore, under the moral point of view, as an Impossibility, and mere deceptive Nonentity, – put together for commercial purposes. Of which sort, nevertheless,

*A lampooning, satirical kind of verse.

how many millions, through all manner of gradations, from the wielder of a king's sceptre to the vendor of brimstone matches, at tea-tables, council-tables, behind shop-counters, in priests' pulpits, incessantly and everywhere, do now, in this world of ours, in this Isle of ours, offer themselves to view! From such, at least from this intolerable overproportion of such, might the merciful Heavens one day deliver us. Glorious, heroic, fruitful for his own Time, and for all Time and all Eternity, is the constant Speaker and Doer of Truth! If no such again, in the present generation, is to be vouchsafed us, let us have at least the melancholy pleasure of beholding a decided Liar. Wretched mortal, who with a single eye to be 'respectable' for ever sittest cobbling together two Inconsistencies, which stick not for an hour, but require ever new gluten and labour, – will it, by no length of experience, no bounty of Time or Chance, be revealed to thee that Truth is of Heaven, and Falsehood is of Hell; that if thou cast not from thee the one or the other, thy existence is wholly an Illusion and optical and tactual Phantasm; that properly thou existest not at all? Respectable! What, in the Devil's name, is the use of Respectability, with never so many gigs and silver spoons, if thou inwardly art the pitifullest of all men? I would thou wert either cold or hot.

One such desirable second-best, perhaps the chief of all such, we have found here in the Count Alessandro di Cagliostro, Pupil of the Sage Althotas, Foster-child of the Scherif of Mecca, probable Son of the last King of Trebisond; named also Acharat, and unfortunate child of Nature; by profession healer of diseases, abolisher of wrinkles, friend of the poor and impotent, grand-master of the Egyptian Mason-lodge of High Science, Spirit-summoner, Gold-cook, Grand Cophta, Prophet, Priest, and thaumaturgic moralist and swindler; really a Liar of the first magnitude, thoroughpaced in all provinces of lying, what one may call the King of Liars. Mendez Pinto, Baron Munchausen, and others, are celebrated in this art, and not without some colour of justice; yet must it in candour remain doubtful whether any of these comparatively were much more than liars from the teeth onwards:

a perfect character of the species in question, who lied not in word only, nor in act and word only, but continually, in thought, word and act; and, so to speak, lived wholly in an element of lying, and from birth to death did nothing but lie, – was still a desideratum. Of which desideratum Count Alessandro offers, we say, if not the fulfilment, perhaps as near an approach to it as the limited human faculties permit. Not in the modern ages, probably not in the ancient (though these had their Autoclytus, their Apollonius, and enough else), did any completer figure of this sort issue out of Chaos and Old Night: a sublime kind of figure, presenting himself with 'the air of calm strength', of sure perfection in his art; whom the heart opens itself to with wonder and a sort of welcome. 'The only vice, I know,' says one, 'is Inconsistency.' At lowest, answer we, he that does his work shall have his work judged of. Indeed, if Satan himself has in these days become a poetic hero, why should not Cagliostro, for some short hour, be a prose one? 'One first question,' says a great Philosopher, 'I ask of every man: Has he an aim, which with undivided soul he follows, and advances towards? Whether his aim is a right one or a wrong one, forms but my second question.' Here then is a small 'human Pasquil', not without poetic interest.

. . . But to proceed with business. The present inquirer, in obstinate investigation of a phenomenon so noteworthy, has searched through the whole not inconsiderable circle which his tether enables him to describe: and, sad to say, with the most imperfect results. He has read Books in various languages; feared not to soil his fingers, hunting through ancient dusty Magazines, to sicken his heart in any labyrinth of iniquity and imbecility; . . . Almost our sole even half half-genuine documents are a small barren Pamphlet, 'Cagliostro démasqué à Varsovie, en 1780'; and a small barren Volume purporting to be his Life, written at Rome, of which latter we have a French version, dated 1791. It is on this 'Vie de Joseph Balsamo, connu sous le Nom de Comte Cagliostro', that our main dependence must be placed; of which Work, meanwhile, whether it is wholly or only half-genuine, the reader may judge by one fact: that it comes to us through the medium of the Roman Inquisition, and the proofs to substantiate it lie in the Holy Office there. Alas, this reporting Familiar of the Inquisition was too probably something of a Liar; and he reports lying Confessions of one who was not so much a Liar as a Lie! In such enigmatic duskiness, and thrice-folded involution, after all inquiries, does the matter yet hang.

•

Disraeli

DANIEL O'CONNELL

During the course of the election of 1835, Disraeli was wrongly reported as having described Daniel O'Connell, the Irish MP, as a traitor. A few days later, in a speech in Dublin, O'Connell made known his opinion of the candidate for Taunton.

I must confess that some of the attacks made on me, particularly one by a Mr Disraeli at Taunton, surprised me. Anything so richly deserving the appellation of superlative blackguardism, or at all equal to that in impudence and assurance, I never before met with. The annals of ruffianism do not furnish anything like it. He is an author, I believe, of a couple of novels, and that was all I knew about him until 1831 or 1832, when he wrote to me, being about to stand for High Wycombe, requesting a letter of recommendation from me to the electors. He took the letter with him to the place, got it printed and placarded all over the place. The next I heard of him was his being a candidate for Marylebone; in this he was also unsuccessful. He got tired of being a Radical any longer after these two defeats, and was determined to try his chance as a Tory. He stands the other day at Taunton, and by way of recommending himself to the electors he calls me an incendiary and a traitor. Now my answer to this piece of gratuitous impertinence is, that he is an egregious liar. He is a liar both in action and words. What! Shall such a vile creature be tolerated in England? Shall the man be received by any constituency who after coming forward on two separate occasions as the advocate of certain opinions, now boldly and unblushingly recants those principles by which his political life had been apparently regulated? He is a living lie; and the British Empire is degraded by tolerating a miscreant of his abominable description. The language is harsh, I must confess; but it is no more than deserved, and if I should apologize for using it, it is because I can find no harsher epithets in the English language by which to convey the utter abhorrence I entertain for such a reptile. He is just fit now, after being twice discarded by the people, to become a Conservative.

•

Malingering, or shamming Abram

ANON.

A very serious evil has existed in the army, resulting from a very general practice of idle and dissolute soldiers in barracks, and even in more active service, feigning diseases and disabilities; for the purpose of either escaping duty, or in the hopes of being altogether discharged from the service, and procuring a pension. This imposture has been termed Malingering, or the simulation of diseases, and the unsuccessful or suspected impostors have been usually called Malingerers. In vulgar English, the trick is called Shamming Abram.

Remarkable ingenuity, and a very considerable knowledge of the powers and effects of medicinal agents, have been shown by those who, *a priori*, would not be suspected of such information: and the pertinacity shown by the impostors, when the object was to procure their discharge, has been often wonderful.

The reasons which call for, or privilege a soldier to expect, his discharge, are chronic and incurable rather than acute diseases. It is natural, therefore, to find the malingerers most expert in simulating the former, though, at the same time, the more acute diseases have not been less faithfully represented, when the object in view was only a temporary evasion of duty.

This practice has prevailed to a greater or less extent at different periods of our medical military history; and it is gratifying to learn, from authentic sources, that in the present period of highly improved discipline in the British army, there are not probably two malingerers for ten who were found in the military hospitals thirty or forty years since. It also occurs more or less according to the manner of forming a regiment. In some of the cavalry regiments, and some of the Highland and other distinguished infantry battalions, in which, along with a mild but exact discipline, there is a strong attachment to the service, and remarkable *esprit de corps*, there is scarcely an instance of any of these disgraceful attempts to deceive the surgeon; while in regiments which have been hastily recruited, and under circumstances unfavourable to progressive and complete discipline, the system of imposition is perfectly understood. Among those who counterfeit diseases, it has been observed that the Irish are the most numerous, the Scotsmen less so, but malingering seems least of all the vice of English soldiers.

There appears to be a species of free-masonry among soldiers, and thus these methods of imposture have been systematized, and handed down for the common benefit. A case occurred of a man having a rupture, which on inspection was found to be artificially formed from some written directions, 'How to make a rupture', which were produced. The man was discharged by his commanding officer, but the discharge not being backed by the surgeon's recommendatory certificate, he lost his pension; the commanding officer after his return from Corunna met this man perfectly well, following the laborious occupation of a porter.

In the year 1804, the great increase of ophthalmia in the 50th regiment, and the reported detection of frauds in other regiments, led to a suspicion in the mind of the surgeon of that corps, and a consequent investigation, by which a regular correspondence was detected between the men under medical treatment and their parents or friends. Those suffering from ophthalmia, within the walls of the hospital, requested that those without would forward to them corrosive sublimate, lime, and blue stone; and by the application of these acrid substances to their eyes, they hoped to get them into such a state of disease, as would enable them to produce their discharge, with a pension. And they mentioned the names of men who had been successful by similar means. Proof of guilt having been established, the delinquents were tried by a court-martial, convicted, and punished.

It is hardly possible to believe, that men would endure not only the inconvenience of a severe ophthalmia, than which, perhaps, nothing is more painful, but would even risk the total loss of sight, for the uncertain prospect of a trifling pension, and with the conviction, that even if they gained it, they reduced themselves to a helpless dependence on others through life. But it is nevertheless certain that whole wards have been filled with soldiers labouring under this artificially excited disease; this inflammation of the eye having been produced, and maintained, by quicklime, strong infusions of tobacco, Spanish flies, nitrate of silver, and other metallic salts. The inflammation thus caused is most painful, yet it has been kept up under every privation which can make life miserable.

Wonderful indeed is the obstinacy some malingerers evince; night and day, they will remain, with the endurance of a fakir, in positions most irksome, for weeks and months; nay, many men for the same period have, with surprising resolution and recollection, sat and walked with their bodies bent double, without forgetting for one moment the character of their assumed infirmity.

These impostors are most easily discovered by a retaliating deception on the part of the surgeon; he should conceal his suspicions, and appear to give credit to all that is related to him of the history of the disease, and propose some sort of treatment accordingly.

The nervous disorders that are simulated are such as to require a constant and unceasing watchfulness, on the part of the impostor, lest he should betray himself.

Paralysis of one arm was feigned, with great perseverance and consistency, for months; the soldier pretending that he had fallen asleep in the open air, and awoke with his arm benumbed and powerless. This farce he kept up with such boldness, that, being suspected, a court-martial was held on him, and he was even tied up to the halberts to be punished; but the commanding officer thought the evidence not sufficiently convincing. Having, however, subsequently undergone very severe treatment, and there being no prospect of a pension, he at last gave in.

. . . The acute diseases have many symptoms which are easily simulated, but as easily detected. The appearance of the white tongue is created by rubbing it with chalk, or whitening from the wall; but washing the mouth with water at once proves the deceit. Dr Hennen, in his Military Surgery, says, 'Profligates have, to my knowledge, boasted that they have often received indulgences from the medical officers in consequence of a febrile attack, by presenting themselves after a night's debauch, which they had purposely protracted, to aid the deception. Febrile symptoms are also produced by swallowing tobacco-juice. One man, if unwilling to be cured *secundum artem*, was at least anxious to enumerate his symptoms in an orthodox manner, for he had purloined some pages from Zimmerman's *Treatise on Dysentery*, (the disease he had thought proper to simulate), from one of the medical officers; and from which he was daily in the habit of recounting a change of symptoms. Stoical indifference to their frequently painful imposture and hardihood in maintaining its character, are the necessary qualifications of malingerers, who have frequently evinced a constancy and fortitude under severe pain and privations, worthy of a better cause.'

. . . Even death itself has been simulated. When some officers, in India, were breakfasting in the commander's tent, the body of a native, said to have been murdered by the sepoys, was brought in and laid down. The crime could not be brought home to any one of them, yet there was the body. A suspicion, however, crossed the adjutant's mind, and, having the kettle in his hand, a thought struck him that he would pour a little boiling water on the body; he did so; upon which the murdered remains started up, and scampered off.

•

On being libelled

THOMAS DE QUINCEY

An advertisement having alerted him to the publication of a new satiric journal libelling him, Thomas De Quincey visited a bookseller in Smithfield Market, where he purchased and read the offending article. Here he recollects his reaction.

Suffice it here to say, that, calm as I am now, and careless on recalling the remembrance of this brutal libel, at that time I was convulsed with wrath. As respected myself, there was a depth of malignity in the article which struck me as perfectly mysterious. How could any man have made an enemy so profound, and not even have suspected it? *That* puzzled me. For, with respect to the other subjects of attack, such as Sir Humphrey Davy, &c., it was clear that the malice was assumed; that, at most, it was the gay impertinence of some man about town, armed with triple Irish brass from original defect of feeling, and willing to raise an income by running amuck at any person just then occupying enough of public interest to make the abuse saleable. But, in my case, the man flew like a bull-dog at the throat, with a pertinacy and *acharnement* of malice that would have caused me to laugh immoderately, had it not been for one intolerable wound to my feelings. These mercenary libellers, whose stiletto is in the market, and at any man's service for a fixed price, callous and insensible as they are, yet retain enough of the principles common to human nature, under every modification, to know where to plant their wounds. Like savage hackney coachmen, they know where there is a *raw*. And the instincts of human nature teach them that every man is vulnerable through his female connexions. There lies his honour; there his strength; there his weakness. In their keeping is the heaven of his happiness; in them and through them the earth of its fragility. Many there are who do not feel the *maternal* relation to be one in which any excessive freight of honour or sensibility is embarked. Neither is the name of *sister*, though tender in early years, and impressive to the fireside sensibilities, universally and through life the same magical sound. A sister is a creature whose very property and tendency (*qua* sister) is to alienate herself, not gather round your centre. But the names of *wife* and *daughter*, these are the supreme and starry charities of life: and he who, under a mask, fighting in darkness, attacks you there, that coward has you at disadvantage. I stood in those hideous shambles of Smithfield: upwards I looked to the clouds, downwards to the earth, for vengeance. I trembled with excessive wrath – such was my infirmity of feeling at that time, and in that condition of health; and had I possessed forty thousand lives, all, and every one individually, I would have sacrificed in vindication of her that was thus cruelly libelled. Shall I give currency to his malice, shall I aid and promote it by repeating it? No. And yet why not? Why should I scruple, as if afraid to challenge his falsehoods? – why should I scruple to cite them? He, this libeller, asserted – But faugh!

This slander seemed to have been built upon some special knowledge of me; for I had often spoken with horror of those who could marry persons in a condition which obliged them to obedience – a case which had happened repeatedly within my own knowledge; and I had spoken on this ground, that the authority of a master might be *supposed* to have been interposed, whether it really were so or not, in favour of his designs; and thus a presumption, however false it might be, always remained that his wooing had been, perhaps, not the wooing of perfect freedom, so essential to the dignity of woman, and, therefore, essential to his own dignity; but that perhaps, it had been favoured by circumstances, and by opportunities created, if it had not even been favoured, by express exertions of authority. The libeller, therefore, *did* seem to have some knowledge of my peculiar opinions: yet, in other points, either from sincere ignorance or from affectation, and by way of turning aside suspicion, he certainly manifested a non-acquaintance with facts relating to me that must have been familiar enough to all within my circle.

Let me pursue the case to its last stage. The reader will say, perhaps, why complain of a paltry journal that assuredly never made any noise; for I, the reader, never heard of it till now. No, that is very possible; for the truth is, and odd enough it seems, this malicious journal prospered so little, that, positively, at the seventh number it stopped. Laugh I did, and laugh I could not help but do, at this picture of baffled malice: writers willing and ready to fire with poisoned bullets, and yet perfectly unable to get an effective aim, from sheer want of co-operation on the part of the public.

. . . but the nature of a printed libel is, continually to renew itself as an insult. The subject of it reads this libel, perhaps in solitude; and, by a great exertion of self-command, resolves to bear it with fortitude and in silence. Some days after, in a public room, he sees strangers reading it also: he hears them scoffing and laughing loudly: in the midst of all this, he sees himself pointed out to their notice by some one of the party who happens to be acquainted with his person; and, possibly, if the libel take that particular shape which excessive malice is most likely to select, he will hear the name of some relative, dearer, it may be, to him, and more sacred in his ears, than all this world beside, bandied about with scorn and mockery by those who have not the poor excuse of the original libellers, but are, in fact, adopting the second-hand malignity of others. Such cases, with respect to libels that are quickened into popularity by interesting circumstances, or by a personal interest attached to any of the parties, or by wit, or by extraordinary malice, or by scenical circumstances, or by circumstances unusually ludicrous, are but too likely to occur; and, with every fresh repetition, the keenness of the original provocation is renewed, and in an accelerated ratio. Again, with reference to my own case, or to any case resembling that, let it be granted that I was immoderately and unreasonably transported by anger at the moment; – I thought so myself, after a time, when the journal which published the libel sank under the public neglect; but this was an after consideration; and, at the moment, how heavy an aggravation was given to the strings of malice, by the deep dejection . . . which then possessed me.

•

Disraeli's hypocrisy

ROBERT BLAKE

Sir Robert Peel's repeal of the Corn Laws in 1846 occasioned on of the most bitter political disputes in parliamentary history. Peel had not always been opposed to the Corn Laws, and Disraeli took the opportunity to embarrass Peel with this reminder, accusing him of intellectual dishonesty. What was not publicly known was that upon Peel's becoming Prime Minister in 1841, Disraeli had written to him, asking for a Cabinet appointment. And not just Disraeli, but his wife too. Peel asked Disraeli why, if he had such a low opinion of him, he should have been so ready to seek office under him. Disraeli lied to the House: 'I can assure the House nothing of the kind ever occurred. I never shall – it is totally foreign to my nature – make any application for any place . . . I never ask a favour of the government, not even one of those mechanical things which persons are obliged to ask . . . and as regards myself I never directly or indirectly solicited office . . . it is entirely unfounded.' One of Disraeli's most recent biographers examines the story.

It is inconceivable that Disraeli had forgotten what he had written to Peel. Nor is it plausible to suggest, as Miss Ramsay does in her life of Peel, that he knew his man and reckoned on Peel being too gentlemanly to produce the letter. It is true that

Disraeli knew of Peel's refusal to read out a damaging letter from Joseph Hume in 1830 in somewhat similar circumstances, but no one would have dared, in the light of cool reason, to gamble upon a repetition; even though, as events turned out, the gamble would have come off. Disraeli had indeed denied asking for office once before – to his constituents at Shrewsbury in 1844. He had not been contradicted then, but that was a different matter from confronting in person the very minister to whom he had written an almost abject letter of solicitation. The most likely explanation is panic, rare though such lapses were in Disraeli's life. He possibly knew that in some circles his reputation was none too good. He may well have been flustered, and he probably blurted out his unconvincing denial without fully considering the risk. He certainly asked for trouble by not only denying that he ever solicited office, but also, and equally untruthfully, that he had ever asked for a favour. Had he forgotten the applications that he had made to Graham and Stanley for his brother? It is unlikely that they had.

Peel did not read out Disraeli's letter, but there is no truth in the story apparently believed by Bukle [Disraeli's official biographer] that he was unable to find it. Goldwin Smith in his reminiscences declares that he had first-hand information on this point from Lord Lincoln, who had walked with Peel to the House in the morning and actually saw the letter in Peel's dispatch-case. Why, then, did he miss such a splendid opportunity? We shall never know for certain. Perhaps Peel, who had the hypersensitivity on points of honour of a man only half belonging to the patrician world, refrained because it would be unfair to read out a personal communication. If so that is to his credit . . . Disraeli was lucky, but the general impression of his conduct seems to have been adverse. No doubt much was said in the Lobbies and the Carlton that has not survived to posterity, and people drew their own conclusions. It is not an episode on which his admirers may care to dwell.

•

The incontinent of tongue

THOMAS CARLYLE

'Be not a Public Orator, thou brave young British man, thou who art now growing to be something,' writes Thomas Carlyle in his pamphlet against stump orators. 'Appeal not to the vulgar, with its long ears and its seats in the Cabinet; not by spoken words to the vulgar; *hate* the profane vulgar, and bid it begone. Appeal by silent work, by silent suffering if there be no work, to the gods, who have nobler than seats in the Cabinet for thee!' Public speaking, he says, is nothing more than incontinence of tongue; screeching and gibbering, words without wisdom, without veracity.

Nature admits no lie; most men profess to be aware of this, but few in any measure lay it to heart. Except in the departments of mere material manipulation, it seems to be taken practically as if this grand truth were merely a polite flourish of rhetoric. What is a lie? The question is worth asking, once and away, by the practical English mind.

A voluntary spoken divergence from the fact as it stands, as it has occurred and will proceed to develop itself: this clearly, if adopted by any man, will so far forth mislead him in all practical dealing with the fact; till he cast that statement out of him, and reject it as an unclean poisonous thing, he can have no success in dealing with the fact. If such spoken divergence from the truth be involuntary, we lament it as a misfortune; and are entitled, at least the speaker of it is, to lament it extremely as the most palpable of all misfortunes, as the indubitablest losing of his way, and turning aside from the goal instead of pressing towards it, in the race set before him. If the divergence is voluntary, – there superadds itself to our sorrow a just indignation: we call the voluntary spoken divergence a lie, and justly abhor it as the essence of human treason and baseness, the desertion of a man to the Enemy of men against himself and his brethren. A lost deserter; who has gone over to the Enemy, called Satan; and cannot *but* be lost in the adventure! Such is every liar with the tongue; and such in all nations is he, at all epochs, considered. Men pull his nose, and kick him out of doors; and by peremptory expressive methods signify that they can and will have no trade with him. Such is spoken divergence from the fact; so fares it with the practiser of that sad art.

But have we well considered a divergence *in thought* from what is the fact? Have we considered the man whose very thought is a lie to him and to us! He too is a frightful man; repeating about this Universe on every hand what is not, and driven to repeat it; the sure herald of ruin to all that follow him, that know with *his* knowledge! And would you learn how to get a mendacious thought, there is no surer recipe than carrying a loose tongue. The lying thought, you already either have it, or will soon get it by that method. He who lies with his very tongue, *he* clearly enough has long ceased to think truly in his mind. Does he, in any sense, 'think'? All his thoughts and imaginations, if they extend beyond mere beaverisms, astucities and sensualisms, are false, incomplete, perverse, untrue even to himself. He has become a false mirror of this Universe; not a small mirror only, but a crooked, bedimmed and utterly deranged one. But all loose tongues too are akin to lying ones; are insincere at the best, and go rattling with little meaning; the thought lying languid at a great distance behind them, if thought there be behind them at all. Gradually there will be none or little! How can the thought of such a man, what he calls thought, be other than false?

Alas, the palpable liar with his tongue does at least know that he is lying, and has or might have some faint vestige of remorse and chance of amendment; but the impalpable liar, whose tongue articulates mere accepted commonplaces, cants and babblement, which means only 'Admire me, call me an excellent stump orator!' – of him what hope is there? His thought, what thought he had, lies dormant, inspired only to invent vocables and plausibilities; while the tongue goes so glib, the thought is absent, gone a-woolgathering; getting itself drugged with the applausive 'Hear, hear!' – what will become of such a man? His idle thought has run all to seed, and grown false and the giver of falsities; the inner light of his mind is gone out; all his light is mere putridity and phosphorescence henceforth. Whosoever is in quest of ruin, let him with assurance follow that man; he or no one is on the right road to it.

Good Heavens, from the wisest Thought of a man to the actual truth of a Thing as it lies in Nature, there is, one would suppose, a sufficient interval! Consider it, – and what other intervals we introduce! The faithfullest, most glowing word of a man is but an imperfect image of the thought, such as it is, that dwells within him; his best word will never but with error convey his thought to other minds: and then between *his* poor thought and Nature's Fact, which is the Thought of the Eternal, there may be supposed to lie some discrepancies, some shortcomings! Speak your sincerest, think your wisest, there is still a great gulf between you and the fact. And now, do *not* speak your sincerest, and, what will inevitably follow out of that, do not think your wisest, but think only of your plausiblest, your showiest for parliamentary purposes, where will you land with that guidance? – I invite the British Parliament, and all the Parliamentary and other Electors of Great Britain, to reflect on this till they have well understood it; and then to ask, each of himself, What probably the horoscopes of the British Parliament, at this epoch of World-History may be?

•

A lying century

THOMAS CARLYLE

Thomas Carlyle devoted the latter part of his life to a history of Frederick the Great. One of Carlyle's problems as a historian, having chosen this subject, was that he had nothing but contempt for the history of the eighteenth century, as this passage from the early pages of the work reveals only too eloquently.

One of the grand difficulties in a History of Friedrich is, all along, this same, That he lived in a Century which has no History and can have little or none. A Century so opulent in accumulated falsities, – sad opulence descending on it by inheritance, always at compound interest, and always largely increased by fresh acquirement on such immensity of standing capital; opulent in that bad way as never Century before was! Which had no longer the consciousness of being false, so false had it grown; and was so steeped in falsity, and impregnated with it to the very bone, that – in fact the measure of the thing was full, and a French Revolution had to end it. To maintain much veracity in such an element, especially for a king, was no doubt doubly remarkable. But now, how extricate the man from his Century? How show the man, who is a Reality worthy of being seen, and yet keep his Century, as a Hypocrisy worthy of being hidden and forgotten, in the due abeyance?

To resuscitate the Eighteenth Century, or call into men's view, beyond what is necessary, the poor and sordid personages and transactions of an epoch so related to us, can be of no purpose of mine on this occasion. The Eighteenth Century, it is well known, does not figure to me as a lovely one; needing to be kept in mind, or spoken of unnecessarily. To me the Eighteenth Century has nothing grand in it, except that grand Universal Suicide, named French Revolution, by which it terminated its otherwise most worthless existence with at least one worthy act; – setting fire to its old home and self; and going up in flames and volcanic explosions, in a truly memorable and important manner. A very fit termination, as I thankfully feel, for such a Century. Century spendthrift, fraudulent-bankrupt; gone at length utterly insolvent, without real *money* of performance in its pocket, and the shops declining to take hypocrisies and speciosities any farther: – what could the poor Century do, but at length admit, 'Well, it is so. I am a swindler-century, and have long been;

having learned the trick of it from my father and grandfather; knowing hardly any trade but that in false bills, which I thought foolishly might last forever, and still bring at least beef and pudding to the favoured of mankind. And behold it ends; and I am a detected swindler, and have nothing even to eat. What remains but that I blow my brains out, and do at length one true action?' Which the poor Century did; many thanks to it, in the circumstances.

For there was need once more of a Divine Revelation to the torpid frivolous children of men, if they were not to sink altogether into the ape condition. And in that whirlwind of the Universe, – lights obliterated, and the torn wrecks of Earth and Hell hurled aloft into the Empyrean; black whirlwind, which made even apes serious, and drove most of them mad, – there was, to men, a voice audible; voice from the heart of things once more, as if to say: 'Lying is not permitted in this Universe. The wages of lying, you behold, are death. Lying means damnation in this Universe; and Beelzebub, never so elaborately decked in crowns and mitres, is *not* God!' This was a revelation truly to be named of the Eternal, in our poor Eighteenth Century; and has greatly altered the complexion of said Century to the Historian ever since.

•

True lies and false lies

JOHN RUSKIN

In his work *Modern Painters*, Ruskin (1819–1900) came to consider the relations of Art to God and Man: 'We have to inquire into the various Powers, Conditions, and Aims of mind involved in the conception or creation of pictures; in the choice of subject, and the mode and order of its history; – the choice of forms, and the modes of their arrangement.' Thus Ruskin comes to consider the nature of gentlemanliness. One of the gentleman's identifying characteristics, says Ruskin, is his desire of truthfulness.

The truthfulness which is opposed to cunning ought, perhaps, rather to be called the desire of truthfulness; it consists more in unwillingness to deceive than in not deceiving, – an unwillingness implying sympathy with and respect for the person deceived; and a fond observance of truth up to the possible point, as in a good soldier's mode of retaining his honour through a *ruse-de-guerre*. A cunning person seeks for opportunities to deceive; a gentleman shuns them. A cunning person triumphs in deceiving; a gentleman is humiliated by his success, or at least by so much of the success as is dependent merely on the falsehood, and not on his intellectual superiority.

The absolute disdain of all lying belongs rather to Christian chivalry than to mere high-breeding; as connected merely with this latter, and with general refinement and courage, the exact relations of truthfulness may be best studied in the well-trained Greek mind. The Greeks believed that mercy and truth were co-relative virtues – cruelty and falsehood, co-relative vices. But they did not call necessary severity, cruelty; nor necessary deception, falsehood. It was needful sometimes to slay men, and sometimes to deceive them. When this had to be done, it should be done well and thoroughly; so that to direct a spear well to its mark, or a lie well to its end, was equally the accomplishment of a perfect gentleman. Hence, in the pretty diamond-cut-diamond scene between Pallas and Ulysses, when she receives him on the coast of Ithaca, the goddess laughs delightedly at her hero's good lying, and gives him her hand upon it; – showing herself then in her woman's form, as just a little more than his match. 'Subtle would he be, and stealthy, who should go beyond thee in deceit, even were he a god, thou many-witted! What! here in thine own land, too, wilt thou not cease from cheating? Knowest thou not me, Pallas Athena, maid of Jove, who am with thee in all thy labours, and gave thee favour with the Phaeacians, and keep thee, and have come now to weave cunning with thee?' But how completely this kind of cunning was looked upon as part of a man's power, and not as a diminution of faithfulness, is perhaps best shown by the single line of praise in which the high qualities of his servant are summed up by Chremulus in the *Plutus* – 'Of all my house servants, I hold you to be the faithfullest, and the greatest cheat (or thief).'

Thus, the primal difference between honourable and base lying in the Greek mind lay in honourable purpose. A man who used his strength wantonly to hurt others was a monster; so, also, a man who used his cunning wantonly to hurt others. Strength and cunning were to be used only in self-defence, or to save the weak, and then were alike admirable. This was their first idea. Then the second, and perhaps the more essential, difference between noble and ignoble lying in the Greek mind, was that the honourable lie – or, if we may use the strange, yet just, expression, the true lie – knew and confessed itself for such – was ready to take full responsibility of what it did. As the sword answered for its blow, so the lie for its snare. But what the Greeks hated with all their heart was the false lie; – the lie that did not know itself, feared to confess itself, which slunk to its aim under a cloak of truth, and sought to do liars' work, and yet not take liars' pay, excusing itself to the conscience by quibble and quirk. Hence the great expression of Jesuit principle by Euripides, 'The tongue has sworn, but not the heart', was a subject of execration throughout Greece, and the satirists exhausted their arrows on it – no audience was ever tired of hearing 'that Euripidean thing' brought to shame.

And this is especially to be insisted on in the early education of young people. It should be pointed out to them with continual earnestness that the essence of lying is in deception, not in words: a lie may be told by silence, by equivocation, by the accent on a syllable, by a glance of the eye attaching a peculiar significance to a sentence; and all these kinds of lies are worse and baser by many degrees than a lie plainly worded; so that no form of blinded conscience is so far sunk as that which comforts itself for having deceived, because the deception was by gesture or silence, instead of utterance; and finally, according to Tennyson's deep and trenchant line, 'A lie which is half a truth is ever the worst of lies.'

•

The accursed lies of David Livingstone

OWEN CHADWICK

The publication of David Livingstone's *Missionary Travels in South Africa* caused a wave of passion for Africa in British churches, and led other missionaries and travellers to the region, expecting a primitive Utopia. But the reality was altogether different, as some found at great personal cost.

But the gravest conviction which Stewart formed – as Rowley before him – was the belief that Livingstone had been guilty, if not of deceit, at least of culpable exaggeration, in his descriptions of the country. Why had Rowley and Procter come out, expecting to find a regular communication with the coast by the *Pioneer* every three months? Why had the Bishop insisted, against so much good advice, in bringing his sister and allowing Mrs Burrup to join her husband? Why had the hard-headed Bishop of Cape Town become a party to the scheme, which Commander Wilson had thought so wild and premature, of planting an English and Christian village in the middle of Central Africa? What had precipitated these little groups of Englishmen into their present and apparently inextricable agony? Missionary endeavour was often enthusiastic, and enthusiasm is not always practical, is sometimes ready to suppose that the faith which moves mountains is a sufficient substitute for foresight and careful planning. It was not to be contested that the wave of altruistic passion for Africa which had swept the churches in Britain had contributed to the rashness of the ven- ture. But Rowley, and now Stewart, believed Livingstone was primarily responsible for the rashness. In his *Missionary Travels*, and his subsequent letters printed in England, he had drawn a Utopian picture – a little primitive paradise endowed with a natural harvest of wealth only waiting for the white man to garner; a land of smiling tribes and game, of corn and cotton, of health and rapid communication by noble rivers, a land of serenity and sanatoria, of natural orchards of orange and lemon trees. The mission had bought a second-hand cotton-gin because it expected to be self-supporting economically within three years: they had been told that they might live off their guns; they had been encouraged to think the land safe for ladies. Procter had supposed, from reading Livingstone's letters, that he was coming to 'a sort of African Arcadia'. Livingstone's far-flung eye had seen a vision – a vision which might yet be justified. But he failed to tell the world of the mountains and seas of toil which lay between his vision and its fulfilment.

Not that he had said anything which could be convicted of being misleading. Nor, as Kirk insisted to Stewart, was it fair to judge Livingstone's picture of Central Africa by the chaos of war and famine which was afflicting the region two or three years later than his descriptions of it. But, though he had not given any detail patently untrue, he failed to state the difficulties and perils which surrounded what he was describing; partly because his own character of heroic perseverance made him suppose that where he could go, everyone else – missionary, commercial traveller, cotton spinner, planter – could go likewise. 'Let me note,' wrote Stewart on 3 October, 1862, 'the fallacy in Livingstone's method. He meets a difficulty, overcomes it by an amount of perseverance and expenditure of strength and money which men will put forth once or twice but which it would be ruinous to carry out as a rule. And then he speaks of insurmountable difficulties being surmounted. They have been for a time, but they remain as before, obstructions to navigation or any other enterprise that may be attempted.' Wherever he went, Stewart measured areas of cotton-growing, diligently testing Livingstone's claim that he had opened the best cotton-field in the world, the counterpoise to American slavery. 'At present,' wrote Stewart, 'it would be as well to purpose some counterpoise to humbug.'

And so Stewart came to believe, like Rowley before him, that Livingstone could even be said to be 'in some respect responsible for the Bishop's death'. 'His accursed lies,' wrote Stewart after an evening's discussion, 'have caused much toil, trouble, anxiety, and loss of life, as well as money and reputation, and I have been led a dance over half the world to accomplish nothing.'

Following the death of a close friend, Stewart could no longer resist the temptation to look around for a scapegoat.

That bright, hot, and clear afternoon, he took his copy of Livingstone's *Missionary Travels in South Africa* and walked a little way down the bank. Then he threw the book with all his strength 'into the turbid, muddy, weed-covered Zambezi . . . The volume was fragrant with odours of and memories of the earnestness with which I studied the book in days gone by. How different it appeared now! It was nothing short of an eyesore, the very sight of its brown covers. I do not think it is as the Rev. R—M—* is said to have called it, "a pack of lies", but it would need a great many additions to make it the truth. Thus I disliked the book, and sent it to sink or swim into the vaunted Zambezi. So perish all that is false in myself and others.'

•

A capital lie

PAUL JOHNSON

The misuse of sources by Marx and Engels was demonstrated as early as the 1880s. This was not simply a matter of recklessness, says Paul Johnson, but amounted to something more systematic.

Marx cannot have been unaware of the weaknesses, indeed

*Robert Moffat.

dishonesties, of Engels's book since many of them were exposed in detail as early as 1848 by the German economist Bruno Hildebrand, in a publication with which Marx was familiar. Moreover Marx himself compounds Engels's misrepresentations knowingly by omitting to tell the reader of the enormous improvements brought about by enforcement of the Factory Acts and other remedial legislation since the book was published and which affected precisely the type of conditions he had highlighted. In any case, Marx brought to the use of primary and secondary written sources the same spirit of gross carelessness, tendentious distortion and downright dishonesty which marked Engels's work. Indeed they were often collaborators in deception, though Marx was the more audacious forger. In one particularly flagrant case he outreached himself. This was the so-called 'Inaugural Address' to the International Working Men's Association, founded in September 1864. With the object of stirring the English working class from its apathy, and anxious therefore to prove that living standards were falling, he deliberately falsified a sentence from W. E. Gladstone's Budget speech of 1863. What Gladstone said, commenting on the increase in national wealth, was: 'I should look almost with apprehension and with pain upon this intoxicating augmentation of wealth and power if it were my belief that it was confined to the class who are in easy circumstances.' But, he added, 'the average condition of the British labourer, we have the happiness to know, has improved during the last twenty years in a degree which we know to be extraordinary, and which we may almost pronounce to be unexampled in the history of any country and of any age'. Marx, in his address, has Gladstone say: 'This intoxicating augmentation of wealth and power is entirely confined to classes of property.' Since what Gladstone actually said was true, and confirmed by a mass of statistical evidence, and since in any case he was known to be obsessed with the need to ensure that wealth was distributed as widely as possible, it would be hard to conceive of a more outrageous reversal of his meaning. Marx gave as his sources the *Morning Star* newspaper; but the *Star*, along with other newspapers and Hansard, gives Gladstone's words correctly. Marx's misquotation was pointed out. None the less, he reproduced it in *Capital*, along with other discrepancies, and when the falsification was again noticed and denounced, he let out a huge discharge of obfuscating ink; he, Engels and later his daughter Eleanor were involved in the row, attempting to defend the indefensible, for twenty years. None of them would ever admit the original, clear falsification and the result of the debate is that some readers are left with the impression, as Marx intended, that there are two sides to the controversy. There are not. Marx knew Gladstone never said any such thing and the cheat was deliberate. It was not unique. Marx similarly falsified quotations from Adam Smith.

•

Broken promises

DEE BROWN

The American Indians were consistently lied to throughout the nineteenth century. 'There is no use talking to these Americans,' Chief Sitting Bull of the Sioux tribe told a Canadian Government Commissioner. 'They are all liars, you cannot believe anything they say.' At a later meeting with one of these lying Americans, General Terry, the Chief told him: 'You come here to tell us lies, but we don't want to hear them. I don't wish any such language to be used to me; that is to tell me such lies in my Great Mother's house. Don't you say two more words. Go back home where you came from . . . The part of the country you gave me you ran me out of. I have come here to stay with these people, and I intend to stay here.' That was in 1874. But it wasn't just government agents and army generals who lied and broke their promises to the Indians. Four years earlier, the American Government had invited Chief Red Cloud to Washington. The following extract reveals the extent of the mendacity that existed towards the Indian delegation.

Secretary of the Interior Jacob Cox opened the proceedings with the sort of oration these Indians had heard many times before. The government would like to give the Indians arms and ammunition for hunting, Cox said, but could not do this until it was sure all the Indians were at peace. 'Keep the peace,' he concluded, 'and then we will do what is right for you.' He said nothing about the Sioux reservation on the Missouri.

Red Cloud responded by shaking hands with secretary Cox and the other officials. 'Look at me,' he said. 'I was raised on this land where the sun rises – now I come from where the sun sets. Whose voice was first sounded on this land? The voice of the red people who had but bows and arrows. The Great Father says he is good and kind to us. I don't think so. I am good to his white people. From the word sent me I have come all the way to his house. My face is red; yours is white. The Great Spirit has made you to read and write, but not me. I have not learned. I come here to tell my Great Father what I do not like in my country. You are all close to the Great Father, and are a great many chiefs. The men the Great Father sends to us have no sense – no heart.

'I do not want my reservation on the Missouri; this is the fourth time I have said so.' He stopped for a moment, and gestured towards Spotted Tail and the Brule delegation. 'Here are some people from there now. Their children are dying off like sheep; the country does not suit them. I was born at the forks of the Platte and I was told that the land belonged to me from north, south, east, and west . . . when you send goods to me, they are stolen all along the road, so when they reach me they are only a handful. They held a paper for me to sign, and this is all I got for my land. I know the people you send out there are liars. Look at me. I am poor and naked. I do not want war with my government . . . I want you to tell all this to my Great Father.'

Donehowaga of the Iroquois, the commissioner, replied: 'We will tell the President what Red Cloud has said today. The President told me he would speak with Red Cloud very soon.'

. . . The meeting with President Grant was on June 9, in the executive office of the White House. Red Cloud repeated much of what he had said at the Interior Department, emphasizing that his people did not want to live on the Missouri River. The treaty of 1868, he added, gave them the right to trade at Fort Laramie and have an agency on the Platte. Grant avoided a direct reply, but he promised to see that justice was done the Sioux. The President knew that the treaty ratified by Congress made no mention of Fort Laramie or the Platte; it specifically stated that the Sioux agency was to be 'at some place on the Missouri'. Privately he suggested to Secretary Cox and Commissioner Parker that they call the Indians together the next day and explain to them the terms of the treaty.

Donehowaga spent a restless night; he knew the Sioux had been tricked. When the printed treaty was read and explained to them, they would not like what they heard. Next morning at the Interior Department, Secretary Cox went through the treaty point by point, while Red Cloud listened patiently to the slow interpretation of the English words. When it was finished he declared firmly: 'This is the first time I have heard of such a treaty. I never heard of it and do not mean to follow it.'

Secretary Cox replied that he did not believe any of the peace commissioners at Laramie would have told a lie about the treaty.

'I do not say the commissioners lied,' Red Cloud retorted, 'but the interpreters were wrong. When the soldiers left the fort, I signed a treaty of peace, but it was not this treaty. We want to straighten things up.' He arose and started to leave the room. Cox offered him a copy of the treaty, suggesting that he have his own interpreter explain it to him and then they would discuss it at another meeting. 'I will not take the paper with me,' Red Cloud replied. 'It is all lies.'

That night in their hotel the Sioux talked of going home the next day. Some said they were ashamed to go home and tell their people how they had been lied to and cheated into signing the treaty of 1868. It would be better to die there in Washington. Only the intercession of Donehowaga, the Little Father, persuaded them to come back for one more meeting. He promised to help them interpret the treaty in a better way. He had seen President Grant and convinced him that there was a solution to the difficulty.

When the difficulties had apparently been removed, Red Cloud was invited to go to New York, where, for the first time, he had the opportunity of speaking to the people instead of to Government officials.

'We want to keep peace,' he told them. 'Will you help us? In 1868 men came and brought papers. We could not read them, and they did not tell us truly what was in them. We thought the treaty was to remove the forts, and that we should cease from fighting. But they wanted to send us traders on the Missouri. We did not want to go to the Missouri, but wanted traders where we were. When I reached Washington the Great Father explained to me what the treaty was, and showed me that the interpreters had deceived me. All I want is right and just. I have tried to get from the Great Father what is right and just. I have not altogether succeeded.'

•

What the catechism says about lying

CARDINAL NEWMAN

Newman sought to defend Catholicism against the charge that his Church suffered from a lack of scruple with regard to truthfulness. This opinion seems hardly surprising when one recollects the Jesuits' use of casuistry. It was Newman's opinion that all men might resort to a lie in extreme circumstances, no matter what their faith.

. . . if Protestants wish to know what our real teaching is, as on other subjects, so on that of lying, let them look, not at our books of casuistry, but at our catechisms. Works on pathology do not give the best insight into the form and the harmony of the human frame; and, as it is with the body, so is it with the mind. The Catechism of the Council of Trent was drawn up for the express purpose of providing preachers with subjects for their Sermons; and as my whole work has been a defence of myself, I may here say that I rarely preach a Sermon, but I go to this beautiful and complete Catechism to get both my matter and my doctrine. There we find the following notices about the duty of Veracity:

'"Thou shalt not bear false witness," &c.: let attention be drawn to two laws contained in this commandment: the one, forbidding false witness; the other bidding, that removing all pretence and deceits, we should measure our words and deeds by simple truth, as the Apostle admonished the Ephesians of that duty in these words: "Doing truth in charity, let us grow in Him through all things."

'To deceive by a lie in joke or for the sake of compliment, though to no one there accrues loss or gain in consequence, nevertheless is altogether unworthy: for thus the Apostle admonishes, "Putting aside lying, speak ye truth." For therein is great danger of lapsing into frequent and more serious lying, and from lies in joke men gain the habit of lying, whence they gain the character of not being truthful. And thence again, in order to gain credence to their words, they find it necessary to make a practice of swearing.

'Nothing is more necessary (for us) than truth of testimony, in those things, which we neither know ourselves, nor can allowably be ignorant of, on which point there is extant that maxim of St Augustine's; Whoso conceals the truth, and whoso puts forth a lie, each is guilty; the one because he is not willing to do a service, the other because he has a wish to do a mischief.

'It is lawful at times to be silent about the truth, but out of a court of law; for in court, when a witness is interrogated by the judge according to law, the truth is wholly to be brought out.

'Witnesses, however, must beware, lest, from over-confidence in their memory, they affirm for certain, what they have not verified.

'In order that the faithful may with more good will avoid the sin of lying, the Parish Priest shall set before them the extreme misery and turpitude of this wickedness. For, in holy writ, the devil is called the father of a lie; for, in that he did not remain in Truth, he is a liar, and the father of a lie. He will add, with the view of ridding men of so great a crime, the evils which follow upon lying; and, whereas they are innumerable, he will point out (at least) the sources and general heads of these mischiefs and calamities, viz. 1. How great is God's displeasure and how great His hatred of a man who is insincere and a liar. 2. What little security there is that a man who is specially hated by God may not be visited by the heaviest punishments. 3. What more unclean and foul, as St James says, than . . . that a fountain by the same jet should send out sweet water and bitter? 4. For that tongue, which just now praised God, next, as far as in it lies, dishonours Him by lying. 5. In consequence, liars are shut out from the possession of heavenly beatitude. 6. That too is the worst evil of lying, that that disease of the mind is generally incurable.

'Moreover, there is this harm too, and one of vast extent, and touching me generally, that by insincerity and lying faith and truth are lost, which are the firmest bonds of human society, and, when they are lost, supreme confusion follows in life, so that men seem nothing to differ from devils.

'Lastly, the parish Priest will set those right who excuse their insincerity and allege the example of wise men, who, they say, are used to lie for an occasion. He will tell them, what is most true, that the wisdom of the flesh is death. He will exhort his hearers to trust in God, when they are in difficulties and straits, nor to have recourse to the expedient of a lie.

'They who throw the blame of their own lie on those who have already by a lie deceived them, are to be taught that men must not revenge themselves, nor make up for one evil by another.' . . .

There is much more in the Catechism to the same effect, and it is of universal obligation; whereas the decision of a particular author in morals need not be accepted by any one.

To one other authority I appeal on this subject, which commands from me attention of a special kind, for it is the teaching of a Father. It will serve to bring my work to a conclusion.

'St Philip,' says the Roman Oratorian who wrote his Life, 'had a particular dislike of affectation both in himself and others, in speaking, in dressing, or in anything else.

'He avoided all ceremony which savoured of worldly compliment, and always showed himself a great stickler for Christian simplicity in every thing; so that, when he had to deal with men of worldly prudence, he did not very readily accommodate himself to them.

'And he avoided, as much as possible, having anything to do with two-faced persons, who did not go simply and straightforwardly to work in their transactions.

'As for liars, he could not endure them, and he was continually reminding his spiritual children, to avoid them as they would a pestilence.'

These are the principles on which I have acted before I was a Catholic; these are the principles which, I trust, will be my stay and guidance to the end.

•

Mother nature's liars

SAMUEL BUTLER

What is 'lying'? Turning for moral guidance to my cousins the lower animals, whose unsophisticated nature proclaims what God has taught them with a directness we may sometimes study, I find the plover lying when she lures us from her young ones under the fiction of a broken wing. Is God angry, think you, with this pretty deviation from the letter of strict accuracy? or was it not He who whispered to her to tell the falsehood – to tell it with a circumstance, without conscientious scruple, not once only, but to make a practice of it, so as to be a plausible, habitual, and professional liar for some six weeks or so in the year? I imagine so. When I was young I used to read in good books that it was God who taught the bird to make her nest, and if so He probably taught each species the other domestic arrangements best suited to it. Or did the nest-building information come from God, and was there an evil one among the birds also who taught them at any rate to steer clear of priggishness?

Think of the spider again – an ugly creature, but I suppose God likes it. What a mean and odious lie is that web which naturalists extol as such a marvel of ingenuity!

Once on a summer afternoon in a far country I met one of those orchids who make it their business to imitate a fly with their petals. This lie they dispose so cunningly that real flies, thinking the honey is being already plundered, pass them without molesting them. Watching intently and keeping very still, methought I heard this orchid speaking to the offspring which she felt within her, though I saw them not. 'My children,' she exclaimed, 'I must soon leave you; think upon the fly, my loved ones, for this is truth; cling to this great thought in your passage through life, for it is the one thing needful, once lose sight of it and you are lost!' Over and over again she sang this burden in a small still voice, and so I left her. Then straightway I came upon some butterflies whose profession it was to pretend to believe in all manner of vital truths which in their inner practice they rejected; thus, asserting themselves to be certain other and hateful butterflies which no bird will eat by reason of their abominable smell, these cunning ones conceal their own sweetness, and live long in the land and see good days. No: lying is so deeply rooted in nature that we may expel it with a fork, and yet it will always come back: it is like the poor, we must always have it with us; we must all eat a peck of moral dirt before we die.

All depends upon who it is that is lying. One man may steal a horse when another may not look over a hedge. The good man who tells no lies wittingly to himself and is never unkindly, may lie and lie and lie whenever he chooses to other people, and he will not be false to any man: his lies become truths as they pass into the hearer's ear. If a man deceives himself and is unkind, the truth is not in him, it turns to falsehood while yet in his mouth, like the quails in the Wilderness of Sinai. How this is so or why, I know not, but that the Lord hath mercy on whom He will have mercy and whom He willeth He hardeneth.

•

Further thoughts on falsehood

SAMUEL BUTLER

i. Truth consists not in never lying but in knowing when to lie and when not to do so. *De minimis non curat veritas.* Yes, but what is a minimum? Sometimes a maximum is a minimum and sometimes it is the other way.

ii. Lying is like borrowing or appropriating in music. It is only a good, sound, truthful person who can lie to any good purpose; if a man is not habitually truthful his very lies will be false to him and betray him. The converse also is true; if a man is not a good, sound, honest, capable liar there is no truth in him.

iii. Any fool can tell the truth, but it requires a man of some sense to know how to lie well.

iv. I do not mind lying, but I hate inaccuracy.

v. A friend who cannot at a pinch remember a thing or two that never happened is as bad as one who does not know how to forget.

vi. Cursed is he that does not know when to shut his mind. An open mind is all very well in its way, but it ought not to be so open that there is no keeping anything in or out of it. It should be capable of shutting its doors sometimes, or it may be found a little draughty.

vii. He who knows not how to wink knows not how to see; and he who knows not how to lie knows not how to speak the truth. So he who cannot suppress his opinions cannot express them.

viii. There can no more be a true statement without falsehood distributed through it, than a note on a well-tuned piano that is not intentionally and deliberately put out of tune to some extent in order to have the piano in the most perfect possible tune. Any perfection of tune as regards one key can only be got at the expense of all the rest.

ix. Lying has a kind of respect and reverence with it. We pay a person the compliment of acknowledging his superiority whenever we lie to him.

x. I seem to see lies crowding and crushing at a narrow gate and working their way in along with truths into the domain of history.

Nature's Double Falsehood

That one great lie she told about the earth being flat when she knew it was round all the time! And again how she stuck to it that the sun went round us when it was we who were going round the sun! This double falsehood has irretrievably ruined my confidence in her. There is no lie which she will not tell and stick to like a Gladstonian. How plausibly she told her tale, and how many ages was it before she was so much as suspected! And then when things did begin to look bad for her, how she brazened it out, and what a desperate business it was to bring her shifts and prevarications to book!

•

Truth of intercourse

R. L. STEVENSON

Among sayings that have a currency in spite of being wholly false upon the face of them for the sake of a half-truth upon another subject which is accidentally combined with the error, one of the grossest and broadest conveys the monstrous proposition that it is easy to tell the truth and hard to tell a lie. I wish heartily it were. But the truth is one; it has first to be discovered, then justly and exactly uttered. Even with instruments specially contrived for the purpose – with a foot-rule, a level, or a theodolite – it is not easy to be exact; it is easier, alas! to be inexact. From those who mark the divisions on a scale to those who measure the boundaries of empires or the distance of the heavenly stars, it is by careful method and minute, unwearying attention that men rise even to material exactness or to sure knowledge even of external and constant things. But it is easier to draw the outline of a mountain than the changing appearance of a face; and truth in human relations is of this more intangible and dubious order: hard to seize, harder to communicate. Veracity to facts in a loose, colloquial sense – not to say that I have been in Malabar when as a matter of fact I was never out of England, not to say that I have read Cervantes in the original when as a matter of fact I know not one syllable of Spanish – this, indeed, is easy and to the same degree unimportant in itself. Lies of this sort, according to circumstances, may or may not be important; in a certain sense even they may or may not be false. The habitual liar may be a very honest fellow, and live truly with his wife and friends; while another man who never told a formal falsehood in his life may yet be himself one lie – heart and face, from top to bottom. This is the kind of lie which poisons intimacy. And, vice versa, veracity to sentiment, truth in a relation, truth to your own heart and your friends, never to feign or falsify emotion – that is the truth which makes love possible and mankind happy.

. . . Truth of intercourse is something more difficult than to refrain from telling open lies. It is possible to avoid falsehood and yet not tell the truth. It is not enough to answer formal questions. To reach the truth by yea and nay communications implies a questioner with a share of inspiration, such as is often found in mutual love. Yea and nay may mean nothing; the meaning must have been related in the question. Many words are often necessary to convey a very simple statement; for in this sort of exercise we never hit the gold; the most that we can hope is by many arrows, more or less far off on different sides, to indicate, in the course of time, for what target we are aiming, and after an hour's talk, back and forward, to convey the purport of a single principle or a single thought. And yet while the curt, pithy speaker misses the point entirely, a wordy, prolegomenous babbler will often add three new offences in the process of excusing one. It is really a most delicate affair. The world was made before the English language, and seemingly upon a different design. Suppose we held our converse not in words, but in music: those who have a bad ear would find themselves cut off from all near commerce, and no better than foreigners in this big world. But we do not consider how many have 'a bad ear' for words, nor how often the most eloquent find nothing to reply. I hate questioners and questions; there are so many that can be spoken to without a lie. 'Do you forgive me?' Madam and sweetheart, so far as I have gone in life I have never yet been able to discover what forgiveness means. 'Is it still the same between us?' Why, how can it be? It is eternally different; and yet you are still the friend of my heart. 'Do you understand me?' God knows; I should think it highly improbable.

The cruellest lies are often told in silence. A man may have sat in a room for hours and not opened his teeth, and yet come out of that room a disloyal friend or a vile calumniator. And how many loves have perished because, from pride, or spite, or diffidence, or that unmanly shame which withholds a man from daring to betray emotion, a lover, at the critical point of the relation, has but hung his head and held his tongue? And, again, a lie may be told by a truth, or a truth conveyed through a lie. Truth to facts is not always truth to sentiment; and part of truth, as often happens in answer to a question, may be the foulest calumny. A fact may be an exception; but the feeling is the law, and it is that which you must neither garble nor belie. The whole tenor of a conversation is part of the meaning of each separate statement; the beginning and the end each define and travesty the intermediate conversation. You never speak to God; you address a fellow-man, full of his own tempers; and to tell the truth, rightly understood, is not to state the true facts, but to convey a true impression; truth in spirit, not truth to the letter, is the true veracity. To reconcile averted friends a Jesuitical discretion is often needed, not so much to gain a kind hearing as to communicate sober truth. Women have an ill name in this connection; yet they live in as true relations; the lie of a good woman is the index of her heart.

•

The Wharton letters

PAGET TOYNBEE AND LEONARD WHIBLEY

This anecdote, from an edition of the correspondence of Thomas Gray, suggests the mendacity of none other than Sir Edmund Gosse with regard to his edition of the poet's works.

Gosse contributed to the English Men of Letters Series a *Life of Gray* which was published in 1882. The biography has many errors of fact and unwarrantable assumptions. Unhappily, it has been accepted as reliable.

Two years later there appeared: *The Works of Thomas Gray in Prose and Verse*, edited by Edmund Gosse, 4 vols., 8vo., London 1884.

The second and third volumes contained the letters written by Gray . . . In printing the letters Gosse 'followed Mitford's latest collations, except as regards the very numerous letters addressed to Wharton'. These, he stated, 'I have scrupulously printed, as though they had never been published before, direct from the originals, which exist, in a thick volume, among the Egerton MSS., in the Manuscript department of the British Museum. The Wharton letters are so numerous and so important, and have hitherto been so carelessly transcribed, that I regard this portion of my labour, mechanical as it is, with great satisfaction.' The statement seems to indicate, without any loop-hole of ambiguity, that whereas the Wharton letters had been carelessly transcribed before (i.e. by Mitford, for no one else had transcribed them) Gosse was scrupulously printing them 'direct from the originals', and had himself undertaken the mechanical labour of transcription. Gosse's statement was put to the proof by Tovey, who, in an Appendix to the first volume of his edition of *Gray's Letters* (published in 1900), pointed out, with a polite irony, the many coincidences of error in the texts of Mitford and Gosse. These could not be explained on any assumption except that Gosse was reproducing (with occasional corrections) Mitford's text and not that of the original letters. Gosse ignored the exposure, and when two years later he issued a 'revised edition' of his book, he left the statement that the letters had been printed 'direct from the originals' as he had written it eighteen years before.

The question remained open until in 1931 the Honourable Sir Evan Charteris, in *The Life and Letters of Sir Edmund Gosse*, offered the following explanation:

> Unfortunately Gosse had employed someone else to copy the letters in the Egerton MSS., and the copyist, wearying of the script, and finding that the letters had been published by Mitford, soon began to copy from the printed word in preference to the MSS. Mitford's edition of the letters differed from the originals, and those differences reappeared in the work of the copyist.

Thus Gosse's reiterated assertion that the Wharton letters had been 'scrupulously printed direct from the originals' and by his own labours of transcription is proved devoid of truth.

•

The Parnell commission

ANON.

In May 1882, Lord Frederick Cavendish, the Secretary for Ireland, and his Under-Secretary, Thomas Burke, were murdered in Phoenix Park, Dublin, by Irish Republicans. In 1887 *The Times* published a letter apparently written by the Irish Nationalist MP, Charles Parnell, in which he condoned the murders. More incriminating letters appeared, and as a result, the Government set up an inquiry, of whose activities the following is an account.

In March, 1887, *The Times* began the publication of a series of articles entitled 'Parnellism and Crime'. Their object was to prove that Parnell's Nationalist Movement was really a revolutionary movement, stained by crime and designed to overthrow British authority in Ireland. Very shortly afterwards the same newspaper published an extraordinary letter, the original of which purported to be in the handwriting of Parnell. 'We do not think it right,' said *The Times*, 'to withhold any longer from public knowledge the fact that we possess, and have in our possession, documentary evidence which has a most serious bearing on the Parnellite conspiracy, and which, after a most careful and minute scrutiny, is, we are satisfied, quite authentic. We produce one document of which the accuracy cannot be impugned, and we invite Mr Parnell to explain how his signature became attached to such a letter.'

The writer of the letter in question – which was addressed to an unknown person, and dated May 15th, 1882, that is, nine days after the Phoenix Park murders – actually attempted to justify that horrible crime.

'Dear Sir,' he wrote, 'I am surprised at your friend's anger, but he and you should know that to denounce the murders was the only course open to us. To do so promptly and plainly was our best policy, but you can tell him, and all concerned, that though I regret the accident of Lord F. Cavendish's death, I cannot refuse to admit that Burke got no more than his deserts. You are at liberty to show him this, and others whom you can trust also. But let not my address be known; he can write to House of Commons. – Yours very truly, Charles S. Parnell.'

No more damaging charge could have been made against the Irish leader, and the fact that it was brought by a newspaper of such repute as *The Times* gave it the strongest weight. But Parnell remained quite unmoved. He simply told the House of Commons that the letter was a bare-faced forgery, as were others of a similar nature which had already been published, and he said that he would willingly have placed his own body between Lord Frederick Cavendish and the assassin's knife, and that he would have done the same for Mr Burke. He then demanded an inquiry by a Select Committee of the House. After some delay the Government offered a judicial instead of a parliamentary inquiry, and to this Parnell agreed. Three High Court judges were appointed to form a Special Commission to inquire into the matter, and also into similar charges against a number of Parnell's followers, and they were given the fullest powers of investigation.

The trial began in the autumn of 1888, and took place in the Law Courts in the Strand, London.

. . . Parnell now pressed through his counsel for an immediate investigation into the source from which the letters had come. Time and again the Attorney-General [appearing for *The Times*] managed to evade this issue, but at length, on the fiftieth day of the trial, the question came before the Court. Mr Soames, the solicitor for *The Times*, proved that the letters were brought to him by Mr McDonnell, the manager of the paper, and that he (Mr Soames) took steps to compare them with the genuine handwriting of Parnell. Then Mr McDonnell went into the box, and he deposed that he had received the letters from a Mr Houston, secretary of the 'Irish Loyal and Patriotic Union'. When cross-examined by Parnell's junior counsel – Mr Henry

Asquith, the future Prime Minister – McDonnell admitted that, though he gave Mr Houston £1,000 for the letters, he had not asked, nor had he been told, where they came from.

Sir Charles Russell [senior counsel for Parnell] now demanded that Houston should be examined. The Attorney-General refused. But, after some further argument, he was overruled by the Bench, and Houston went into the box.

Mr Houston stated that . . . it was part of his work to collect evidence of Nationalist complicity in crime, and stated that for this purpose he had made use of the services of a penurious Dublin journalist called Richard Pigott. This man was paid a guinea a day to hunt up documents likely to incriminate Parnell and his followers, and Houston said that he eventually produced a bundle of letters which he said he had obtained from two Fenians called Brown and Murphy. This was in the summer of 1886, and Houston went over to Paris, where he met Pigott and handed him the sum of £605 for the letters. Houston further stated that he never saw Brown or Murphy, but that £500 of the money he gave Pigott was supposed to be paid to them. In the packet there were eleven letters. Five were said to be signed by Parnell, and the others by Patrick Egan, who was treasurer of the Irish Land League.

It was now impossible for *The Times* to prevent Pigott giving evidence, and accordingly, on the 20th of February 1889, a greasy man, with a dirty grey beard and an enormous bald head, followed the usher into the witness box. On being sworn he gave his name as Richard Pigott, bowing obsequiously to the three judges as he did so. He looked a thoroughly pugnacious character, but he gave his evidence quite calmly and clearly. However, his jaunty manner soon changed when Sir Charles Russell rose to begin his deadly cross-examination. A sheet of paper was handed to the witness.

'Mr Pigott,' said Russell, 'would you be good enough, with my Lord's permission, to write some words on that sheet of paper for me?' The witness obliged, though he was seen to be a little flurried. Now one of the words was 'hesitancy', and the reason why Russell put it to Pigott was that in one of the letters, purporting to be signed by Egan, it had been wrongly spelt – the letter coming after 't' being 'e' instead of 'a'. When the sheet of paper was handed back Russell noticed, as he had hoped, that Pigott had made the same mistake. For the moment, however, he said nothing, but proceeded to question the witness about the first articles in *The Times*.

Russell first asked Pigott if, at the time the articles started, he knew of the intended publication of the letters. Pigott said no. Russell then produced a letter written by Pigott to the Catholic Archbishop of Dublin from which it was quite plain that he did know. Pigott, now thoroughly confused, floundered on from lie to lie, and when Russell suddenly turned round and taxed him with the letter of Egan's and his incorrect spelling of the word 'hesitancy', he collapsed like a pricked bubble. When the Court rose for the day Pigott protested, as he left the witness box, that he had not forged the letters, and that if he had he would not be where he was. 'Not if you could help it,' said Russell. 'Why couldn't I help it?' retorted Pigott. To this retort Russell answered quietly, 'You will hear presently, I think, Mr Pigott.'

But Pigott did not stay to hear. Next morning when his name was called he failed to answer, and the Attorney-General could offer no reason for his non-appearance. Russell now applied for, and was granted, a warrant for his arrest. Pigott, however, must have foreseen this, for he had fled the country, leaving behind him a written confession that he had forged the letters. This confession, which was made in the presence of two well-known journalists, one of whom was Henry Labouchere, the editor of *Truth*, was subsequently read out in court. Parnell's rehabilitation followed as a matter of course not only before the Court, but in the eyes of the wider general public. Pigott was eventually tracked down by the police to an hotel in Madrid, and there, as he was on the point of being arrested in his bedroom, he blew out his brains.

•

The decay of lying

OSCAR WILDE

Wilde's brilliant 'observation', extracted here, takes the form of a dialogue between two young gentlemen, Cyril and Vivian, in the library of a country house in Nottinghamshire. Cyril comes across Vivian who tells him that he is writing an article.

CYRIL: What is the subject?

VIVIAN: I intend to call it 'The Decay of Lying: A Protest'.

CYRIL: Lying! I should have thought that our politicians kept up that habit.

VIVIAN: I assure you that they do not. They never rise beyond the level of misrepresentation, and actually condescend to prove, to discuss, to argue. How different from the temper of the true liar, with his frank, fearless statements, his superb irresponsibility, his healthy, natural disdain of proof of any kind! After all, what is a fine lie? Simply that which is its own evidence. If a man is sufficiently unimaginative to produce evidence in support of a lie, he might just as well speak the truth at once. No, the politicians won't do. Something may, perhaps, be urged on behalf of the Bar. The mantle of the Sophist has fallen on its members. Their feigned ardours and unreal rhetoric are delightful. They can make the worse appear the better cause, as though they were fresh from Leontine schools, and have been known to wrest from reluctant juries triumphant verdicts of acquittal for their clients, even when those clients, as often happens, were clearly and unmistakably innocent. But they are briefed by the prosaic, and are not ashamed to appeal to precedent. In spite of their endeavours, the truth will out. Newspapers, even, have degenerated. They may now be absolutely relied upon. One feels it as one wades through their columns. It is always the unreadable that occurs. I am afraid that there is not much to be said in favour of either the lawyer or the journalist. Besides, what I am pleading for is Lying in art. Shall I read you what I have written? It might do you a great deal of good.

. . .

CYRIL: You will find me all attention.

VIVIAN (reading in a very clear voice): 'THE DECAY OF LYING: A PROTEST. – One of the chief causes that can be assigned for the curiously commonplace character of most of the literature of our age is undoubtedly the decay of Lying as an art, a science, and a social pleasure. The ancient historians gave us delightful fiction in the form of fact; the modern novelist presents us with dull facts under the guise of fiction. The Blue-Book is rapidly becoming his ideal both for method and manner. He has his tedious *document humain*, his miserable little *coin de la création* [corner of the universe] into which he peers with his microscope. He is to be found at the Librairie Nationale, or at the British Museum, shamelessly reading up his subject. He has not even the courage of other people's ideas, but insists on going directly to life for everything, and ultimately, between encyclopedias and personal experience, he comes to the ground, having drawn his types from the family circle or from the weekly washerwoman, and having acquired an amount of useful information from which never, even in his most meditative moments, can he thoroughly free himself.

'The loss that results to literature in general from this false ideal of our time can hardly be overestimated. People have a careless way of talking about a "born liar", just as they talk about a born poet. But in both cases they are wrong. Lying and poetry are arts – arts, as Plato saw, not unconnected with each other – and they require the most careful study, the most disinterested devotion. Indeed, they have their technique, just as the more material arts of painting and sculpture have their subtle secrets of form and colour, their craft-mysteries, their deliberate artistic methods. As one knows the poet by his fine music, so one can recognize the liar by his rich rhythmic utterance, and in neither case will the casual inspiration of the moment suffice.

Here, as elsewhere, practice must precede perfection. But in modern days while the fashion of writing poetry has become far too common, and should, if possible, be discouraged, the fashion of lying has almost fallen into disrepute. Many a young man starts in life with a natural gift for exaggeration which, if nurtured in congenial and sympathetic surroundings, or by the imitation of the best models, might grow into something really great and wonderful. But, as a rule, he comes to nothing. He either falls into careless habits of accuracy . . ., or takes to frequenting the society of the aged and well-informed. Both things are equally fatal to his imagination, as indeed, they would be fatal to the imagination of anybody, and in a short time he develops a morbid and unhealthy faculty of truth-telling, begins to verify all statements made in his presence, has no hesitation in contradicting people who are much younger than himself, and often ends by writing novels which are so life-like that no one can possibly believe in their probability. This is no isolated instance that we are giving. It is simply one example out of many; and if something cannot be done to check, or at least to modify, our monstrous worship of facts, Art will become sterile and beauty will pass away from the land.

. . . 'We need not say anything about the poets, for they, with the unfortunate exception of Mr Wordsworth, have been really faithful to their high mission, and are universally unreliable. But in the works of Herodotus, who in spite of the shallow and ungenerous attempts of modern sciolists to verify his history, may justly be called the "Father of Lies"; in the published speeches of Cicero and the biographies of Suetonius; in Tacitus at his best; in Pliny's *Natural History*; in Hanno's *Periplus*; in all the early chronicles; in the Lives of the Saints; in Froissart and Sir Thomas Malory; in the travels of Marco Polo; in Olaus Magnus, and Aldrovandus, and Conrad Lycosthenes, with his magnificent *Prodigiorum et Ostentorum Chronicon*; in the autobiography of Benvenuto Cellini; in the memoirs of Casanova; in Defoe's *History of the Plague*; in Boswell's *Life of Johnson*; in Napoleon's despatches, and in the works of our own Carlyle, whose *French Revolution* is one of the most fascinating historical novels ever written, facts are either kept in their proper subordinate position, or else entirely excluded on the general ground of dullness. Now everything is changed. Facts are not merely finding a footing-place in history, but they are usurping the domain of Fancy, and have invaded the kingdom of Romance. Their chilling touch is over everything. They are vulgarizing mankind. The crude commercialism of America, its materializing spirit, its indifference to the poetical side of things, and its lack of imagination and of high unattainable ideals, are entirely due to that country having adopted for its national hero a man who, according to his own confession, was incapable of telling a lie, and it is not too much to say that the story of George Washington and the cherry-tree has done more harm, and in a shorter space of time, than any other moral tale in the whole of literature.'

CYRIL: My dear boy!

VIVIAN: I assure you it is the case, and the amusing part of the whole thing is that the story of the cherry-tree is an absolute myth. However, you must not think that I am too despondent about the artistic future either of America or of our own country. Listen to this:

'That some change will take place before this century has drawn to its close we have no doubt whatsoever. Bored by the tedious and improving conversation of those who have neither the wit to exaggerate nor the genius to romance, tired of the intelligent person whose reminiscences are always based on memory, whose statements are invariably limited by probability, and who is at any time liable to be corroborated by the merest Philistine who happens to be present, Society sooner or later must return to its lost leader, the cultured and fascinating liar. Who he was who first, without ever having gone out to the rude chase, told the wandering caveman at sunset how he had dragged the Megatherium from the purple darkness of its jasper cave, or slain the Mammoth in single combat and brought back its gilded tusks, we cannot tell, and not one of our modern anthropologists, for all their much-boasted science, has had the ordinary courage to tell us. Whatever was his name or race, he certainly was the true founder of social intercourse. For the aim of the liar is simply to charm, to delight, to give pleasure. He is the very basis of civilized society, and without him a dinner-party, even at the mansions of the great, is as dull as a lecture at the Royal Society, or a debate at the Incorporated Authors, or one of Mr Burnand's farcical comedies.

'Nor will he be welcomed by society alone. Art, breaking from the prison-house of realism, will run to greet him, and will kiss his false, beautiful lips, knowing that he alone is in possession of the great secret of all her manifestations, the secret that Truth is entirely and absolutely a matter of style; while Life – poor, probable, uninteresting human life – tired of repeating herself for the benefit of Mr Herbert Spencer, scientific historians, and the compilers of statistics in general, will follow meekly after him, and try to reproduce in her own simple and untutored way, some of the marvels of which he talks.

'No doubt there will always be critics who, like a certain writer in the *Saturday Review*, will gravely censure the teller of fairy tales for his defective knowledge of natural history, who will measure imaginative work by their own lack of any imaginative faculty, and will hold up their ink-stained hands in horror if some honest gentleman, who has never been farther than the yew-trees of his own garden, pens a fascinating book of travels like Sir John Mandeville, or, like great Raleigh, writes a whole history of the world, without knowing anything whatsoever about the past. To excuse themselves they will try and shelter under the shield of him who made Prospero the magician, and gave him Caliban and Ariel as his servants, who heard the Tritons blowing their horns, round the coral reefs of the Enchanted Isle, and the fairies singing to each other in a wood near Athens, who led the phantom kings in dim procession across the misty Scottish heath, and hid Hecate in a cave with the weird sisters. They will call upon Shakespeare – they always do – and will quote that hackneyed passage forgetting that this unfortunate aphorism about Art holding the mirror up to Nature, is deliberately said by Hamlet in order to convince the bystanders of his absolute insanity in all art-matters.'

. . .

'What we have to do, what at any rate it is our duty to do, is to revive this old art of Lying. Much, of course, may be done in the way of educating the public, by amateurs in the domestic circles, at literary lunches, and at afternoon teas. But this is merely the light and graceful side of lying, such as was probably heard at Cretan dinner-parties. There are many other forms. Lying for the sake of gaining some immediate personal advantage, for instance – lying with a moral purpose, as it is usually called – though of late it has been rather looked down upon, was extremely popular with the antique world. Athena laughs when Odysseus tells her "his words of sly devising", as William Morris phrases it, and the glory of mendacity illumines the pale brow of the stainless hero of Euripidean tragedy, and sets among the noble women of the past the young bride of one of Horace's most exquisite odes. Later on, what at first had been merely a natural instinct was elevated into a self-conscious science. Elaborate rules were laid down for the guidance of mankind, and an important school of literature grew up around the subject. Indeed, when one remembers the excellent philosophical treatise of Sanchez on the whole question, one cannot help regretting that no one has ever thought of publishing a cheap and condensed edition of the works of that great Casuist. A short primer, "When to Lie and How", if brought out in an attractive and not too expensive a form, would no doubt command a large sale, and would prove of real practical service to many earnest and deep-thinking people. Lying for the sake of the improvement of the young, which is the basis of home education, still lingers amongst us, and its advantages are so admirably set forth in the early books of Plato's *Republic* that it is unnecessary to dwell upon them here. It is a mode of lying for which all good mothers have peculiar capabilities, but it is capable of still further development, and has been sadly overlooked by the School Board. Lying for the sake of a monthly salary is, of course, well known in Fleet Street, and the profession of a political leader-writer is not without its advantages. But it is said to be a somewhat dull occupation, and it certainly does not lead to much beyond a kind of ostentatious obscurity. The only form of lying that is absolutely beyond reproach is lying for its own sake, and the highest development of this is, as we have already pointed out, Lying in Art. Just as those who do not love Plato more than Truth cannot pass beyond the threshold of the Academe, so those who do not love Beauty more than Truth never know the inmost shrine of Art. The solid, stolid British intellect lies in the desert sands like the Sphinx in Flaubert's marvellous tale, and fantasy, *La Chimère*, dances round it, and calls to it with her false, flute-toned voice. It may not hear her now, but surely some day, when we are all bored to death with the commonplace character of modern fiction, it will hearken to her and try to borrow her wings.

'And when that day dawns, or sunset reddens, how joyous we shall all be! Facts will be regarded as discreditable, Truth will be found mourning over her fetters, and Romance, with her temper of wonder, will return to the land. The very aspect of the world will change to our startled eyes. Out of the sea will rise Behemoth and Leviathan, and sail round the high-pooped galleys, as they do on the delightful maps of those ages when books on geography were actually readable. Dragons will wander about the waste places, and the phoenix will soar from her nest of fire into the air. We shall lay our hands upon the basilisk, and see the jewel in the toad's head. Champing his gilded oats, the Hippogriff will stand in our stalls, and over our heads will float the Blue Bird singing of beautiful and impossible things, of things that are lovely and that never happen, of things that are not and that should be. But before this comes to pass we must cultivate the lost art of Lying.'

•

The holy lie

FRIEDRICH NIETZSCHE

I suggested long ago that convictions might be more dangerous enemies of truth than lies. This time I should like to pose the decisive question: is there any difference whatever between a lie and a conviction? – All the world believes there is, but what does all the world not believe! – Every conviction has its history, its preliminary forms, its tentative shapes, its blunders: it *becomes* a conviction after *not* being one for a long time, after *hardly* being one for an even longer time. What? could the lie not be among these embryonic forms of conviction? – Sometimes it requires merely a change in persons: in the son that becomes conviction which in the father was still a lie. – I call a lie: wanting *not* to see something one does see, wanting not to see something *as* one sees it: whether the lie takes place before witnesses or without witnesses is of no consequence. The most common lie is the lie one tells to oneself; lying to others is relatively the exception. Now this desiring *not* to see what one sees, this desiring not to see as one sees, is virtually the primary condition for all who are in any sense *party*: the party man necessarily becomes a liar. German historiography, for example, is convinced that Rome was despotism, that the Teutons brought the spirit of freedom into the world: what difference is there between this conviction and a lie? Is there any further need to be surprised if all parties, German historians included, instinctively have the big moral words in their mouths – that morality *continues to exist* virtually because the party man of every sort has need of it every moment? – 'This is *our* conviction: we confess it before all the world, we live and die for it – respect everything that has convictions!' – I have heard this kind of thing even from the lips of anti-Semites. On the contrary, gentlemen! An anti-Semite is certainly not made more decent by the fact that he lies on principle . . . The priests, who are subtler in such things and understand very well the objection that can be raised to the concept of a conviction, that is to say mendaciousness on principle *because* serving a purpose, have taken over from the Jews the prudence of inserting the concept 'God', 'the will of God', 'the revelation of God' in its place. Kant too, with his categorical imperative, was on the same road: his reason became *practical* in this matter . – There are questions whose truth or untruth *cannot* be decided by man; all the supreme questions, all the supreme problems of value are beyond human reason . . . To grasp the limits of reason – only *this* is truly philosophy . . . To what end did God give mankind revelation? Would God have done anything superfluous? Mankind *cannot* of itself know what is good and what evil, therefore God taught mankind his will . . . Moral: the priest does *not* lie – the question 'true' or 'untrue' does not *arise* in such things as priests speak of; these things do not permit of lying at all. For in order to lie one would have to be able to decide what is true here. But this is precisely what mankind *cannot* do; the priest is thus only God's mouthpiece. – This kind of priestly syllogism is by no means only Jewish and Christian; the right to lie and the *shrewdness* of a 'revelation' pertains to the type priest, to priests of *decadence* as much as to priests of paganism (– pagans are all who say Yes to life, to whom 'God' is the word for the great Yes to all things). – The 'Law', the 'will of God', the 'sacred book', 'inspiration' – all merely words for the conditions *under* which the priest comes to power, *by* which he maintains his power – these concepts are to be found at the basis of all priestly organizations, all priestly or priestly-philosophical power-structures. The 'holy lie' – common to Confucius, the Law-Book of Manu, Mohammed, the Christian Church –: it is not lacking in Plato. 'The truth exists': this means, wherever it is heard, *the priest is lying* . . .

•

J'accuse

EMILE ZOLA

In 1894 a French artillery officer of Jewish descent, Alfred Dreyfus, was convicted of treason, court-martialled, and sent to Devil's Island. He was, however, innocent, and the victim of the most mendacious military conspiracy in the history of modern France. But Dreyfus was not forgotten, and in 1898 the novelist Emile Zola wrote his famous open letter to the French President. As a result the trial was re-opened, although it was not until 1906 that Dreyfus was finally cleared. The extract printed here concludes Zola's letter.

. . . I do not despair in the least of ultimate triumph. I repeat with more intense conviction: the truth is on the march and nothing will stop it! It is only today that this affair has begun, since it is only now that sides have definitely been taken; on the one hand, the culprits who want no light at all on this business; on the other, lovers of justice who would lay down their lives for it. I have said elsewhere and I say again, when the truth is buried underground, it grows, it chokes, it gathers such an explosive force that on the day when it bursts out, it blows everything up with it. We shall soon see whether we have not laid the mines for a most far-reaching disaster of the near future.

But this letter is long, Mr President, and it is time to conclude.

I accuse Colonel Du Paty de Clam of having been the diabolical agent of the judicial error, unconsciously, I prefer to believe, and of having continued to defend his deadly work during the past three years through the most absurd and revolting machinations.

I accuse General Mercier of being an accomplice in one of the greatest crimes of history, probably through weak-mindedness.

I accuse General Billot of having had in his hands the decisive proofs of the innocence of Dreyfus and of having concealed them, and of having rendered himself guilty of the crime of lèse-humanity and lèse-justice, from political motives and to save the face of the General Staff.

I accuse General de Boisdeffre and General Gonse of being accomplices in the same crime, the former no doubt through religious prejudice, the latter out of *esprit de corps*.

I accuse General de Pellieux and Major Ravary of having carried out a villainous inquest, I mean an inquest of the most monstrous partiality, the complete report of which is an imperishable monument of naive effrontery.

I accuse three handwriting experts, Mm. Belhomme, Varinard and Couard, of having made lying and fraudulent reports, unless a medical examination will certify them to be deficient in sight and judgement.

I accuse the War Office of having led a vile campaign in the press, particularly in *L'Éclair* and in *L'Écho de Paris*, in order to misdirect public opinion and cover up its sins.

I accuse, lastly, the first court-martial of having violated all human rights in condemning a prisoner on testimony kept secret from him, and I accuse the second court-martial of having covered up this illegality by order, committing in turn the judicial crime of acquitting a guilty man with full knowledge of his guilt.

In making these accusations I am aware that I render myself liable to articles 30 and 31 of the Libel Laws of July 29, 1881, which punish acts of defamation. I expose myself voluntarily . . .

I have one passion only, for light, in the name of humanity which has borne so much and has a right to happiness . . . Let them dare then to take me to the court of appeals, and let there be an inquest in the full light of day!

I am waiting.

•

Truth suppression in Freudian analysis

SIGMUND FREUD

Even a careful liar may betray himself by a slip of the tongue. For Freud, a slip of the tongue was indicative of 'the suppression of the speaker's intention to say something'. Freud gave many examples of what we now call 'Freudian slips', but perhaps the best one he quoted relates to the following experience of one of Freud's own followers, an American doctor by the name of Brill, who recalls the following experience.

I went for a walk one evening with Dr Frink, and we discussed some of the business of the New York Psychoanalytic Society. We met a colleague, Dr R., who I had not seen for years and of whose private life I knew nothing. We were very pleased to meet again, and on my invitation he accompanied us to a café, where we sat two hours in lively conversation. He seemed to know some details about me, for after the usual greetings he asked after my small child and told me that he heard about me from time to time from a mutual friend and had been interested in my work ever since he had read about it in the medical press. To my question as to whether he was married he gave a negative answer, and added: 'Why should a man like me marry?'

On leaving the café, he suddenly turned to me and said: 'I should like to know what you would do in a case like this: I know a nurse who was named as co-respondent in a divorce case. The wife sued the husband and named her as co-respondent, and *he* got the divorce.' I interrupted him, saying: 'You mean *she* got the divorce.' He immediately corrected himself, saying: 'Yes, of course, *she* got the divorce,' and continued to tell how the nurse had been so affected by the divorce proceedings and the scandal that she had taken to drink, had become very nervous, and so on; and he wanted me to advise him how to treat her.

As soon as I had corrected his mistake I asked him to explain it, but I received the usual surprised answers: had not everyone a right to make a slip of the tongue? It was only an accident, there was nothing behind it, and so on. I replied that there must be a reason for every mistake in speaking, and that had he not told me earlier that he was unmarried, I would be tempted to suppose he himself was the hero of the story; for in that case the slip could be explained by his wish that he had obtained the divorce rather than his wife, so that he should not have (by our matrimonial laws) to pay alimony, and so that he could marry again in New York State. He stoutly denied my conjecture, but the exaggerated emotional reaction which accompanied it, in which he showed marked signs of agitation followed by laughter, only strengthened my suspicions. To my appeal that he should tell the truth in the interests of science, he answered: 'Unless you wish me to lie you must believe that I was never married, and hence your psycho-analytic interpretation is wrong.' He added that someone who paid attention to every triviality was positively dangerous. Then he suddenly remembered that he had another appointment and left us.

Both Dr Frink and I were still convinced that my interpretation of his slip of the tongue was correct, and I decided to corroborate or disprove it by further investigation. Some days later I visited a neighbour, an old friend of Dr R., who was able to confirm my explanation in every particular. The divorce proceedings had taken place some weeks before, and the nurse was cited as co-respondent.

•

Protocols of the Elders of Zion

UNIVERSAL JEWISH ENCYCLOPEDIA

The Protocols first appeared in Russia as part of anti-semitic propaganda used by reactionaries in an effort to discredit liberal elements intent on economic reform. But the effects of the Protocols were most strikingly felt in Germany, and while this was initially part of an anti-Soviet, White Russian effort to discredit the Revolution, the Protocols were quickly taken up by the Nazis as evidence of an international Jewish conspiracy. One of the first people to find positive proof that the Protocols were a blatant lie was the Constantinople correspondent of *The Times*, Philip Graves. He had been given a book by a Russian who had obtained it from a member of the Czar's secret police, and was struck by the similarity between some of its passages and sections of the Protocols. The book was the *Dialogue* of Maurice Joly, and it is certain that the Protocols were largely drawn from it. Another important disclosure came from a French Count named du Chayla, who told a French newspaper that the Protocols had originated with General Rachkovskii, head of the Russian police in Paris. Here, the origin and content of the Protocols are examined.

Introduction

Origin The Protocols of the Elders of Zion (Russian Protokoly Sionskikh Mudretsov) first appeared in Russia in the early twentieth century. Apparently the earliest edition was that of Paul Krushevan, who published an abbreviated version in his Kishinev newspaper *Znamia* (*The Banner*) in August 1903. Most subsequent reprints and translations, however, are based upon the longer version published by Sergius Nilus in his book *Velikoe v Malom* (*The Great in the Little*), 2nd ed., Tsarskoe Selo, 1905, and republished in 1911 and in 1917. Another early version was that of G. Butmi, in the third and fourth editions of *Vragi Roda Chelovecheskago* (*Enemies of the Human Race*), published in St Petersburg in 1906 and 1907.

Content The Protocols consist of twenty-four sections (Butmi has twenty-seven), which allegedly were read by a leader of Zion to a secret gathering of Elders. The protocols, somewhat illogically arranged, set forth the alleged schemes of the leaders of Zion to overthrow all governments, and their proposals for organizing a Jewish world empire. The speaker boasts that by the use of terror, and through the debilitating effects of liberalism and class strife, the Gentile states have been weakened. Other weapons used are a monopoly of gold, which is entirely in Jewish hands, and control of the press, as well as immorality and economic crises. As non-Jewish allies of these supposed Elders the leader lists Free Masons, political parties, and atheists; speculators and corrupt politicians are ready to do the bidding of the Jews; and if any people dares to rebel, their capital will be blown up by explosions in its subway system, or the Elders will turn up against them 'American or Chinese or Japanese cannon'. After the terrorized and bewildered people have submitted to the inevitable, the leaders of Zion will set up their world empire. Instead of the gold standard they will introduce a flexible paper currency; the press will be censored and licensed; financial stability will be insured by skilful taxation and public works; credit monopolies will be instituted, and prosperity will result, so that the people will rejoice in their good fortune. As for the hostile few, their secret societies will be broken up, and the police will keep close watch over each potential enemy. Dangerous foes of the new regime will be arrested and treated like common criminals. Thus the people will enjoy the blessings of prosperity and security, and will be glad that they dwell under the House of David.

Evidence as to Authenticity

Statements of Original Publishers Krushevan, the first to print the Protocols, did not claim that they actually originated with the Jews, but stated that they might well be the secret Jewish program. Nilus and Butmi, however, state positively that the Protocols are an authentic Jewish product. Nevertheless, neither one claims to have seen the original Protocols. What the reader is given is a copy of the original, made in France by an unknown, and which, after passing through several hands, finally was translated from the French and published. (In one place Nilus states that the copy came from the Zionist headquarters, in another, from a leading Free Mason.) No signatures of the Elders are given, and indeed, in his earlier editions Nilus did not attempt to identify the Jewish leaders to whom the Protocols were read. In the 1917 edition, however, Nilus states that he had just learned from Jewish sources that the Protocols were read by Theodor Herzl at the time of the Zionist Congress in August, 1897.

Butmi sheds little light on the origin of the Protocols. In his book they are accompanied by what is termed the explanation of the translator, who says they were taken from the vaults of the Zionist Central Headquarters, and were signed by the representatives of Zion, who, however, were not the same as the representatives of the Zionist movement. Butmi himself cautions his readers against this distinction; Herzl's group, he states, is really a dangerous revolutionary organization, and there is no difference between these Zionists and those who signed the Protocols. Thus there are several contradictory explanations offered concerning the origin of the Protocols, and it is only in the 1917 edition of Nilus that an attempt is made definitely to connect them with a specific category of Jews – Herzl and the Basel Congress.

Internal Evidence Neither Nilus or Butmi is an unimpeachable witness. Butmi dedicated his book to the 'Union of the Russian People', a notorious terrorist society, and in his introduction made statements so extreme that his veracity is doubtful. Nilus was a mystic, much concerned over the imminent coming of Antichrist. In his 1911 edition he had much to say of the symbol of Antichrist, a six-pointed star, composed of an ordinary and inverted triangle. He complained that the ordinary triangle, the sign of good, was found on the soles of galoshes, and the inverted triangle, the sign of evil, was on Russian railroad cars. Such were the sponsors of the Protocols.

The Protocols themselves contain a number of doubtful passages. There is the famous statement that the Elders would ensure the election of docile puppets – men who had in their past some 'Panama' or other. The word Panama was perhaps used as a generic term for corruption, as the Panama scandal was already known by 1897, the year of the Zionist Congress – or, on the other hand, it may have referred to the election of President

Loubet in 1899, as he was accused of complicity in the Panama affair. If Loubet's election was meant, then the Protocols could not have been read at the Zionist Congress of 1897. Then there is the threat to blow up recalcitrant capitals by explosions in their subway systems – allegedly uttered when only two European capitals had subways, and only two others were building them. The boast that all Europe was in a state of turmoil, thanks to the machinations of the Elders, does not fit the situation in 1897, when Europe was fairly peaceful, instead of being 'in torture' and subject to disorders and revolution. Likewise the claim that the financial straits of the powers were calamitous does not correspond with the world situation at that time. And the threat of using 'American or Chinese or Japanese cannon' was an empty one.

In other places the Elders are pictured as boasting that they controlled the French Revolution of 1789, and that they invented the phrase 'Liberty, Equality, Fraternity' – although these statements are untrue. The Protocols contain only one quotation from the Bible – and that, strange to say, is from the Vulgate, the Latin Bible used by the Catholic Church. And another suspicious contradiction is that the Jews, who are depicted as boasting about their mastery of gold, are made to propose the abolition of the gold standard after their rise to power.

Conclusions The case for the authenticity of the Protocols is weak. It is based upon the statements of Nilus and Butmi, two unreliable witnesses. No facsimile of the original is available, no signatures, or other concrete proof. Moreover, both men admit that the manuscript passed through several hands before reaching them. Furthermore, there are conflicting versions to account for their possession of the manuscript, and it was only in 1917 that Nilus assigned the work to a specific group of Jews. The Protocols themselves contain a number of internal contradictions and possible anachronisms.

There is, moreover, evidence to show how the Protocols really originated. We have the testimony of du Chayla, who talked with Nilus and heard him admit that they came from

Rachkovskii, and of Graves, who found the prototype, the *Dialogue* of Joly, the indisputable source for much of the material of the Protocols. Then at the Bern trial reputable witnesses – Burtsev, Svatikov, and others – gave evidence as to the Russian origin of the Protocols. Burtsev cited what he had learned from former police chiefs like Lopukhin, Beletskii, and Globachev – all of whom implicated Rachkovskii in the fabrication. Svatikov reported his conversation with Bint of the Russian police in Paris, who admitted that under Rachkovskii he had helped in forging the Protocols; the attempts of Russian conservatives to disprove this testimony are not convincing. Thus, while there is no valid evidence to connect the Protocols with Zionists or other Jews, all the evidence there is tends to show that the Protocols originated with Rachkovskii, head of the Russian police in Paris.

•

George Washington and the cherry-tree

MARK TWAIN

I am suffering now from the fact that I, who have told the truth a good many times in my life, have lately received more letters than anybody else urging me to lead a righteous life. I have more friends who want to see me develop on a higher level than anybody else.

Young John D. Rockefeller, two weeks ago, taught his Bible class all about veracity, and why it was better that everybody should always keep a plentiful supply on hand. Some of the letters I have received suggest that I ought to attend his class and learn, too. Why, I know Mr Rockefeller, and he is a good fellow. He is competent in many ways to teach a Bible class, but when it comes to veracity he is only thirty-five years old. I'm seventy years old. I have been familiar with veracity twice as long as he.

And the story about George Washington and the little hatchet has also been suggested to me in these letters – in a fugitive way, as if I needed some of George Washington and his hatchet in my constitution. Why, dear me, they overlook the real point in that story. The point is not the one that is usually suggested, and you can readily see that.

The point is not that George said to his father, 'Yes, father, I cut down the cherry-tree; I can't tell a lie,' but that the little boy – only seven years old – should have his sagacity developed under such circumstances. He was a boy wise beyond his years. His conduct then was a prophecy of later years. Yes, I think he was the most remarkable man the country ever produced – up to my time, anyway.

Now then, little George realized that circumstantial evidence was against him. He knew that his father would know from the size of the chips that no full-grown hatchet cut that tree down, and that no man would have haggled it so. He knew that his father would send around the plantation and inquire for a small boy with a hatchet, and he had the wisdom to come out and confess it. Now, the idea that his father was overjoyed when he told little George that he would rather have him cut down a thousand cherry-trees than tell a lie is a nonsense. What did he really mean? Why, that he was absolutely astonished that he had a son who had the chance to tell a lie and didn't.

I admire old George – if that was his name – for his discernment. He knew when he said that his son couldn't tell a lie that he was stretching it a good deal. He wouldn't have to go to John D. Rockefeller's Bible class to find that out. The way the old George Washington story goes down it doesn't do anybody any good. It only discourages people who can tell a lie.

•

Telling stories

EDMUND GOSSE

Brought up among the Plymouth Brethren, Sir Edmund Gosse had the sternest upbringing imaginable. In this extract from *Father and Son* he describes the fantastic lengths to which his mother took her abhorrence of lies.

... I found my greatest pleasure in the pages of books. The range of these was limited, for story-books of every description were sternly excluded. No fiction of any kind, religious or secular, was admitted into the house. In this it was to my Mother, not to my Father, that the prohibition was due. She had a remarkable, I confess to me still unaccountable impression, that to 'tell a story', that is, to compose fictitious narrative of any kind, was a sin. She carried this conviction to extreme lengths. My Father, in later years, gave me some interesting examples of her firmness. As a young man in America, he had been deeply impressed by *Salathiel*, a pious prose romance by that then popular writer, the Rev. George Croly. When he first met my Mother, he recommended it to her, but she would not consent to open it. Nor would she read the chivalrous tales in verse of Sir Walter Scott, obstinately alleging that they were not 'true'. She would read none but lyrical and subjective poetry. Her secret diary reveals the history of this singular aversion to the fictitious, although it cannot be said to explain the cause of it. As a child, however, she had possessed a passion for making up stories, and so considerable a skill in it that she was constantly being begged to indulge others with its exercise. But I will, on so curious a point, leave her to speak for herself:

> 'When I was a very little child, I used to amuse myself and my brothers with inventing stories, such as I read. Having, as I suppose, naturally a restless mind and busy imagination, this soon became the chief pleasure of my life. Unfortunately, my brothers were always fond of encouraging this propensity, and I found in Taylor, my maid, a still greater tempter. I had not known there was any harm in it, until Miss Shore [a Calvinist governess], finding it out, lectured me severely, and told me it was wicked. From that time forth I considered that to invent a story of any kind

> was a sin. But the desire to do so was too deeply rooted in my affections to be resisted in my own strength [she was at that time nine years of age], and unfortunately I knew neither my corruption nor my weakness, nor did I know where to gain strength. The longing to invent stories grew with violence; everything I heard or read became food for my distemper. The simplicity of truth was not sufficient for me; I must needs embroider imagination upon it, and the folly, vanity and wickedness which disgraced my heart are more than I am able to express. Even now [at the age of twenty-nine], tho' watched, prayed and striven against, this is still the sin that most easily besets me. It has hindered my prayers and prevented my improvement, and therefore has humbled me very much.'

. . . My own state, however, was, I should think, almost unique among the children of cultivated parents. In consequence of the stern ordinance which I have prescribed, not a single fiction was read or told to me during my infancy. The rapture of the child who delays the process of going to bed by cajoling 'a story' out of his mother or his nurse, as he sits upon her knee, well tucked up, at the corner of the nursery fire, – this was unknown to me. Never, in all my early childhood, did any one address to me the affecting preamble 'Once upon a time!'. I was told about missionaries, but never about pirates, I was familiar with humming birds, but I had never heard of fairies. Jack the Giant-Killer, Rumpelstiltskin and Robin Hood were not of my acquaintance, and though I understood about wolves, Little Red Riding Hood was a stranger even by name. So far as my 'dedication' was concerned, I can but think that my parents were in error thus to exclude the imaginary from my outlook upon facts. They desired to make me truthful; the tendency was to make me positive and sceptical. Had they wrapped me in the soft folds of supernatural fancy, my mind might have been longer content to follow their traditions in an unquestioning spirit.

Baron Corvo

A. J. A. SYMONS

The bizarre life of Frederick Rolfe, the self-styled Baron Corvo, failed priest and painter, novelist, and liar, was the subject of A. J. A. Symons's biography, *The Quest for Corvo*. Rolfe had been dead – he died, destitute, in Venice – for over a decade by the time Symons embarked upon his 'quest', which was a work of some considerable detection given the attitude of Rolfe's family to what they considered to be the scandal of his homosexuality. Symons believed that Rolfe's rejection for the priesthood (it was decided by his superiors that he had no vocation) had a tremendous impact on his psychology, and its attendant fantasy life. 'This rejection must have been a tremendous blow to Rolfe. He knew very well his unfitness to pass unnoticed among ordinary men (since indeed he was not ordinary), and he had set his heart on the dignity and mystery of spiritual rank. What remained? Only one course, to deny the rightness of the verdict; to assert that it was the Athenians who had lost him, not he the Athenians; and this, the easiest way, he took. It was the first stage of the *paranoia* that darkened his life. On the fact of his un-ordinariness (which his subconsciousness could not ignore) he built up a phantasy picture of an abnormal Rolfe (abnormal since he had a priestly Vocation) thwarted unreasonably by those who should have known the truth.' It was in this mood, Symons explains, that he distilled the title or pseudonym of Baron Corvo. This extract, with its generous apology for Corvo's habitual mendacity, reveals a little of that precarious psychology, and how Rolfe managed to gain one benefactor by maligning others.

Rolfe had got through his first Venetian winter by a skilful manipulation of credit and excuses. It was a remarkable feat; but his credit had several buttresses. In the first place, Rolfe had paid handsomely while he could, and was positive that he would not be long without funds. In the second, landlords of hotels in seasonal places welcome regular residents; and since 'Mr Rolfe' had expressed his intention of remaining permanently, Signor Barbieri, proprietor of the Hotel Belle Vue et de Russie, had no wish to lose this customer, unless there was a good cause. Further, Rolfe received many letters from England, mostly written on thick or official paper, the more-hopeful-seeming of which he showed to the landlord, who saw this 'English' had friends who were concerned on his behalf. But what proved the most convincing demonstration to the Italian hotel-keeper of the truth of his queer guest's claim to have property in England, which would presently be profitable, was Mr Taylor's official letter (enclosing cheque in advance) offering, on behalf of Benson, Dawkins, and Pirie-Gordon, to make a regular payment in respect of Rolfe for three months. Rolfe's anger when he heard of the proposal was genuine and impressive; but the return of the money, on which he insisted, was more impressive still, and convinced Signor Barbieri that if he waited he would be paid.

. . . During the winter, while Signor Barbieri's tolerance persisted, Rolfe became an observed figure at the Hotel Belle Vue. Though he kept very much to himself, he was constantly to be seen armed with his vast fountain pen and oddly-shaped manuscript books . . .; he became, as at Holywell, a 'man of mystery' by his almost ostentatious reticence: and naturally, other English residents, in and out of the hotel, became curious concerning their reserved fellow-countryman. Not least among the curious was Canon Lonsdale Ragg, Anglican chaplain to the English colony.

The Canon was wintering with his wife in the Hotel Belle Vue, working on the final draft of a study in ecclesiastical history, *The Church of the Apostles*. Both Canon and Mrs Ragg were impressed and interested by the silent author (for such Rolfe was known to be) who for week after week seemed at pains to avoid their society. So marked a desire for privacy could only be broken by Rolfe himself; and one day he broke it. He left an exquisitely written note in the hall, asking in brief and formal phrases for an interview.

At the subsequent meeting, Rolfe gave reasons for his stand-offishness and his note. Both, he explained, were due to the difficulties in which he was plunged by the unscrupulous actions of his agent in England, and the perfidy of his friends. While his affairs were entangled he had preferred to make no new acquaintances; but they had now reached such a pass that he felt justified by desperation in approaching one who, though professing a different form of faith, was nevertheless a Christian and an Englishman, and (probably) able to distinguish his abysmal ignorance of business affairs, and advise concerning the best action to be taken. Like the Wedding-Guest, the Canon could not 'choose but hear'.

Rolfe then disclosed those circumstances of which the reader is aware, but set them in a very different light. His troubles began, in this account, when he lost his lawsuit against Col. Thomas. In order to meet the costs of that case, he told the interested Canon, he had been forced to pledge his present and future work in favour of his solicitor, who had undertaken to collect royalties earned by the various books so assigned, and make the author a modest allowance on which to live. Letters from Mr Taylor supporting these statements were produced. But now Mr Taylor, moved by his own cupidity and by the malevolent counsels of the Rev. Robert Hugh Benson and Mr Pirie-Gordon (who wished to force him to write books for them), had ceased to pay what he had promised, or to deliver any accounts showing the position. For months, Rolfe said, he had withstood this tyranny, refusing to return to England to act as 'ghost' so that others should get fame, determined to remain in Venice, where he felt well and able to do good work. To resist the coercion to which he was subjected he had pawned all that he could pawn, and overdrawn at the bank. Yet, notwithstanding, he had been unable, for some time, to pay his bill, and now he was threatened with ejection from the hotel. What should he do?

Canon Ragg, though flattered by this appeal to his business

sense, was (not surprisingly) at a loss for a ready answer. Rolfe, however, supplied his own. What was required, he pointed out, was a new agent who would extricate his affairs from the malfeasance of his present one, administer them as they should be administered, and make him that small allowance for lack of which he was now in need. The Canon agreed that such a solution would be excellent if it could be attained and promised to think the matter over.

How much of his distorted version of the facts did Rolfe believe? In a way, the whole. The psychology of *paranoia* is now well documented, if not well understood. It is in part an exaggeration of the normal human power to believe what is known to be untrue. Who is there who does not reject and conceal from himself certain disagreeable facts which, if accepted consciously, would unfavourably affect the course of life? The coward who performs acts of heroism rather than admit to himself the fact of cowardice is a well-worn example of the process at one end of the scale, as the thief who retains his own self-respect and sense of honesty is of the other. This ability to suppress what is undesirable for the mind to dwell upon is part of the basis of personality, and expresses itself in those unreasonable (but satisfactory) prejudices which we retain even after they have been logically disproved. Within limits it is a beneficent gift. But there are those in whom early circumstances or later misfortune unduly widen the limits within which this power can safely operate; and then arises a 'fixed idea' which, despite all evidence to the contrary, becomes the point from which reasoning proceeds. Whatever conflicts with this 'fixed idea' and the (perfectly logical) consequences which would necessarily follow, is flatly regarded by the sufferer as non-existent or untrue.

. . . Such conviction gave him force when relating his wrongs to his new benefactor. For Canon Ragg became his benefactor. Whatever doubts he may have had of some details of Rolfe's story, he accepted it as substantially true. He was so far convinced, indeed, that he took the venturesome step of assuring the hotel-keeper of his confidence in Rolfe's bona-fides; and so the impending eviction was postponed.

Behind every great man stands a perjured wife

EARL LLOYD-GEORGE

While Chancellor of the Exchequer, David Lloyd-George was accused – correctly – of having an affair with a married woman. Having decided to sue, and to swear on oath that it was not true, he then persuaded his wife similarly to perjure herself. Lloyd-George's eldest son, the 2nd Earl Lloyd-George, relates how his father went about this sensitive mission.

Father knew that, win or lose, his career was greatly endangered. He had an unerring instinct about the public temper. 'You must stand by me, Maggie. Otherwise it's all over with me.' My father was forty-six, holding a post second in importance only to that of the Prime Minister. He knew that he would be attacked mercilessly if my mother expressed open doubt as to his innocence, if it were shown that she did not support him in his rejection of the accusation. There was great danger even if she remained uncommitted to his cause. I know that my mother, a deeply religious woman, was in torment in giving support to the lie to be sworn on oath. As a woman, she had been mortally hurt by his infidelities. As a wife, she had been gravely wronged. I know exactly the extent of her conflict.

'You must help me, Maggie. If I get over this, I give my oath you shall never have to suffer this ordeal again.' 'You will go into the witness box?' 'Yes.' 'And you will give your oath that this story is untrue?' 'I have to.' 'And you give *me* your oath that I shall not have to suffer this sort of thing again. How can I rely on your "oath"?' 'I can make it true. Maggie, I put my life in jeopardy for my beliefs. One day I shall be Prime Minister. I shall be a force for the public good. If you help me, you shall never regret your decision.'

My mother told me about the conversations she had with

father at this time. (She was never to forget them.) She did not want him to plead with her to save his career 'for the public good'. She did not care about that; she wanted simply to help him because he was hurt and frightened and in grave trouble. She could not deny him help then.

On 12 March 1909 the Chancellor of the Exchequer drove to the Law Courts in the Strand . . . There were rumours that Mrs Lloyd-George was leaving her husband, that papers had been submitted to solicitors. Her carriage, packed with trunks, had been seen bound for the station where she was to take the train to Criccieth. Others believed that she was at home, but estranged from her husband and waiting the outcome of the case before filing a suit against him. Mr Lloyd-George alighted from his car, and it was then seen that his wife had accompanied him. Together they entered the courtroom. Throughout the hearing she sat at his side.

He was called into the witness box. 'Have you read the allegations made in the *People*?' his counsel asked him. 'Yes.' 'Are they true in substance or in fact?' 'The paragraphs are an absolute invention,' he said firmly, 'every line of them.' Cross examination? None. Carson, for the defence, offered 'a sincere and frank apology' for the allegations, saying that they were without foundation or justification. The case was over, and damages for the plaintiff were put at £1,000, a modest sum indeed for an 'unfounded and unjustified' attack on the reputation of the Chancellor of the Exchequer. But father was glad to settle the matter without further parley. This money too went to a local Welsh cause. Even my father's worst enemies were silenced by mother's presence at his side during the hearing, and the anticipated aftermath of privileged sniping in the Commons did not take place; nor did anyone refer to the meagre estimate of damages awarded to the Chancellor. The general feeling was that, innocent or not, if Maggie stood by him, that was good enough. The chapter was closed.

•

The hidden life of Sir Edmund Backhouse

HUGH TREVOR-ROPER

Sir Edmund Backhouse, self-styled 'marquis Pa k'o-ssu' in the Manchu peerage, was one of the century's greatest liars and forgers, and not dissimilar to that other great liar, Baron Corvo, whom we have already met. He was, writes Sir Hugh Trevor-Roper, 'the spendthrift aesthete of the 1890s who became the sinologue and recluse of the next century, the spiritual fascist of the Second World War; the brilliant linguist who used his gifts to diddle successive patrons; the enchanter whose spells softened the hard heads of businessmen and diplomats . . . the secret war-time agent who led his own government on a ludicrous wild-goose chase; the scholar who created a "masterpiece" of historical writing and produced a masterpiece of forgery . . .' Here Trevor-Roper examines the mendacity of Backhouse's memoirs, and in particular his claim to have known the French poet, Paul Verlaine.

Like many men whose life excites conventional disapproval, Backhouse ascribed his eccentricity to a misunderstood childhood. His early years, he wrote, had been 'ideally unhappy'. He detested both his mother and his father, and used the most violent language about both of them. Indeed, he twice describes the scene of his mother's funeral, in October 1902, when (he tells us) he stood at the graveside and, much to the surprise of his widowed father, cursed her 'detestable memory' in 'ten different tongues'. He was then thirty years old and, according to his own account, had not seen his mother for eight years; but time and absence had not abated his detestation, his need to avenge the sufferings of the past. Nor was he any happier at school than at home; for St George's, Ascot, the school to which he had been sent at the age of nine, was, he tells us, merely another scene of torture. It was 'a nursery of stereotyped intellects', and the boys which it turned out were 'prigs and snobs': only the companionship of Winston Churchill, Maurice Baring and some others made life bearable. The headmaster, Herbert Sneyd-Kynnersley, was 'a sadistic tyrant of colossal self-adulation, who loved to flog his pupils' and who, he suggests, had homosexual relations with some of them. However, after four years, the horrors of school life at Ascot were suddenly compensated, says Backhouse, by the arrival of a new teacher to whom he became devoted and who was to be the greatest influence in his life, redeeming it from insularity and philistinism. This new master, who arrived in February 1886 and stayed till July of the same year, teaching French, was none other than the poet Paul Verlaine.

Verlaine, according to Backhouse, stayed at St George's, Ascot, for six months teaching French . . . On Verlaine's arrival at St George's, Backhouse (he tells us) at once became his favoured friend and protégé. With the consent of his parents (which seems surprising), he accompanied Verlaine to Paris in the Easter holidays, and thus found his way, at an early age, into French literary circles. Through Verlaine, then or on later visits, he became familiar with most of the French writers of the time, and the Ganymede of some of them. He mentions Mallarmé, Barrès, Villiers de l'Isle Adam, Pierre Loti, Pierre Louys, J. K. Huysmans. In the first draft of *The Dead Past* he also mentioned Rimbaud, but when Hoeppli pointed out an insuperable chronological difficulty, he deftly changed the poet into a cobbler called Rimbot whose name had occasioned a temporary and pardonable confusion.

. . . Backhouse's pretended relations with Verlaine are central to his whole romance about his early life and literary friendships, and he took great trouble to ensure that his account of them was irrefutable by the factual knowledge available at the time. Unfortunately, in this case his ingenuity was in vain. Later research has filled gaps in our knowledge of Verlaine's life, and consequently Backhouse's story dissolves, dragging down with it the whole elaborate edifice of the literary part of the memoirs and, by a logical consequence, everything else too. . . . When Backhouse wrote about his relations with Verlaine, he had beside him – it is clear because he quotes page-references – the biography of Verlaine by his friend Edmond Lepelletier. Now Lepelletier leaves a blank in Verlaine's life between 10 February 1886, when he wrote from Paris after the death of his mother, and July 1886 when he entered the Teno hospital in Paris. Backhouse knew that Verlaine had, on several earlier occasions, taught French briefly at English private schools, and he knew that, on one of these occasions, he had been accompanied by his young protégé Lucien Letinois. What Backhouse has done is to fill in this convenient blank period, bringing Verlaine to another English school – his own – between those dates, and substituting himself for Letinois. The operation has been artfully carried out, known dates are respected, contemporary events worked in, predictable inconsistencies avoided. His story would be technically irrefutable if that blank period had not since been filled in from authentic sources which show that Verlaine was in Paris during the whole time.

•

Piltdown man

CHARLES DAWSON

The 'discovery' of Piltdown Man by Arthur Smith Woodward and Charles Dawson ranks as one of the most audacious scientific frauds of all time. Here at last, it was believed, was incontrovertible proof of man's ape-like ancestry, and a confirmation of evolutionary theory. What seems certain, however, is that the fragment of skull which Dawson found in his quarry had been planted, most probably by Dawson himself. The piece of skull had been the subject of gypsum staining, which gave the appearance of fossilization. But as with all great lies – which this one truly was – the reason for the swift acceptance by the scientific establishment was simple: scientists wanted to believe it. Piltdown Man fitted in with existing preconceptions about human evolution. Nevertheless, the skull was guarded from scientific scrutiny for several decades, and was only proved to be fake in 1955. An excerpt from Dawson's own lying paper, entitled 'On the Discovery of a Palaeolithic Human Skull and Mandible in a Flint-Bearing Gravel overlying the Wealden (Hastings Beds) at Piltdown, Fletching, Sussex', is printed here.

Several years ago I was walking along a farm-road close to Piltdown Common, Fletching (Sussex), when I noticed that the road had been mended with some peculiar brown flints not usual in the district. On inquiry I was astonished to learn that they were dug from a gravel-bed on the farm, and shortly afterwards I visited the place, where two labourers were at work digging the gravel for small repairs to the roads. As this excavation was situated about four miles north of the limit where the occurrence of flints overlying the Wealden strata is recorded, I was much interested, and made a close examination of the bed. I asked the workmen if they had found bones or other fossils there. As they did not appear to have noticed anything of the sort, I urged them to preserve anything that they might find. Upon one of my subsequent visits to the pit, one of the men handed to me a small portion of unusually thick human parietal bone. I immediately made a search, but could find nothing more, nor had the men noticed anything else. The bed is full of tabular pieces of ironstone closely resembling this piece of skull in colour and thickness; and, although I made many subsequent searches, I could not hear of any further find nor discover anything – in fact, the bed seemed to be quite unfossiliferous.

It was not until some years later, in the autumn of 1911, on a visit to the spot, that I picked up, among the rain-washed spoil heaps of the gravel pit, another and larger piece belonging to the frontal region of the same skull, including a portion of the left superciliary ridge. As I had examined a cast of the Heidelberg jaw, it occurred to me that the proportions of this skull were similar to those of that specimen. I accordingly took it to Dr A.

Smith Woodward at the British Museum (Natural History) for comparison and determination. He was immediately impressed with the importance of the discovery, and we decided to employ labour and to make a systematic search among the spoil heaps and gravel, as soon as the floods had abated; for the gravel pit is more or less under water during five or six months of the year. We accordingly gave up as much time as we could spare since last spring (1912), and completely turned over and sifted what spoil-material remained; we also dug up and sifted such portions of the gravel as had been left undisturbed by the workmen.

. . . From these facts it appears probable that the skull and mandible cannot safely be described as being of earlier date than the first half of the Pleistocene Epoch. The individual probably lived during a warm cycle in that age.

•

Infantile mental life: two lies told by children

SIGMUND FREUD

It is comprehensible that children should tell lies when in doing so they mimic the lies of grown-up people. But a number of the lies of well-brought-up children have a peculiar significance, and should cause their instructors to reflect rather than to be angry. These lies proceed from the influence of an excessive love motive, and become momentous if they lead to a misunderstanding between the child and the person whom it loves.

I

A girl of seven (in her second year at school) had asked her father for money to buy colours for painting Easter eggs. The father had refused, saying he had no money. Shortly afterwards the girl again asked for some money for a contribution towards a wreath for the funeral of the late reigning princess. Each of the school-children was to bring fifty pfennigs. The father gave her ten marks; she paid her contribution, put nine marks on her father's writing table, and with the remaining fifty pfennigs bought paints, which she hid in her toy-cupboard.

At dinner the father asked suspiciously what she had done with the missing pfennigs, and whether she had not bought the colours with them. She denied it; but her brother, who was two years older, and together with whom she had planned to paint the eggs, betrayed her; the colours were found in the cupboard. The father, very angry, handed the culprit over to her mother for punishment, which was severely administered. Afterwards the mother herself was overwhelmed when she saw the child's extreme despair. She caressed the little girl after punishing her, and took her for a walk to console her. But the effects of this experience, described by the patient herself as the 'turning-point' of her life, proved to be immitigable. She had hitherto been a wild, self-confident child; thenceforth she became timid and vacillating. During her engagement she flew into a rage that was incomprehensible even to herself, when her mother was buying furniture and trousseau-garments for her. She had the feeling that after all it was *her* money, and no one else ought to buy anything with it. As a young wife she was shy of asking her husband for any expenditure for her personal needs, and made an unnecessary distinction between 'her' money and his. During the course of her treatment it happened now and again that her husband's remittances to her were delayed, so that she was resourceless in the foreign city. After she had once told me this, I made her promise that if it happened again she would borrow the small necessary sum from me. She gave the promise, but on the next occasion of embarrassment she did not keep it and preferred to pawn her jewellery. She explained that she could not take money from me.

The appropriation of the fifty pfennigs in her childhood had a significance which the father could not divine. Some time before she began going to school, she had played a singular little prank with money. A neighbour with whom she was friendly had sent the girl with a small sum of money, as companion for her own still younger little boy, to make some purchase in a shop. As the elder of the two, she was bringing the change from the purchase back to the house. But when she met the neighbour's servant-maid in the street, she flung the money down on the pavement. In the analysis of this action, even to herself inexplicable, the thought of Judas occurred to her, when he flung away the silver pieces gained by him through the betrayal of his Master. She declared that she was certainly acquainted with the story of the Passion before she went to school. But in what manner could she have identified herself with Judas?

At the age of three and a half she had a nursemaid of whom she was extremely fond. This girl had a love-affair with a doctor, and visited his surgery with the child. It appears that the child was the witness of various sexual proceedings. Whether she saw the doctor give money to the nursemaid or not is not certainly established; there is, however, no doubt that the girl gave the child little presents of money to ensure her silence, and that purchases (probably sweets) were made with these on the way home. It is possible, too, that the doctor himself occasionally gave money to the child. Nevertheless, the child betrayed the girl to her mother out of jealousy. She played so ostentatiously with the pfennigs she had brought home that her mother could not but ask: 'Where did you get that money?' The maid was dismissed.

To take money from anyone had thus early come to mean for her the yielding of the body, the erotic relation. To take money from her father was equivalent to a declaration of love. The phantasy that her father was her lover was so seductive that the childish desire for colours for the Easter eggs was easily, by its aid, indulged in in spite of the prohibition. But she could not confess to the appropriation of the money; she was obliged to disavow it, because the motive of the deed, unknown to herself, could not be confessed. The father's chastisement was thus a refusal of the tenderness offered him, a humiliation, and so it broke her spirit. During the treatment a period of severe depression ensued, the explanation of which led to her remembering the events described, when I was once obliged to copy that humiliation by asking her not to bring me any more flowers.

It will scarcely be necessary, for the psycho-analyst, to insist upon the fact that in this child's little experience we are confronted with one of those extremely common cases of persistence of early anal erotism in the later erotic life. Even the desire to paint the eggs with colours derives from the same source.

II

A woman, now very ill as the consequence of a disappointment in life, was in earlier years a particularly healthy, truth-loving, earnest and admirable girl, and became a tender-natured woman. But still earlier, in the first years of her life, she had been a wilful and discontented child, and though she developed fairly early into an excessively good and conscientious one, there were occurrences in her schooldays which, when she fell ill, caused her deep remorse and were regarded by her as proofs of fundamental depravity. Memory told her that she had frequently in those days bragged and lied. Once, on the way home, a schoolfellow boasted: 'Yesterday we had ice at dinner.' She answered: 'Oh, we have ice every day.' In reality she did not know what ice at dinner could mean; she knew ice only in the long blocks in which it is carted about, but she perceived that there was something grand in having it for dinner, and so she would not be excelled by her schoolfellow.

When she was ten years old they were given in their drawing lessons the task of drawing a circle in free-hand. But she made use of the compasses, thus easily producing a perfect circle, and showed her achievement triumphantly to her neighbour in class. The teacher came up, heard her boasting, discovered the marks of the compasses in the delineation of the circle, and took the girl to task. But she stubbornly denied it, would not be abashed by any proofs, and took refuge in stubborn silence. The teacher conferred with her father; both were influenced by the girl's usual good behaviour to decide against any further notice of the occurrence.

This child's two lies were instigated by the same complex. As the eldest of five children, the little girl early manifested an unusually strong attachment to her father, which was destined in later years to wreck her happiness in life. But she could not long escape the discovery that her beloved father was not so great a personage as she was inclined to think him. He had to struggle against money-difficulties; he was not so powerful nor so distinguished as she had imagined. This departure from her ideal she could not put up with. Since, as women do, she based all her ambition upon the beloved man, it became a dominating idea with her that she must support her father against the world. So she boasted to her schoolfellows, in order not to have to belittle her father. When, later on, she learnt to translate ice for dinner by 'glace', the path lay open for her remorse about this reminiscence to take its course as a dread of pieces or splinters of glass.

The father was an excellent draughtsman, and had often enough called forth the delight and wonderment of the children by exhibitions of his skill. In her identification of herself with her father, she had in school drawn that circle which she could produce successfully only by underhand means. It was as though she wanted to boast: 'Look here – see what my father can do!' The consciousness of guilt that hung around her excessive fondness for her father found its outlet in the attempted deception; a confession was impossible for the same reason that was given in the earlier observation – it could not but have been the confession of the hidden incestuous love.

We should not think lightly of such episodes in child-life. It would be a grave misconception to read into such childish errors the prognosis of a developing immoral character. Nevertheless, they are intimately connected with the most powerful motivations of the childish soul, and are prophetic of tendencies which will take shape either in the later destiny or in a future neurosis.

•

German atrocities

THE BRYCE REPORT

During the First World War there were many reports of German atrocities in Belgium and France, and in order to establish the truth or falsehood of these rumours the British Government set up an investigating committee under the chairmanship of Lord Bryce. The report, issued in 1915, elicited a powerful response in British and American newspapers. In fact it was largely invented: there was no real evidence for the majority of the gruesome stories appearing in the report; and certainly, no attempt was made to evaluate even what little evidence there was. The Bryce Report is nothing more than a piece of official propaganda pretending to be a legal investigation. Not surprisingly, the historian H. C. Peterson has called the Bryce Report 'one of the worst atrocities of the war'.

The Treatment of Women and Children

The evidence shows that the German authorities, when carrying out a policy of systematic arson and plunder in selected districts, usually drew some distinction between the adult male population on the one hand and the women and children on the other. It was a frequent practice to set apart the adult males of the condemned district with a view to the execution of a suitable number – preferably of the younger and more vigorous – and to reserve the women and children for milder treatment. The depositions, however, present many instances of calculated cruelty, often going the length of murder, towards the women and children of the condemned area.

. . . Apart from the crimes committed in special areas and belonging to a scheme of systematic reprisals for the alleged shooting by civilians, there is evidence of offences committed against women and children by individual soldiers, or by small groups of soldiers, both in the advance through Belgium and France as in the retreat from the Marne. Indeed, the discipline appears to have been loose during the retreat, and there is evidence as to the burning of villages, and the murder and violation of their female inhabitants during this episode of the war.

In this tale of horrors hideous forms of mutilation occur with some frequency in the depositions, two of which may be connected in some instances with a perverted form of sexual instinct.

A third form of mutilation, the cutting of one or both hands, is frequently said to have taken place. In some instances where this form of mutilation is said to have occurred it may be the consequence of a cavalry charge up a village street, hacking and slashing at everything in the way; in others a victim may possibly have held a weapon, in others the motive may have been the theft of rings.

We find many well-established cases of the slaughter (often accompanied by mutilation) of whole families, including not infrequently that of quite small children. In two cases it seems to be clear that preparations were made to burn a family alive. These crimes were committed over a period of many weeks and simultaneously in many places, and the authorities must have known or ought to have known that cruelties of this character were being perpetrated, nor can anyone doubt that they could have been stopped by swift and decisive action on the part of the heads of the German army.

. . . The cases of violation, sometimes under threat of death, are numerous and clearly proved. We refer here to comparatively few out of the many that have been placed in the Appendix, because the circumstances are in most instances much the same. They are often accompanied with cruelty, and the slaughter of women after violation is more than once credibly attested . . .

23rd August I went with two friends (names given) to see what we could see. About three hours out of Malines we were taken prisoner by a German patrol – an officer and six men – and marched off into a little wood of saplings, where there was a house. The officer spoke Flemish. He knocked at the door; the peasant did not come. The officer ordered the soldiers to break down the door, which two of them did. The peasant came and asked what they were doing. The officer said he did not come quickly enough, and that they had 'trained up' plenty of others. His hands were tied behind his back, and he was shot at once without a moment's delay. The wife came out with a suckling child. She put the child down and sprang at the Germans like a lioness. She clawed their faces. One of the Germans took a rifle and struck her a tremendous blow with the butt on the head. Another took his bayonet and fixed it and thrust it through the child. He then put his rifle on his shoulder with the child up it, its little arms stretched out once or twice. The officers ordered the houses to be set on fire, and straw was obtained, and it was done. The man and his wife and his child were thrown on top of the straw. There were about forty other peasants there also, and the officer said: 'I am doing this as a lesson and example to you. When a German tells you to do something next time you must move more quickly.' The regiment of Germans was a regiment of Hussars, with cross-bones and a death's head on the cap.

Can anyone think that such acts as these, committed by women in the circumstances created by the invasion of Belgium, were deserving of the extreme form of vengeance attested by these and other depositions?

In considering the question of provocation it is pertinent to take into account the numerous cases in which old women and very small children have been shot, bayoneted, and even mutilated. Whatever excuse may be offered by the Germans for the killing of grown-up women, there can be no possible defence for the murder of children, and if it can be shown that infants and small children were not infrequently bayoneted and shot it is a fair inference that many of the offences against women require no explanation more recondite than the unbridled violence of brutal or drunken criminals.

It is clearly shown that many offences were committed against infants and quite young children. On one occasion children were even roped together and used as a military screen against the enemy, on another three soldiers went into action carrying small children to protect themselves from flank fire.

... The number and character of these murders constitute the most distressing feature connected with the conduct of the war so far as it is revealed in the depositions submitted to the Committee.

•

Lloyd George's bluff

FRANCES STEVENSON

Frances Stevenson was for many years Lloyd George's mistress – many years after Wales's greatest liar had, as we have already seen (page 283), given Mrs Lloyd George his word that 'you shall never have to suffer this ordeal again'. Stevenson kept a diary, and it is here that we find yet another example of the mendacity of David Lloyd George.

21 November 1916 D. had a great row in the Cabinet with McKenna today. The question of Sir W. Robertson going to Russia was discussed. D. said that he left the decision in the hands of the Cabinet, that he did not wish to press for it, but that what he objected to was the impression that one of his colleagues in the Cabinet was trying to give Sir W. Robertson, that D. was urging the proposal in order to get rid of Robertson. Immediately all the others demanded to know the name of the person he was alluding to. D. demurred and said that he would prefer to disclose it to the PM alone. But the others would not have it: several of them, they said, had been in Robertson's company, & it was only fair to them that they should be absolved from the accusation. 'Very well,' said D., 'then I will tell you. It is the Chancellor of the Exchequer!' Of course McKenna denied it flatly, but D. insisted, saying 'One of two people then is lying, and I think I know which to believe.' Eventually D. wrung it out of him in the end that 'perhaps he had not denied the suggestion that Robertson was being sent because D. wanted him out of the way'. That was enough for the others. The prestige of McKenna is now lower than it was before. D. literally hates him, & I do not think he will rest until he has utterly broken him. I said to D.: 'Who was it who actually told you that McKenna had said this to Robertson?' 'No one,' he said, 'but I guessed that he had said it.' 'Then whom did you mean when you said that one of two people was lying? Who was the second person?' 'That was pure bluff,' said D. laughing, 'but I was right, and that was how I got it out of him.'

•

How I killed Rasputin

PRINCE YOUSSOPOV

Rasputin was the *éminence grise* of the last of the Tsars. His baneful influence brought him many enemies, among them Prince Felix Youssopov, who murdered Rasputin in December 1916 and later wrote a book about it. There is no doubt that Rasputin was murdered by Youssopov and other army officers, but the details of the murder, as recounted by him, are so fantastic as to warrant inclusion here. According to Youssopov, he prepared some poisoned cakes and wine, which Rasputin consumed, but which did not kill him. The conspirators were then obliged to shoot him. Rasputin's daughter Maria has said that her father had a horror of sweet things, and that he would not have eaten the cakes. As for the wine, she believes that the cyanide crystals simply had not dissolved. The later details of Rasputin's assassination, she suggests, were lies added 'partly to make the story more picturesque and partly to excuse the slaughter; for since it was a question of doing away with a being whose devilish vitality resisted cyanide, it would be understandable that the five conspirators, in their terror, should riddle him with bullets'. But even then Rasputin did not die . . .

Rasputin lay motionless, but on touching him I discovered that he was still warm.

I felt his pulse. There was no beat.

From his wounds drops of blood trickled, and fell on the granite floor.

It was an awe-inspiring and revolting sight.

I cannot explain why, but I suddenly seized him by both arms and violently shook him. The body rose, leant sideways, and fell back into its former position, the head hanging lifelessly to one side.

I stood over him for a little time longer, and was on the point of going away when my attention was arrested by a slight trembling of his left eyelid . . . I bent down over him, and attentively examined his face . . . It began to twitch convulsively. The movements became more and more pronounced. Suddenly the left eye half-opened . . . An instant later the right lid trembled and lifted . . . And both eyes . . . eyes of Rasputin – fixed themselves upon me with an expression of devilish hatred.

My blood froze in speechless horror. I was petrified . . . I wanted to run, to call for help; but my feet would not move, and no sound came from me.

I stood riveted to the floor as if in a nightmare.

Then the incredible happened . . . With a violent movement Rasputin jumped to his feet. I was horror-stricken. The room resounded with a wild roar. His fingers, convulsively knotted, flashed through the air . . . Like red-hot iron they grasped my shoulder and tried to grip me by the throat. His eyes were crossed, and obtruded terribly; he was foaming at the mouth.

And in a hoarse whisper he constantly repeated my name.

I cannot convey in words the fear which possessed me.

I tried to tear myself away, but his iron clutch held me with incredible strength. A terrible struggle ensued.

This dying, poisoned, and shot-ridden creature, raised by the powers of darkness to avenge his destruction, inspired me with a feeling so terrifying, so ghastly, that the memory of it haunts me to this day.

At that moment I understood and felt in the fullest degree the real power of Rasputin. It seemed that the devil himself, incarnate in this muzhik, was holding me in vice-like fingers, never to let me go.

But with a supreme effort I tore myself free.

Rasputin groaned, and fell backwards, still gripping my epaulet which he had torn off in the struggle. I looked at him; he lay all huddled and motionless.

But again he stirred.

I rushed upstairs, calling on Purishkevich, who was in my study, to come to my aid.

'Quick! quick! the revolver! He is still alive!' I shouted.

I myself was unarmed. I had given my revolver to the Grand Duke Dmitri Pavlovich. At the door of my study I met Purishkevich, who had heard my desperate call for assistance. He was amazed to learn that Rasputin was still alive, and hurriedly took out his revolver from its holster. At that moment I heard sounds behind me. I realized that it was Rasputin, and in an instant I found myself in my study. Here on the writing-table I had left the loaded-stick, which Maklakov had given me 'in case I might ever want it'. I seized it and rushed out.

Rasputin, on all-fours, was rapidly making his way up the staircase, bellowing and snorting like a wounded animal.

Suddenly he gathered himself up and made a final leap towards the wicket door leading to the courtyard.

In the full certainty that the door was locked, and that the key was in the possession of those who had left us, I stood on the staircase landing, firmly grasping the loaded-stick.

But to my horror and surprise, the wicket door opened, and Rasputin vanished through it into the darkness.

Purishkevich immediately rushed after him. Two shots rang out, resounding all over the yard.

I was beside myself with the idea that he might escape us. I rushed to the main entrance and ran along the Moika quayside, towards the courtyard, hoping, in case Purishkevich had missed him, to stop Rasputin at the gates.

There were three entrances to the courtyard and only the centre gates were locked. Through the railing I saw that it was just to those gates that Rasputin, led by instinct, was heading.

A third shot rang out, and a fourth . . .

Rasputin stumbled and fell near a snow-heap. Purishkevich ran up to him, stood still for a few seconds, and evidently having decided that everything was now over, and that Rasputin was killed, with rapid steps turned back to the house. I called out to him, but he did not hear me.

After looking round and finding that the streets were empty and that the shots had not attracted attention, I entered the courtyard and went up to the snow-mound where Rasputin was lying.

He showed no signs of life.

•

The German corpse factory

THE TIMES

This, the most popular atrocity story of the First World War, was invented by a Brigadier-General seeking to influence Chinese public opinion against Germany. In the House of Commons on 2 December 1925, the story was finally admitted to have been a complete lie.

> We pass through Everynicourt. There is a dull smell in the air, as if lime were being burnt. We are passing the great Corpse Exploitation Establishment (*Kadaververwertungsanstalt*) of this Army Group. The fat that is won here is turned into lubricating oils, and everything else is ground down in the bones mill into a powder, which is used for mixing with pigs' food and as manure.

In our column 'Through German Eyes' yesterday we published the above callous description of a German 'Corpse Exploitation Establishment' situated behind the enemy's lines north of Reims. This description was furnished by Herr Karl Rosner, special correspondent of the Berlin *Lokalanzeiger* on the Western front.

This statement corroborates a striking account of this new and horrible German industry which appeared in the *Indépendance Belge* for April 10, as extracted from *La Belgique*, of Leyden in Holland.

This version, omitting some of the most repulsive details, is as follows:

> We have known for long that the Germans stripped their dead behind the firing line, fastened them into bundles of three or four bodies with iron wire, and then dispatched these grisly bundles to the rear. Until recently the trains laden with the dead were sent to Seraing, near Liège, and a point north of Brussels, where were refuse consumers. Much surprise was caused by the fact that of late this traffic has proceeded in the direction of Gerolstein and it was noted that on each wagon was written 'D.A.V.G.'.
>
> German science is responsible for the ghoulish idea of the formation of the German Offal Utilization Company (Limited) ('D.A.V.G.' or 'Deutsche Abfall-Verwertungs Gesellschaft'), a dividend-earning company with a capital of £250,000, the chief factory of which has been constructed 1,000 yards from the railway connecting St Vith, near the Belgian frontier, with Gerolstein, in the lonely, little-frequented Eifel district, south-west of Coblentz. This factory deals specially with the dead from the Western front. If the results are as good as the company hopes, another will be established to deal with corpses on the Eastern front.
>
> The factory is invisible from the railway. It is placed deep in forest country, with a specially thick growth of trees about it. Live wires surround it. A special double track leads to it. The works are about 700 ft. long and 110 ft. broad, and the railway runs completely round them. In the

north-west corner of the works the discharge of the trains takes place.

The trains arrive full of bare bodies, which are unloaded by the workers who live at the works. The men wear oilskin overalls and masks with mica eye-pieces. They are equipped with long hooked poles, and push the bundles of bodies to an endless chain, which picks them with big hooks, attached at intervals of 2 ft. The bodies are transported on this endless chain into a long, narrow compartment, where they pass through a bath which disinfects them. They then go through a drying chamber, and finally are automatically carried into a digester or great cauldron, in which they are dropped by an apparatus which detaches them from the chain. In the digester they remain for six to eight hours, and are treated by steam, which breaks them up while they are slowly stirred by machinery.

From this treatment result several products. The fats are broken up into stearine, a form of tallow, and oils, which require to be redistilled before they can be used. The process of distillation is carried out by boiling the oil with carbonate of soda, and some of the by-products resulting from this are used by German soapmakers. The oil distillery and refinery lie in the south-eastern corner of the works. The refined oil is sent out in small casks like those used for petroleum, and is of a yellowish brown colour.

The fumes are exhausted from the buildings by a great pipe to the north-eastern corner, where they are condensed and the refuse resulting is discharged into a sewer. There is no high chimney, as the boiler furnaces are supplied with air by electric fans.

There is a laboratory and in charge of the works is a chief chemist with two assistants and seventy-three men. All the employees are soldiers and are attached to the 8th Army Corps. There is a sanatorium by the works, and under no pretext is any man permitted to leave them. They are guarded as prisoners at their appalling work.

It will be remembered that one of the American Consuls, on leaving Germany in February, stated in Switzerland that the Germans were distilling glycerine for nitro-glycerine from the bodies of their dead, and thus were obtaining some part of their explosives.

•

The Boche

RUDYARD KIPLING

Many writers undertook propaganda work for the British Government during the First World War, including G. K. Chesterton, Arnold Bennett, Hilaire Belloc, John Galsworthy, Ford Madox Hueffer, Sir Arthur Conan Doyle and John Buchan. This piece of nonsense came from the pen of Rudyard Kipling.

A shell must fall somewhere, and by the law of averages occasionally lights straight as a homing pigeon on the one spot where it can wreck most. The earth opens for yards around, and men must be dug out – some merely breathless, who shake their ears, swear, and carry on, and others whose souls have gone loose among the terrors. These have to be dealt with as their psychology demands, and the French officer is a good psychologist. One of them said: 'Our national psychology has changed. I do not recognize it myself.'

'What made the change?'

'The Boche. If he had been quiet for another twenty years the world might have been his – rotten, but all his. Now he is saving the world.'

'How?'

'Because he has shown us what Evil is. We – you and I, England and the rest – had begun to doubt the existence of Evil. The Boche is saving us.'

. . . And in the meantime, Rheims goes about what business it may have with that iron nerve and endurance and faith which is the new inheritance of France. There is agony enough when the big shells come in; there is pain and terror among the people; and always fresh desecration to watch and suffer. The old men and the women and the children drink of that cup daily, and yet the bitterness does not enter their souls. Mere words of admiration are impertinent, but the exquisite quality of the French soul has been the marvel to me throughout. They say themselves, when they talk, 'We did not know what our nation was. Frankly, we did not expect it ourselves. But the thing came, and – you see, we go on.'

Or as a woman put it more logically, 'What else can we do? Remember, *we* knew the Boche in '70 when *you* did not. We know what he has done in the last year. This is not war. It is against wild beasts that we fight. There is no arrangement possible with wild beasts.' This is the one vital point which we in England *must* realize. We are dealing with animals who have scientifically and philosophically removed themselves inconceivably outside civilization. When you have heard a few – only a few – tales of their doings, you begin to understand a little. When you have seen Rheims, you understand a little more. When you have looked long enough at the faces of the women, you are inclined to think that the women will have a large say in the final judgement. They have earned it a thousand times.

. . . The great building must once have been a monastery. Twilight softened its gaunt wings, in an angle of which were collected fifty prisoners, picked up among the hills behind the mists.

They stood in some sort of military formation preparatory to being marched off. They were dressed in khaki, the colour of gassed grass, that might have belonged to any army. Two wore spectacles, and I counted eight faces of the fifty which were asymmetrical – out of drawing on one side.

'Some of their later drafts give us that type,' said the Interpreter. One of them had been wounded in the head and roughly bandaged. The others seemed all sound. Most of them looked at nothing, but several were vividly alive with terror that cannot keep the eyelids still, and a few wavered on the grey edge of collapse.

They were the breed which, at the word of command, had stolen out to drown women and children; had raped women in the streets at the word of command; and, always at the word of command, had sprayed petrol, or squirted flame; or voided their excrements on the property and persons of their captives. They stood there outside all humanity. Yet they were made in the likeness of humanity. One realized it with a shock when the bandaged creature began to shiver, and they shuffled off in response to the orders of civilized men.

•

The rape at Deraa

T. E. LAWRENCE

The incident at Deraa is one of the most important myths in the legend of Lawrence of Arabia, and for this extraordinary story Lawrence's own account, in his *Seven Pillars of Wisdom* (1926), remains the only source. But the story is both incoherent and at odds with the facts regarding the Bey of Deraa, as established by the Arab historian Suleiman Mousa, by Phillip Knightly and Colin Simpson in their book *The Secret Lives of Lawrence of Arabia*, and by Desmond Stewart in his biography of Lawrence. Given Lawrence's sado-masochistic predilections, the story is little more than sexual fantasy: to this extent it is a valuable insight into the character of Lawrence, but as an historical event it is sheer fabrication.

Properly to round off this spying of the hollow land of Hauran, it was necessary to visit Deraa, its chief town. We could cut it off on north and west and south, by destroying the three railways; but it would be more tidy to rush the junction first and work outwards. Tala, however, could not venture in with me since he was too well known in the place. So we parted with him with many thanks on both sides, and rode southward along the line until near Deraa. There we dismounted.

. . . At the corner of the aerodrome by the south end of the station we struck over towards the town. There were old Albatross machines in the sheds, and men lounging about. One of these, a Syrian soldier, began to question us about our villages, and if there was much 'government' where we lived. He was probably an intending deserter, fishing for a refuge. We shook him off at last and turned away. Someone called out in Turkish. We walked on deafly; but a sergeant came after, and took me roughly by the arm, saying 'The Bey wants you.' There were too many witnesses for fight or flight, so I went readily. He took no notice of Faris.

I was marched through the tall fence into a compound set about with many huts and a few buildings. We passed to a mud room, outside which was an earth platform, whereon sat a fleshy Turkish officer, one leg tucked under him. He hardly glanced at me when the sergeant brought me up and made a long report in Turkish. He asked my name: I told him Ahmed ibn Bagr, a Circassian from Kuneitra. 'A deserter?' 'But we Circassians have no military service.' He turned, stared at me, and said very slowly 'You are a liar. Enrol him in your section, Hassan Chowish, and do what is necessary till the Bey sends for him.'

They led me on into a guard-room, mostly taken up by large wooden cribs, on which lay or sat a dozen men in untidy uniforms. They took away my belt, and my knife, made me wash myself carefully, and fed me. I passed a long day there. They would not let me go on any terms, but tried to reassure me. A soldier's life was not all bad. Tomorrow, perhaps, leave would be permitted, if I fulfilled the Bey's pleasure this evening. The Bey seemed to be Nahi, the Governor. If he was angry, they said, I would be drafted for infantry training to the depot in Baalbek. I tried to look as though, to my mind, there was nothing worse in the world than that.

Soon after dark three men came for me. It had seemed a

chance to get away, but one held me all the time. I cursed my littleness. Our march crossed the railway, where were six tracks, besides the sidings of the engine shop. We went through a side gate, down a street, past a square, to a detached, two-storied house. There was a sentry outside, and a glimpse of others lolling in the dark entry. They took me upstairs to the Bey's room; or to his bedroom, rather. He was another bulky man, a Circassian himself, perhaps, and sat on the bed in a night-gown, trembling and sweating as though with fever. When I was pushed in he kept his head down, and waved the guard out. In a breathless voice he told me to sit on the floor in front of him, and after that was dumb; while I gazed at the top of his great head, on which the bristling hair stood up, no longer than the dark stubble on his cheeks and chin. And last he looked me over, and told me stand up: then to turn round. I obeyed; he flung himself back on the bed, and dragged me down with him in his arms. When I saw what he wanted I twisted round and up again, glad to find myself equal to him, at any rate in wrestling.

He began to fawn on me, saying how white and fresh I was, how fine my hands and feet, and how he would let me off the drills and duties, make me his orderly, even pay me wages, if I would love him.

I was obdurate, so he changed his tone, and sharply ordered me to take off my drawers. When I hesitated he snatched at me; and I pushed him back. He clapped his hands for the sentry, who hurried in and pinioned me. The Bey cursed me with horrible threats: and made the man holding me tear my clothes away, bit by bit. His eyes rounded at the half-healed places where the bullets had flicked through my skin a little while ago. Finally he lumbered to his feet, with a glitter in his look, and began to paw me over. I bore it for a little, till he got too beastly; and then jerked my knee into him.

He staggered to his bed, squeezing himself together and groaning with pain, while the soldier shouted for the corporal and the other three men to grip me hand and foot. As soon as I was helpless the Governor regained courage, and spat at me, swearing he would make me ask pardon. He took off his slipper, and hit me repeatedly with it in the face, while the corporal braced my head back by the hair to receive the blows. He leaned forward, fixed his teeth in my neck and bit till the blood came. Then he kissed me. Afterwards he drew one of the men's bayonets. I thought he was going to kill me, and was sorry: but he only pulled up a fold of the flesh over my ribs, worked the point through, after considerable trouble, and gave the blade a half-turn. This hurt, and I winced, while the blood wavered down my side and dripped to the front of my thigh. He looked pleased and dabbled it over my stomach with his finger-tips.

In my despair I spoke. His face changed and he stood still, then controlled his voice with an effort, to say significantly, 'You must understand that I know: and it will be easier if you do as I wish.' I was dumbfounded, and we stared silently at one another, while the men who felt an inner meaning beyond their experience, shifted uncomfortably. But it was evidently a chance shot, by which he himself did not, or would not, mean what I feared. I could not again trust my twitching mouth, which faltered always in emergencies, so at last threw up my chin, which was the sign for 'No' in the East; then he sat down, and half-whispered to the corporal to take me out and teach me everything.

They kicked me to the head of the stairs, and stretched me over a guard-bench, pommelling me. Two knelt on my ankles, bearing down on the back of my knees, while two more twisted my wrists till they cracked, and then crushed them and my neck against the wood. The corporal had run downstairs; and now came back with a whip of the Circassian sort, a thong of supple black hide, rounded, and tapering from the thickness of a thumb at the grip (which was wrapped in silver) down to a hard point finer than a pencil.

He saw me shivering, partly I think, with cold, and made it whistle over my ear, taunting me that before his tenth cut I would howl for mercy, and at the twentieth beg for the caresses of the Bey; and then he began to lash me madly across and across with all his might, while I locked my teeth to endure this thing which wrapped itself like flaming wire about my body.

To keep my mind in control I numbered the blows, but after twenty lost count, and could only feel the shapeless weight of pain, not tearing claws, for which I had prepared, but a gradual cracking apart of my whole being by some too-great force whose waves rolled up my spine till they were pent within my brain, to clash terribly together. Somewhere in the place a cheap clock ticked loudly, and it distressed me that their beating was not in its time. I writhed and twisted, but was held so tight that my struggles were useless. After the corporal ceased, the men took up, very deliberately, giving me so many, and then an interval during which they would squabble for the next turn, ease themselves, and play unspeakably with me. This was repeated often, for what may have been no more than ten minutes. Always for the first of every new series, my head would be pulled round, to see how a hard white ridge, like a railway, darkening slowly to crimson, leaped over my skin at the instant of each stroke, with a bead of blood where the two ridges crossed. As the punishment proceeded the whip fell more and more upon existing weals, biting blacker or more wet, till my flesh quivered with accumulated pain, and with terror of the next blow coming. They soon conquered my determination not to cry, but while my will ruled my lips I used only Arabic, and before the end a merciful sickness choked my utterance.

At last when I was completely broken they seemed satisfied. Somehow I found myself off the bench, lying on my back on the dirty floor, where I snuggled down, dazed, panting for breath, but vaguely comfortable. I had strung myself to learn all pain until I died, and no longer actor, but spectator, thought not to care how my body jerked and squealed. Yet I knew or imagined what passed about me.

I remember the corporal kicking with his nailed boot to get me up; and this was true, for the next day my right side was dark and lacerated, and a damaged rib made each breath stab me sharply. I remembered smiling idly at him, for a delicious warmth, probably sexual, was swelling through me: and then that he flung up his arm and hacked with the full length of his whip into my groin. This doubled me half-over, screaming, or, rather, trying impotently to scream, only shuddering through my open mouth. One giggled with amusement. A voice cried, 'Shame, you've killed him.' Another slash followed. A roaring, and my eyes went black: while within me the core of life seemed to heave slowly up through the rending nerves, expelled from its body by this last indescribable pang.

•

Frank Harris

HUGH KINGSMILL

Frank Harris, sometime editor of the *Saturday Review* and *Vanity Fair*, memoirist, polymath and bon viveur, was exposed to the public as a liar and a charlatan by Hugh Kingsmill in his biography of 1932. Of his memoirs, *My Life and Loves*, Kingsmill says, 'no one but a salamander would risk the stake for the accuracy of a single statement in Harris's autobiography . . .' 'On what foundation of actual fact Harris has erected the superstructure of his youthful triumphs, even the most indulgent reader will pause to wonder. At the age of thirteen he was already in the school cricket eleven; he had learnt *Paradise Lost* by heart in a week; as Shylock he had anticipated the particular piece of business so much applauded fifteen years later in Henry Irving's rendering of that part; he had made love to a girl of his own age in church, and had come within measurable distance of overpowering a French governess in a rustic summerhouse; . . . and he had thrashed the school bully, a boy of seventeen or eighteen, the captain of the cricket eleven.' Kingsmill was intimately acquainted with Harris, but it was some time before he could see Harris for the poseur he was. Not the least of Harris's many deceits was his claim to have known so many personalities of the day.

Before leaving England Harris arranged for the publication of the first volume of *Contemporary Portraits*, which came out in

1915. Four more volumes were published by himself in subsequent years.

In the course of his life Harris met, or thought he met, every remarkable man between Carlyle and Trotsky, between Wagner and Gaudier-Brzeska. During his last twenty years, from 1911, the greater part of his writing was occupied with his impressions of these men.

. . . Harris's subjects may be arranged in three classes: those whom he knew fairly intimately, and met on a number of occasions, as, for example, Oscar Wilde, Randolph Churchill, Bernard Shaw, George Moore, Wells, Sir Herbert Tree, Richard Middleton; those whom there is either a certainty or a reasonable presumption that he met between once and half a dozen times: Carlyle, Renan, Maupassant, Sir Richard Burton, George Meredith, Browning, Swinburne, Matthew Arnold, A. E. Housman, Ernest Dowson, Walter Pater, Herbert Spencer, Balfour; and those whom he may have seen, or even spoken to, but who certainly neither revealed themselves to him in characteristic sayings, nor interchanged opinions with him. Among these are Wagner, Thomas Hardy and Tennyson.

This last class is chiefly composed of those about whom he wrote after the war, when his memory was failing, and when his control over his inventive faculty, always spasmodic, had almost ceased to operate.

In his autobiography he tells how he met Tennyson at a London house, where the poet sat throned like a god and surrounded by worshippers, male and female. Harris heard him saying: 'Moral good is the crown of life. But what value is it without immortality? If I knew my life was coming to an end in an hour, should I give anything to a beggar? Not a penny; if I didn't believe myself immortal . . . At the same time I can't believe in Hell, endless punishments seem stupid to me.'

One might almost as easily believe that Harris was passing through an ante-chamber of Whitehall Palace, when Shakespeare put it to Queen Elizabeth that the quality of mercy becomes the throned monarch better than his or her crown, as that he happened to be present at the precise moment when Tennyson made these celebrated remarks so often quoted in print.

The lecture he reads Thomas Hardy on *Tess* is equally fantastic. In his great days in London he was, as he says in his *Life of Wilde*, almost unaware of Hardy. But in his old age, when he was editing *Pearson's Magazine* in New York, he perceived that Hardy had become famous and that a talk between Hardy and Harris would please and impress his American public. He therefore dug up a brilliant essay on Hardy, written in the 'nineties by a friend of Harris's, Francis Adams, and dramatized it as a dialogue in which Hardy appears as discouraged and bemused by Harris's searching criticism, but not flexible enough to admit his own incompetence, indeed rather stupidly dogged.

The point at issue is the love felt by Tess and her three dairymaid friends for Angel Clare. All four, Harris reminds Hardy, come to grief because of Clare, one taking to drink, another drowning herself, and the third going half-crazy, while Tess herself is completely distraught. 'But,' Harris says, 'before this could even seem possible to us, Hardy, you would have to endow Angel Clare with extraordinary qualities.' Even, Harris insists, had Hardy painted Clare as handsome as Adonis, tongued like Shakespeare, and with a personality like Napoleon's, one still couldn't find four women all confessing to each other that they loved him.

Moved by Hardy's distress, Harris explained that he could only tell him what he regarded as the truth. 'I'm sure of that,' Hardy replies, 'but it is a blow to me.' The torture begins again, and Hardy at last rebels: 'I can't believe you,' he exclaims, 'for the life of me I can't see it with your eyes.'

Harris's conversations with Wagner, in the fourth volume of his *Portraits*, published in 1924, were analysed by Mr Ernest Newman in three long articles in the *Sunday Times* and shown to be a very slipshod dramatization in dialogue form of facts about Wagner gathered from various books. After giving dozens of lesser reasons for believing that Harris's meeting with Wagner never took place, Mr Newman points out that Cosima, who was always with Wagner at this time, guarding his failing strength from all unnecessary taxes on it, is not once mentioned by Harris. Even Harris felt this shaft, and a year later, in his autobiography, tried to staunch the wound by explaining that in his portrait of Wagner he had left out, half-consciously, two or three features which it seemed to him hardly right to publish as long as Cosima Wagner was alive. He does not give his reasons for believing Cosima to be dead in 1925.

•

The lie that is man's good character

MARK TWAIN

In an early part of Twain's autobiography he considers the nature of man, and argues that man is the only creature possessed of malice. Moreover he is the only creature that is possessed of a nasty mind. But what of man's noble qualities?

. . . There are certain sweet-smelling, sugar-coated lies current in the world which all politic men have apparently tacitly conspired together to support and perpetuate. One of these is, that there is such a thing in the world as independence: independence of thought, independence of opinion, independence of action. Another is, that the world loves to *see* independence – admires it, applauds it. Another is, that there is such a thing in the world as toleration – in religion, in politics, and such matters; and with it trains that already mentioned auxiliary lie that toleration is admired and applauded. Out of these trunk-lies spring many branch ones: to wit, the lie that not all men are slaves; the lie that men are glad when other men succeed; glad when they prosper; glad to see them reach lofty heights; sorry to see them fall again. And yet other branch lies: to wit, that there is heroism in man; that there is something about him that ought to be perpetuated – in heaven, or hell, or somewhere. And these other branch lies, to wit: that conscience, man's moral medicine chest, is not only created by the Creator, but is put into man ready charged with the right and only true and authentic correctives of conduct – and the duplicate chest, with the self-same correctives, unchanged, unmodified, distributed to all nations and epochs. And yet one other branch lie: to wit, that I am I, and you are you; that we are units, individuals, and have natures of our own, instead of being the tail end of a tapeworm eternity of ancestors extending in linked procession back and back and back – to our source in the monkeys, with this so-called individuality of ours a decayed and rancid mush of inherited instincts and teachings derived, atom by atom, stench by stench, from the entire line of that sorry column, and not so much new and original matter in it as you could balance on a needle point and examine under a microscope. This makes well-nigh fantastic the suggestion that there can be such a thing as a personal, original, and responsible nature in a man, separable from that in him which is not original, and findable in such a quantity as to enable the observer to say, this is a man, not a procession.

. . . Consider the first-mentioned lie: that there is such a thing in the world as independence; that it exists in individuals; that it exists in bodies of men. Surely if anything *is* proven, by whole oceans and continents of evidence, it is that the quality of independence was almost wholly left out of the human race. The scattering exceptions to the rule only emphasize it, light it up, make it glare. The whole population of New England meekly took their turns, for years, in standing up in the railway trains, without so much as a complaint above their breath, till at last these uncounted millions were able to produce exactly one single independent man, who stood to his rights and made the railroad give him a seat. Statistics and the law of probabilities warrant the assumption that it will take New England forty years to breed this fellow. There is a law, with penalty attached, forbidding trains to occupy the Asylum Street crossing for more than five minutes at a time. For years people and carriages used to wait there nightly as much as twenty minutes on a stretch while New

England trains monopolized that crossing. I used to hear men use vigorous language about that insolent wrong – but they waited just the same.

We are discrete sheep; we wait to see how the drove is going, and then go with the drove.

. . . If we would learn what the human race really *is* at bottom, we need only observe it in election times. A Hartford clergyman met me in the street and spoke of a new nominee – denounced the nomination, in strong, earnest words – words that were refreshing for their independence, their manliness. He said, 'I ought to be proud, perhaps, for this nominee is a relative of mine; on the contrary, I am humiliated and disgusted, for I know him intimately – familiarly – and I know that he is an unscrupulous scoundrel, and always has been.' You should have seen this clergyman preside at a political meeting forty days later, and urge, and plead, and gush – and you should have heard him paint the character of this same nominee. You would have supposed he was describing the Cid, and Greatheart, and Sir Galahad, and Bayard the Spotless all rolled into one. Was he sincere? Yes – by that time; and therein lies the pathos of it all, the hopelessness of it all. It shows at what trivial cost of effort a man can teach himself to lie, and learn to believe it, when he perceives, by the general drift, that it is the popular thing to do. Does he believe his lie *yet*? Oh, probably not; he has no further use for it. It was but a passing incident; he spared to it the moment that was its due, then hastened back to the serious business of his life.

And what a paltry poor lie is that one which teaches that independence of action and opinion is prized in men, admired, honored, rewarded. When a man leaves a political party, he is treated as if the party owned him – as if he were its bond slave, as most party men plainly are – and had stolen himself, gone off with what was not his own. And he is traduced, derided, despised, held up to public obloquy and loathing. His character is remorselessly assassinated; no means, however vile, are spared to injure his property and his business.

The preacher who casts a vote for conscience' sake runs the

risk of starving. And is rightly served, for he has been teaching a falsity – that men respect and honor independence of thought and action.

Mr Beecher may be charged with a *crime*, and his whole following will rise as one man, and stand by him to the bitter end; but who so poor to be his friend when he is charged with casting a vote for conscience' sake. Take the editor so charged – take – take anybody.

All the talk about tolerance, in anything or anywhere, is plainly a gentle lie. It does not exist. It is in no man's heart; but it unconsciously, and by moss-grown inherited habit, drivels and slobbers from all men's lips. Intolerance is everything for oneself, and nothing for the other person. The mainspring of man's nature is just that – selfishness.

Let us skip the other lies, for brevity's sake. To consider them would prove nothing, except that man is what he is – loving toward his own, lovable to his own – his family, his friends – and otherwise the buzzing, busy, trivial enemy of his race – who tarries his little day, does his little dirt, commends himself to God, and then goes out into the darkness, to return no more, and send no messages back – selfish even in death.

•

The art eternal

H. L. MENCKEN

One of the laudable by-products of Freudian necromancy is the discovery that lying, in most cases, is involuntary and inevitable – that the liar can no more avoid it than he can avoid blinking his eyes when a light flashes or jumping when a bomb goes off behind him. At its worst, indeed, this necessity takes on a downright pathological character, and is thus as innocent as sciatica or albuminaria. It is part of the morbid baggage of hysterics and neurasthenics: their lying is simply a symptom of their compulsive effort to adjust themselves to an environment which bears upon them too harshly for endurance. The rest of us are not quite so hard pushed, but pushed we all are. In us the thing works through the inferiority complex, which no man can escape. He who lacks it entirely is actually reckoned insane by the fact: his satisfaction with his situation in the world is indistinguishable from a delusion of grandeur. The great majority of us – all, in brief, who are normal – pass through life in constant revolt against our limitations, objective and subjective. Our conscious thought is largely devoted to plans and specifications for cutting a better figure in human society, and in our unconscious the business goes on much more steadily and powerfully. No healthy man, in his secret heart, is content with his destiny. Even the late Woodrow, during his lazy term as the peer of Lincoln and Washington, was obviously tantalized by the reflection that, in earlier ages, there had been Martin Luther, St Ignatius Loyola and Paul of Tarsus. We are tortured by such dreams and images as a child is tortured by the thought of a state of existence in which it would live in a candy-store and have two stomachs. The more we try to put the obscene apparition away, the more it haunts and badgers us.

Lying is the product of the unconscious yearning to realize such visions, and if the policeman, conscience, prevents the lie being put into plain words, then it is at least put into more or less plausible acts. We all play parts when we face our fellow-men, as even poets have noticed. No man could bring himself to reveal his true character, and, above all, his true limitations as a citizen and a Christian, his true meannesses, his true imbecilities, to his friends, or even to his wife. Honest autobiography is therefore a contradiction in terms: the moment a man considers himself, even *in petto*, he tries to gild and fresco himself. Thus a man's wife, however realistic her view of him, always flatters him in the end, for the worst she sees in him is appreciably better, by the time she sees it, than what is actually there. What she sees, even at times of the most appalling domestic revelation and confidence, is not the authentic man at all, but a compound made up in part of the authentic man and in part of his projection of a gaudy ideal. The man who is most respected by his wife is the one who makes this projection most vivid – that is, the one who is the most daring and ingratiating liar. He can never, of course, deceive her utterly, but if he is skilful he may at least deceive her enough to make her happy.

Omnis homo mendax: thus the Psalmist. So far the Freudians merely parrot him. What is new in their gospel is the doctrine that lying is instinctive, normal, and unavoidable – that a man is forced into it by his very will-to-live. This doctrine purges the business of certain ancient embarrassments, and restores innocence to the heart. Think of a lie as a compulsion neurose, and you think of it more kindly. I need not add, I hope, that this transfer of it from the department of free will to that of determinism by no means disposes of the penalty that traditionally pursues it, supposing it to be detected and resented. The proponents of the free will always make the mistake of assuming that the determinists are simply evil fellows looking for a way to escape the just consequences of their transgressing. No sense is in that assumption. If I lie on the witness-stand and am detected by the judge, I am jailed for perjury forthwith, regardless of my helplessness under compulsion. Here justice refuses absolutely to distinguish between a misfortune and a tort: the overt act is all it is concerned with. But as jurisprudence grows more intelligent and more civilized it may change its tune, to the benefit of liars, which is to say, to the benefit of humanity. Science is unflinchingly deterministic, and it has begun to force its determinism into morals. We no longer flog a child afflicted with nocturnal enuresis: we have substituted concepts of mental aberration for concepts of crime in a whole series of cases: kleptomania-shoplifting, pyromania-arson, &c.; and, in the United States at least, the old savage punishment of murderers is now ameliorated by considerations of psychiatry and even of honor. On some shining tomorrow a psychoanalyst may be put into the box to prove that perjury is simply a compulsion neurose, like beating time with the foot at a concert or counting the lamp-posts along the highway.

However, I have but small faith in millenniums, and do not formally predict this one. Nor do I pronounce any moral judgement, pro or con: moral judgements, as old Friedrich used to say, are foreign to my nature. But let us not forget that lying, *per se*, is not forbidden by the moral code of Christendom. Holy Writ dismisses it cynically, and the statutes of all civilized states are silent about it. Only the Chinese, indeed, make it a penal offense. Perjury, of course, is prohibited everywhere, and also any mendacity which amounts to fraud and deprives a fellowman of his property, but that far more common form of truth-stretching which has only the lesser aim of augmenting the liar's personal dignity and consequence – this is looked upon with a very charitable eye. So is that form which has the aim of helping another person in the same way. In the latter direction lying may even take on the stature of a positive virtue. The late King Edward VII, when Prince of Wales, attained to great popularity throughout Christendom by venturing into downright perjury. Summoned into a court of law to give expert testimony regarding some act of adultery, he lied like a gentleman, as the phrase goes, to protect a woman. The lie, to be sure, was intrinsically useless; no one believed that the lady was innocent. Nevertheless, every decent Christian applauded the perjurer for his good intentions, including even the judge on the bench, sworn to combat false witness by every resource of forensics. All of us, worms that we are, occasionally face the alternatives that confronted Edward. On the one hand, we may tell the truth, regardless of consequences, and on the other hand we may mellow it and sophisticate it to make it humane and tolerable. It is universally held that the man who chooses the first course is despicable. He may be highly moral, but he is nevertheless a cad – as highly moral men have so curious a way of being. But if he lies boldly, then he is held to be a man of honor, and is respected as such by all other men of honor.

For the habitual truth-teller and truth-seeker, indeed, the world has very little liking. He is always unpopular, and not infrequently his unpopularity is so excessive that it endangers his life. Run your eye back over the list of martyrs, lay and clerical: nine-tenths of them, you will find, stood accused of nothing worse than honest efforts to find out and announce the truth. Even today, with the scientific passion become familiar in the world, the general view of such fellows is highly unfavorable. The typical scientist, the typical truth-seeker in every field is held under suspicion by the great majority of men, and variously beset by posses of relentless foes. If he tries to find out the truth about arterio-sclerosis, or surgical shock, or cancer, he is denounced as a scoundrel by the Christian Scientists, the osteopaths and the anti-vivisectionists. If he tries to tell the truth about the government, its agents seek to silence him and punish him. If he turns to fiction and endeavors to depict his fellow-men accurately, he has the Comstocks on his hands. In no field can he count upon a friendly audience, and freedom from assault. Especially in the United States is his whole enterprise viewed with bilious eye. The men the American people admire most extravagantly are the most daring liars; the men they detest most violently are those who try to tell them the truth. A Galileo could no more be elected President of the United States than he could be elected Pope of Rome. Both high posts are reserved for men favored by God with an extraordinary genius for swathing the bitter facts of life in bandages of soft illusion.

Behind this almost unanimous distrust of the truth-teller there is a sound and sure instinct, as there is behind every other manifestation of crowd feeling. What it shows is simply this: that the truth is something too harsh and devastating for the majority of men to bear. In their secret hearts they know themselves, and they can suffer the thought of themselves only by idealizing the facts. The more trivial, loathsome and degraded the reality, the more powerful and relentless must be the idealization. An Aristotle, I daresay, may be able occasionally to regard himself searchingly and dispassionately – but certainly not an ordinary man. Here we come back to what we began with: the inferiority complex. The truth-seeker forgets it, and so comes to grief. He forgets that the ordinary man, at bottom, is always afraid of himself, as of some horrible monster. He refuses to sanction the lie whereby the ordinary man maintains his self-respect, just as the bounder, put upon the stand, refuses to support the lie whereby a woman maintains the necessary theory of her chastity. Thus he is unpopular, and deserves to be.

Then why does he go on? Why does he kick up such a bother and suffer such barbarous contumely, all to no end – for the majority of so-called truths, it must be evident, perish as soon as they are born: no one will believe them. The answer probably is that the truth-seeker is moved by the same obscure inner necessity (in Joseph Conrad's phrase) that animates the artist. Something within him, something entirely beyond his volition, forces him to pursue his fanatical and useless quest – some impulse as blind as that which moves a puppy to chase its tail. Again the compulsion neurose! But this one differs materially from that of the liar. The latter is hygenic; it makes for peace, health, happiness. The former makes only for strife and discontent. It invades the immemorial pruderies of the human race. It breeds scandals and heart-burnings. It is essentially anti-social, and hence, by modern theories of criminology, diseased. The truth-seeker thus becomes a pathological case. The average man is happily free from any such malaise. He avoids truth as diligently as he avoids arson, regicide or piracy on the high seas: because he believes that it is dangerous, that no good can come of it, that it doesn't pay. The very thought of it is abhorrent to him. This average man, I believe, must be accepted as the normal man, the natural man, the healthy and useful man. He presents a character that is general in the race, and favorable to its security and contentment. The truth never caresses; it stings – and life is surely too short for sane men to be stinging themselves unnecessarily. One would regard it as idiotic even in a flea.

Thus the truth about the truth emerges, and with it the truth about lying. Lying is not only excusable; it is not only innocent, and instinctive; it is, above all, necessary and unavoidable. Without the ameliorations that it offers life would become a mere syllogism, and hence too metallic to be borne. The man who lies simply submits himself sensibly to the grand sweep and ripple of the cosmic process. The man who seeks and tells the truth is a rebel against the inner nature of all of us.

•

War propaganda

ADOLF HITLER

The following is an extract from Hitler's *Mein Kampf*, first published in July 1925.

At the time when I was following all political events with attention, the business of propaganda was always of extreme interest to me. In it I saw an instrument which the Socialist-Marxist organization had long controlled with masterly skill and employed to the full. I soon came to realize that the right use of propaganda was a regular art, which was practically unknown to the bourgeois Parties. The Christian-Socialist movement alone, in Lueger's time especially, applied the instrument with a certain virtuosity and owed many of their successes to it.

Had we any propaganda at all?

Alas! I can only reply no. All that was undertaken in that direction was so inadequate and wrong-headed from the start as to be not of the slightest use – sometimes it did actual harm.

Insufficient in form, wrong psychologically; there can be no other outcome of a systematic examination of the German war propaganda. They even seem to have been uncertain as to the first question: Is propaganda a means or an end?

It is a means, and must be judged from the point of view of the objective it is to serve. It must be suitably shaped so as to assist that objective. It is also clear that the importance of the objective may vary from the standpoint of general necessity, and that the essential qualities of propaganda must vary so as to be in harmony with it. The objective we fought for, as the War went on, was the noblest and most compelling which is imaginable to man. It was the freedom and independence of our nation, security for future nourishment and – the nation's honour.

As regards the question of humanity, Moltke has said that in war the essential is to bring the matter to a finish quickly, and that the severest methods conduce most effectually to that end.

Propaganda in the War was a means to an end. It was a struggle for the life of the German nation; therefore propaganda could only be founded on principles which were of value to that objective. The cruellest weapons were humane, if they conduced to a speedier victory, and indeed they were the only method which helped the nation to secure a dignity of freedom.

This was the only possible attitude to adopt towards the question of war propaganda in a life and death struggle such as this.

If those in high positions had been clear about the foregoing there would have been no uncertainty as to the form and employment of this weapon; for it is nothing more nor less than a weapon, but a really terrible one in the hands of one who understands it.

All propaganda should be popular and should adapt its intellectual level to the receptive ability of the least intellectual of those whom it is desired to address. Thus it must sink its mental elevation deeper in proportion to the numbers of the mass whom it has to grip. If it is, as it is with propaganda for carrying through a war, a matter of gathering a whole nation within its circle of influence, there cannot be enough attention paid to avoidance of too high a level of intellectuality.

The receptive ability of the masses is very limited, their understanding small; on the other hand, they have great power of forgetting. This being so, all effective propaganda must be confined to very few points, which must be brought out in the form of slogans, until the very last man is enabled to comprehend what is meant by any slogan. If this principle is sacrificed to the desire to be many-sided, it will dissipate the effectual working of the propaganda, for the crowd will be unable to digest or retain the material that is offered them. It will, moreover, weaken and finally cancel its own effectiveness.

It was, for instance, fundamentally wrong to paint the enemy in a ridiculous light, as the Austrian and German comic papers made a point of doing in their propaganda; wrong because, when the enemy was actually met with in the flesh, it was bound at once to produce on our men a totally different impression of him, which subsequently took its revenge in a most terrible manner; for the German soldier, under the direct impression of the enemy's power of resistance, now felt he had been deceived by the fabricators of his information up to that moment, and instead of strengthening or at least confirming his fighting keenness, it did the opposite. The men broke down under it.

On the other hand, the British and American war propaganda was psychologically correct. By displaying the German to their own people as a barbarian and a Hun, they were preparing the individual soldier for the horrors of war, and so helped to spare him disappointments. The most terrible of the weapons which now came against him were now, for him, merely a confirmation of the information which he had already received and reinforced his faith in the truth of his Government's assertions, whilst it heightened his rage and hatred against the villainous enemy.

Thus the British soldier never felt that the information he got from home was untrue, and this alas! was so much the case with the German, that he ended by rejecting all that came from that quarter as pure swindle and *Krampf*.

What, for instance, should we say about a poster advertising a new soap, if it described other soaps as being 'good'? We should shake our heads over it.

It was fundamentally wrong, when discussing the subject of war guilt, to suggest that Germany could not be counted as alone responsible for the outbreak of that catastrophe; the proper thing would have been to lay the burden of it without cease upon the enemy, even if this did not correspond with the true course of events, as was nevertheless the actual fact.

The masses are in no position to distinguish where foreign illegality begins and our own ends.

An immense majority of the people are so feminine in nature and point of view, that their thoughts and actions are governed more by feeling and sentiment than by reasoned consideration.

This sentiment is, however, not complicated, but very simple and consistent. It does not differentiate much, but it is either positive or negative, love or hate, truth or lies, never half one and half the other, and so on.

This was realized by the British propaganda with very real genius. In England there were no half statements which might have given rise to doubts.

The proof of their brilliant understanding of the primitiveness of sentiment in the mass of the people lay in the publication of horrors, which suited this condition and both cleverly and ruthlessly prepared the ground for moral solidity at the front even when great defeats came along, and further, in nailing down the German enemy as being the sole cause of the War – a lie, the unqualified impudence of which, and the way it was put before the nation, took account of the sentimental and extremist nature of the public, and so gained credence.

Alteration of methods should not alter the essence of what propaganda is meant to effect, but its purport must be the same at the end as at the start. The slogan may have various lights thrown upon it, but any treatment applied to it should always finish with the slogan. Propaganda can work solidly and consistently in no other way.

The success of any advertisement, whether in business or politics, is due to the continuity and consistency with which it is employed.

The example of enemy propaganda was typical of this also. It confined itself to a few points of view, was addressed solely to the masses, and was pursued with untiring perseverance. Throughout the whole War use was made of the basic ideas and forms of expression found to be right at the beginning, and even the slightest alteration was never considered. At first it appeared lunatic from the impudence of its assertions – later on it became unpleasant and was finally believed. At the end of four and a half years revolution broke out in Germany, and its war-cries were inspired by the enemy's propaganda.

The British understood yet another thing – that this intellectual weapon can only be used successfully with the masses, but that, if successful, it richly repays what it costs.

Propaganda counted with them as a weapon of the first class, whereas with us it was the last way for officeless politicians to make a living and a tiny berth for modest heroes.

Taken all in all, its success was just nil.

•

The big lie

ADOLF HITLER

In *Mein Kampf*, Hitler 'analyses' the causes of the collapse of the German Reich after the First World War. The easiest explanation of the collapse, he says, is that it was brought about by the consequences of the lost war. But, argues Hitler, this is simply not so.

There may be many who will seriously believe this nonsense, but there are still more from whose mouth such an explanation can only be a lie and conscious falsehood. This last applies to all those who today feed at the government's cribs. For didn't the prophets of the revolution again and again point out most urgently to the people that it was a matter of complete indifference to the broad masses how this War turned out? Did they not, on the contrary, gravely assure us that at most the 'big capitalist' could have an interest in a victorious end of the gigantic struggle of nations, but never the German people as such, let alone the German worker? Indeed, didn't these apostles of world conciliation maintain the exact opposite: didn't they say that by a

German defeat 'militarism' would be destroyed, but that the German nation would celebrate its most glorious resurrection? Didn't these circles glorify the benevolence of the Entente, and didn't they shove the blame for the whole bloody struggle on Germany? And could they have done this without special consequences for the nation? Wasn't the whole revolution embroidered with the phrase that it would prevent the victory of the German flag, but that through it the German people would at last begin advancing towards freedom at home and abroad?

Will you claim that this was not so, you wretched, lying scoundrels?

It takes a truly Jewish effrontery to attribute the blame for the collapse solely to the military defeat when the central organ of all traitors to the nation, the Berlin *Vorwarts*, wrote that this time the German people must not bring its banner home victorious!

And now this is supposed to be the cause of our collapse?

Of course, it would be perfectly futile to fight with such forgetful liars. I wouldn't waste my words on them if unfortunately this nonsense were not parroted by so many thoughtless people, who do not seem inspired by malice or conscious insincerity. Furthermore, these discussions are intended to give our propaganda fighters an instrument which is very much needed at a time when the spoken word is often twisted in our mouths.

. . . The collapse of the army was not the cause of our present-day misfortune, but only the consequence of other crimes, a consequence which itself again, it must be admitted, ushered in the beginning of a further and this time visible collapse.

The truth of this can be seen from the following:

Must a military defeat lead to so complete a collapse of a nation and a state? Since when is this the result of an unfortunate war? Do peoples perish in consequence of lost wars as such?

The answer to this can be very brief: always, when military defeat is the payment meted out to peoples for their inner rottenness, cowardice, lack of character, in short, unworthiness. If this is not the case, the military defeat will rather be the inspiration of a great future resurrection than the tombstone of national existence.

. . . In the way in which the German people received its defeat, we can recognize most clearly that the true cause of our collapse must be sought in an entirely different place from the purely military loss of a few positions or in the failure of an offensive; for if the front as such had really flagged and if its downfall had really encompassed the doom of the fatherland, the German people would have received the defeat quite differently. Then they would have borne the ensuing misfortune with gritted teeth or would have mourned it, overpowered by grief; then all hearts would have been filled with rage and anger towards the enemy who had become victorious through a trick of chance or the will of fate; then, like the Roman Senate, the nation would have received the defeated divisions with the thanks of the fatherland for the sacrifices they had made and besought them not to despair of the Reich. The capitulation would have been signed only with the reason, while the heart even then would have beaten for the resurrection to come.

This is how a defeat for which only fate was responsible would have been received. Then people would not have laughed and danced, they would not have boasted of cowardice and glorified the defeat, they would not have scoffed at the embattled troops and dragged their banner and cockade in the mud. But above all: then we should never have had the terrible state of affairs which prompted a British officer, Colonel Repington [the Military Correspondent of *The Times*], to make the contemptuous statement: 'Of the Germans, every third man is a traitor.' No, this plague would never have been able to rise into the stifling flood which for five years now has been drowning the very last remnant of respect for us on the part of the rest of the world.

This most of all shows the assertion that the lost War was the cause of the German collapse to be a lie. No, this military collapse was itself only the consequence of a large number of symptoms of disease and their causes, which even in peacetime were with the German nation. This was the first consequence, catastrophic and visible to all, of an ethical and moral poisoning, of a diminution in the instinct of self-preservation and its preconditions, which for many years had begun to undermine the foundations of the people and the Reich.

It required the whole bottomless falsehood of the Jews and their Marxist fighting organization to lay the blame for the collapse on that very man who alone, with superhuman energy and will power, tried to prevent the catastrophe he foresaw and save the nation from its time of deepest humiliation and disgrace. By branding Ludendorff as guilty for the loss of the World War, they took the weapon of moral right from the one dangerous accuser who could have risen against the traitors to the fatherland. In this they proceeded on the sound principle that the magnitude of a lie always contains a certain factor of credibility, since the great masses of the people in the very bottom of their hearts tend to be corrupted rather than consciously and purposely evil, and that, therefore, in view of the primitive simplicity of their minds, they more easily lie in little things, but would be ashamed of lies that were too big. Such a falsehood will never enter their heads, and they will not be able to believe in the possibility of such monstrous effrontery and infamous misrepresentations in others; yes, even when enlightened on the subject, they will long doubt and waver, and continue to accept at least one of these causes as true. Therefore, something of even the most insolent lie will always remain and stick – a fact which all the great lie-virtuosi and lying-clubs in this world know only too well and also make the most treacherous use of.

The foremost connoisseurs of this truth regarding the possibilities in the use of falsehood and slander have always been the Jews; for after all, their whole existence is based on one single great lie, to wit, that they are a religious community while actually they are a race – and what a race! One of the greatest minds of humanity has nailed them forever as such in an eternally correct phrase of fundamental truth: he called them 'the great masters of the lie'. And anyone who does not recognize this or does not want to believe it will never in this world be able to help the truth to victory.

All the nice girls love a sailor

H. MONTGOMERY HYDE

Norman Birkett was one of the most brilliant advocates practising at the Bar between the wars. In 1946 he was one of the two British judges at the international War Crimes Tribunal at Nuremberg. As a King's Counsel he appeared in a great many murder cases, most usually for the defence. In this case, however, Birkett found himself on the side of the plaintiff in an action for libel. The plaintiff was none other than Lady Louis Mountbatten, the wife of Lord Louis Mountbatten, and given what we now know about Edwina's sexual appetite – she had numerous affairs – the case looks very different from the way in which it appeared to Birkett's biographer, H. Montgomery Hyde, when he came to write about it.

The libel, which Birkett rightly described as 'atrocious and abominable', was published in a gossip column entitled 'Behind the Scenes' in *The People* on May 20, 1932, and written by an anonymous contributor who signed himself 'The Watcher'. It said:

FAMOUS HOSTESS EXILED

SOCIETY SHAKEN BY TERRIBLE SCANDAL

I am able to reveal today the sequel to a scandal which has shaken society to the very depths. It concerns one of the leading hostesses in the country, a woman highly connected and immensely rich.

Associations with a coloured man became so marked that they were the talk of the West End. Then one day the couple were caught in compromising circumstances.

The sequel is that the Society woman has been given the hint to clear out of England for a couple of years to let the affair blow over, and the hint comes from a quarter which cannot be ignored.

'It is not too much to say that it is the most monstrous and most atrocious libel of which I myself in all my experience in these courts have ever heard,' said Birkett in opening the case before the Lord Chief Justice, Lord Hewart. 'Your Lordship may think that the word "scandal" at the top of the article coupled with the words, "the hint comes from a quarter which cannot be ignored", puts it beyond all doubt that the writer deliberately intended to defame Lady Louis Mountbatten. It is unnecessary to say that there is not one word of truth in these horrible allegations. Nor is there the faintest ground upon which these lying rumours could be brought into existence at all.' Birkett went on to say that the defendants were willing to pay damages, and there was not the smallest doubt that a jury would have awarded heavy damages, but Lady Louis refused to accept one single penny which would be to her 'in the highest degree distasteful'. What she did desire was that there should be a speedy and public vindication of her name in the fullest possible manner, and with this end in view her counsel asked that 'in the very exceptional circumstances of this case', she and her husband might be allowed to go into the witness box. Lord Hewart agreed.

Lord Louis Mountbatten was the first to give evidence. He told the court how, as a naval officer attached to the Mediterranean Fleet, he had been ordered to Malta for two years and it was natural that his wife and children should follow him there for the duration of his appointment. Lady Louis then entered the witness box. Replying to her counsel's questions, she declared that she had returned to this country from Malta solely in order to give evidence in this case.

Birkett held up a copy of the offending journal. 'The second paragraph in this publication deals with a coloured man,' he said. 'Is there one single word of truth in the allegation there made?'

'Not one single word,' Lady Louis answered in ringing tones.

'In fact, I have never in the whole course of my life met the man referred to.'*

'Your friends have named to you the coloured man supposed to be referred to in the paragraph?' continued Birkett.

'They have,' admitted Lady Louis.

'And you have never had anything to do with him in any shape or form?'

'The whole thing is a preposterous story.'

'Was it your desire, when the article was brought to your notice, that you should have the opportunity of going into the box to deny this horrible thing on oath?'

'It was my express wish.'

For the defendants, Sir Patrick Hastings made an unqualified apology, coupled with 'genuine and deep regrets', and reiterated the newspaper's willingness to pay damages, which Hastings agreed if awarded by a jury must have been extremely heavy. It was also intimated that the person responsible for the gossip column had been dismissed as soon as the proprietors of *The People* had received Lady Louis Mountbatten's complaint.

'One does not wonder that in these circumstances the plaintiff does not desire damages,' Lord Hewart observed. 'I should have been astonished if she had accepted them because there are some libels which are crimes on the part of everybody concerned.'

In agreeing to Birkett's request that the record should be withdrawn on the terms that the defendants apologized and paid all the plaintiff's costs and expenses, the Lord Chief Justice made it clear that he did so 'with considerable doubt and hesitation' in view of the possibility of criminal proceedings being instituted. As it was, Lord Hewart ordered that a copy of the paper should be kept in the custody of the court, and the editor was fortunate in escaping prosecution for criminal libel.

•

*It was said that the actor Paul Robeson never got over Edwina's public rejection of him, not to mention the evidence of her colour prejudice. See Richard Hough's book *Edwina* for a full account of their affair.

Famine in the Ukraine: the inhuman power of the lie

ROBERT CONQUEST

The dekulakization of the Ukraine between 1929 and 1932, in which millions of peasant families were dispossessed of their land which was then concentrated in Party hands in collective farms, resulted in widespread famine and the deaths of millions of people. The historian Robert Conquest has estimated that as many as fourteen million may have perished. Here he considers how the fact of the famine was concealed from the West.

A major element in Stalin's operations against the peasantry was what Pasternak calls the 'inhuman power of the lie'. Deception was practised on a giant scale. In particular every effort was made to persuade the West that no famine was taking place, and later that none had in fact taken place.

On the face of it, this might appear to have been an impossible undertaking. A great number of true accounts reached Western Europe and America, some of them from impeccable Western eyewitnesses. (It was not found feasible, at least in 1932, to keep all foreigners out of the famine areas.)

But Stalin had a profound understanding of the possibilities of what Hitler approvingly calls the Big Lie. He knew that even though the truth may be readily available, the deceiver need not give up. He saw that flat denial on the one hand, and the injection into the pool of information of a corpus of positive falsehood on the other, were sufficient to confuse the issue for the passively uninstructed foreign audience, and to induce acceptance of the Stalinist version by those actively seeking to be deceived. The Famine was the first major instance of the exercise of this technique of influencing world opinion, but it was to be followed by a number of others such as the campaign over the

Moscow Trials of 1936–8, the denial of the existence of the forced labour camp system, and so on. Indeed, it can hardly be said to be extinct today.

Edouard Herriot, the French Radical leader, twice premier of his country, was in the USSR in August and September 1933. He spent five days in the Ukraine: half this time was devoted to official receptions and banquets, and the other half to a conducted tour. As a result he felt able to claim that no famine existed, and to blame reports of such on elements pursuing an anti-Soviet policy. *Pravda* (13 September 1933) was able to announce that 'he categorically denied the lies of the bourgeois press about a famine in the Soviet Union'.

Such comments, from a widely known statesman, had, we are told, a great effect on European opinion. The irresponsibility shown must have greatly encouraged Stalin in his view of the gullibility of the West, on which he was to play so effectively in later years.

A visitor to Kiev describes the preparations for Herriot. The day before his arrival the population was required to work from 2 a.m. cleaning the streets and decorating the houses. Food-distribution centres were closed. Queues were prohibited. Homeless children, beggars, and starving people disappeared. A local inhabitant adds that shop windows were filled with food, but the police dispersed or arrested even local citizens who pressed too close (and the purchase of food was forbidden). The streets were washed, the hotel he was to stay in was refurbished, with new carpets and furniture and new uniforms for the staff. And similarly in Kharkov.

But the closest co-operator of all with the Soviet lies about the famine, reveals Conquest, was an American named Walter Duranty, correspondent of *The New York Times*.

In November 1932 Duranty had reported that 'there is no famine or actual starvation, nor is there likely to be'.

When the famine became widely known in the West, and reported in his own paper and by his colleagues, playing down, rather than denial, became his method. Still denying famine he spoke of 'malnutrition', 'food shortages', 'lowered resistance'.

On 23 August 1933 he wrote that 'any report of a famine in Russia is today an exaggeration or malignant propaganda', going on to say that 'the food shortage which has affected almost the whole population in the last year and particularly the grain-producing provinces – that is the Ukraine, the North Caucasus, the Lower Volga Region – has, however, caused heavy loss of life'. He estimated the death rate as nearly four times the usual rate. This usual rate would, in the regions named, 'have been about 1,000,000' and this was now in all probability 'at least trebled'.

This admission of two million extra deaths was thus made to appear regrettable, but not overwhelmingly important and not amounting to 'famine'. (Moreover he blamed it in part on the 'flight of some peasants and the passive resistance of others'.)

In September 1933 he was the first correspondent to be admitted to the famine regions, and reported that 'the use of the word famine in connection with the North Caucasus is a sheer absurdity', adding that he now felt that for this area at least his earlier estimate of excess deaths had been 'exaggerated'. He also spoke of 'plump babies' and 'fat calves' as typical of the Kuban. (Litvinov found it useful to cite these despatches in answering Congressman Kopelmann's letter of inquiry.)

Duranty blamed famine stories on emigrés, encouraged by the rise of Hitler, and spoke of 'the famine stories then current in Berlin, Riga, Vienna and other places, where elements hostile to the Soviet Union were making an eleventh-hour attempt to avert American recognition by picturing the Soviet Union as a land of ruin and despair'.

The reputation Duranty had already acquired by the autumn of 1933 is dryly expressed in a despatch from the British Embassy about the visit Duranty (an Englishman) had now been permitted to make to the grain areas of the Ukraine: 'I have no doubt that

. . . he will have no difficulty in obtaining sufficient quantitative experience in tour hours to enable him to say whatever he may wish to say on return.' It also described him as 'Mr Duranty, *The New York Times* Correspondent, whom the Soviet Union is probably more anxious to conciliate than any other'.

Malcolm Muggeridge, Joseph Alsop and other experienced journalists held the plain opinion that Duranty was a liar – as Muggeridge later put it 'the greatest liar of any journalist I have met in fifty years of journalism'.

This lobby of the blind and the blindfold could not actually prevent true accounts by those who were neither dupes nor liars from reaching the West. But they could, and did, succeed in giving the impression that there was at least a genuine doubt about what was happening and insinuating that reports of starvation came only from those hostile to the Soviet government and hence of dubious reliability. Reporters of the truth like Muggeridge and Chamberlain were under continuous and violent attack by pro-Communist elements in the West over the next generation.

For the falsification was not temporary. It had entered the field of 'scholarship' with the Webbs* and others. It continued to produce results – such as one scandalous piece of active, rather than merely conniving, falsification coming as late as in the 1940s, with the production in Hollywood of the film *North Star*, which represented a Soviet collective farm as a hygienic, well-fed village of happy peasants – a travesty greater than could have been shown on Soviet screens to audiences used to lies, but experienced in this particular matter to a degree requiring at least a minimum of restraint.

One Communist gave as the reason, or one of the reasons, for the suppression of truth, the fact that the USSR could only win the support of workers in the capitalist countries if the human

*Sidney and Beatrice Webb published *Soviet Communism: A New Civilization* in 1937.

cost of its policies was concealed. It seems not in practice to have been so much a matter of the workers as of the intellectuals and formers of public opinion.

As George Orwell complained (of England), 'Huge events like the Ukraine famine of 1933, involving the deaths of millions of people, have actually escaped the attention of the majority of English russophiles.' But it was not only a matter of pure russophiles, but also a large and influential body of Western thought.

The scandal is not that they justified the Soviet actions, but that they refused to hear about them, that they were not prepared to hear about them, that they were not prepared to face the evidence.

•

The Reichstag fire

HANS BERND GISEVIUS

Late one cold February night in 1933, the building that housed the German Reichstag went up in flames; and with the immediate enactment of 'emergency decrees for the protection of nation and state' against 'Communist assaults', so did democracy. A Dutchman and Communist, Marinus van der Lubbe, was found guilty of incendiarism, and executed. Nevertheless, suspicions remained that it was the Nazis themselves who had set fire to the building. Not the least of the difficulties in accepting the idea of a lone arsonist was that it was logistically impossible for one man to have caused fires in so many separate parts of the building. These suspicions were intensified when the body of a man by the name of Rall was found in a shallow grave outside Berlin. Prior to his death, Rall, a prisoner on a burglary charge, had one day appeared before magistrates and made an unexpected statement about the Reichstag fire. His story was that he and named members of the SA had set fire to the Reichstag. Hans Bernd

Gisevius, one of the few survivors of the 1944 plot to kill Hitler, was a member of the Gestapo at the time of the fire. Here he examines the lie that was supposed to have sheltered the guilty parties, but which went wrong.

Rall's rather primitive confession was sufficient, so to speak, to loosen the bonds of propriety which had restrained all talk about the Reichstag fire. After a few drinks Ernst or Diels or Geissel would recapitulate their memories of the night of the fire. The untimely discovery of Rall's body broke the seal of silence which had been placed on the case. Consequently, Nebe and I received enough hints to put together a fairly exact sketch of the more obscure aspects of the fire. A harmless, casual question or two put to other participants rounded out the picture for us.

The sensational element for us – and we had a hard time convincing ourselves that it was true – was that Goebbels, not Goering, was the real Reichstag incendiary. It was Goebbels who first thought of it. Goebbels had held the preliminary conferences with Karl Ernst. Goebbels had approved the choice of the squad. Goebbels had indicated the rooms where the fire would get the best foothold. Goebbels had 'facilitated' the execution of the business by giving his sanction to the shooting-down of any chance witnesses.

Goebbels had guaranteed that no one would conduct a search in the group headquarters or in the palace of the Reichstag president. Goebbels had promised that any action against SA men would be denounced as a libellous attack on the Nazi movement itself. Goebbels had originated the plan of not merely accusing the Communists, but of generously turning over the problem of solving the crime to the police.

Goebbels had clearly perceived the value of muzzling the entire Left press as a device for concealing the truth. Goebbels had therefore vigorously urged the proclamation of the vicious emergency decrees. It was this point that Goebbels had discussed at length with Goering. In the course of this discussion Goebbels had mysteriously hinted that the Führer was aware that something dramatic and thorough had to take place – perhaps an attempted assassination, perhaps a fire – but that Hitler wished to be surprised.

And Goebbels had then taken the responsibility for 'preparing' the Führer for the game, laying the ground for Hitler's outburst of fury on the night of the fire. Let us remember that Hitler was dining with Goebbels when he was startled by the news of the fire!

Goering had simply given his consent to the whole plot. The Reich propaganda minister's plot appealed to him; he particularly liked the fact that no participation would be required of him. He was perfectly willing to place the palace and the underground tunnel at their disposal, but if Goebbels and Karl Ernst wanted to do the rest, to turn the trick by themselves, so much the better for him. That way was far safer: he need only wait to see Hitler's or Hindenburg's reaction. Naturally Goebbels could depend on Goering's willingness to seize the slightest and most fantastic pretext to strike out at the Marxists. Goering did, of course, have some part to play. He took the precaution of talking the matter over with Diels and dropping a few hints to Daluege. But for the rest he merely let the affair run its course.

Helldorf had no part at all. This SA group leader was enjoying champagne and caviar in a luxurious nightclub when the sirens began howling and the word was passed around that the Reichstag was on fire. Accompanied by his SA comrade, von Arnim, the rector of the Technical High School, Helldorf went out into the street and convinced himself that the sky was indeed blood-red. The two men debated whether they ought to drive to the scene. But learning that the fire-engines had already arrived, and that the Führer, Goebbels, Goering and Papen were also on the spot, Helldorf decided to return to his good food and his tête-à-tête.

I heard Helldorf give this account of the scene repeatedly. It was widely believed that he must have participated as one of the leaders in the affair – the impression arose from Lubbe's momentary reaction at the trial when Helldorf sharply ordered him to raise his head. To my mind this was a mere bit of drama whose significance was greatly magnified. Unlike other SA leaders who testified before the Leipzig court, Helldorf moved in these lofty circles with complete social ease. Men like Heines, the SA group leader and police chief of Breslau, would have been incapable of the nonchalance with which Count Helldorf, in response to the question of whether he had ever seen Lubbe before, condescendingly ordered the Dutchman: 'Lift up your head for once.' All the other SA toughs who killed every day without the slightest compunction were in agony every time they had to appear before the court and the throng of foreign correspondents. Their discomfort was plainly visible, and they stood rigidly at attention while they poured out their perjuries. Such men would never have ventured to address Lubbe that way in the solemn atmosphere of the court.

The key question still remains: How did Lubbe become involved in the diabolic business? We already know that this poor fellow was not needed to set the Reichstag on fire. We did not need Rall to certify to this obvious fact. On the other hand, Lubbe could not very well have stood around in a corner until the flames were shooting high.

The first fact that we determined with certainty was that the performance would have been given even without Lubbe. The date, the incendiaries, the inflammable fluid were all prepared down to the last detail before this blunderer into world history put in his appearance.

Naturally, he was eagerly welcomed. It is hard to say, however, whether Goebbels did not have occasion later on to curse the chance that made him stumble across Lubbe. For the original plan had envisioned nothing more than a crude swindle, a raw piece of election propaganda. Basically it had been merely a matter of burning to the ground a building with ugly associations for the Nazis. An absurd act whose immediate effect was to disconcert the Opposition, followed by a reign of terror that would silence all doubters – such was ever the Nazi logic.

This crude plan was rudely disturbed when Lubbe made his bid to become a second Herostratus. Goebbels, of course, would not have been Goebbels if his perverted imagination had failed to reach out at once to grasp at this unfortunate Dutchman. What an obvious and splendid stroke of propaganda the man afforded! Not only would they accuse his Communist fellows: they would also produce a living, and moreover an alien, Bolshevist caught *in flagrante delicto*. Then, according to the plan, as soon as they had placarded the man's picture all over town, he would be hanged in an outburst of public fury. Lynch justice, the Americans called it. What could go wrong with such a plan?

But things did go wrong – the cunning Goebbels had not foreseen two possibilities. In the first place, Lubbe's arrest introduced a complication which would not have been present if there had simply been a conflagration and the police had found no incendiary. For now the formalities had to be observed; there had to be hearings, investigations, indictments, and ultimately a trial. And the more involved these public activities became, the more the swindle was imperilled. Moreover – and this is the second feature that the propaganda minister overlooked – Goebbels' imagination was not the only one that set to work. The spark ignited another mind – Hitler, too, let his imagination work on the alien who provided so picturesque a subject for the impending tribunal.

It does not matter whether Hitler knew or suspected anything before the fire; for the moment the flames leaped into the night sky, the moment the populace thronged to the scene and Lubbe's wretched figure stepped out of the burning building, the Führer was no longer the man he had been half an hour before. Hitler himself was enchanted; as in all dramatic moments he became the victim of his capacity for self-hypnosis. From that moment all he could think of was the great show-trial in which he, who was so fond of making revelations, would be able to say all manner of things to an astonished world.

•

The importance of being Ernest

JEFFREY MEYERS

To a great extent, Ernest Hemingway invented his own myth. He was a liar, and he knew it, admitted it even. Jeffrey Meyers examines Hemingway, 'the Ham'.

Hemingway was committed more to art than to action (though action stimulated his art), more to legend than to truth. When opportunity offered, he was capable of heroism; when it did not he escaped into mythomania. He followed the tradition of Mark Twain and frontier humor (which he had exploited in his high-school days), of exaggerated exploits and tall tales. In *Soldier's Home*, the most accurate portrayal of his feelings just after the war, Krebs is ashamed of his own need for mendacity: 'To be listened to at all he had to *lie*, and after he had done this twice he, too, had a reaction against the war and talking about it . . . His lies were quite unimportant lies and consisted in attributing to himself things other men had seen, done or heard of, and stating as facts certain apocryphal incidents familiar to all soldiers.' But later, when boasting and prevarication were more a sign of gregarious self-confidence than of security, Hemingway defended interesting lies as a vital expression of the writer's imagination: 'It is not *unnatural* that the best writers are liars. A major part of their trade is to lie or invent and they will lie when they are drunk, or to themselves, or to strangers. They often lie unconsciously and then remember their lies with deep remorse. If they knew all other writers were liars too it would cheer them up . . . A liar in full flower . . . is as beautiful as cherry trees, or apple trees when they are in full blossom. Who should ever discourage a liar?'

Hemingway always embroidered the events in his life. His

exaggerations, lies and heroic image were related to the traditions and myths of frontier humor that had inspired his youthful works. But he not only helped to create the myths about himself, he also seemed to believe them. He felt he could write only about what he had actually experienced and his literary credo was to tell it as it was. But he combined scrupulous honesty in his fiction with a tendency to distort and rewrite the story of his life. Given his predisposition to mythomania, his reluctance to disappoint either his own expectations or those of his audience, and the difficulty of refuting and verifying certain facts of his life, he felt virtually forced to invent an exciting and imaginative alternative to commonplace reality.

Hemingway turned his lies into legends and was able to live out his private fantasies. Like Vincent Berger, the hero of Malraux's *The Walnut Trees of Altenburg*, 'he could perhaps have found some means of destroying the mythical person he was growing into, had he been compelled. But he had no wish to do so. His reputation was flattering. What was more important, he enjoyed it.'

. . . Two of Hemingway's most successful public images were the soldier and the sage. He was a natural leader and claimed that he had 'fought in all the wars', though he had actually fought in none of them. When the journalist Vincent Sheean denied that Hemingway was a combatant in Spain, Pauline insisted that he had merely pretended to be a newspaperman 'while in fact holding a high combat command with the Loyalists. "This legendary, mythogenic quality," adds Sheean, "was not Ernest's fault; it was intrinsic to his character; he created such stories as unthinkingly as others breathe."'

. . . During his lifetime, the Hemingway legends took hold and replaced reality. Matthew Bruccoli has noted 'how difficult it is to establish the truth about virtually everything involving Hemingway', how 'difficult to differentiate the public Papa from the private writer'. As Joyce observed: 'the unfacts, did we possess them, are too imprecisely few to warrant our certitude'. Everyone believed that Hemingway had Indian blood, was kept out of school for a year to play the 'cello, ran away from home, injured his eye while boxing, associated with gangsters, had affairs with the actress Mae Marsh and the spy Mata Hari, fought with the Italian *Arditi*, was fitted with an aluminium kneecap, kept a mistress in Sicily, reported the battles of the Greco-Turkish War in the wilds of Anatolia. Yet virtually all the drinking, boxing, hunting, fishing and fornicating stories are exaggerations or fantasies. Edmund Wilson, who turned against Hemingway in *The Wound and the Bow*, observed that by 1939 he had already passed 'into a phase where he is occupied with building up his public personality . . . Hemingway has created a Hemingway who is not only incredible but obnoxious. He is certainly his own worst-invented character.'

•

Jewish ritual murder

DER STÜRMER

Der Stürmer is probably the most infamous newspaper in history. For over two decades it was the chief organ of Nazi-orchestrated anti-Semitism, although it was owned privately by Julius Streicher, who was hanged at Nuremberg for war crimes. At the height of its popularity, *Der Stürmer* had a circulation of nearly half a million, and a readership many times that number. This article is taken from the notorious ritual murder special of 1934.

JEWISH MURDER PLAN AGAINST GENTILE HUMANITY EXPOSED

THE MURDEROUS PEOPLE

The Jews are under a terrible suspicion the world over. Who does not know this, does not understand the Jewish problem. Anyone who merely sees the Jews, as Heinrich Heine (Chaim

Bueckberg) described them, 'a tribe which secures its existence with exchange and old trousers, and whose uniforms are the long noses', is being misled. But anyone who knows the monstrous accusation which has been raised against the Jews since the beginning of time, will view these people in a different light. He will begin to see not only a peculiar, strangely fascinating nation; but criminals, murderers, and devils in human form. He will be filled with holy anger and hatred against these people.

The suspicion under which the Jews are held is murder. They are charged with enticing Gentile children and Gentile adults, butchering them and draining the blood. They are charged with mixing this blood into their masses [sic] (unleaven [sic] bread) and using it to practise superstitious magic. They are charged with torturing their victims, especially children; and during this torture they shout threats, curse, and cast spells against the Gentiles. This systematic murder has a special name. It is called

RITUAL MURDER

The knowledge of Jewish ritual murder is thousands of years old. It is as old as the Jews themselves. The Gentiles have passed the knowledge of it from generation to generation, and it has been passed down to us through writings. It is known of throughout the nation. Knowledge of ritual murder can be found even in the most secluded rural villages. The grandfather told his grandchildren, who passed it on to his children, and his children's children, until we have inherited the knowledge today.

It is also befalling other nations. The accusation is loudly raised immediately, anywhere in the world, where a body is found which bears the marks of ritual murder. This accusation is raised only against the Jews. Hundreds and hundreds of nations, tribes, and races live on this earth, but no one ever thought to accuse them of the planned murdering of children or to call them murderers. All nations have hurled this accusation only against the Jews. And many great men have raised such an accusation. Dr Martin Luther writes in his book *Of the Jews and Their Lies*:

'They stabbed and pierced the body of the young boy Simon of Trent. They have also murdered other children . . . The sun never did shine on a more bloodthirsty and revengeful people as they, who imagine themselves to be the people of God, and who desire to and think they must murder and crush the heathen. Jesus Christ, the Almighty Preacher from Nazareth, spoke to the Jews: "Ye are of your father the devil, and the lusts of your father ye will do. He was a murderer from the beginning." '

THE STRUGGLE OF *DER STÜRMER*

The only newspaper in Germany, yes, in the whole world, which often screams the accusation of ritual murder into the Jewish face is *Der Stürmer*. For more than ten years *Der Stürmer* has led a gigantic battle against Judaism. This has caused *Der Stürmer* to be under constant attack by the Jews. Dozens of times it has been confiscated and prohibited. Its workers, most of all its editor Julius Streicher, have been dragged to court hundreds of times. They were convicted, punished and locked into prisons. *Der Stürmer* has come to know the Jew from the confession which Dr Conrad Alberti-Sittenfeld, a Jew, wrote in 1899 in No 12 of the magazine *Gesellschaft*:

> One of the most dangerous Jewish qualities is the brutal, direct barbaric intolerance. A worse tyranny cannot be practised than that which the Jewish clique practises. If you try to move against this Jewish clique, they will, without hesitating, use brutal methods to overcome you. Mainly the Jew tries to destroy his enemy in the mental area, by which he takes his material gain away, and undermines his civil existence. The vilest of all forms of retaliation, the boycott, is characteristically Jewish.

Der Stürmer has never been stopped. Just in Nuremberg alone there have been fought dozens of Talmudic and ritual murder cases in the courts. Because of the Jewish protests the attention of the whole world was focused on these cases. Thereafter heavy convictions followed. At first no judge had the guts to expose the Jewish problem. Finally in 1931 (court case lasting from Oct. 30th to Nov. 4th) *Der Stürmer* won its first victory. The jury found the following:

1. *Der Stürmer* is not fighting against the Jewish religion, but against the Jewish race.
2. The Talmud and Schulchan aruch are not religious books. They have no right to be protected under the religious paragraphs.
3. The laws of the Talmud which are quoted and published in *Der Stürmer* are exact quotations from the Talmud.
4. The laws of the Talmud are in harsh contradiction to German morals.
5. The Jews of today are being taught from the Talmud.

With this verdict *Der Stürmer* brought about the first big breach in the Jewish–Roman Administration of Justice, which was given the job before the National Socialist revolution to protect Judaism and its government. The Jews, of course, became greatly agitated about it all. But for *Der Stürmer* this success was an omen of victory yet to come. Of course, *Der Stürmer* does not stop half-way. It knows what must be done. It is our duty! to frustrate the gigantic murder plot of Judaism against humanity. It is our duty! to brand this nation before the whole world, to uncover its crimes and to render it harmless. It is our duty! to free the world from this national pest and parasitic race. *Der Stürmer* will fulfil its mission. It will light up the darkness with the truth which shall rule the world. And it will always direct itself according to the following proverb: 'He who knows the truth and does not speak it truly is a miserable creature.'

•

Agitprop

ARTHUR KOESTLER

Ernest Hemingway said that 'fascism is a lie told by bullies. A writer who will not lie cannot live and work under fascism.' There were, however, many who did just that. Equally there were many who told the Communist lie. During the Spanish Civil War, there came into being a Paris-based organization which went by the name of Agitprop – the Agitation and Propaganda Department of the Comintern. This group was made up of several correspondents who knowingly wrote lies on behalf of the Republican cause, which were disseminated as honest reporting. Among these was Arthur Koestler. He later described his efforts, and it is with this 'confession' that we are now concerned.

Arriving in Paris from Spain unexpectedly one day during the Spanish Civil War, I telephoned Katz at the office of the Agence Espagne, the news agency of the Republican Government which he organized and directed. As was usual when one telephoned any office run by Katz, an excited voice said, 'Si, si, mais, s'il vous plaît, be so good speak deutsch, bitten schoen, momentito,' and then Katz came on the line shouting, 'Thank God you're here, come at once, urgent.' He plunged immediately into business. 'Have I ever told you that you are considered by many, myself included, the best journalist in the world?'

'Often, when you wanted to get something for nothing out of me.'

'Well, what I want now is a tip-top, smashing, eye-witness account of the great anti-Franco revolt which occurred yesterday at Tetuan, the news of it having been hitherto suppressed by censorship.'

I said I had never been to Tetuan and knew of no revolt there.

'Not the point at all,' he said impatiently. 'Nor have I heard of any such thing.' The point, he explained, was that a crucial moment had been reached in the supply of arms to the battling Spanish Republicans.

Occasionally, despite non-intervention, the government of Léon Blum, under pressure from the Left, agreed that all concerned should shut both eyes tight while military supplies were rushed across the Catalan frontier. At this moment a major battle was being mounted in Spain. On the frontier a big consignment of field guns was ready. The outcome of the battle might depend on its getting through. Next morning a strong deputation of Communist deputies and others was to call on Blum, asking for a little shut-eye. Blum, naturally, was always more malleable when anything happened to suggest that Franco might, after all, lose the war. It was thus essential, Katz pointed out, that a jolt of that kind should be administered now. Something with a clear psychological impact. What better for the purpose than news of a sudden revolt against Franco at the very origin and source of his first onslaught, Spanish Morocco? Why not, for instance, Tetuan? That, he said, would have impact.

There seemed to be just a chance, and we worked on that story at a high pitch of anxiety and excitement. Our chief anxiety was that, with nothing to go on but the plans in the guide-books, which were without contours, we might have Democrats and Fascists firing at one another from either end of an avenue which some travelled night-editor would know had a great hump in the middle. The fighting, accordingly, took place in very short streets and open squares. As we saw it, an important feature of the affair was that sections of the Moorish soldiery, sickened by losses in Spain, had joined with civilian victims of colonial oppression and Spanish anti-Fascists in united, if desperate, action. It meant that the same thing might happen in Spain itself. Katz was insistent we use a lot of names, of both heroes and villains, but express uncertainty over some of them – thus in the confusion of the struggle outside the barracks it had been impossible to ascertain whether Captain Murillo who died so gallantly was the same Captain Murillo who, months ago in Madrid . . .

In the end it emerged as one of the most factual, inspiring and yet sober pieces of war reporting I ever saw, and the night-editors loved it. When the deputation saw Blum in the morning he had been reading it in newspaper after newspaper and appreciating its significance. He was receptive to the deputation's suggestions. The guns got through all right, and the Republicans won that battle.

. . . Many people to whom I have at one time and another told this little story of the Tetuan revolt have been themselves revolted, profoundly shocked. Or at least they said they were. When I first published it as part of an article in a weekly paper, Mr R. H. Crossman, Labour Member of Parliament, referred to it with disgust in a piece he wrote for the *News Chronicle*. Aware that Mr Crossman had himself played a considerable role in British wartime propaganda, I was in turn taken aback. Was it, then, possible that throughout the life-and-death struggle with Hitler our propagandists had all along taken the view that their paramount duty was to be gentlemen, and not to tell lies, however damagingly misleading these might be to the enemy? What about, I thought as I noted Mr Crossman's disdain for the Tetuan trick, the 'Man Who Never Was' and suchlike episodes?

Reading on, I was fascinated to find that what fretted Mr Crossman was not that the thing had been done, but that I seemed to be quite happy, retrospectively, to have had a hand in it. According to him, it was true that he and colleagues had done that sort of thing during the war, but they had done it with gentlemanly distaste. '"Black" propaganda,' wrote Mr Crossman, 'may be necessary in war, but most of us who practised it detested what we were doing.'

A comfortable ethical position, if you can stop laughing. To me, at least, there seems nothing risible in the spectacle of a man firing off his propaganda-lies as, one presumes, effectively as he knows how, but keeping his conscience clear by 'detesting' his own activities. After all, if he does not think the cause for which he is fighting is worth lying for, he does not have to lie at all, any more than the man who sincerely feels that killing is murder is forced to shoot at those enemy soldiers. He can become a conscientious objector, or run away. *'Paris vaut bien une messe'*, and I do not recall that Henry of Navarre ever claimed that he had detested his own 'cynical' behaviour.

At any rate, Katz had none of these inhibitions and did his work *con amore*.

•

We lied damnably

HANSARD/HAROLD NICOLSON

On 16 February 1938, in the House of Commons, Harold Nicolson spoke on the subject of British propaganda in a debate on the supply of British news abroad. He opposed the idea of broadcasting abroad with the aim of 'trying either to imitate or refute the lies of others'. The only sort of propaganda he could envisage would work 'not by telling any lies ourselves; but by thinking out calmly, quietly, what we do really represent in terms of culture, and by spending a great deal of money in order to see that theory is enhanced, fortified, and spread abroad'. With regard to the dangers of propaganda, Nicolson spoke as follows:

It is valuable that we should talk about this subject in the House, but if we are to achieve any creative unanimity . . . we must have some idea of what is the sound philosophy, or the sound theory, of British propaganda. I think the presence of the three words I have mentioned indicates the line – *not by retaliation*; and by that we not only mean not abusing the other side, but also . . . not imitating the methods adopted by the other side. I think that is vitally important. I think we must realize – and we do realize as the speeches made already show – that this question of propaganda is a new, multiple and highly dangerous instrument in international policy. We must bear in mind something more. It is an instrument which is uncongenial to ourselves. I do not want to be self-righteous, but I think it will be agreed that propaganda, in the first place, is based upon avoidance of the truth and I think it will also be agreed that in this country, in general, we object to untruths.

As I say, I do not want to be self-righteous, because in a national emergency we can be as untruthful as, or more untruthful than, anybody else. During the War we lied damnably. Let us be clear about that. [An Hon. Member: 'Splendidly?'] No, damnably, not splendidly. I think some of our lies have done us tremendous harm and I should not myself like to see such propaganda again. It has done us harm in several ways. If you read the early chapters of Hitler's book *Mein Kampf* you will find that the impression which was made by our propaganda upon the then Corporal Hitler was damaging and persistent and is now a dangerous impression. He thought it tremendous. He admired it very much. I think also that if you follow the lists of books published in the United States you will find, even at this moment, an enormous number of books being published devoted solely to the subject of the effects and methods of British propaganda in 1917 and 1918. It is most unfortunate. Therefore, we must not be self-righteous and say that we could never practise propaganda by such untruthful and dirty methods – because we can. But that was in time of war. In peace, the ordinary Englishman does not like telling lies and that is one reason why the whole thing is uncongenial.

There is another and more subtle reason. Propaganda, like commercial advertisement, is based on over-statement, and that over-statement is not adapted to our national temperament, whether English or Scottish. Our national temperament is based on under-statement and when we have to compete in terms of superlatives with Italy or Germany or even America, we do so half-heartedly. If propaganda is half-hearted it is bad. We have to get our propaganda whole-hearted. We have to get it on a basis which accords with our national temperament and that must be a basis of truth. Therefore, we cannot compete with or imitate other countries . . .

•

Hitler's Munich lie

ADOLF HITLER

Following his annexation of Austria – the *Anschluss* – Hitler turned his attention to the Sudetenland, that part of Czechoslovakia whose population was largely made up of Germans. Hitler demanded that they be allowed the right to self-determination; in other words, that they should become part of the greater German Reich. The Czech Government refused to consider such a proposition, and Hitler sent troops to the Czech border. Throughout September 1938, Europe held its breath while it waited to see if Hitler would invade the Sudetenland; and there was much diplomatic coming and going, culminating in the Munich agreement by which the British Prime Minister, Neville Chamberlain, achieved 'peace in our time'. A couple of days before Chamberlain's arrival in Munich, the Führer made a speech in Berlin in which he played the role of the reasonable man merely wanting a fair solution to the problem, and most mendaciously of all, denying any further territorial ambitions in Europe.

At this time I have also sought gradually to establish good and lasting relations with other nations. We have given guarantees for the States in the West, and to all those States bordering on our frontiers we have given our assurances of the inviolability of their territory so far as Germany is concerned. These are no mere words. This is our sacred determination. We have no interest in breaking the peace.

. . . I went further and offered the hand to England.

. . . I went further. Directly after the restoration of the Saar territory which was decided by a plebiscite I declared to France that there were now absolutely no differences outstanding between us. I said that for us the Alsace-Lorraine question no longer existed. It is a frontier district. The people of this country during the most recent decades has never really been asked its own opinion. We have the feeling that the inhabitants of this province will be happiest if they are not fought over again. All of us do not wish for any war with France. We want nothing from France – positively nothing. And when the Saar territory had returned to the Reich thanks to the loyal execution of the treaties by France – that I desire to reaffirm in this place – I solemnly declared for the future all territorial differences between France and Germany have been removed. Today I cannot see any difference between us. Here are two great peoples who both wish to work and live. And they will live their lives best if they work together.

. . . And now before us stands the last problem that must be solved and will be solved. It is the last territorial claim which I have to make in Europe, but it is the claim from which I will not recede, and which, God willing, I will make good.

This history of the problem is as follows: in 1918 under the watchword 'The Right of the Peoples to Self-Determination' Central Europe was torn in pieces and was newly formed by certain crazy, so-called 'statesmen'. Without regard for the origin of the peoples, without regard for either their wish as a nation or the economic necessities, Central Europe at that time was broken into atoms and new so-called States were arbitrarily formed. To this procedure Czechoslovakia owes its existence. This Czech State began with a single lie and the father of this lie was named Benes [President of Czechoslovakia]. This Mr Benes at that time appeared in Versailles and he first of all gave the assurance that there was a Czechoslovak nation. He was forced to invent this lie in order to give to the slender number of his own fellow countrymen a somewhat greater range and then a fuller justification. And the Anglo-Saxon statesmen, who were, as always, not very adequately versed in respect of questions of geography or nationality, did not at that time find it necessary to test these assertions of Mr Benes. Had they done so, they could have established the fact that there is no such thing as a Czechoslovak nation but only Czechs and Slovaks and that the Slovaks did not wish to have anything to do with the Czechs, but . . .

I am grateful to Mr Chamberlain for all his efforts. I have assured him that the German people desires nothing else than peace, but I have also told him that I cannot go back behind the limits set to our patience. I have further assured him, and I repeat it here, that when the problem is solved there is for Germany no further territorial problem in Europe. And I have still further assured him that at the moment when Czechoslovakia solves her problems, that means when the Czechs have come to terms with their other minorities, and that peaceably and not through oppression, then I have no further interest in the Czech State. And that is guaranteed to him! We want no Czechs!

But in the same way I desire to state before the German people that with regard to the problem of the Sudeten Germans my patience is now at an end! I have made Mr Benes an offer which is nothing but the carrying into effect of what he himself has promised. The decision now lies in his hands: peace or war! He will either accept this offer and now at last give to the Germans their freedom, or we will go and fetch this freedom for ourselves.

. . . In this hour we all wish to form a common will and that will must be stronger than every hardship and every danger. And if this will is stronger than hardship and danger then one day it will break down hardship and danger.

We are determined!

Now let Mr Benes make his choice.

•

Truth on a toilet wall

ALEKSANDER WAT

Aleksander Wat was a Polish intellectual, imprisoned by Stalin following the outbreak of the Second World War. His remarkable memoirs have been compared with Solzhenitsyn's work. Here, he recalls his time in Kiev Prison in the Soviet Union, where writing on the latrine walls provided the only truth in a world perverted by Soviet lies. Wat considers one of these pieces of graffiti which read: 'A curse on whoever invented the name Corrective Labour Camps'.

'A curse on whoever invented the name . . .' – anger about a name, the meaning of words, semantics. The loss of freedom, tyranny, abuse, hunger would all have been easier to bear if not for the compulsion to call them freedom, justice, the good of the people. Mass exterminations are not an exception in history; cruelty is part of human nature, part of society. But a new, third, dimension had been added that was more deeply and subtly oppressive: a vast enterprise to deform language. Had it been only lies and hypocrisy – lying is part of human nature and all governments are hypocritical. The rulers' hypocrisy can cause rebellion, but here any possible rebellion had been nipped in the bud once and for all. A lie is an infirmity, a disease of language. The natural function of language is to ascertain the truth, or truths. Lies, by their very nature partial and ephemeral, are revealed as lies when confronted with language's striving for truth. But here all the means of disclosure had been permanently confiscated by the police. The customary or even the logical, natural connections between words and things, facts, had been taken from the individual, expropriated everywhere, and nationalized for good, so that now any word could mean whatever suited the whims of the usurper of all words, meanings, things, and souls. The viler the deed, the more grandiloquent the name. But if only this procedure were used to mask criminal means and ignoble ends – that too had happened often enough in history, the history of wars, tyrannies, and annexations; Tacitus knew about all that. But in this case a coherent set of grandiloquent terms and the opposing monstrous reality were kept side by side, ostentatiously and with diabolical thoroughness and perseverance, and under threat of extermination a person was coerced into fully believing that the terms and the facts were identical. Such things had been anticipated and attempted in history's darker hours, but this was the first time that the 'reforging of souls' was carried out by the police on such a colossal scale, with such speed and such logic. Collective farmers dying of starvation were herded to films in which the tables buckled under the weight of food; under threat of death they *had* to believe that these banquets, and not their wretched poverty, their collective farms, were true and typical. Young enthusiasts sang rapturously: 'I know no other land/ Where a man can breathe so free' while their fathers perished in the camps. But for souls that had not been reforged yet, nothing was as hateful as that total corruption of language. It drove them to their wits' end. It suffocated them like a nightmare, like a noose around their necks.

When I was at liberty in Russia, which by then had been pacified until it was like a cemetery, I saw some old people who risked their lives to shout out, if only once, that slavery is slavery and not freedom. That was to be a common thing later on in post-war Poland, even during the blackest years. I was one of that large number, and I paid dearly for it.

So in the prison latrines you could read the plain human truth about Stalin's Russia – there, and only there.

•

Lord Haw-Haw and the anti-lie bureau

W. J. WEST

The voice called 'Oxford Accent' by those journalists monitoring German broadcasts, and christened 'Lord Haw-Haw', was not that of William Joyce, who was executed for treason in 1946. The voice had been broadcasting from Berlin before Joyce left Britain. It is not known whose voice first drew that sobriquet, but as we shall see, Joyce made the fatal mistake of assuming the role of the 'real' Lord Haw-Haw after his arrival in Germany.

William Joyce had been warned by a contact in MI5 that he was about to be arrested under the Emergency Powers Regulation 18(B). Instead of going to Ireland, as members of his family had thought most likely, he took advantage of an introduction he believed he had to Goebbels' Propaganda Ministry in Berlin. Unfortunately his contact, who both he and MI5 thought was a German agent, was nothing of the sort, merely a journalist who was dabbling in the espionage field. Joyce found to his horror that he was stranded in Berlin with almost no funds, war had been declared and his approaches to the authorities had got nowhere. One day early in September he and his wife had ended a fruitless day, searching for somewhere to live, having tea at one of the main Berlin hotels, and there, by chance, they were seen by Mrs Eckersley* who knew Joyce and had made small contributions to his party before the war. On her advice Joyce approached the authorities running the English-language radio station and got employment in a junior capacity carrying out translations. In a short while his actual position as leader of one of the principal National Socialist

*Mrs P. P. Eckersley, a Mosleyite fascist who, at the outbreak of war, had found employment with the English-language radio station in Berlin.

parties in Britain was recognized and he embarked on his radio career.

Joyce had obtained a first-class degree in English Literature at Bedford College, University of London, and he had subsequently embarked on a Ph.D. at King's College, London. His literary interests and political thought both developed rapidly in Berlin into one of the most sustained outbursts of political polemic in British letters, rivalling the achievements of such masters of the political pamphlet as William Prynne in the seventeenth century. Later in the war Joyce made the mistake of deciding to trade on the British propaganda triumph of Lord Haw-Haw and started a programme in which he himself spoke featuring as the 'real' Lord Haw-Haw. Many listeners in England at the time knew that this was not the voice they had got to know and hate, but the fiction had now become fact, a fact that was to take Joyce to the gallows.

Joyce's scripts, especially those written for the clandestine stations, were so convincing that they created a particular problem for the counter-propagandists at the Ministry of Information. This was the seemingly unstoppable spread of rumours which were given a spurious authenticity by being attributed to 'Lord Haw-Haw'. The old tag 'I read it in the papers' had long been replaced by 'I heard it on the radio'. This now became 'Haw-Haw said'. The department which dealt with these so-called 'Haw-Haw rumours' was the appropriately named 'Anti-Lie Bureau' of the Ministry of Information. The purpose of this bureau was originally to counteract supposed German propaganda lies with the truth. More often they found themselves in the position of giving the lie to rumours which were in fact true. Joyce and the other script writers soon realized that information from spies was unnecessary when writing for the average member of the British public. It was quite sufficient to tell them things directly related to their own environment, things happening around them, for everything else to be carried along with it, including demoralizing half-truths and embarrassing political facts. The sources of the 'rumours' most used were those that Mrs Eckersley and her colleagues worked from that inexhaustible quarry, the British newspapers. It is clear from evidence given in interrogations after the war that Joyce had access to the full range of the British Press within twenty-four hours of publication. Britain had German and other enemy papers in the same time; the planes which carried them arrived at specially arranged points at neutral airports, usually in Spain and Sweden, where waiting porters rapidly exchanged the bundles of newspapers from one plane to another.

Anyone who now reads the wartime British press, censored though it was by a variety of means, can soon see how the most 'authentic' rumours could be broadcast within hours of the things referred to actually happening.

. . . the whole matter of rumour and the activities of the Anti-Lie Bureau would have remained merely an embarrassing episode in British history, of limited importance and of significance only as an example of the sort of thing that could happen even within a democratic society when faced with a situation of total war. But unfortunately the tinge of totalitarianism became stronger when it was decided, on the model of similar legislation in Nazi Germany, to prosecute people who spread these rumours. It is difficult, at first, to see how a prosecution of someone for the spreading of a 'Haw-Haw rumour' could be carried out, and on what evidence a Court would be able to convict, especially when it is borne in mind that many of these rumours were known to be true and were only denied for reasons of security and morale. The method used was to arrest someone who had without doubt been spreading a rumour and attributing it to Lord Haw-Haw. The BBC was then approached and asked if the Monitors had taken down any similar 'rumour' at the time. If the answer was positive a prosecution took place at which the BBC gave evidence.

•

Bodyguard of lies: Churchill and the D-Day deceptions

ANTHONY CAVE-BROWN

'Neptune' was the code-word for the invasion of the Normandy coast of France in the spring of 1944, and 'Plan Jael' the overall deception policy of the Allied High Command to mislead Hitler about Allied strategy and tactics in the months ahead. The historian Anthony Cave-Brown describes how the British Prime Minister, Winston Churchill, made himself largely responsible for the central role that deceptions and stratagems would play in 'Neptune'.

The British Political Warfare Executive (PWE) and, to a lesser extent, the American Office of War Information (OWI) had been created expressly to wage, in concert with the LCS,* a war of words against the Third Reich. Their credo was 'to approach the German mind through a deception and through elaborately sustained fictions, calculated to throw it off its guard and to appeal to the selfish, disloyal, individualist motives in the [German soldier and citizen]'. Their main weapon was rumour – the theory that you may not be able to bomb a currency but you can certainly destroy it with a whisper; and their objective was 'to drive a wedge between the Nazi leaders and the people, and to create an intensification of war-weariness and defeatism by every means, open and clandestine . . .'

But words are not bullets, rumours are not bombs, and there were few indications that the obedience of the German people to their Führer was wavering, or that the German soldier was

*London Controlling Section: a secret bureau established by Churchill within his personal HQ to plan stratagems to deceive the Germans about Allied operations.

weakening in his determination to repulse an invasion. The Neptune planners knew of the serious disagreements between Hitler and his generals; many of the highest officers of the German General Staff were, in fact, members of the Schwarze Kapelle.* Thus far their conspiracies had come to little, and Hitler retained his iron grip over his generals, the German people and the continent of Europe. But any manoeuvre, any expedient, was worthy of consideration. For this was total war. The Allies had demanded, in the resounding – and some commanders believed ill-considered – proclamation of 'Unconditional Surrender', the complete capitulation of Germany. And Germany would not surrender without a monumental fight. Neptune would be the decisive encounter in a war that had to be fought to the bitter end, and the secret war that attended Neptune would be equally bitter. As Foot† later wrote: 'Nothing quite like it had ever been seen before; probably nothing quite like it will be seen again, for the circumstances of Hitler's war were unique, and called out this among other unique responses.'

The most unique of those responses was the fifth area of covert activity proposed in Plan Jael – deception, the ultimate secret weapon and the most secret of all secret operations. Deception was the province of the LCS, and its special assignment was to plant upon the enemy, along the channels open to it through the Allied High Command, hundreds, perhaps thousands of splinters of information that, when assembled by the enemy intelligence services, would form a plausible and acceptable – but false – picture of Allied military intentions. The LCS had refined the arts of deception in its past operations; now Jael proposed that Hitler be led to believe that the Allies intended to attack not Normandy but elsewhere in France. It was a deception that would decide the fate of Neptune. The LCS would have to use every conduit at its disposal in a carefully conceived and

*The 'Black Orchestra': a small group of officers conspiring to overthrow Hitler.

†Captain M. R. D. Foot, Special Air Service.

timed scenario of special means to send this fiction to the desk of Hitler. Those special means would involve whispers and rumours, the services of double and even triple agents, the careers and reputations of famous generals, sacrificial military and clandestine operations, wireless games, the creation of fictitious armies and the manipulation of resistance forces and the Schwarze Kapelle. In short, nothing could be overlooked in the attempt to convince the Germans that the invasion would strike at a different time and a different place than was actually intended.

. . . A plaque hung on the wall behind the men who frequently met beneath the pavements of Westminster to discuss the intricacies of Plan Jael. It was placed there as if in answer to the criticisms that were, perhaps, inevitable when the existence of this super-secret agency finally became known some fifteen years after the war was over. On the plaque were the words of Sir Garnet Wolseley, a former Commander-in-Chief of the British army, who wrote in *The Soldier's Handbook* in 1869:

> We are bred up to feel it a disgrace ever to succeed by falsehood . . . we will keep hammering along with the conviction that honesty is the best policy, and that truth always wins in the long run. These pretty little sentiments do well for a child's copy book, but a man who acts on them had better sheath his sword forever.

It was clear that Churchill and the LCS would stop at nothing to ensure secrecy and surprise for Neptune. Even Churchill's choice of code-name for the cover and deception operations that would attend Neptune revealed something of their cunning, merciless and intent. Jael was the woman in the Song of Deborah in the Old Testament who committed one of the blackest acts of treachery in that long, dark chronicle. For the Song tells how Deborah the Prophetess plotted with Barak, the commander of the Israelite army, to defeat Jabin, the King of Canaan, and Sisera, the Canaanite commander who, with 'nine hundred chariots of iron', had ruled the Israelites for twenty years. Their stratagem succeeded and Sisera was lured to battle at the foot of Mount Tabor on the Plain of Esdraelon. There was a heaven-sent rainstorm, Sisera's chariots bogged down, Barak and his men emerged from their hiding place on the mountainside, 'And the Lord discomfited Sisera, and all his chariots . . . and all the host of Sisera fell upon the edge of the sword; and there was not a man left.'

Sisera himself survived and fled the battlefield on foot; and as he was trying to reach Canaan, he happened upon the encampment of Heber the Kenite, who was absent that day. But his wife Jael greeted him cordially; and believing that a treaty of friendship existed between the Canaanites and the Kenites, Sisera asked for food and a place to rest. To this Jael agreed, and exhausted by battle and his flight, Sisera lay down upon her bed. Jael brought him goat's milk and promised to stand guard at the tent door, but when Sisera was deeply asleep, she took a hammer and a tent peg and 'smote the nail into his temples, and fastened it into the ground . . .'

> Thus ended the Canaanites' rule of the Israelites. And thus, it was hoped, would Plan Jael help the Allies end the rule of Hitler.

By December of 1943, as every other Allied agency prepared for its part in Neptune, the finishing touches had been put on Plan Jael and it was ready to be sent for approval to the Combined Chiefs of Staff at Washington, the highest Allied war council. It was little more than a formality, for Jael had already been agreed upon as the overall deception policy of the Grand Alliance at the conference between Churchill, Roosevelt and Marshal Josef Stalin at Teheran in November 1943. There remained only one further consideration: the question of the code-name for the plan. Appropriate as it was, it was decided, reluctantly, to change the name of the plan. For only a few days before, at Teheran, Churchill, in describing the special means of Plan Jael, had made a remark that would become a classic epigram.

> 'In war-time, truth is so precious, that she should always be attended by a bodyguard of lies.'

And so Plan Jael was renamed 'Plan Bodyguard', a *ruse de guerre* that would come to be compared with the Trojan Horse – a stratagem for which the totem was that graceful but wicked little sprite* at the centre of the LCS conference table.

Plan Bodyguard, and the intricate special means that would be employed in its execution, had been designed for a single purpose – to enable the best and finest of the young men of the Allied armies to get ashore – and stay ashore – in the first tumultuous hours of D-Day. No one could predict the success of Bodyguard until Neptune actually emerged from the sea. No one could be certain that the influences symbolized by the Dancing Faun would work to achieve surprise on June 6, 1944. For as General Sir Frederick Morgan, one of the planners of Neptune, later remarked, corrupting slightly the words of Wellington after Waterloo:

> It was going to be a close-run thing, a damned close-run thing – the closest-run thing you ever saw in your life.

•

Wasch und desinfektionsraum

CENTRAL COMMISSION FOR INVESTIGATION OF GERMAN CRIMES IN POLAND

From the evidence of witnesses who as prisoners were employed at the gas-chambers in Auschwitz, the operation of gassing prisoners wholesale relied heavily on the cooperation of the victims themselves, which was

*A dancing faun – 'the Greco-Roman numen that suggested dark and evil spirits at work in tangled forests'.

achieved partly by fear, and partly by the lies and deceptions of the SS.

Prisoners, selected for gassing straight from the trains on the railway line, and others selected in the camp, were driven to the crematoria on foot; those who were unable to walk were taken in motor trucks. Between the railway platform and the gas-chambers there was an uninterrupted procession of people towards the chambers as they were steadily cleared of corpses. In the middle of the road lorries were continually fetching the weak, old, sick, and children, from the railway. In the ditches at the road-sides lay SS-men with machine guns ready to fire. An SS-man addressed the crowd huddled in the yard telling them that they were going to the baths for disinfection as they were dirty and lousy, and in such a state they could not be admitted into the camp. The gassing was carried out under the personal supervision of the doctor SS-Hauptsturmführer Mengele. The prisoners who arrived in the yard of the crematorium were driven to the dressing-room, over the door of which was the inscription 'Wasch und Desinfektionsraum' and the same inscription in the language of the victims destined for gassing. From plans and remains which have been found, and from the evidence of witnesses, it appears that in the dressing-room there were clothing pegs with numbers. The SS-men advised the victims huddled in the cloakroom each of them to remember the number of the peg on which he had hung his clothes so that he might find them again easily afterwards. After undressing they were driven through a corridor to the actual gas-chamber, which had previously been heated with the aid of portable coke-braziers. This heating was necessary for the better evaporation of the hydrogen cyanide. By beating them with rods and setting dogs on them, about 2,000 victims were packed into a space of 210 square metres (250 square yards).

From the ceiling of this chamber, the better to deceive the victims, hung imitation shower-baths, from which water never poured. After the gas-tight doors had been closed, the air was pumped out and through four special openings in the ceiling, the contents of cans of cyclon, producing cyanide-hydrogen gas,* were poured in.

•

Why we must lie to children

GEORGE BERNARD SHAW

When my father, after conscientiously fulfilling his parental duty by expiating to me on the supreme excellence and authority of the Bible as a source of enlightenment and instruction, was tempted by his love of anti-climax to add that it is 'the damnedest parcel of lies ever invented', he was not uttering a blasphemous falsehood: he was only exaggerating a fact for the sake of a chuckle. For the Bible does contain a good many lies which ought never to be told to children, and which are yet inculcated by all the Christian Churches as divine truths. Who can defend teaching children, or adults either, that there are such beings as witches, and that it is our duty to kill them? Or that the universe was made and is ruled by a tribal deity who was so shocked by the wickedness of the human race he had himself created that he sent a flood to drown it, but was persuaded to spare one family because its patriarch put him in a good humour by roasting a joint of beef to put under his nose? Or that a later deity, equally shocked by his own handiwork, sent his innocent son into the world to be horribly tortured and slain to expiate our crimes, and that those of us who believe this will go to heaven no matter what sins we commit, and those who do not will be damned everlastingly however virtuously they have lived? What civilization could any State build on these savage superstitions of vindictive theism and blood sacrifice? And who would now be obsessed by them if they had not been inculcated during

*The cyclon needed for the killing of the victims locked in the chamber was brought by an SS doctor in a car with the Red Cross on it.

infancy? Surely the Russian Government, the German Government, the Voltairean French Government are right in decreeing that children in their jurisdiction shall be protected against such inculcation, and better informed. Should not the British Government in the present crisis warn the Church of England that it will be disestablished and disendowed if it does not at once stop declaring in the eighteenth of its Thirty-nine articles that the majority of the human race, including our Russian allies, are to be held accursed?

What shall we tell our naughty children? They are all naughty occasionally, sometimes in a crisis of nerves, sometimes more rationally because they do not see why they should not do as they like. It is easy for a Ministry of Education to rule that the parent or teacher or nurse must not tell lies nor beat it nor drug it. But suppose its mother says, 'I find that the best and only means of discharging a crisis of nerves is a smacking. Can you suggest anything better?' Suppose the teacher says, 'When a child asks why it should not do as it pleases I cannot ask it to read Hobbes's *Leviathan* or Herbert Spencer's *Data of Ethics*: I have to tell it that there is such a place as hell and that it will be sent there if it does not do what it is told. This is a lie; but the child believes it and understands it and behaves itself. If I may not tell it this lie, what lie am I to tell it? seeing that the truth is beyond comprehension.' My own nursemaid kept me in order by threatening that if I persisted in disobeying her 'the cock would come down the chimney.' To me the cock was an avenging deity. And I doubt whether the most enlightened Ministry of Education could have managed me at that age more effectually than the nursemaid. Mahomet, one of the wisest men who ever had this problem to tackle, could not govern the Arabs, nor wean them from the worship of sacred stones, without inventing a hell which was not only terrifying but disgusting, and substituting for the stones a God (Allah) who was certainly a great improvement on Jehovah, but in whose existence we can no longer believe as naively as Mahomet did. Dante elaborated the picture for the Christian Churches. Many people still believe quite seriously in hell; and though a considerable number of influential persons scoff at it, the results are not reassuring: those who no longer fear anything beyond the grave are sometimes dangerously unscrupulous on this side of it. In the Middle Ages men committed crimes; but they made very substantial efforts to expiate them. Our criminals within the law are left to their consciences (when they have any); and though they subscribe to charities to mitigate the poverty and disease their selfishness creates, they leave us neither the cathedrals nor the great charities and schools we owe to William the Conqueror and his like.

It seems then that the State must tell its citizens lies of some sort to keep them in order, and that the lies must vary according to their ages; for a boy or a girl of ten will not be afraid of the cock coming down the chimney.

•

The party is always right: the prevention of literature

GEORGE ORWELL

Freedom of thought and of the Press are usually attacked by arguments which are not worth bothering about. Anyone who has experience of lecturing and debating knows them off backwards. Here I am not trying to deal with the familiar claim that freedom is an illusion, or with the claim that there is more freedom in totalitarian countries than in democratic ones, but with the much more tenable and dangerous proposition that freedom is *undesirable* and that intellectual honesty is a form of anti-social selfishness. Although other aspects of the question are usually in the foreground, the controversy over freedom of speech and of the Press is at bottom a controversy over the desirability or otherwise of telling lies. What is really at issue is the right to report contemporary events truthfully, or as truthfully as is consistent with the ignorance, bias and self-deception from which every observer necessarily suffers. In saying this I may seem to be saying that straightforward 'reportage' is the only branch of literature that matters: but I will try to show later that at every literary level, and probably in every one of the arts, the same issue arises in more or less subtilized forms. Meanwhile, it is necessary to strip away the irrelevancies in which this controversy is usually wrapped up.

The enemies of intellectual liberty always try to present their case as a plea for discipline versus individualism. The issue truth-versus-untruth is as far as possible kept in the background. Although the point of emphasis may vary, the writer who refuses to sell his opinions is always branded as a mere *egoist*. He is accused, that is, either of wanting to shut himself up in an ivory tower, or of making an exhibitionist display of his own personality, or of resisting the inevitable current of history in an attempt to cling to unjustified privileges. The Catholic and the Communist are alike in assuming that an opponent cannot be both honest and intelligent. Each of them tacitly claims that 'the truth' has already been revealed, and that the heretic, if he is not simply a fool, is secretly aware of 'the truth' and merely resists it out of selfish motives. In Communist literature the attack on 'petty-bourgeois individualism', 'the illusions of nineteenth-century liberalism', etc., are backed up by words of abuse such as 'romantic' and 'sentimental', which, since they do not have any agreed meaning, are difficult to answer. In this way the controversy is manoeuvred away from its real issue. One can accept, and most enlightened people would accept, the Communist thesis that pure freedom will only exist in a classless society, and that one is most nearly free when one is working to bring such a society about. But slipped in with this is the quite unfounded claim that the Communist Party is itself aiming at the establishment of the classless society, and that in the USSR this aim is actually on the way to being realized. If the first claim is allowed to entail the second, there is almost no assault on common sense and common decency that cannot be justified. But meanwhile, the real point has been dodged. Freedom of the intellect means the freedom to report what one has seen, heard, and felt, and not to be obliged to fabricate imaginary facts and feelings. The familiar tirades against 'escapism', and 'individualism', 'romanticism' and so forth, are merely a forensic device, the aim of which is to make the perversion of history seem respectable.

The organized lying practised by totalitarian states is not, as is sometimes claimed, a temporary expedient of the same nature as military deception. It is something integral to totalitarianism, something that would still continue even if concentration camps and secret police forces had ceased to be necessary. Among intelligent Communists there is an underground legend to the effect that although the Russian government is obliged *now* to deal in lying propaganda, frame-up trials, and so forth, it is secretly recording the true facts and will publish them at some future date. We can, I believe, be quite certain that this is not the case, because the mentality implied by such an action is that of a liberal historian who believes that the past cannot be altered and that a correct knowledge of history is valuable as a matter of course. From the totalitarian point of view history is something to be created rather than learned. A totalitarian state is in effect a theocracy, and its ruling caste, in order to keep its position, has to be thought of as infallible. But since, in practice, no one is infallible, it is frequently necessary to rearrange past events in order to show that this or that mistake was not made, or that this or that imaginary triumph actually happened. Then again, every major change in policy demands a corresponding change of doctrine and a revaluation of prominent historical figures. This kind of thing happens everywhere, but is clearly likelier to lead to outright falsification in societies where only *one* opinion is permissible at any given moment. Totalitarianism demands, in fact, the continuous alteration of the past, and in the long run probably demands a disbelief in the very existence of objective truth. The friends of totalitarianism in this country usually tend to argue that since absolute truth is not attainable, a big lie is no worse than a little lie. It is pointed out that *all* historical records are biased and inaccurate, or, on the other hand, that modern physics has proved that what seems to us the real world is an illusion, so that to believe in the evidence of one's senses is simply vulgar philistinism. A totalitarian society which succeeded in perpetuating itself would probably set up a schizophrenic system of thought, in which the laws of common sense held good in everyday life and in certain exact sciences, but could be disregarded by the politician, the historian, and the sociologist. Already there are countless people who would think it scandalous to falsify a scientific textbook, but would see nothing wrong in falsifying a historical fact. It is at the point where literature and politics cross that totalitarianism exerts its greatest pressure on the intellectual. The exact sciences are not, at this date, menaced to anything like the same extent. This partly accounts for the fact that in all countries it is easier for the scientists than for the writers to line up behind their respective governments.

Literature has sometimes flourished under despotic regimes, but, as has often been pointed out, the despotisms of the past were not totalitarian. Their respective apparatus was always inefficient, their ruling classes were usually either corrupt or apathetic or half-liberal in outlook, and the prevailing religious doctrines usually worked against perfectionism and the notion of human infallibility. Even so it is broadly true that prose literature has reached its highest levels in periods of democracy and free speculation. What is new in totalitarianism is that its doctrines are not only unchallengeable but also unstable. They have to be accepted on pain of damnation, but on the other hand they are always liable to be altered at a moment's notice. Consider, for example, the various attitudes, completely incompatible with one another, which an English Communist or 'fellow-traveller' has had to adopt towards the war between Britain and Germany. For years before September, 1939, he was expected to be in a continuous stew about 'the horrors of Nazism' and to twist everything he wrote into a denunciation of Hitler: after September, 1939,* for twenty months, he had to believe that Germany was more sinned against than sinning, and the word 'Nazi', at least as far as print went, had to drop right out of his vocabulary. Immediately after hearing the 8 o'clock news bulletin on the morning of 22nd June, 1941, he had to start believing once again that Nazism was the most hideous evil the world had ever seen.† Now, it is easy for a politician to make such changes: for a writer the case is somewhat different. If he is to switch his allegiance at exactly the right moment, he must either tell lies about his subjective feelings, or else suppress them altogether. In either case he has destroyed his dynamo. Not only will ideas refuse to come to him, but the very words he uses will seem to stiffen under his touch. Political writing in our time consists almost entirely of prefabricated phrases bolted together like the pieces of a child's Meccano set. It is the unavoidable result of self-censorship. To write in plain, vigorous language one has to think fearlessly, and if one thinks fearlessly one cannot be politically orthodox. It might be otherwise in an 'age of faith', when the prevailing orthodoxy has been long established and is not taken too seriously. In that case it would be possible, or might be possible, for large areas of one's mind to remain unaffected by what one officially believed. Even so, it is worth noticing that prose literature almost disappeared during the only age of faith that Europe has ever enjoyed. Throughout the whole of the Middle Ages there was almost no imaginative prose literature and very little in the way of historical writing: and the intellectual leaders in society expressed their most serious thoughts in a dead language which barely altered during a thousand years.

Totalitarianism, however, does not so much promise an age of faith as an age of schizophrenia. A society becomes totalitarian when its structures become flagrantly artificial: that is, when its ruling class has lost its function but succeeds in clinging to power by force or fraud. Such a society, no matter how long it

*Hitler's non-aggression pact with Stalin was signed in September 1939.
†The German army attacked the Soviet Union on 22 June 1941.

persists, can never afford to become either tolerant or intellectually stable. It can never permit either the truthful recording of facts, or the emotional sincerity, that literary creation demands. But to be corrupted by totalitarianism one does not have to live in a totalitarian country. The mere prevalence of certain ideas can spread a kind of poison that makes one subject after another impossible for literary purposes. Wherever there is an enforced orthodoxy – or even two orthodoxies, as often happens – good writing stops. This is well illustrated by the Spanish Civil War. To many English intellectuals the war was a deeply moving experience about which they could write sincerely. There were only two things that you were allowed to say, and both of them were palpable lies: as a result, the war produced acres of print but almost nothing worth reading.

•

Kaltenbrunner's denial

ANN AND JOHN TUSA

Of all the charges brought at Nuremberg, the indictment against Ernst Kaltenbrunner, former head of the Gestapo and SD,* was the longest. Himmler, Heydrich and Muller were dead, and Eichmann had disappeared; therefore Kaltenbrunner was the sole representative of the organization which had implemented Hitler's policy of genocide.

Kaltenbrunner made no attempt to deny the crimes of the Gestapo and the SD. As Dean observed in a cable with some understatement: 'this should prove useful in the case against these organizations'. Indeed Kaltenbrunner denied no crimes. Like Keitel he simply denied he had any connection with them. But he extended this line of defence to an unparalleled length and thinness. It was no wonder he looked pale and nervous as he

**Sicherheitsdienst*: the Nazi security service.

gave evidence and stretched credulity, that he twitched incessantly as he tried to maintain the untenable. Keitel had at least admitted to drafting orders, even to signing them. Kaltenbrunner would admit to nothing. He claimed that orders were issued in his name without his knowledge; that he was constantly bypassed in the chain of command; that he was never informed of policies in operation when he took office and remained unaware of them. His examination in chief took only a morning. It had been a session of breathtaking high-wire lying, made all the more amazing because he was such a clumsy performer. The *Daily Telegraph* thought Kaltenbrunner must be 'surely the most inept Nazi apologist to enter the witness box'. *The Times* thought he had put forward 'the ugliest defence yet heard at the Nuremberg trial . . . a flood of clumsy denial that would look stupid were it not a sorry attempt to hide behind dead men' – Himmler and Muller in particular. Birkett, like everyone else, had to accept that 'it is impossible to think of the position occupied by Kaltenbrunner and at the same time to believe that he was ignorant of so many matters'. Yet Birkett suffered from the problem experienced so often by those at Nuremberg: 'It is always difficult to imagine that one human person can have been the head and fount of such scenes of misery and bloodshed.'

But once the cross-examination of Kaltenbrunner began, it became certain that he had indeed been the originator of so many of the most loathsome of all Nazi crimes. For a day and a half Amen* laid bare his lies. Amen had collected damning affidavits and documents and he used them with remorseless efficiency. Out came example after example of Kaltenbrunner as the vital cog in the machine by which Himmler had processed arrests, punishments, executions. There in court were Kaltenbrunner's own orders for British and American commandos to be shot, for anti-Jewish measures to begin in Denmark, for SD members to be drafted into Einsatzkommandos, for 65,000 prisoners to be murdered in Mauthausen, for Hungarian Jews to be worked to

*Colonel John Amen, member of the US prosecuting team.

death. Kaltenbrunner denied them all, of course. He tried to claim that his signatures were only facsimiles; when that failed, he claimed they were forgeries. He attempted to explain that he had negotiated with the Red Cross for the hand-over of prisoners, that thanks to his efforts the extermination of the Jews had stopped in 1944. He swore he had only ever seen one concentration camp and that was Mauthausen, which he called a labour camp where stone was quarried for the pavements of Vienna. He declared he had never even heard of Auschwitz until 1943 when Himmler told him it was an armaments factory; that he never saw a gas-chamber; that he had never heard of a policy to kill Jews – it was all settled when he took office (and this minutes after he had claimed to have stopped extermination).

But all Amen's evidence made nonsense of Kaltenbrunner's disclaimers. Affidavits told of his three visits to Mauthausen, of how he 'went laughing into a gas-chamber' and enjoyed demonstrations of the three methods of execution: hanging, gassing and shooting in the back of the neck. 'Lies,' said Kaltenbrunner. Another affidavit explained that SD units engaged in wiping out the Warsaw Ghetto got their orders direct from Kaltenbrunner. The man who wrote it, said Kaltenbrunner, 'comes from North Germany and knows nothing about history or politics'. As Amen pressed his case, Kaltenbrunner became hysterical: 'For a whole year I have had to submit to this insult of being a liar,' he screamed. Then in a characteristic flash of self-pity he whimpered: 'My mother who died in 1943 was called a whore and many similar things were hurled at me.'

The other defendants thought it a contemptible exhibition. They all expressed horror at the lies the man was telling – though they were all prepared to perjure themselves, they could not stomach the sheer quantity of brazen perjury Kaltenbrunner was indulging in. Nor, in spite of their own proclivities, could they countenance such gross claims of ignorance and lack of responsibility. From the first session in Kaltenbrunner's defence 'his fellow prisoners in the dock began to look embarrassed', *The Times* reported. 'Goering absented himself in the afternoon with a slight cold.' When Kaltenbrunner returned to the dock on the second day, Jodl 'was the only co-defendant who said a word to him'.

Ernst Kaltenbrunner was hanged for war crimes on 16 October 1946.

•

Shifting the blame

ANN AND JOHN TUSA

After the end of the Second World War, the International Military Tribunal at Nuremberg, which was made up of representatives of the four powers, America, Britain, the Soviet Union and France, sought to try those who were guilty of war crimes. But the trial was also a convenient opportunity for the Soviets to try and shift the blame for the Katyn massacre – in which 11,000 Polish officers had been rounded up and shot – on to the Germans.

. . . [The] judges had to clear a problem which had occasionally surfaced from the time the indictment was drawn up – the Russian allegation that the German army had murdered up to 11,000 Polish officers in Katyn wood near Smolensk. The Russians had embarrassed their colleagues by insisting on including this charge; most people suspected that the Russians themselves had been responsible for the killings. Their subsequent handling of the matter had increased that embarrassment, incensed the defence, and irritated the judges. When first raised in court in February during the Russian prosecution case, Pokrovsky had called the Katyn murders 'one of the most important criminal acts for which the major war criminals are responsible'. Yet in spite of such a large verbal claim he had considered it adequate to summarize briefly a report on the atrocity by the Soviet Extraordinary State Commission and then to submit that report as the sole evidence for his allegation. The defence clamoured for a fuller hearing of the charge. Had they merely called for a chance to prove Russian guilt in order to establish a damaging case of *tu quoque*, they would undoubtedly have been overruled by the Tribunal. As it was the judges themselves were far from satisfied with Pokrovsky's perfunctory presentation of such a grave matter. On 12 March they summoned the Russian chief prosecutor, Rudenko, and insisted he call witnesses to substantiate the charge and to face cross-examination. Rudenko's high-handed response increased their determination to hold a more thorough examination – he not only protested against their ruling on witnesses, he made the indefensible claim that the report of the Extraordinary State Commission must be treated as irrefutable evidence. On 6 April Biddle expressed to him in no uncertain terms the judges' view that the report would only be given as much weight as any other official report – that is to say, just as much as the Tribunal deemed appropriate. And, furthermore, they had now decided they wished to hear three witnesses each for the defence as well as the prosecution in this matter.

When the hearing on the Katyn massacre finally took place on 1 and 2 July, scepticism about the Russian charge can only have been increased by their evidence, and doubts about the desirability of raising it at all deepened by the peculiarly inept way in which the Russians did it. Both the Russian and the defence cases turned on establishing the date when the Polish officers died. The Russians claimed that the shootings had taken place in the autumn of 1941 when German troops occupied the area. They brought as witness a Bulgarian pathologist who had been a member of an international investigation team set up by the Germans in 1943 which had fixed the date of the massacre as early 1940 – when the Russians were still in control of the district. He now, however, denounced that report, stating that its medical arguments were faulty, that the experts had only been allowed to examine a few bodies chosen for them by the Germans and had signed a prepared summary of their findings while waiting to leave from a military airport (more or less, he implied, as a condition of take-off).

The Bulgarian now declared that forensic evidence clearly pointed to autumn 1941 as the date of the murders, as did a Russian pathologist who had taken part in the State Commission's examination of 925 corpses at Katyn in 1944. The Russian added that papers, letters and diaries found on the bodies supported this dating, and that the calibre of bullet and method of execution (shooting in the head or back of the neck) were exclusively German. The Russian case became even more specific. They named as culprits a unit 'camouflaged' under the title 'Staff Engineer Battalion 537' commanded by a 'Lieutenant-Colonel Arnes'.

This attempt at precision rebounded on them. The defence produced in court not 'Lieutenant-Colonel Arnes' but Colonel Ahrens, the former commander of the Signals Regiment 537, units of which had moved into the Katyn area from the late summer of 1941. Ahrens said he had seen the mound containing the Polish bodies soon after he arrived in November, that he had ordered an investigation in 1943 after wolves had disinterred bones and when local people told him they had always feared that bodies had been buried there since hearing shots and screams in the wood in 1940. He, too, claimed to have seen written evidence on the bodies, but that it was never dated later than early 1940. Ahrens and two other German witnesses, both from his regiment, emphasized that a Signals Regiment would never have been considered suitable for carrying out executions, let alone on such a scale, when they were already overstretched by the tasks of moving into Smolensk; and that they were never equipped with automatic weapons of the calibre used to kill the Polish officers (though some Russian units were).

The Tribunal did not investigate the facts of the Katyn murders extensively during this two-day hearing. Its duty was not to act as a commission of inquiry into the atrocity. Rather it was to open the Russian allegation to defence challenge, a challenge the Russians had not withstood. As their case was exposed, they veered away from their confident accusation against the 'Staff Engineer Battalion' and replaced it in court with the sudden allegation that an Einsatzgruppen was present in the district in autumn 1941 – but without producing any evidence to connect it with the crime. The Russians were perhaps fortunate that the judges chose to make no mention of the Katyn massacre in their judgement. Conclusions very different from those they desired might well have been drawn from the evidence they presented: a tacit hint that they had merely failed to prove their case let them off lightly.

•

Denazification

GEORGE CLARE

George Clare, an Austrian-Jewish refugee from Hitler, found himself serving with the British Army's Intelligence Section of Information Services Control, with responsibility for clearing as 'free from Nazi infection' those Germans who were applying for jobs in the administrative and cultural life of the new Germany. There were many attempts by former Nazis to mislead Clare and his colleagues. Here he describes one particular lying Nazi, a journalist named Mohr who had already been given a provisional clearance by the Düsseldorf Information Control unit. Mohr was at the time working on the editorial staff of a Cologne illustrated weekly, and was applying for a licence to publish a magazine.

When he came into my office I welcomed him, according to the interview protocol, with the words: 'So you're the man who hates filling in our Fragebogens.* Anyway, that's what my Düsseldorf colleagues have told me. Why, if you've nothing to hide?'

'I've filled in about twenty since the end of the war,' Mohr said. 'Enough for one lifetime, wouldn't you agree, Mr Clare?'

*Questionnaire.

'I would, I suppose,' I said, 'but you overlooked some of the questions on the one I've got here. Tell you what, let's go through it together and do the thing properly now.'

I started to read: 'Father's name: Hermann Mohr; Profession: Architect; Mother: Maria Mohr née Derichs. Fine, but you did not fill in your parental home address . . .'

'Oversight, sorry,' Mohr said. 'Cologne, Stadtwaldgurtel 69.'

'Right. Now you write here that you went to Paris to study at the Sorbonne. And you go on to say you didn't want to stay at German universities because you objected to their militarist and National Socialist outlook. That's interesting. But you don't give any dates for your stay in France.'

'Oh, it's true. I went there in 1937. I can prove it. I've managed to save all my French documents,' Mohr said. Opening his briefcase, he took out his Sorbonne registration certificate and handed it to me.

'Thank you,' I said. 'Now let's read on. You say here that you had trouble with the Gestapo because of your friendship with Jews at the Sorbonne, some of them refugees from Germany.'

'Yes, the Gestapo in Paris reported me to the Gestapo in Cologne because of it.'

'I would have thought that the few Gestapo men in Paris in 1937, the year of the Paris World Fair, would have had more important things to do than watching a student.'

'Perhaps it wasn't the Gestapo who reported me,' he replied. 'Apart from the Jews from Germany there were also other students from the Reich there, and most of them belonged to the National Socialist Students' League. One of them must have spied on me.'

'Were you a member of that organization?'

'Oh no, of course not.'

'Ah yes, you did say you went to France because you disliked how things were at German universities. Yet what about those other German students? If, as you say, most of them were Nazis why did they, like you the anti-Nazi, study at a French university?'

'I don't know,' Mohr answered. 'One didn't talk about those things. It was too dangerous.'

'Yet you befriended Jews. Wasn't that just as dangerous?'

'Well, yes, and that was how I got into trouble. When I went back home in the summer of 1939 because of the enemy war-threat the Gestapo interrogated me for two hours, accusing me of having been chummy with the Jewish clique. They let me go after I told them a lot of lies – for instance, that I had Jewish contacts only because one could get a first-rate lunch at the Jewish students' canteen for a mere two francs.'

'And that was not your motive?'

'Well, I was short of money, but no. I lied to the Gestapo but not to you.'

'Fine. Now you say here that you were sent to a concentration camp, yet again you don't give the date.'

'That was before the war. They arrested me on 23 January 1943,' Mohr answered, 'but I expressed myself badly on that Fragebogen. That's what comes of having to fill in so many.'

He paused. Maybe he expected some reaction from me to his little joke.

When none came he went on, 'I was supposed to be sent to a concentration camp, but wasn't actually because of my health. I had had meningitis with bone-marrow complications, could hardly see and had to walk with a stick. It was very painful.'

'You must have been very fortunate to fall into the hands of such humane Gestapo men,' I commented. 'I'm sorry, but I find that story difficult to believe.'

'Well, I also had a friend, a Nazi high-up. He helped me.'

'Isn't that a bit surprising in your case? You have repeatedly stressed that, even though you were only eighteen-and-a-half when Hitler came to power, you were always an anti-Nazi and never wanted to have anything to do with them. Yet such an important Nazi was a friend of yours? Tell me, Herr Mohr, do you know that we have documents where we can check the truth of what you're saying?'

'Yes, I've heard,' he said.

'Do you perhaps want to amend or change anything you've written on your Fragebogen or told me?'

'No.'

'All right. I'll now read out from your Fragebogen the questions concerning membership of the NSDAP and its organizations and how you answered them. Please listen. "Were you a member of the National Socialist Party?" Your reply: "No." "Were you a member of the National Socialist Students' League?" Answer: "No." "Were you a member of the Reichs-Chamber for the Press?" "No." "Did you ever fill in a Reichskulturkammer* Fragebogen?" "No." Those were your statements, Herr Mohr, and the young lady there who's writing down everything we're saying has also recorded your assurances that you lied to the Gestapo but not to me. Yet here,' I said, taking his Kulturkammer folder out of my desk drawer, 'is your file and here, over what is undoubtedly your signature, is the Fragebogen you just said you never filled in. According to it you joined the Nazi Party on 1 May 1933, immediately after your eighteenth birthday, when you became eligible for membership. At the first opportunity. And here, look, you, who so disliked the Third Reich's universities, give your membership in the League of National Socialist Students. You have some explaining to do, haven't you?'

'Well, Mr Clare,' Mohr said, 'that's a long story.'

'It's my job to listen to long stories. Go ahead,' I replied.

'As you've stressed,' he began, 'I was just over eighteen in 1933. So when the Nazis took over my parents thought it would be a good idea and help my future if I joined the party. So somehow this was done . . .'

'Somehow?' I interrupted. 'What is that supposed to mean? You applied for membership, completed and signed the application form and were accepted.'

*The Reichs-Chamber of Culture. Germans either conformed with Nazism, or were refused membership of the main Chamber and its subsidiaries for theatre, film, literature, music, the press and the visual arts. Without membership they could not work.

'Well, yes, I forgot about that. I know everybody you talk to will tell you the same. It's no excuse, but you see inwardly I always was an anti-Nazi. I can produce dozens of witnesses who can testify to that. I did everything I could against them. That they eventually arrested me and almost sent me to a concentration camp proves my true political convictions.'

'And so you felt inwardly justified in falsifying all your twenty British Military Government Fragebogen?'

'Honestly, it's been a burden on my conscience. But knowing what I truly felt during the Third Reich I did not think the mistakes I made in my youth need haunt me for ever. Especially as I resigned from the party in 1943.'

'Oh come off it, Herr Mohr!' I exclaimed. 'Stop playing games with me. You did not resign; they threw you out because you had forged documents, the very same reason you're in trouble now. That's why you were arrested.'

'I did help a Jew to get out of Germany. Like you he's now a sergeant in the British Army. And I also faked papers so some soldier friends of mine could get special Berlin leave. But by now you probably won't believe anything I say.'

'Sorry, but that's how it is,' I said. 'You've been stupid beyond belief. Had you told the truth you would have gone before a denazification panel which might well have decided in your favour. As it is you will be tried by a Military Government court and you'll never get a licence.'

'But to err is human, can't you understand that?'

'A man who had the courage, as you say, actively to oppose the Nazis must also have the courage to tell the full truth about himself.'

'I feared for my job. I am a passionate journalist. It's my whole life. I love my work, so much so it destroyed my marriage. Surely you have the humanity to understand my motives.'

'I am not judging those or you, Herr Mohr,' I replied, 'or the truth of your anti-Nazi convictions. That's not my job. You can explain all that to the court. I'm only concerned with the fact that you lied on your Fragebogen. I now want you to write a confession.'

Mohr did and when he gave it to me he asked, 'May I say one last word and please don't think I'm merely saying it to move you. This will be the death of me.'

According to the protocol I lost my patience at this point.

'For heaven's sake, don't give me that tragic death or suicide bullshit,' I snapped. 'Take what's coming to you. You've nobody to blame but yourself.'

•

Young Mr Nixon

MORTON AND MICHAEL LEVITT

Richard Nixon's father was a strict Quaker. 'He had a hot temper, and I learned early that the only way to deal with him was to abide by the rules he laid down. Otherwise I would have felt . . . the ruler or the strap as my brothers did.' He had to be very persuasive to escape his father's anger, and this may well have been the origin of Nixon's tendency to lie his way out of trouble, or when the truth conflicted with his purposes as he perceived them. This is well illustrated by an account of what took place in Nixon's first election to Congress, a campaign which he fought against a Democrat called Jerry Voorhis.

The campaign began with Nixon fresh from the Navy, identifying Voorhis as someone who 'stayed safely behind the front in Washington' while Nixon was, according to his own campaign circulars, 'a clean, forthright young American who fought in the defense of his country in the stinking mud and jungles of the Solomons'.

Voorhis came from a wealthy family, was a Phi Beta Kappa at Yale, and had a pleasantly radical streak which led him to try life as a laborer after college graduation. He went to Congress in 1936 as a Roosevelt man and in 1940 demonstrated his conservative tendencies by sponsoring a bill to register Communists. By 1946 he was regarded by the Washington press corps as the 'hardest-working Congressman in Washington'. He was a markedly liberal man, although he openly opposed the CIO's Political Action Committee (PAC), which he said was Communist-dominated. Despite Voorhis' rejection of it, the PAC chose to support him. Nixon leaped with a vengeance on Voorhis' statement that he did not have any PAC support. When Nixon produced a letter on CIO stationery which endorsed Voorhis, the trap was sprung. Garry Wills's review of the campaign follows below:

> He [Voorhis] was off balance, explaining, splitting hairs all the rest of the campaign, which reached a climax in the fifth debate at San Gabriel Mission. Nixon, of course, went to Congress, to the Un-American Activities Committee, to Hiss.*

In truth, Voorhis was every inch a responsible Congressman. Earl Mazo recounts that Nixon told him that his first move after securing the Republican Congressional nomination was to decide that Voorhis' 'conservative reputation must be blasted'. He branded Voorhis as a man who stood for federal controls (hardly popular after the war) and as an enemy of free enterprise. Nixon called his opponent 'a lip-service American, a front for un-American elements'. When the Republican campaign headquarters came out with a statement accusing Voorhis of voting the 'Moscow line' and calling Nixon 'a man who will talk American and at the same time Vote American in Congress', the election was all but over.

Voorhis was simply not a radical, and Nixon's campaign was palpably dishonest in its effort to suggest that this was a fair statement of the particulars. Moreover, while Voorhis had remained in Washington as a Congressman during the war, this

*Alger Hiss. See page 388.

was by no means an unusual circumstance. It was also not true that Nixon was fighting during the same time in the 'jungles of the Solomons'.

Nixon was commissioned as a Navy officer and was shipped to New Caledonia, where he served as a supply officer in the Naval Air Transport Command. There is no evidence of Nixon seeing combat, and his military career has been described by an old Navy friend, Lester Wroble, as consisting of three essentials: (1) he set up a service where men could buy whiskey, food, and other staples not available as general use, (2) he consistently made money in poker games, and (3) he always knew what he was going to do after the war. Thus, there is some question about whose war service was more meritorious, the hard-working Congressman or the soft-berthed naval officer.

•

The Alger Hiss case

MORTON AND MICHAEL LEVITT

In 1948 Alger Hiss, a former senior State Department official, was publicly accused of being a Communist by *Time* magazine editor and 'reformed' Communist, Whittaker Chambers. The matter came to the attention of the House of Representatives Un-American Activities Committee (HUAC), whose most junior member was a young Congressman by the name of Richard Nixon. Recognizing the political capital that was to be gained, Nixon made a target out of Hiss, and by the end of the year the original charges by Whittaker Chambers of membership of the Party had escalated to espionage, for which Hiss was indicted by a grand jury. As Morton and Michael Levitt have proved, both Hiss and Nixon lied during the case: Hiss refused to admit that he knew Whittaker Chambers; Nixon lied to Hiss about his prior knowledge of Chambers's testimony. 'The final irony in the Hiss–Nixon relationship,' say Morton and Michael Levitt, 'is its absolute symmetry. A small lie escalates, and before the liar looks around, his fortune is imperilled. So it was with Alger Hiss and Richard Nixon. The former was an all-American boy laid low for an untruth. The scenario that brought about his downfall was masterminded by an ambitious young California Congressman whose own career was built on untruths and who finally ended public life in disgrace after being exposed in a monumental series of lies.'

[The] crucial lie for Hiss was, in our opinion, his refusal to admit to knowing Whittaker Chambers by that name or any of the eight or nine other names he used over the years. That first denial led unfortunately to the necessity for further denials. When Hiss asserted that a man's name and his picture did not summon up any recollection at all, he was then forced into being logically consistent even in the face of the enlarging evidentiary field. There was at first no relationship recalled, then only a very small one, almost forgettable really; then just a little more, a car, a flat, a rug, a picture painted by one woman and accepted by another, but still no more than that, still easily forgettable; and then finally, thirty years later, the offhand comment that contained the suggestion of something much closer, a relationship in which Chambers was jealous to the point of cold hostility towards Priscilla Hiss and evinced an 'almost paternal attitude' towards Hiss himself.

When Stripling asked Hiss at the first hearing, 'You say you have never seen Mr Chambers?' Hiss's response – 'The name means absolutely nothing to me' – was evasive. Hiss had more to go on for this identification than just the man's name. In the next exchange he admitted, 'I have looked at all the pictures [of Whittaker Chambers] I was able to get hold of in, I think it was yesterday's paper which had the pictures.' His response was, as Nixon described it, '. . . qualified carefully'. In one sense, Hiss admitted being covert. He told his son, Anthony, and others that he remembered hearing the name 'Whittaker Chambers' when interviewed by the FBI in 1947.

The Chambers name game became mightily complicated for Hiss at the subsequent hearing when he gave his accuser the name of 'George Crosley' but was unable – and, as it later turned out, unwilling – to produce any other witnesses to substantiate this recollection. Although the Nye Committee receptionist was by then dead, certainly there were other reporters covering the committee's hearing who could not remember this 'gregarious' – at least this was Hiss's estimation – writer by this or any other name.

When Hiss found the man who remembered publishing poems by Chambers during the years 1925 and 1926 under the nom de plume George Crosley, this witness was not called to the stand. Why? Hiss says his attorney dissuaded him because the publisher, Samuel Roth, who had been convicted under the obscenity laws, would be viewed by the jury as a man of dubious credibility. Moreover it was feared that his association with the defense might reflect adversely on their client. These were their conclusions, but another argument could be offered that the testimony could reflect adversely on Chambers, who, after all, had submitted the erotic poems under a false name to a man who would eventually be convicted for obscenity. A Hiss lie or blunder? It is impossible to say, but many have concluded that the decision to keep Roth off the stand was one of the biggest blunders in the defense's case.

While it is often claimed that legal verdicts derive from the relationship between facts and the law . . . it would seem . . . that the more important facts for a jury are the human ones – the man's demeanor, whether he 'appears' to be innocent or guilty – in effect, does his story make human sense?

And it was here that Hiss failed badly. No one believed that a man could not recognize another with whom he lunched occasionally, who spent a week or so in his home, whom he loaned or gave a car, and from whom he received a rug.

. . . Hiss was lying about knowing Chambers, and all the birds were coming home to roost, for this was the very first issue in the case, whether Hiss knew Chambers or not, and from then on Hiss's credibility was badly shattered; he was in – nay, he had deliberately put himself in – the position of being an absolutely honest man. Chambers, of course, had no such obstacles to overcome. He had lied much, sometimes too often even to straighten out in his own mind, sometimes only yesterday or the day before, but this time it was the truth, the whole truth, so help him, God. Chambers, the confessed sinner, had now found religion and with it, in inevitable accompaniment, the truth as well. Hiss, the professed saint, was really a Communist, a man who lied about the most simple issue, personal recollection, and thus must be lying about much else as well.

And so Alger Hiss . . . may well have come to his sad end because he felt compelled to deny his relationship with the shabby Chambers and, not making that denial stick, could not then be believed by his peers in a number of far more important issues. Remarkably, this was Nixon's conclusion, although he never informed the public of his posture. In a letter Nixon wrote to John Foster Dulles before the first trial, he said of Hiss: 'Whether he was guilty of technical perjury or whether it has been established definitely that he was a member of the Communist Party are issues which may still be open to debate, but there is no longer any doubt in my mind that for reasons only he can give, he was trying to keep the [HUAC] committee from learning the truth in regard to his relationship with Chambers.'*

•

Lying lawyers

CHARLES P. CURTIS†

I will start with the story of Sam the Lookout.

A distinguished New York lawyer was once called over to sit in a conference of admiralty lawyers with the crew of a ship

*The truth about the relationship between the two men, suggest the authors, may have been that Hiss had had a homosexual relationship with Chambers, and was unwilling to confess to it in order to protect his wife. Convicted after two trials and sent to prison for perjury, the Statute of Limitations having precluded a charge of espionage, Hiss served four years of a five-year sentence. Having lost his licence to practise law, he went on to live an anonymous life selling stationery.

†The author is a member of the Massachusetts bar.

which had been in collision. The lawyers were going over the testimony which the members of the crew would give at the approaching trial. Finally they came to the lookout, and the Captain, who was asking the questions, turned to him and said, 'You, of course, were up in the eyes on the forecastle keeping a sharp lookout.' The seaman squirmed in his chair, twisted his cap, and said, 'The truth is, Captain, I was in the head having a smoke.' The lawyers leaned forward, but the Captain turned to reassure them. 'That's all right, gentlemen, he'll testify that he was keeping a sharp lookout. Won't you Sam?' 'No,' said Sam, 'I guess I can't do that.'

And then, this lawyer said, such a storm of indignation burst over Sam as he had never seen. The Captain and the rest of the crew cursed him for betraying his ship. Let him go to the head if he had to. Let him even have his smoke if he must. But when he did, let him also take the consequences. The collision was not his fault, they agreed. The fog was too thick for him to have seen the other vessel in time, but was he going to let his own ship down? If he left his post on his own affairs, he had no right to make the ship pay the penalty. What if it was perjury? He'd taken that risk. Not the ship, but he had taken the risk of perjury.

The admiralty lawyers sat back and listened. They seemed to recognize that there were special peculiarities in the ethics of the sea which they could not but respect, though distinctly they were not a part of admiralty law. The meeting broke up with Sam still obstinately refusing to do what, the Captain insisted, any good seaman ought to know he was in honor bound to do.

Then I tried to find a situation in which a lawyer may be in duty bound to lie for his client. I asked an eminent and very practical judge. He told me he hoped I was joking. I went to two leaders of the bar, both ex-presidents of bar associations. One said, 'No, I don't believe there is such a situation.' The other said, 'Why, of course, there are.' But he has not yet given me one.

Finally I thought I had one. It was the case of a lawyer who, I felt very sure, had lied to me when he told me that he did not represent a certain man. I was secretary of the Grievance Committee of the Bar Association at the time, and I was trying to find out whether this man had been blackmailed by some other lawyers. I went to this lawyer and asked him. If he had even admitted to me that he had represented this man, I should have been pretty sure that the man had indeed been blackmailed, for I knew that he had not gone to his regular counsel, but to a different lawyer, in order to keep the whole affair secret. The lawyer told me he did not even know the man.

I recall thinking then, that this lawyer was doing just right by lying to me, but I don't know who else agreed with me. My lawyer had gone to make the same denial to the Grievance Committee, and later, when the Bar Association brought proceedings for his disbarment, in the course of the proceedings, persisted in his denial before the court itself. He was not disbarred, but he was subsequently reprimanded and suspended.

I take it that it is inadmissible to lie to the court. A lawyer's duty to his client cannot rise higher than its source, which is the court. Perhaps my lawyer did wrong to lie to the Grievance Committee, but I am not so sure. I know he did right to lie to me, and I am inclined to hope that in his place I should have lied to the Grievance Committee as well.

It may be that it all depends on whether you are asked the question by someone who has a right to ask it. If he has no right to ask and if simple silence would, or even might, lead him to the truth, then, I believe your lawyer is in duty bound to lie. For the truth is not his, but yours. It belongs to you and he is bound to keep it for you, even more vigorously than if it were only his own. He must lie, then, beyond the point where he could permissibly lie for himself. But this only illuminates the problem from a different angle, the right to ask instead of the duty to answer. Let me give you a situation in which a lawyer must lie to someone who does have the right to ask him the question.

A lawyer is called on the telephone by a former client who is unfortunately at the time a fugitive from justice. The police want him and he wants advice. The lawyer goes to where his client is, hears the whole story, and advises him to surrender. Finally he succeeds in persuading him that this is the best thing to do, and they make an appointment to go to police headquarters. Meanwhile the client is to have two days to wind up his affairs and make his farewells. When the lawyer gets back to his office, a police inspector is waiting for him, and asks him whether his client is in town and where he is. Here are questions which the police have every right to ask of anybody, and even a little hesitation in this unfortunate lawyer's denials will reveal enough to betray his client. Of course he lies.

And why not? The relation between a lawyer and his client is one of the intimate relations. You would lie for your wife. You would lie for your child. There are others with whom you are intimate enough, close enough, to lie for them when you would not lie for yourself. At what point do you stop lying for them? I don't know and you are not sure.

To every one of us come occasions when we don't want to tell the truth, not all of it, certainly not all of it at once, when we want to be something less than candid, a little disingenuous. Indeed, to be candid with ourselves, there are times when we deliberately and more or less justifiably undertake to tell something less or something different. Complete candor to anyone but ourselves is a virtue that belongs to the saints, to the secure, and to the very courageous. Even when we do want to tell the truth, all of it, ultimately, we see no reason why we should not take our own time, tell it as skilfully and as gracefully as we can, and most of us doubt our own ability to do this as well by ourselves as another could do it for us. So we go to a lawyer. He will make a better fist of it than we can.

I don't see why we should not come out roundly and say that one of the functions of a lawyer is to lie for his client; and on rare occasions, as I think I have shown, I believe it is. Happily they are few and far between, only when his duty gets him into a corner or puts him on the spot. Day in, day out, a lawyer can be as truthful as anyone. But not ingenuous.

A lawyer is required to be disingenuous. He is required to

make statements as well as arguments which he does not believe in. But the further his statements descend toward the particular, the more truthful he may be, indeed must be, because no one appreciates the significance of the particular better than a lawyer. In the higher brackets of generality, he has to be freed from his own beliefs and prejudices, for they are irrelevant, unless they are pressed into service for the client. But his insincerity does not extend to the particular, except, of course, particulars which do not belong to him, but are his client's secrets. Barring these, when he is talking for his client, a lawyer is absolved from veracity down to a certain point of particularity. And he must never lose the reputation of lacking veracity, because his freedom from the strict bonds of veracity and of the law are the two chief assets of the profession.

•

The Third Man

KIM PHILBY

H. A. R. 'Kim' Philby was recruited into the Soviet Secret Service while still an undergraduate at Cambridge. In 1940 he joined the British Secret Intelligence Service (MI6), and by 1949 had become the principal liaison officer with the CIA and FBI. All the time he was passing secrets to the Soviets, as were several others, who were also known to Philby. But for the defection to the Soviet Union of Guy Burgess and Donald Maclean, which had the effect of bringing Philby under suspicion, he might have become the head of SIS itself. Here Philby reveals how he lied to his MI5 interrogators, successfully convincing them of his innocence. Obliged to resign from the Foreign Service because of his association with Burgess, Philby managed to remain in Intelligence until the early 1960s, when, fearing that his role as 'the Third Man' was about to be discovered, he disappeared in Beirut, reappearing in Moscow several months later.

Easton told me that Dick White was anxious to see us both as soon as possible, so we drove across the park to Leconfield House, off Curzon Street, where MI5 had set up their headquarters. This was to be the first of many interrogations, although an attempt was made, at this early stage, to conceal that ugly fact. Easton sat in while White asked the questions; the role of the former was presumably to see fair play. It may be imagined that there was some apprehension on my side, some embarrassment on theirs. I could not claim White as a close friend; but our personal and official relations had always been excellent, and he had undoubtedly been pleased when I superseded Cowgill. He was bad at dissembling, but he did his best to put our talk on a friendly footing. He wanted my help, he said, in clearing up this appalling Burgess-Maclean affair. I gave him a lot of information about Burgess's past and impressions of his personality, taking the line that it was inconceivable that anyone like Burgess, who courted the limelight instead of avoiding it and was generally notorious for indiscretion, could have been a secret agent, let alone a Soviet agent from whom strictest security standards would be required. I did not expect this line to be in any way convincing as to the facts of the case; but I hoped it would give the impression that I was implicitly defending myself against the unspoken charge that I, a trained counter-espionage officer, had been completely fooled by Burgess. Of Maclean, I disclaimed all knowledge. I had heard of him, of course, and might even have met him here or there, but offhand I could not have put a face to him. As I had only met him twice, for about half an hour in all and both times on a conspiratorial basis, since 1937, I felt that I could safely indulge in this slight distortion of the truth.

I offered to put a summary of what I had said on paper. It was possible that our talk was bugged, and I wanted a written record to correct any bias that the microphone might have betrayed. When I went back for my second interrogation a few days later, White gave my note a cursory glance, then edged towards the real focus of his interest. We might clarify matters, he said, if I gave him an account of my relations with Burgess. To that end, a detailed statement of my own career would be useful. As I have explained . . . there were some awkward zig-zags to be negotiated, but I explained them away as best I could. In doing so, I gave White a piece of gratuitous information, a slip which I regretted bitterly at the time. But it is virtually certain that they would have dug it out for themselves in time, and it is perhaps just as well that I drew attention to it myself at an early stage.

This information related to a trip which I had made to Franco's Spain before *The Times* sent me as their accredited correspondent. It seemed that MI5 had no record of that trip and had assumed that *The Times* had sent me to Spain direct from a desk in Fleet Street. When I corrected White on this point, he did not take long to ask me if I had paid for the first journey out of my own resources. It was a nasty little question because the enterprise had been suggested to me and financed by the Soviet service, just as Krivitsky had said, and a glance at my bank balance for the period would have shown that I had no means for gallivanting around Spain. Embedded in this episode was also the dangerous little fact that Burgess had been used to replenish my funds. My explanation was that the Spanish journey had been an attempt to break into the world of high-grade journalism on which I had staked everything, selling all my effects (mostly books and gramophone records) to pay for the trip. It was reasonably plausible and quite impossible to disprove. Burgess's connection with my Spanish adventure was never found out. I had an explanation ready, but already had quite enough to explain.

When I offered to produce a second summary of our talks, White agreed, but asked me rather impatiently to harp less on Burgess and concentrate on my own record. All but the tip of the cat's tail was now out of the bag, and I was not surprised to receive a summons from the Chief. He told me that he had received a strong letter from Bedell-Smith, the terms of which precluded any possibility of my returning to Washington . . . After this, it was almost a formality when the Chief called me a second time and told me, with obvious distress, that he would have to ask for my resignation.

... I spent the summer house-hunting and settled for a small place near Rickmansworth. It was already November when the Chief telephoned me and asked me to see him at ten o'clock on the following morning. I drove up to London on a beautiful wintry morning with the hedgerows bending low under inch-thick rime. The Chief explained that a judicial inquiry had been opened into the circumstances of the Burgess-Maclean escape. The inquiry was in the hands of H. J. P. Milmo, a King's Counsellor who had worked for MI5 during the war. I was required to give evidence, and the Chief hoped I would have no objection. The mention of Milmo indicated that a crisis was at hand. I knew him and of him. He was a skilled interrogator; he was the man whom MI5 usually brought in for the kill. As I drove with the Chief across St James's Park to Leconfield House, I braced myself for a sticky ordeal. I was still confident that I could survive an examination, however robust, on the basis of the evidence known to me. But I could not be sure that new evidence had not come to hand for Milmo to shoot at me.

On arrival at Leconfield House, I was introduced to the head of the legal branch of MI5 and then ushered into the presence of Milmo. He was a burly fellow with a florid, round face, matching his nickname, 'Buster'. On his left sat Arthur Martin, a quiet young man who had been one of the principal investigators of the Maclean case. He remained silent throughout, watching my movements. When I looked out of the window, he made a note; when I twiddled my thumbs, he made another note. After sketchy greetings, Milmo adopted a formal manner, asking me to refrain from smoking as this was a 'judicial inquiry'.

It was all flummery, of course. It crossed my mind to ask Milmo for his credentials or to suggest that the headquarters of MI5 were an odd venue for a judicial inquiry. But that would have been out of character for the part which I had decided to play; that of a cooperative ex-member of SIS as keen as Milmo himself to establish the truth about Burgess and Maclean. So, for the best part of three hours, I answered or parried questions meekly enough, only permitting a note of anger when my character was directly attacked. It was useless, I knew, to try to convince the ex-intelligence officer in Milmo; my job was simply to deny him the confession which he required as a lawyer.

I was too closely involved in Milmo's interrogation to form an objective opinion of its merits. Much of the ground that he covered was familiar and my answers, excogitated long before, left him little to do but shout. Early in the interview, he betrayed the weakness of his position by accusing me of entrusting to Burgess 'intimate personal papers'. The charge was so obviously nonsensical that I did not even have to feign bewilderment. It appeared that my Cambridge degree had been found in Burgess's flat . . . It was flimsy stuff and went far to strengthen my confidence in the outcome.

. . . Several times in the following weeks, Skardon came down to continue his interrogations. He was scrupulously courteous, his manner verging on the exquisite; nothing could have been more flattering than the cosy warmth of his interest in my views and actions. He was far more dangerous than the ineffective White or the blustering Milmo. I was helped to resist his polite advances by the knowledge that it was Skardon who had wormed his way into Fuchs's confidence with such disastrous results. During our first long conversation, I detected and evaded two little traps which he laid for me with deftness and precision. But I had scarcely begun congratulating myself when the thought struck me that he might have laid others which I had not detected.

Yet even Skardon made mistakes. He began one interview by asking me for written authority to examine my bank balance. He could have got legal authority to do so whether I approved or not; so I raised no objection – especially since he would find no trace of irregular payments because no irregular payments had ever been made. But, with the authority in his hands, he began to question me on my finances, and I took the opportunity of giving him some harmless misinformation. My object in doing so was a serious one. I had been able to invent plausible explanations for most of the oddities of my career, but not all of them.

Where my invention failed, I could only plead lapses of memory. I just could not remember this person or that incident. The probing of my finances gave me a chance of confirming the erratic workings of my memory. If I could not remember my financial transactions, I could scarcely be expected to remember all the details of my social and professional life.

After several such interrogations, Skardon came no more. He did not tell me that he was satisfied or dissatisfied; he just left the matter hanging. He was doubtless convinced that I was concealing from him almost everything that mattered, and I would have given a lot to have glimpsed his summing-up. There was no doubt that the evidence against me was impressive, but it was not yet conclusive. That it was not so regarded emerged from yet another summons to Broadway, this time to be interrogated by Sinclair and Easton. It was distasteful to lie in my teeth to the honest Sinclair; I hope he now realizes that in lying to him I was standing as firmly on principle as he ever did. But I enjoyed my duel with Easton. After my experiences with White, Milmo and Skardon, I was moving on very familiar ground, and did not think he could succeed where they had failed. He didn't.

•

The great Powers lie

STEPHEN E. AMBROSE

On the afternoon of 1 May 1960, an American U-2 reconnaissance plane piloted by Francis Gary Powers was shot down by the Soviets. The Soviet premier, Nikita Khrushchev, made a speech to the Supreme Soviet denouncing America for its aggressive provocation, and suggested, mischievously perhaps, that the militarists might have been acting without the knowledge of the U S President, Dwight D. Eisenhower. The news was communicated to the President while he was preparing to fly to Paris for a heads of government summit; the main topic on the agenda was nuclear disarmament. Eisenhower's biographer takes up the story.

Khrushchev's charge that Eisenhower did not know what was going on in his own Administration, which dovetailed so nicely with the ongoing Democratic campaign, angered the President. Still, he decided to make no rejoinder, nor any explanation. He could have refuted the charges immediately. He might have issued a statement taking full responsibility, pointing out that no U-2 flight ever left the ground without his personal approval, insisting that because of the closed nature of the Soviet Union and because of fears of a nuclear Pearl Harbor, the overflights were necessary to the security of his country. In the process, he could have reminded the world that, as everyone knew, the KGB was far more active in spying on the West than the CIA was in spying on Russia. He might have given a brief outline of the history of the U-2, then made the most fundamental point of all – that the evidence gathered by the overflights provided convincing proof that there was no missile gap, despite Khrushchev's boasting about Soviet rockets, and that as a result of the photographs, the United States had been able to keep some kind of control on its own defense spending.

But he did none of these things, because he had a fetish about keeping the U-2 secret. The odd thing about this fetish was that the U-2 was no secret to the Soviets, and had not been since the very first flight, back in 1956. Indeed, all the governments involved – British, French, Turkish, Norwegian, Formosan, and others – knew about the U-2. The people who did not know were the Americans and their elected representatives.

Another option available to Eisenhower would have been to state that since the Soviets had turned down Open Skies*, he had decided to unilaterally put it into effect anyway, and then invite Khrushchev to fly all he wanted across the United States. To do that, however, Eisenhower would have had to make public the U-2 flights. Although it is difficult to see, a quarter of a century

*A proposal at the Geneva summit whereby the United States and the Soviet Union should open their skies to provide facilities for aerial photography to the other country.

later, when Russian and American spy satellites are constantly in orbit around the world, what damage could have resulted, Eisenhower decided to make a desperate effort to keep the overflights a secret, or at least to deny their existence. Instead of confessing, he launched a cover-up.

He did so because he thought a cover-up would work. Acting on the assumption that Powers was dead and his plane in ruins, Eisenhower believed that Khrushchev could prove nothing. The irony – or perhaps the tragedy, considering what was at stake at the summit – was that Eisenhower himself had pointed out that his greatest single asset was his 'reputation for honesty', and that if a U-2 were lost 'when we are engaged in apparently sincere deliberations, it could be put on display in Moscow and ruin the President's effectiveness'. But he clung to the hope that Khrushchev, without any physical evidence, would be unconvincing.

On the afternoon of May 5, after returning to Washington, Eisenhower approved a statement that was then issued by the National Aeronautics and Space Administration. It began, 'One of NASA's U-2 research airplanes, in use since 1956 in a continuing program to study meteorological conditions found at high altitude, has been missing since May 1, when its pilot reported he was having oxygen difficulties over the Lake Van, Turkey area.' Presumably, the U-2 had strayed off course, perhaps crossing the border into Russia. The unstated assumption was that Powers' weather plane was the one the Russians had shot down.

The following day, Khrushchev released a photograph of a wrecked airplane, describing it as the U-2 Powers had flown. It was not, however, a U-2, but another airplane. The premier was setting a trap. He wanted Eisenhower to continue to believe that Powers was dead, the U-2 destroyed, so that the United States would stick to its 'weather research' story, as it did. Then, on May 7, Khrushchev sprang his great surprise. He jubilantly reported to a 'wildly cheering' Supreme Soviet that 'we have parts of the plane and we also have the pilot, who is quite alive and kicking. The pilot is in Moscow and so are the parts of the plane.' Khrushchev made his account a story of high drama and low skulduggery interspersed with bitingly sarcastic remarks about Eisenhower's cover story. Cries of 'Shame, Shame!' rose from the deputies as Khrushchev heaped scorn on the CIA mixed with cries of 'Bandits, Bandits!'

Upon receiving the news of Powers' capture by the Russians alive, news that he had found 'unbelievable', Eisenhower knew that since Khrushchev had both the plane and the pilot (and the film), there was little point in denying any further the real purpose of the overflights. He was not ready, however, to tell the American people, and the world, that he personally was involved in the distasteful business of spying. Dulles, Herter, and other top officials were frantically trying to find ways to protect the President. (During a 4.30 p.m. phone call, Dulles referred to a statement Herter wanted to release saying 'There is an inconsistency.' Herter replied that 'this was to get the President off the hook. Mr Dulles said he would do anything he could.') On Herter's recommendation, Eisenhower then authorized the State Department to issue a statement denying that Powers had any authorization to fly over the Soviet Union.

That statement was so ill conceived and so poorly timed that it made a bad situation much worse. As James Reston reported in *The New York Times*,

> The United States admitted tonight that one of this country's planes equipped for intelligence purposes had 'probably' flown over Soviet territory.
>
> An official statement stressed, however, that 'there was no authorization for any such flight' from authorities in Washington.
>
> As to who might have authorized the flight, officials refused to comment. If this particular flight of the U-2 was not authorized here, it could only be assumed that someone in the chain of command in the Middle East or Europe had given the order.

The following morning, May 9, an agitated Secretary of Defense called a disturbed Secretary of State on the telephone. Gates did not like at all the implication that his officers in the field were authorizing unapproved flights over Soviet territory. According to the summary of the conversation, 'Gates said we should say that it is a matter of national policy and we have been doing it because everything else has failed. Gates said somebody has to take responsibility for the policy and while the President can say he didn't know about this one flight,* he did approve the policy.' Herter replied that 'the President didn't argue with this but for the moment doesn't want to say anything and we have been trying to keep the President clear on this'.

Twenty-five minutes later, Eisenhower himself called Herter. The President wanted Herter to issue a statement admitting that the overflights had been going on for years, under orders from the President, to 'get adequate knowledge of the composition of the Russian military and industrial complex'. Eisenhower said the statement should also point out that while he, the President, 'realizes at times that unusual and unorthodox things are needed to do this', he did not get the details of spying or reconnaissance trips.

The attempt to cover up continued that afternoon, when Goodpaster called Herter to say that Eisenhower wanted a statement from State that would indicate that the U-2 flights were carried out under 'a very broad directive from the President given at the earliest point of his Administration to protect us from surprise attack'. But, Goodpaster added, 'The President wants no specific tie to him of this particular event.'

The resulting statements added to a national sense of humiliation, shame, and confusion. Reston reported,

> This is a sad and perplexed capital tonight, caught in a swirl of charges of clumsy administration, bad judgement and bad faith.

*In fact, Eisenhower did specifically authorize that flight.

> It was depressed and humiliated by the United States having been caught spying over the Soviet Union and trying to cover up its activities in a series of misleading official announcements.

. . . Over the next two days, humiliation gave way to fright as the headlines became increasingly alarmist. 'Krushchev Warns of Rocket Attack on Bases Used by US Spying Planes', *The Times* announced on May 10. The following morning, the headline read, 'US Vows to Defend Allies if Russians Attack Bases'.

Khrushchev, at an impromptu news conference in Moscow, announced that he was putting Powers on trial and added, 'You understand that if such aggressive actions continue this might lead to war.' Eisenhower held his own news conference, where he read a prepared statement. In firm, measured tones, without a hint of regret or apology, Eisenhower said Khrushchev's antics over the 'flight of an unarmed nonmilitary plane can only reflect a fetish of secrecy'. Because of the nature of the Soviet system, spying 'is a distasteful but vital necessity'. When asked whether his trip to Russia had been cancelled, he replied, 'I expect to go.' When asked if the outlook for the summit had changed, he replied, 'Not decisively at all, no.'

But of course it had. No one in Washington could have supposed for a minute that Khrushchev would not exploit the fact that he had caught the Americans red-handed, and that they had lied about it.

•

Lie-checking during the Cuban missile crisis

PAUL EKMANN

Paul Ekmann, an expert in 'non-verbal communication', describes a meeting between President Kennedy and Andrei Gromyko, the Soviet Foreign Minister, which took place during the Cuban missile crisis of

1962, and analyses the lies that were perpetrated by both sides. He concludes that both Kennedy and Gromyko were 'natural liars, inventive and clever in fabricating, smooth talkers, with a convincing manner', and that 'any politician who comes to power, in part through his skill in debate and public speeches, who is agile in handling questions at news conferences, with a glistening TV or radio image, has the conversational talents to be a natural liar'.

During the Cuban missile crisis, two days before a meeting between President John F. Kennedy and Soviet Foreign Minister Andrei Gromyko, on Tuesday, October 14, 1962, President Kennedy was informed by McGeorge Bundy that a U-2 flight over Cuba had yielded incontrovertible evidence that the Soviet Union was placing missiles in Cuba. There had been repeated rumors to that effect, and with an election coming up in November, Khrushchev (in the words of political scientist Graham Allison) 'had assured the President, through the most direct and personal channels, that he understood Kennedy's domestic problem and would do nothing to complicate it. Specifically, Khrushchev had given the President solemn assurances that the Soviet Union would not put offensive missiles in Cuba.' Kennedy was 'furious' (according to Arthur Schlesinger); although '. . . angry at Khrushchev's efforts to deceive him . . . [he] . . . took the news calmly but with an expression of surprise' (Theodore Sorenson's account). In the words of Robert Kennedy, '. . . as the representatives of the CIA explained the photographs that morning . . . we realized that it had all been lies, one gigantic fabric of lies'. The President's chief advisers began to meet that day to consider what actions the government should take. The President decided that '. . . there should be no public disclosure of the fact that we knew of the Soviet missiles in Cuba until a course of action had been decided upon and readied . . . Security was essential, and the President made it clear that he was determined that for once in the history of Washington there should be no leaks whatsoever' (Roger Hilsman, then in the State Department).

Two days later, on Thursday, October 16, as his advisers still debated what course the country should take, President Kennedy saw Gromyko. 'Gromyko had been in the United States for over a week, but no American official knew exactly why . . . [He] had asked for an audience at the White House. The request had come in about the same time as the . . . [U-2 photographic evidence]. Had the Russians spotted the U-2 plane? Did they wish to talk to Kennedy to feel out his reactions? Would they use this talk to inform Washington that Khrushchev was at this moment going public about the missiles, revealing his coup before the United States could spring its reaction?' Kennedy '. . . was anxious as the meeting approached, but managed to smile as he welcomed Gromyko and [Anatoly] Dobrynin [the Soviet Ambassador] to his office' (Sorenson). Not yet ready to act, Kennedy believed it important to conceal his discovery of the missiles from Gromyko, to avoid the Soviets having a further advantage.

The meeting began at 5 p.m. and lasted until 7.15. Secretary of State Dean Rusk, Llewellyn Thompson (former United States Ambassador to the Soviet Union), and Martin Hildebrand (director of the Office of German Affairs) watched and listened from one side, while Dobrynin, Vladimir Semenor (Soviet Deputy Minister of Foreign Affairs), and a third Soviet official watched from the other side. Translators from each side were also present. 'Kennedy sat in his rocker facing the fireplace, Gromyko to his right on one of the beige sofas. Cameramen came in, took pictures for posterity, then left. The Russian leaned back against a striped cushion and began speaking . . .'

After talking at some length about Berlin, Gromyko finally spoke of Cuba. According to Robert Kennedy's account, 'Gromyko said he wished to appeal to the United States and to President Kennedy on behalf of Premier Khrushchev and the Soviet Union to lessen the tensions that existed with regard to Cuba. President Kennedy listened, astonished, but also with some admiration for the boldness of Gromyko's position . . . [the President spoke] . . . firmly, but with great restraint considering the provocation . . .' Journalist Elie Abel relates: 'The President gave Gromyko a clear opportunity to set the record straight by referring back to the repeated assurances of Krushchev and Dobrynin that the missiles in Cuba were nothing but anti-aircraft weapons . . . Gromyko stubbornly repeated the old assurances, which the President now knew to be lies. Kennedy did not confront him with the facts.' Kennedy 'remained impassive . . . he gave no sign of tension or anger' (Sorenson).

Gromyko was in a mood of 'unwonted joviality' (Abel) when he left the White House. Reporters asked him what was said in the meeting. Gromyko smiled at them, obviously in a good mood, and said that the talks had been 'useful, very useful'. Robert Kennedy reports, 'I came by shortly after Gromyko left the White House. The President of the United States, it can be said, was displeased with the spokesman of the Soviet Union.' 'I was dying to confront him with our evidence,' Kennedy said, according to political scientist David Detzer. In his office Kennedy commented to Robert Lovett and McBundy, who had come in: 'Gromyko . . . in this very room not over ten minutes ago, told more bare-faced lies than I have ever heard in so short a time. All during his denial . . . I had the low-level pictures in the center drawer of my desk and it was an enormous temptation to show them to him.'

Let us consider Ambassador Dobrynin first. He was probably the only one at the meeting who was not lying. Robert Kennedy thought that the Soviets had lied to Dobrynin, not trusting Dobrynin's skill as a liar, and that Dobrynin had been truthful, as he knew it, in denying there were any missiles in Cuba in his earlier meetings with Robert Kennedy. It would not be unusual for an ambassador to be so misled by his own government for such a purpose. John F. Kennedy had done just that with Adlai Stevenson, not informing him about the Bay of Pigs, and, as Allison points out, 'similarly the Japanese Ambassador was not informed of Pearl Harbor; the German Ambassador in Moscow was not informed of Barbarossa [the German plan to invade Russia]'. In the period between June 1962, when the Soviets are presumed to have decided to put missiles in Cuba, and this meeting in mid-October, the Soviets used Dobrynin and Georg

Bolshakov, a public information official at the Soviet Embassy, to repeatedly assure members of the Kennedy administration . . . that no offensive missiles were being put in Cuba. Bolshakov and Dobrynin did not need to know the truth and probably, in fact, did not. Neither Khrushchev, Gromyko, nor anyone else who did know the truth ever directly met with their opponents until October 14, two days before the meeting between Gromyko and Kennedy. Khrushchev met in Moscow with the American Ambassador, Foy Kohler, and denied there were any missiles in Cuba. It was only then that the Soviets for the first time took the risk that their lies could have been discovered if Krushchev, or, two days later, Gromyko, made a mistake.

At the meeting in the White House, there were two lies, one by Kennedy and the other by Gromyko. Some readers may find it strange that I use the word *lie* to describe Kennedy and not just Gromyko. Most people do not like to use that word about someone who is admired, because they, but not I, consider lying inherently evil. Kennedy's actions at that meeting fit my definition of a concealment lie. Both men, Kennedy and Gromyko, concealed from each other what each knew to be true – that there were missiles in Cuba. My analysis suggests why Kennedy was more likely than Gromyko to have provided a clue to his deceit.

As long as each had worked out his line in advance – and each would have had opportunity to do so – there should have been no problem in concealing from each other the knowledge they shared. Both men might have felt detection apprehension because the stakes involved were so great. Presumably the anxiety Kennedy is reported to have felt when he greeted Gromyko was detection apprehension. The stakes (and therefore the detection apprehension) may have been greater for Kennedy than for Gromyko. The United States still had not decided what to do. Not even the intelligence information about just how many missiles were in Cuba, in what stage of readiness, was complete. Kennedy's advisers thought that he must keep the discovery secret, for if Khrushchev were to learn before the United States acted, they feared Khrushchev would, through evasions and threats, complicate American action and gain a tactical advantage. According to McGeorge Bundy, 'It made all the difference – I felt then and have felt since – that the Russians were caught pretending, in a clumsy way, that they had not done what it was clear to the whole world they had in fact done.' The Soviets, too, wanted time, to complete the construction of their missile bases, but it did not matter much if the Americans were to learn about the missiles now. The Soviets knew that American U-2 planes would soon discover the missiles if they had not done so already.

Even if one does not grant any difference in the stakes, Kennedy might have felt more detection apprehension than Gromyko, because he probably felt less confident about his ability to lie. Certainly he was less practiced than Gromyko. Also, Gromyko probably would feel more confident if he shared Khrushchev's opinion of Kennedy, formed at the Vienna summit meeting a year earlier, that Kennedy was not very tough.

. . . The point is not to determine whether Kennedy's concealment was uncovered but to explain why there was a chance it might have been and to demonstrate that, even then, recognizing clues to deceit would not have been an easy, uncomplicated matter. Reportedly, Kennedy sensed no mistakes in Gromyko's lies. Since Kennedy already knew the truth he had no need to spot clues to deceit. Armed with that knowledge Kennedy could admire Gromyko's skill.

•

The Profumo affair

HANSARD/SIR PETER RAWLINSON

John 'Jack' Profumo was Secretary of State for War, a Privy Counsellor, and a prominent member of Harold Macmillan's Conservative Government. Profumo had an affair with Christine Keeler, a call-girl to whom he had been introduced by Dr Stephen Ward, whose circle of friends included a Captain Ivanov, then Assistant Naval Attaché at the Russian

Embassy in London, who was also a member of GRU, the Soviet secret military intelligence directorate. Following an incident in which Keeler was threatened with a gun by one of her other lovers, Johnny Edgecombe, she was ordered to appear at Edgecombe's trial. Instead she went to Spain, and there sold her story to the newspapers. As a result, Profumo decided to make a statement to the House of Commons, denying the relationship. Six weeks later, Profumo admitted that this statement had been a lie, and resigned his office. The full text of Profumo's lie to the House appears below. The then Solicitor-General, Peter Rawlinson, subsequently revealed how he and members of the Cabinet were themselves deceived by Profumo, and how he came to draft the minister's untruthful statement to the House.

Personal Statement

The Secretary of State for War (Mr John Profumo): With permission, Sir, I wish to make a personal statement.

I understand that in the debate on the Consolidated Fund Bill last night, under protection of Parliamentary Privilege, the hon. Gentlemen the Members for Dudley (Mr Wigg) and for Coventry, East (Mr Crossman) and the hon. Lady the Member for Blackburn (Mrs Castle), opposite, spoke of rumours connecting a Minister with a Miss Keeler and a recent trial at the Central Criminal Court. It was alleged that people in high places might have been responsible for concealing information concerning the disappearance of a witness and the perversion of justice.

I understand that my name has been connected with the rumours about the disappearance of Miss Keeler.

I would like to take this opportunity of making a personal statement about these matters.

I last saw Miss Keeler in December 1961, and I have not seen her since. I have no idea where she is now. Any suggestion that I was in any way connected with or responsible for her absence from the trial at the Old Bailey is wholly and completely untrue.

My wife and I first met Miss Keeler at a house party in July,

1961, at Cliveden. Among a number of people there was Dr Stephen Ward, whom we already knew slightly, and a Mr Ivanov, who was an attaché at the Russian Embassy.

The only other occasion that my wife or I met Mr Ivanov was for a moment at the official reception for Major Gagarin at the Soviet Embassy.

My wife and I had a standing invitation to visit Dr Ward.

Between July and December, 1961, I met Miss Keeler on about half a dozen occasions at Dr Ward's flat, when I called to see him and his friends. Miss Keeler and I were on friendly terms. There was no impropriety whatsoever in my acquaintanceship with Miss Keeler.

Mr Speaker, I have made this personal statement because of what was said in the House last evening by the three hon. Members, and which, of course, was protected by Privilege. I shall not hesitate to issue writs for libel and slander if scandalous allegations are made or repeated outside the House.

Rawlinson: A few days later I went with John* to Jack Profumo's room. John told me that Jack Profumo had denied any impropriety with the girl and that the whole story was a malevolent newspaper stunt. Now John wanted me to hear for myself what Profumo had to say. In the Secretary of State's room I listened to Jack's categorical and emphatic denials of any impropriety with the girl, who in 1961, he emphasized was certainly not a prostitute nor involved in the kind of world into which two years later she had apparently sunk. I asked if the Minister was prepared to issue a writ for slander or libel if opportunity presented itself. I warned him that in any lawsuit a defendant might well seek to prove that he had committed adultery and then his whole life and his conduct would come under close investigation and, when it came to court, under a public searchlight. I said that once he had issued a writ he would have to pursue the case to its end either in settlement and apology, or in the verdict of a jury.

*John Hobson, then Attorney-General.

The reply was vehement, a declaration that he would sue anyone who ever published this libel about him. The newspaper, he said, had a note from him to the girl addressed as 'Darling'; but not everyone who called a woman darling (and this was a common form of address in the theatre circles in which he and his wife moved) had committed adultery with her. It must be remembered, he insisted, that when he had met Christine Keeler she was vastly different from that which she had apparently become.

It may be, he concluded, that in the present climate of press hostility to the government arising from the Radcliffe Tribunal* and the imprisonment of the two journalists, he might not at first be believed. But he was determined that he would not be driven out of public life and ruined by lies and gossip of the kind which had so recently destroyed our colleague, Tam Galbraith. He repeated that he had not slept with the girl; that he was being dragged into her present story solely because he was a minister, probably to get money out of him or to make a better story to sell; and that the liars were using elements in the press who were determined to get their own back on the government. He would be damned if he would tamely let himself be destroyed.

. . . John had told what he knew to Martin Redmayne, the Chief Whip. There followed discussions between the Chief Whip, the Prime Minister's Principal Private Secretary Tim Bligh, and the Prime Minister himself. The position, then, at that time was that Profumo emphatically denied the rumours. He was advised by a distinguished and experienced solicitor who told us (although he had no obligation to say so) that he himself wholly believed his client. Instructions had been given to issue writs for libel, and the Director of Public Prosecutions had been informed

*A tribunal set up to investigate the circumstances of the Vassall case: Peter Vassall was an English Admiralty clerk who, as a result of his homosexuality, had been blackmailed into spying for the Russians. The Civil Lord of the Admiralty, Tam Galbraith, had been falsely accused of having had a homosexual affair with Vassall – an accusation which broke his spirit.

that the Minister would give evidence if any blackmail charges arose.

But my practice at the Bar had made me perhaps more wary in such matters than John [Hobson]. I remained uneasy. I spoke with John. I said that if all was not as it appeared he would be blamed and there would be no mercy. I reminded him that the Conservative Party was in the business of winning and keeping power; it had no scruple in sacrificing any of its servants should interest demand it. John said quietly that there was no alternative. Statements had been made to him on honour. On those assurances of honour, and in the light of the pledges to sue or to prosecute (promises which it seemed were being redeemed), he must support to the hilt. Otherwise he said all confidence in colleagues was finished. There had to be standards of trust between colleagues and this was between him and a life-long friend. Similar words about the need for trust between colleagues were used by the Prime Minister in the House of Commons later in the summer.

. . . The Chief Whip spoke to the Prime Minister, who agreed that Profumo could now substantiate the assurances to his colleagues which he had given in private, and that Profumo should make a personal statement in the House to clear his name. Iain Macleod, the Leader of the House, who would be concerned if a personal statement were to be made, joined us. We moved to a larger room. Jack Profumo was telephoned, and John and I suggested that Derek Clogg, Profumo's solicitor, should come since this fortuitous opportunity could be used to rebut all the rumours and allegations. Derek Clogg would be able not only to suggest what he thought should be included but he would also be needed to ensure that the personal statement did not prejudice any of the litigation which had been started on Jack's behalf. So it was essential that he should come with Jack.

I, myself, felt glad that at last the moment of truth had arrived. Any refusal to make the statement would lead over the weekend to exploitation of the story based upon what George Wigg and the others had said under the cloak of Parliamentary Privilege and which could therefore safely be published in the newspapers. After such comments in the House, the crisis had certainly been brought to the boil. The only explanation for any refusal to answer in public the comments would be that all the protestations made in private had been false. But none of us for one moment expected that there would be any refusal to make a statement. We believed that Jack Profumo would be as eager as we to seize this chance to clear his name. So we waited, relieved that the climax had arrived.

Jack Profumo and Derek Clogg joined the five of us who were still in the House. The three lawyers then went into another room, and we drafted the statement. Derek Clogg did indeed require that it should be comprehensive so that it met all the known rumours and gossip which had been circulating for so many weeks and he ensured that its terms would not prejudice the litigation that had been launched. I wrote out the draft statement.

We re-joined the others . . . who had been talking and awaiting our return. I read out what we suggested that the personal statement should include. When I came to the words, 'Miss Keeler and I were on friendly terms', Jack Profumo interjected, 'Do I have to say that? It sounds so awful.'

I thought that he was referring to the wording. The words were certainly trite and stilted, but at the time I could think of none better. I asked how else it could be put. The matter was then discussed. It was agreed that the statement had to cover the accepted fact that Profumo had known the girl two years before but that he emphatically denied any adultery or impropriety. So in the end he accepted the words and shortly thereafter we broke up, the statement settled.

At the time I did not gain any impression of drowsiness; his interjection belied any lack of understanding. There was also plenty of time later that morning to recant if there was to be any recantation, for the statement would not be made until 11 a.m., several hours ahead. I certainly did not expect any as I went home and got into bed at 5 a.m. I rose again at 7.30. I did not go to the House, but went early to my work at the Law Courts. There I suddenly began to think about that interjection. Did it mean more than I thought that it had at the time? I waited, for the first time, with some anxiety. Then John told me that the statement had been made as it had been written. I felt ashamed that, for a moment, I had doubted.

On 3 June Jack Profumo made his confession that what he had said to the House on March 22nd was false, and he resigned . . .

Several days after Profumo's confession, Rawlinson wrote to the Chief Whip, Martin Redmayne: 'I presume that both you and I will be accused of gullibility over our part in the Profumo deceit. For my part I should like to make it plain that in the interviews I had with him in February I pressed him firmly over his story and received clear, categorical and what seemed convincing denials of any guilt whatsoever . . . We were in the event deceived. And so was his solicitor, Derek Clogg, a man of the highest reputation and great experience. Moreover I think that I have had as much experience of this kind of legal practice as anyone in my profession, and my professional judgement was as completely deceived as was your judgement as a man of the world by what was not only a wicked series of lies, but was also a most brazen and convincing performance which led to the application to the DPP and even an action in the courts.

•

Security smears and Harold Wilson

DAVID LEIGH

The journalist David Leigh has alleged that, after the General Election of 1964, Conservative Central Office asked MI5 to 'investigate' the Prime Minister and leader of the Labour Party, Harold Wilson. There was a current theory that by going to the Soviet Union with his secretary, Mrs Marcia Williams, Wilson might have 'laid himself open to blackmail' and thus become a 'security risk'. This theory, says Leigh, represented an interesting conjunction of rumours, largely based on two lies quarried from an early period in Wilson's life, which were subsequently circulated by the intelligence services – 'that Wilson got on badly with his wife, and that while in Canada, he had slept with Barbara Castle, who was, twenty years later, to become his Cabinet colleague'.

In April 1949 Wilson launched a new drive for dollar exports. Because of an economic recession in the US, fewer British goods were being bought, and 'Export or Die' was the slogan of the day. Firms which could sell to the US or Canada basked in ministerial favour, and Wilson threw himself into the role of Britain's chief commercial traveller. The following month he invited Barbara Castle to fly out to Canada with him on an extended sales tour.

It was scarcely a seduction ploy – the energetic young Castle had been badgering him for months not to be excluded from trips merely because she was a woman. His other PPS, Tom Cook, had accompanied him on the plum trip to Moscow to get the trade agreement. Wilson's sexuality – of an entirely blameless kind – was to prove of far less significance in his life than the fact that he liked talented women and he liked to give them political opportunities. He was not, despite his masculine-minded Yorkshire background, a male chauvinist pig. The same could not be said of many of those who spread false gossip about him later.

In the event, male chauvinism made the trip rather a fiasco from Barbara Castle's point of view. The Canadians had a strictly limited view of women. In each town at which the plane touched down, the routine was the same. First the young political aide had to listen to a repeat of Harold Wilson's basic speech in which he praised British goods. His audience of businessmen would then point out that British goods were too expensive . . . and that British manufacturers insisted on exporting styles no one wanted to buy . . . After these predictable exchanges, Wilson would retire to a stag dinner with the local male politicians, from which

Barbara Castle was excluded. When she finally protested at the last port of call, a dinner was duly arranged for her as well – with the politicians' wives in a separate anteroom. By all accounts, she ended the trip in a very bad temper. 'No, I did not go to bed with him,' she says, laughing at the thought forty years later, 'far from it.'

The other element in Wilson's early life which was later fastened on by MI5 was his relationship with his wife. Mary Baldwin, the shy, unshowy daughter of a Lancashire congregational minister, met Wilson when he was a schoolboy and married him in 1940, when he was a young don about to be directed into work in the war-time civil service. She thought she was marrying a university lecturer, and made it clear in subsequent years that she did not relish the hectic and aggressive scramble of life in international politics.

... In the early years of his career as a rising young minister, Wilson spent far too many days and even months away from home. At the end of 1946, for example, Attlee sent him to Washington for almost three months to negotiate the setting-up of FAO, the international Food and Agriculture Organisation. Mary remained alone in Oxford with their small son Robin. The foreign trips were frequent; Mary's hopes of continuing to live in the academic atmosphere of Oxford soon foundered while her husband camped in a London flat. As she said in 1947, 'He is supposed to visit us at weekends, but out of the last fifteen, he's had two free ones.' The family eventually moved into a London house, but Mary still refused to have it turned into a political salon. This meant that Wilson did his socializing and political conspiring elsewhere, accidentally laying himself open to repeated attempts to associate his name with sexual scandal. When he became more firmly entrenched in power, his widely assorted enemies resorted to increasingly outrageous slanders; they suggested that his wife wanted to divorce him; that he had slept with not only Barbara Castle but later his political secretary Marcia Williams; that he had fathered children on Mrs Williams; that he had exposed himself to blackmail by the KGB in Moscow by sexual misconduct. All these false stories were collected up by the Intelligence services of London and Washington, there to be circulated by officers or former officers of MI6, MI5, the CIA and the FBI.

The earliest of these stories dates back even before the Canadian trip with Barbara Castle in 1949. It was alleged that in 1947, at the time of Wilson's prolonged Washington visit, the strain on his marriage became acute. As a result, his wife met a Polish academic in Oxford and they fell in love. In order to maintain his political career, the false story went, Wilson patched his marriage up. A similar story, with different circumstances, was to surface thirteen years later, again in an attempt to discredit Wilson when he looked likely to win the Labour leadership. Wilson manifested understandable resentment when a version of the false 1947 story finally appeared in print in a 1977 biography, *Harold Wilson, Yorkshire Walter Mitty*, by a reputable Canadian political journalist, Andrew Roth. Roth said that Mary Wilson 'met another man' in 1947, and quoted one of Mary Wilson's own poems as rather unlikely evidence. Wilson issued a libel writ challenging a variety of points in the book – on the 1947 story, Roth was unable to mount any defence, and Wilson was awarded £10,000 in damages. The book was withdrawn.

The sexual stories were untrue. It is, however, worth asking a question that will recur in the history of rumour and innuendo attached to Harold Wilson. What if the stories had actually been accurate? What would it have mattered if – like most other people – the Wilsons had occasionally found their long marriage in difficulties and the occasional outside sexual relationship had occurred? After all, even if every one of the false rumours had been correct, they would scarcely have added up to a picture of depravity reminiscent of the Borgias. Far from it. They might have fluttered an eyebrow or two in Hampstead Garden Suburb.

What made the difference was the growing post-war world of 'security'. As evidence mounted that sexual blackmail was a regular Soviet Intelligence technique, the British and US Intelligence agencies found themselves increasingly licensed to pry into the possible sexual peccadilloes of an ever-widening range of officials and employees who had access to so-called 'secrets'. Once it was ruled that 'character defects' could turn the average adulterer, homosexual, or drunkard into a 'security risk', it was open season on human frailty. Over a generation MI5 thus came to exercise a new and unpleasant power in the intimate lives not merely of prime ministers, but of many hundreds of thousands of people.

•

Dezinformatsiya

JOHN BARRON

'The system of secrecy,' says the Soviet writer Alexander Zinoviev, 'is one of the essential features of Communist power. It penetrates the whole life of society . . . The system of secrecy is supplemented by a system of disinformation which is carried through so completely that even its instigators can no longer draw a line between fact and fiction.' Here, John Barron describes something of the Soviet system of disinformation, and of how, sometimes, it backfires.

In practising what it calls disinformation, the Soviet Union has for years sponsored grand deceptions calculated to mislead, confound, or inflame foreign opinion. Some of these subterfuges have had a considerable impact on world affairs. Some also have had unforeseeable consequences severely detrimental to Soviet interests. Ultimately, they have made the Soviet Union the victim of its own deceit.

. . . With KGB approval and support, the Czech STB in the autumn of 1964 initiated a vast deception campaign to arouse Indonesian passions against the United States. Through an Indonesian ambassador they had compromised with female agents, the Czechs purveyed to President Sukarno a series of forged documents and fictitious reports conjuring up CIA plots against him. One forgery suggested that the CIA planned to assassinate Sukarno; another 'revealed' a joint American–British plan to invade Indonesia from Malaysia. The unstable Sukarno responded with anti-American diatribes, which some Indonesian journalists in the pay of the KGB and STB amplified and Radio Moscow played back to the Indonesian people. Incited mobs besieged American offices in Djakarta, anti-American hysteria raged throughout the country, and US influence was eradicated. The former STB deception specialist Ladislav Bittman has written a history and analysis of the operation in which he participated. He states, 'We ourselves were surprised by the monstrous proportions to which the provocation grew.'

This brilliant tactical success, however, ended in a débâcle. Bittman notes: 'Czechoslovak and Soviet disinformation departments, intoxicated by potential gains in the battle against the main enemy, deliberately shut their eyes to the danger that the consequences could also be the heightening of internal tension and intensification of Chinese influence in the country.' Encouraged by the increasingly influential Chinese and misled by the climate the Czechs and Russians had created, Indonesian communists concluded that the time was propitious for a coup. The night of September 30, 1965, they murdered six Indonesian generals and attempted to seize the government. The Indonesian military reacted by slaughtering tens of thousands of communists and annihilating the Party, then one of the largest in the world. Indonesia, which seemed destined to slip irretrievably into the communist orbit, emerged as an independent nation with a strong government determined to retain its independence.

Despite such fiascos, Soviet rulers have shown no disposition to abandon organized deception as an instrument of national policy. The practice is another legacy of Lenin embedded in Soviet custom. Just as Lenin admired terror, he extolled the 'poisoned weapons' of deceit, duplicity, and slander. He wrote: 'The communists must be prepared to make every sacrifice and, if necessary, even resort to all sorts of cunning schemes and stratagems, to employ illegal methods, to evade and conceal the truth . . . The practical part of communist policy is to incite one [enemy] against another . . . We communists must use one country against another . . . My words were calculated to evoke hatred, aversion, and contempt . . . not to convince but to break up the ranks of the opponent, not to correct an opponent's mistake but to destroy him, to wipe his organization off the face of the earth. This formulation is indeed of such a nature as to evoke the worst thoughts, the worst suspicions about the opponent.'

Out of these 'Principles of Leninism' the contemporary Soviet concept of *dezinformatsiya*, or disinformation, has evolved. The Russians define disinformation as 'the dissemination of false and provocative information'. As practiced by the KGB, disinformation is far more complex than the definition implies. It entails the distribution of forged or fabricated documents, letters, manuscripts, and photographs; the propagation of misleading or malicious rumours and erroneous intelligence by agents; the duping of visitors to the Soviet Union; and physical acts committed for psychological effect. These techniques are used variously to influence policies of foreign governments, disrupt relations among other nations, undermine the confidence of foreign populations in their leaders and institutions, discredit individuals and groups opposed to Soviet policies, deceive foreigners about Soviet intentions and conditions within the Soviet Union, and, at times, simply to obscure depredations and blunders of the KGB itself.

Disinformation operations differ from conventional propaganda in that their true origins are concealed, and they usually involve some form of clandestine action. For this reason, Soviet rulers always have charged their clandestine apparatus with primary responsibility for disinformation.

The Cheka and each of its organizational descendants had a 'Disinformation Desk' until reorganization of the KGB in 1959 produced a full-fledged Disinformation Department known as Department D of the First Chief Directorate. The first director was General Ivan Ivanovich Agayants, a tall aloof Armenian with grizzled hair and a thin gray mustache. Ascetic and solemn, Agayants combined personal puritanism with a penchant for professional ruthlessness. He gathered a staff of some fifty officers at the Center and stationed another fifteen to twenty at the KGB's Karlshorst Residency in East Berlin. Additionally, he received authorization to engage scientists, technical specialists, and military officers as consultants whenever needed. After the death of Agayants and another reorganization in 1968, the Disinformation Department became Department A, acquiring more stature in the Foreign Directorate bureaucracy and, reportedly, more personnel.

Occasionally Disinformation Department officers travel abroad to participate in operations. Agayants slipped into Sweden in 1963 and Pakistan in 1965. He also went to Indonesia in 1965 and periodically visited Eastern Europe to inspect satellite disinformation departments. His deputy, Sergei Aleksandrovich Kondrashev, traveled to Bonn in 1966 hunting material for slandering West German political leaders. Another Disinformation Department Officer, Yuri Ivanovich Lyudin, using the alias Yuri Ivanovich Modin, spent ten months in New Delhi preparing the forgeries that the KGB released to influence the 1967 Indian elections. A few disinformation officers, such as Vladimir Aleksandrovich Chuchukin, a first secretary of the Soviet UN mission in New York, are permanently stationed abroad. However, for most field work abroad, Department A relies upon officers and agents from the First Chief Directorate's geographic divisions. It also may avail itself of saboteurs from Department V or bona fide Soviet diplomats who at times are employed to plant rumors, wittingly or unwittingly.

•

Business 'bluffing'

ALBERT Z. CARR

A respected businessman with whom I discussed the theme of this article remarked with some heat, 'You mean to say you're going to encourage men to bluff? Why, bluffing is nothing more than a form of lying! You're advising them to lie!'

I agreed that the basis of private morality is a respect for truth and that the closer a businessman comes to the truth, the more he deserves respect. At the same time, I suggested that most bluffing in business might be regarded simply as game strategy – much like bluffing in poker, which does not reflect on the morality of the bluffer.

I quoted Henry Taylor, the British statesman who pointed out that 'falsehood ceases to be falsehood when it is understood on all sides that the truth is not expected to be spoken' – an exact description of bluffing in poker, diplomacy, and business. I cited the analogy of the criminal court, where the criminal is not expected to tell the truth when he pleads 'not guilty'. Everyone from the judge down takes it for granted that the job of the defendant's attorney is to get his client off, not to reveal the truth; and this is considered ethical practice. I mentioned Representative Omar Burleson, the Democrat from Texas, who was quoted as saying, in regard to the ethics of Congress, 'Ethics is a barrel of worms' – a pungent summing-up of the problem of deciding who is ethical in politics.

I reminded my friend that millions of businessmen feel constrained every day to say *yes* to their bosses when they secretly believe *no* and that this is generally accepted as permissible strategy when the alternative might be the loss of a job. The essential point, I said, is that the ethics of business are game ethics, different from the ethics of religion.

He remained unconvinced. Referring to the company of which he is president, he declared: 'Maybe that's good enough for some business-men, but I can tell you that we pride ourselves on our ethics.' . . . But this same fine man, at that very time, was allowing one of his products to be advertised in a way that made it sound a great deal better than it actually was. Another item in his product line was notorious among dealers for its 'built-in obsolescence'. He was holding back from the market a much-improved product because he did not want it to interfere with sales of the inferior item it would have replaced . . . In his view these things had nothing to do with business ethics; they were merely normal business practice. He himself undoubtedly avoided outright falsehoods – never lied in so many words. But the entire organization that he ruled was deeply involved in numerous strategies of deception.

Most executives from time to time are almost compelled, in the interests of their companies or themselves, to practice some form of deception when negotiating with customers, dealers, labor unions, government officials, or even other departments of their companies. By conscious misstatements, concealment of pertinent facts, or exaggeration – in short, by bluffing – they seek to persuade others to agree with them. I think it is fair to say that if the individual executive refuses to bluff from time to time – if he feels obligated to tell the truth, the whole truth, and nothing but the truth – he is ignoring opportunities permitted under the rules and is at a heavy disadvantage in his business dealings.

But here and there a businessman is unable to reconcile himself to the bluff in which he plays a part. His conscience, perhaps spurred by religious idealism, troubles him. He feels guilty; he may develop an ulcer or a nervous tic. Before any executive can make profitable use of the strategy of the bluff, he needs to make sure that in bluffing he will not lose self-respect or become emotionally disturbed. If he is to reconcile personal integrity and high standards of honesty with the practical requirements of business, he must feel that his bluffs are ethically justified. The justification rests on the fact that business, as practiced by individuals as well as by corporations, has the impersonal character of a game – a game that demands both special strategy and an understanding of its special ethics.

The game is played at all levels of corporate life, from the highest to the lowest. At the very instant that a man decides to enter business, he may be forced into a game situation, as is shown by the recent experience of a Cornell honor graduate who applied for a job with a large company:

This applicant was given a psychological test which included the statement, 'Of the following magazines, check any that you have read either regularly or from time to time, and double-check those which interest you most. *Reader's Digest*, *Time*, *Fortune*, *Saturday Evening Post*, *The New Republic*, *Life*, *Look*, *Ramparts*, *Newsweek*, *Business Week*, *US News & World Report*, *The Nation*, *Playboy*, *Esquire*, *Harper's*, *Sports Illustrated*.' His tastes in reading were broad, and at one time or another he had read almost all of these magazines. He was a subscriber to *The New Republic*, an enthusiast for *Ramparts*, and an avid student of the pictures in *Playboy*. He was not sure whether his interest in *Playboy* would be held against him, but he had a shrewd suspicion that if he confessed to an interest in *Ramparts* and *The New Republic*, he would be thought a liberal, a radical, or at least an intellectual, and his chances of getting the job, which he needed, would greatly diminish. He therefore checked five of the more conservative magazines. Apparently it was a sound decision, for he got the job. He had made a game player's decision, consistent with business ethics.

A similar case is that of a magazine space salesman who, owing to a merger, suddenly found himself out of a job:

This man was fifty-eight, and, in spite of a good record, his chance of getting a job elsewhere in a business where youth is favored in hiring practice was not good. He was a vigorous, healthy man, and only a considerable amount of gray in his hair suggested his age. Before beginning his job search he touched up his hair with a black dye to confine the gray to his temples. He knew that the truth about his age might well come out in time, but he calculated that he could deal with that situation when it arose. He and his wife decided that he could easily pass for forty-five, and so he stated his age on his résumé.

This was a lie; yet within the accepted rules of the business game, no moral culpability attaches to it.

... All sensible businessmen prefer to be truthful, but they seldom feel inclined to tell the *whole* truth. In the business game truth-telling usually has to be kept within narrow limits if trouble is to be avoided. The point was neatly made a long time ago (in 1888) by one of John D. Rockefeller's associates, Paul Babcock, to Standard Oil Company executives who were about to testify before a government investigating committee: 'Parry every question with answers which, while perfectly truthful, are evasive of *bottom* facts.' This was, is, and probably always will be regarded as wise and permissible business strategy.

... To be a winner, a man must play to win. This does not mean that he must be ruthless, cruel, harsh, or treacherous. On the contrary, the better his reputation for integrity, honesty, and decency, the better his chances of victory will be in the long run. But from time to time every businessman, like every poker player, is offered a choice between certain loss or bluffing within the legal rules of the game. If he is not resigned to losing, if he wants to rise in his company and industry, then in a crisis he will bluff – and bluff hard.

Every now and then one meets a successful businessman who has conveniently forgotten the small or large deceptions that he practiced on his way to fortune. 'God gave me my money,' old John D. Rockefeller once piously told a Sunday School class. It would be a rare tycoon in our time who would risk the horse laugh with which such a remark would be greeted.

In the last third of the twentieth century even children are aware that if a man has become prosperous in business, he has sometimes departed from the strict truth in order to overcome obstacles or has practiced the more subtle deceptions of the half-truth or the misleading omission. Whatever the form of the bluff, it is an integral part of the game, and the executive who does not master its techniques is not likely to accumulate much money or power.

•

President Johnson and the half-truth

JOHN TEBBEL AND SARAH MILES WATTS

. . . academic researchers, by training, examine every piece of available evidence, consider all the alternatives, and inevitably come to conclusions that can only be open to further questions. If they marshal their evidence to prove a thesis, other scholars selectively assemble evidence from the same sources (and sometimes others) to prove them wrong.

In the case of Lyndon Johnson this kind of methodology was offered particularly rich supplies of source materials because of the president's highly ambiguous nature, in which he was often apparently unable to distinguish between what was true and what was not, handling the facts in whatever way would serve him best. Some biographers have attempted to explain this by picturing him as a true product of the American frontier, a Texan who exemplified the tendency of the pioneer culture to create instant myths – the tall tale, the exaggeration for the sake of humor or emphasis, the larger-than-life approach to everything.

While this theory may be convenient enough to satisfy the psychohistorians, the reality that the reporters who covered Johnson every day had to face was the dense, tangled web of lies, half-truths, evasions, and image-making about Vietnam, begun in the Kennedy administration but reaching its full flowering under Johnson. In his speech of March 31, 1968, during which he proclaimed a partial pause in the bombing of North Vietnam and at the same time announced he would not run for the presidency again, it was significant that neither statement was believed by much of the press, or by many other Americans in and out of the government. It was soon clear that the first statement was another mishandling of the truth; it took time to prove him correct on the second.

When the bombing 'pause' was attacked, Senator Mike Mansfield defended the president by asserting that he '. . . did not lie. Technically he is correct.' That was exactly the point, as Deakin has observed: 'Technically he was correct. That is the story of so much of the credibility gap – the half-truth, the manipulation, the distortion.'

It is worth remembering that the credibility gap between the president and the press initially, then the public, began in August 1964 with the Tonkin Gulf Resolution. This was the result of a claim that the destroyer *Maddox*, along with other naval units, had been fired on by North Vietnamese torpedo patrol boats. The clash, if it actually occurred, took place outside the three-mile limit recognized by the United States but inside the twelve-mile limit claimed by Hanoi. A second encounter, of more dubious validity, occurred the next day. What actually occurred in the Gulf of Tonkin is still a matter of dispute, but there is no doubt about what happened in Washington. The president asked for a congressional resolution that would give him the authority to take 'all necessary measures to repel armed attack', and although there was great uneasiness and controversy in Congress, he got it on August 7. It gave Johnson what he wanted: a blank check for the president to make war. An incident whose authenticity was challenged almost at once by some portions of the press became the starting point for America's real entry into the Vietnam quagmire.

In the summer of 1964 the Republican candidate, Senator Barry Goldwater, was portrayed by the Democrats as a dangerous hawk, while *their* candidate, the accidental president, was cited as a man who, in his own words, would never send American boys to fight a war that should be fought by the young men of Asia. Within months of the election, however, Johnson was at work escalating the war, substantially increasing the American commitment, and the press began to learn more about his credibility.

It took much longer for the public to learn about it, so skilfully was the lying done, and because of the reluctance of so many people to believe what their government was doing. Presidents did not lie. Military leaders in the field did not lie. That was the national mythology. For a long time, until the overwhelming rush of events proved otherwise – events that television made appallingly plain – the public generally believed that it was the media that were lying. Everyone knew the press did not tell the truth, as presidents had always reminded them. Millions still embrace this doctrine, in spite of all the evidence to the contrary.

Johnson was obsessed with secrecy, as his successor proved to be. He concealed facts not only from the press but from his own staff, even from cabinet members. Some had to read the newspapers to find out what was happening to them. The regular White House correspondents were the first to understand that such obsessive secrecy, with its consequent evasions and outright lies, was Johnson's disease. Day by day, incident by incident, this relatively small group of newsmen watched the disease spread like a rapid cancer. But when they tried to tell the public about it, their efforts often not only antagonized the president but sometimes threatened their own credibility as well.

Gradually, and grudgingly, the truth emerged in bits and pieces, leading to the miasma of alienation, withdrawal, suspicion, cynicism, the revolt of the young, the disquiet of parents, the polarization of America – all the agonizing elements that characterized the Vietnam era. The public reluctantly came to understand the difference between Johnson's public and private personae. What they saw was so ugly they did not want to believe it, but the words and pictures they were confronted with could hardly be denied, although strenuous efforts were made to do so.

•

This is not an invasion of Cambodia

WILLIAM SHAWCROSS

Cambodia was neutral during the Vietnam War, but it became a refuge for Communist guerillas. In 1969 it was decided in secret by President

Nixon, Henry Kissinger and only a few members of the military that Cambodian guerilla enclaves should be bombed. This violation of Cambodian neutrality should have come before Congress, whose constitutional duty it is to authorize and fund war when it deems it appropriate to do so. Over the next fourteen months there were 3,630 B-52 bombing raids against suspected Communist bases along Cambodia's border; collectively, the operation was known as 'Menu'. That many innocent civilians were killed is hardly surprising: a single B-52 squadron dropped in one year half the tonnage dropped by US planes in the entire Pacific Theater in the Second World War. Although many newspapermen suspected and reported that Communist positions had been attacked, Nixon, Kissinger, William Rogers (US Secretary of State), Melvin Laird (Secretary of Defense) and others continued to lie to Congress, press and public that there had been no attack. In 1970, President Nixon went on television to explain why US troops were going to attack Communists in Cambodia, and repeated the lie that it had never happened before. Indeed the truth was not established until 1973, but neither Nixon nor Kissinger had any problem in justifying the deception. William Shawcross explains how Nixon went on television and, not for the first time, lied to the world.

Nixon disregarded advice that Abrams simply make a routine announcement of the invasion from Saigon. He was apparently determined to make the most of the occasion and he worked on his speech himself until 4.15 a.m. on the morning of April 30, the day it was to be delivered. A few hours later he called Haldeman and Kissinger into his office and, slumped in his chair, he read it to them. They had only minor comments.

It was much later in the afternoon that the speech was taken over to Laird and Rogers. They were horrified. 'This will cause an uproar,' Rogers told his staff, and Laird called Kissinger to suggest fundamental changes. Under his prodding Kissinger did now suggest some; Nixon rejected almost all of them. The final speech was very much his own, and as delivered, it ranks with 'Checkers', the 1962 'last' press conference, and the 1974 'farewell' to the White House staff, as among the key Nixon texts. As

Jonathan Schell, of the *New Yorker*, pointed out, it reflected his attitudes toward himself, his place in America and America's place in the world, and it explains much about why he acted as he did. It had almost nothing to do with the realities of Cambodia.

Ignoring Menu, Nixon began with the lie that the United States had 'scrupulously respected' Cambodia's neutrality for the last five years and had not 'moved against' the sanctuaries. This falsehood was repeated by Kissinger in his background briefings to the press. That same evening he told reporters that the Communists had been using Cambodia for five years but, 'As long as Sihanouk was in power in Cambodia we had to weigh the benefits in long-range historical terms of Cambodian neutrality as against any temporary military advantages and we made no efforts during the first fifteen months of this administration to move against the sanctuary.' The next day he told of Sihanouk's rule, 'We had no incentive to change it. We made no effort to change it. We were surprised by the development. One reason why we showed such great restraint against the base areas was in order not to change this situation.'

In his announcement of the invasion, Nixon stated that his action was taken 'not for the purpose of expanding the war into Cambodia, but for the purpose of ending the war in Vietnam'; he would give aid to Cambodia, but only to enable it 'to defend its neutrality and not for the purpose of making it an active belligerent on one side or the other'.

He promised that in the Fish Hook area American and South Vietnamese troops 'will attack the headquarters for the entire Communist military operation in Vietnam'; Laird had repeatedly told him that except in the wider reaches of military fantasy, no such 'key control center', as Nixon put it, existed. He alleged that 'the enemy . . . is concentrating his main forces in the sanctuaries, where they are building up to launch massive attacks on our forces and those of South Vietnam'. Melvin Laird had, in fact, reluctantly approved the invasion only because he was sure that the movement of the Communists westward *out of* the sanctuaries would render the United States casualties tolerably low. Nixon then 'noted' – incorrectly – that 'there has been a great deal of discussion with regard to this decision I have made'.

. . . Nixon introduced himself, as he so often did, into the discussion by promising that 'I would rather be a one-term President and do what is right than to be a two-term President at the cost of seeing America become a second-rate power and to see this nation accept the first defeat in its proud 190-year history.' He compared his action with the 'great decisions' made by Woodrow Wilson in the First World War, Franklin Roosevelt in the Second, Eisenhower in Korea, and Kennedy during the missile crisis. 'It is not our power but our will and character that is being tested tonight,' he intoned. Would America have the strength to stand up to 'a group' – by which he presumably meant the entire North Vietnamese population and the Viet Cong together with their supporters in Moscow, in Peking and across the world – that flouted its President's will? 'If we fail to meet this challenge, all other nations will be on notice that despite its overwhelming power the United States, when a real crisis comes, will be found wanting.'

Despite the secrecy and the rhetoric, this was not, it seems, a *real crisis*. Cambodia was a test, a trial through which Nixon was putting the American people, let alone the Cambodians, so that if a real crisis did come one day, the world would beware. 'This is not an invasion of Cambodia,' Nixon insisted. (Officials were ordered to call it an 'incursion' instead.) At one level this was just another lie, but at another it was true. Cambodia was a testing ground for United States resolve.

•

This young man who has now become so alien to me

ALBERT SPEER

Formerly Hitler's architect, Albert Speer became Minister of Armaments and War Production in 1942, and showed absolutely no scruples in exploiting all the slave labour he could get his hands on. As a result he was able to perform miracles in rapidly expanding the Nazi war production capacity, despite heavy Allied bombing. In 1970, following his release from a twenty-year prison sentence for crimes against humanity, Speer published his memoirs – a sanitized account of his participation in one of the greatest crimes of the century. His deceitful account of his concern for 'prisoners' is entirely typical. Of the daily round of executions and beatings, he says nothing. Tom Bower has contrasted the fate of Fritz Sauckel, the Minister of Labour, with that of Speer: 'A crude uneducated man, it was Sauckel's job to obey Speer's orders and find the slave labour in Europe. Speer impatiently criticized Sauckel for delivering too many women and children among the two million in 1942, and in September 1943 he demanded that the Minister of Labour find another 1.2 million to work in Germany's factories. Sauckel obeyed and was hanged.' It was, says Bower, British snobbery that kept Speer alive in the face of the verdict of the French, American and Russian judges that he too should have been hanged.

Our hard-won independence in matters of armaments was broken by Hitler's order to erect a large rocket-production plant dependent on the SS.

In a lonely valley in the Harz Mountains a widely ramified system of caves had been established before the war for the storage of vital military chemicals. Here, on December 10, 1943, I inspected the extensive underground installations where the V-2 was to be produced. In enormous long halls prisoners were kept busy setting up machinery and shifting plumbing. Expressionlessly, they looked right through me, mechanically removing their prisoners' caps of blue twill until our group had passed them.

I cannot forget a professor of the Pasteur Institute in Paris who testified as a witness at the Nuremberg Trial. He too was in the Central Works which I inspected that day. Objectively, without any dramatics, he explained the inhuman conditions in this inhuman factory. The memory is especially painful, the more so because he made his charge without hatred, sadly and brokenly, and also astonished at so much human degeneracy.

The conditions for these prisoners were in fact barbarous, and a sense of profound involvement and personal guilt seizes me whenever I think of them. As I learned from the overseers after the inspection was over, the sanitary conditions were inadequate, disease rampant; the prisoners were quartered right there in the damp caves, and as a result the mortality among them was extraordinarily high.* That same day I allocated the necessary materials and set all the machinery in motion to build a barracks camp immediately on an adjacent hill. In addition, I pressed the SS camp command to take all necessary measures to improve sanitary conditions and upgrade the food. They pledged that they would do so.†

Up to this time I actually paid almost no attention to these problems, and the assurances of the camp commanders persuaded me that matters would be corrected. I did not take action again until January 14, 1944. On January 13, Dr Poschmann, the medical supervisor for all the departments in my Ministry, described the hygenic conditions at the Central Works in the blackest colors. The next day I sent one of my department heads to the plant. Simultaneously, Dr Poschmann started taking various medical measures. A few days later my own illness partially put a halt to these actions. But on May 26, soon after I was back at my post, Dr Poschmann told me that he had arranged for the assignment of civilian doctors to many of the labor camps. But there were difficulties. On the same day, I received a rude letter from Robert Ley in which he protested against Dr Poschmann's interference on formal grounds. Medical treatment in camps was his province, he declared, and angrily demanded that I reprimand

*A hundred men died every day in Nordhausen, the facility described by Speer. By the end of the war, some 20,000 had died in this factory alone. Hanged prisoners (as many as fifty-seven in one day) were left dangling from piano wire for days afterwards, as an example to others.

†Knowing the SS as he did, Speer must have been aware that this 'pledge', if it was ever made at all, would be worthless. For all his pious claims of concern for prisoner welfare, Speer did not lessen the production quotas – the help that was really in his power.

Dr Poschmann, forbid him any further meddling, and discipline him for the steps he had already taken.

I answered immediately that I had no interest to meet his demands, that on the contrary we had the greatest interest in adequate medical treatment for the prisoners. That same day I discussed further medical measures with Dr Poschmann. Since I was making all these arrangements in cooperation with Dr Brandt, and since apart from all humanitarian considerations, the rational arguments were on our side, I did not give a hang about Ley's reaction. I was confident that Hitler would rebuke the party bureaucracy which we had passed over and would even make scornful remarks about the bureaucrats . . . I heard no more from Ley.

During the war the supply of labor became the key factor in any industrial unit. At the beginning of the forties, and subsequently at a faster and faster pace, the SS began secretly building labor camps and making sure they were kept full. In a letter of May 7, 1944, Walter Schieber, one of my department heads, called my attention to the efforts of the SS to use its powers over labor in order to promote its economic expansion. Moreover, the SS was casting eyes on the foreign workers in our factories and became more and more zealous in arresting them for trivial violations of rules and transferring them to its own camps.* My assistants estimated that by this technique we were being deprived of thirty to forty thousand workers a month during the spring of 1944.

At the beginning of June 1944, I protested to Hitler that I could not 'stand the loss of half a million workers a year . . . all the more so because a majority of them were skilled workers trained with considerable effort'. I said that they simply had to

*Speer fails to mention that these labour camps would have included those whose products would have been required by his own ministry; I. G. Farben's factory at Auschwitz, for example, where tens of thousands of prisoners were worked to death producing artificial rubber.

be 'returned to their original occupations as quickly as possible'. Hitler told me to discuss the matter with Himmler; he would then make a decision in my favor. But in defiance of the facts Himmler denied both to me and to Hitler that any such practices were being pursued.*

The prisoners themselves, as I sometimes had a chance to observe, also feared Himmler's growing economic ambitions. I recall a tour through the Linz steelworks in the summer of 1944 where prisoners were moving about freely among the other workers. They stood at the machines in the lofty workshops, served as helpers to trained workers, and talked unconstrainedly with the free workers. It was not the SS but the army soldiers who were guarding them. When we came upon a group of twenty Russians, I had the interpreter ask them whether they were satisfied with their treatment. They made gestures of passionate assent. Their appearance confirmed what they said. In contrast to the people in the caves of the Central Works, who were obviously wasting away, these prisoners were well fed. And when I asked them, just to make conversation, whether they would prefer to return to the regular camp, they gave a start of fright. Their faces expressed purest horror.

But I asked no further questions. Why should I have done so; their expressions told me everything. If I were to try today to probe the feelings that stirred me then, if across the span of a lifetime I attempt to analyse what I really felt – pity, irritation, embarrassment, or indignation – it seems to me that the desperate race with time, my obsessional fixation on production and output statistics, blurred all considerations and feelings of humanity. An American historian has said of me that I loved machines more than people. He is not wrong. I realize that the sight of suffering people influenced only my emotions, but not my conduct. On the plane of feelings only sentimentality emerged; in the realm of

*It is difficult to conceive of what kind of slave labour would have been devoted on a large scale to anything other than the war effort. This really is a lie.

decisions, on the other hand, I continued to be ruled by the principles of utility. In the Nuremberg Trial the indictment against me was based on the use of prisoners in the armaments factories.

By the court's standard of judgement, which was purely numerical, my guilt would have been greater had I prevailed over Himmler and raised the number of prisoners in our labor force, thus increasing the chances of more people for survival. Paradoxically, I would feel better today if in this sense I had been guiltier. But what preys on my mind nowadays has little to do with the standards of Nuremberg nor the figures on lives I saved or might have saved. For in either case I was moving within the system. What disturbs me more is that I failed to read the physiognomy of the regime mirrored in the faces of those prisoners – the regime whose existence I was so obsessively trying to prolong during those weeks and months. I did not see any moral ground outside the system where I should have taken my stand. And sometimes I ask myself who this young man really was, this young man who has now become so alien to me, who walked through the workshops of the Linz steelworks or descended into the caverns of the Central Works twenty-five years ago.

•

No whitewash in the White House

RICHARD NIXON

On 18 June 1972 several men were arrested while breaking into the Democratic Party headquarters in the Watergate complex in Washington. The evidence pointed to their having intended to bug the telephones and to collect information that might prove useful to the Republican campaign to re-elect the President, Richard Nixon. Thanks to the persistence of two reporters, Carl Bernstein and Bob Woodward of the *Washington Post*, and despite the very best efforts of the White House staff at concealment, the trail led right into the Oval Office. Nixon had of course authorized the bugging personally; nevertheless, he was still capable of denying on television, on 30 April 1973, that he had anything to do with it, choosing instead to put the blame on others. The speech, which is vintage Nixon, is one of the most spectacular examples of lying this century has witnessed, and as such the full text is included here.

I want to talk to you tonight from my heart on a subject of deep concern to every American.

In recent months, members of my Administration and officials of the Committee for the Re-election of the President, including some of my closest friends and most trusted aides, have been charged with involvement in what has come to be known as the Watergate affair.

These include charges of illegal activity during and preceding the 1972 Presidential election and charges that responsible officials participated in efforts to cover up that illegal activity.

The inevitable result of these charges has been to raise serious questions about the integrity of the White House itself. Tonight I wish to address those questions.

Last June 17, while I was in Florida trying to get a few days' rest after my visit to Moscow, I first learned from news reports of the Watergate break-in. I was appalled at this senseless, illegal action, and I was shocked to learn that employees of the re-election committee were apparently among those guilty.

I immediately ordered an investigation by appropriate Government authorities. On September 15, as you will recall, indictments were brought against seven defendants in the case. As the investigation went forward, I repeatedly asked those conducting the investigation whether there was any reason to believe that members of my Administration were in any way involved. I received repeated assurances that they were not. Because of these continuing reassurances – because I believed the reports I was getting, because I had faith in the persons from whom I was getting them – I discounted the stories in the press that appeared to implicate members of my Administration or other officials of the campaign committee. Until March of this year, I remained convinced that the denials were true and that the charges of involvement by members of the White House staff were false.

The comments I made during this period, and the comments made by my Press Secretary on my behalf, were based on the information provided to us at the time we made those comments. However, new information then came to me which persuaded me that there was a real possibility that some of these charges were true, and suggesting further that there had been an effort to conceal the facts both from the public, from you, and from me. As a result, on March 21, I personally assumed the responsibility for coordinating intensive new inquiries into the matter, and I personally ordered those conducting the investigations to get all the facts and to report them directly to me, right here in this office.

I again ordered that all persons in the Government or at the re-election committee should cooperate fully with the FBI, the prosecutors and the grand jury. I also ordered that anyone who refused to cooperate in telling the truth would be asked to resign from Government service.

And, with ground rules adopted that would preserve the basic constitutional separation of powers between the Congress and the Presidency, I directed that members of the White House staff should appear and testify voluntarily under oath before the senate committee investigating Watergate.

I was determined that we should get to the bottom of the matter, and that the truth should be fully brought out – no matter who was involved. At the same time, I was determined not to take precipitate action, and to avoid, if at all possible, any action that would appear to reflect on innocent people. I wanted to be fair. But I knew that in the final analysis, the integrity of this office – public faith in the integrity of this office – would have to take priority over all personal considerations.

Today, in one of the most difficult decisions of my Presidency,

I accepted the resignations of two of my closest associates in the White House – Bob Haldeman, and John Ehrlichman* – two of the finest public servants it has been my privilege to know. I want to stress that in accepting these resignations, I mean to leave no implication whatever of personal wrongdoing on their part, and I leave no implication tonight of implication on the part of others who have been charged in this matter. But in matters as sensitive as guarding the integrity of our democratic process, it is essential not only that rigorous legal and ethical standards be observed, but also that the public, you, have total confidence that they are both being observed and enforced by those in authority and particularly by the President of the United States. They agreed with me that this move was necessary in order to restore that confidence.

Because Attorney General Kleindienst – though a distinguished public servant, my personal friend for twenty years, with no personal involvement whatever in this matter – has been a close personal and professional associate of some of those who are involved in this case, he and I both felt that it was also necessary to name a new Attorney General.

The counsel to the President, John Dean, has also resigned.

As the new Attorney General, I have today named Elliot Richardson, a man of unimpeachable integrity and rigorously high principle. I have directed him to do everything necessary to ensure that the Department of Justice has the confidence and trust of every law-abiding person in this country. I have given him absolute authority to make all decisions bearing upon the prosecution of the Watergate case and related matters. I have instructed him that if he should consider it appropriate, he has the authority to name a special supervising prosecutor for matters arising out of the case.

Whatever may have appeared to have been the case before – whatever improper activities may yet be discovered in connexion

*The White House Chief of Staff and Chief Domestic Affairs Advisor, respectively.

with this whole sordid affair – I want the American people, I want you, to know beyond the shadow of a doubt that during my term as President, justice will be pursued fairly, fully, and impartially, no matter who is involved. This office is a sacred trust and I am determined to be worthy of that trust.

Looking back at the history of this case, two questions arise: How could it have happened? Who is to blame?

Political observers have correctly observed that during my twenty-seven years in politics I have always previously insisted on running my own campaigns for office. But 1972 presented a very different situation. In both domestic and foreign policy, 1972 was a year of crucially important negotiations, of vital new directions, particularly in working toward the goal which has been my overriding concern throughout my political career – the goal of bringing peace to America and peace to the world. That is why I decided, as the 1972 campaign approached, that the Presidency should come first and politics second. To the maximum extent possible, therefore, I sought to delegate campaign operations, and to remove the day-to-day campaign decisions from the President's office and from the White House. I also, as you recall, severely limited the number of my own campaign appearances.

Who, then, is to blame for what happened in this case?

For specific criminal actions by specific individuals, those who committed those actions must, of course, bear the liability and pay the penalty. For the fact that alleged improper actions took place within the White House or within my campaign organization, the easiest course would be for me to blame those to whom I delegated the responsibility to run the campaign. But that would be a cowardly thing to do. I will not place the blame on subordinates – on people whose zeal exceeded their judgement, and who may have done wrong in a cause they deeply believed to be right. In any organization, the man at the top must bear the responsibility. That responsibility, therefore, belongs here, in this office. I accept it. And I pledge to you tonight, from this office, that I will do everything in my power to ensure that the guilty are brought to justice, and that such abuses are purged from our political processes in the years to come, long after I have left this office.

Some people, quite properly appalled at the abuses that occurred, will say that Watergate demonstrates the bankruptcy of the American political system. I believe precisely the opposite is true. Watergate represented a series of illegal acts and bad judgements by a number of individuals. It was the system that has brought the facts to light and that will bring the guilty to justice – a system that in this case has included a determined grand jury, honest prosecutors, a courageous judge, John Sirica, and a vigorous free press.

It is essential now that we place our faith in that system – and especially in the judicial system. It is essential that we let the judicial process go forward, respecting those safeguards that are established to protect the innocent as well as to convict the guilty. It is essential that in reacting to the excesses of others, we do not fall into excesses ourselves. It is also essential that we not be so distracted by events such as this that we neglect the vital work before us, before this nation, before America, at a time of critical importance to America and the world.

Since March, when I first learned the Watergate affair might in fact be far more serious than I had been led to believe, it has claimed far too much of my time and attention. Whatever may now transpire in the case – whatever the actions of the grand jury, whatever the outcome of any eventual trials – I must now turn my full attention once again to the larger duties of this office. I owe it to this great office that I hold, and I owe it to you – to our country. I know that, as Attorney General, Elliot Richardson will be both fair and fearless in pursuing this case wherever it leads. I am confident that with him in charge, justice will be done.

There is vital work to be done towards our goal of a lasting structure of peace in the world – work that cannot wait. Work that I must do. Tomorrow, for example, Chancellor Brandt of West Germany will visit the White House for talks that are a vital element of 'The Year of Europe' as 1973 has been called. We are already preparing for the next Soviet–American summit meeting, later this year. This is also a year in which we are seeking to negotiate a mutual and balanced reduction of armed forces in Europe, which will reduce our defense budget and allow us to have funds for other purposes at home so desperately needed. It is the year when the United States and Soviet negotiators will seek to work out the second and even more important round of our talks on limiting nuclear arms, and of reducing the danger of a nuclear war that would destroy civilization as we know it. It is a year in which we confront the difficult tasks of maintaining peace in South-East Asia, and in the potentially explosive Middle East. There is also vital work to be done right here in America – to ensure prosperity, and that means a good job for everyone who wants to work; to control inflation, that I know worries every housewife, everyone who tries to balance a family budget in America; to set in motion new and better ways of ensuring progress towards a better life for all Americans.

When I think of this office – of what it means – I think of all the things that I want to accomplish for this nation – of all the things I want to accomplish for you.

On Christmas Eve, during my terrible personal ordeal of the renewed bombing of North Vietnam, which after twelve years of war, finally helped to bring America peace with honor, I wrote out some of the goals for my second term as President. Let me read them to you.

'To make it possible for our children, and for our children's children, to live in a world of peace.

'To make this country be more than ever a land of opportunity – of equal opportunity, full opportunity for every American.

'To provide jobs for all who can work, and generous help for all who cannot.

'To establish a climate of decency, and civility, in which each person respects the feelings and dignity and the God-given rights of his neighbor.

'To make this a land in which each person can dare to dream, can live his dreams – not in fear, but in hope – proud of his community, proud of his country, proud of what America has meant to himself and the world.'

These are great goals. I believe we can, we must work for them. We can achieve them. But we cannot achieve these goals unless we dedicate ourselves to another goal.

We must maintain the integrity of the White House, and that integrity must be real, not transparent. There can be no whitewash in the White House.

We must reform our political process – ridding it not only of violations of the law, but also of the ugly mob violence, and other inexcusable campaign tactics that have been too often practiced and too readily accepted by one side to the excesses or expected excesses of the other side. Two wrongs do not make a right.

I have been in public life for more than a quarter of a century. Like any other calling, politics has good people, and bad people. And let me tell you, the great majority in politics, in the Congress, in the Federal Government, in the state governments, are good people.

I know that it can be very easy, under the intensive pressures of a campaign, for even well-intentioned people to fall into shady tactics – to rationalize this on the grounds that what is at stake is of such importance to the nation that the end justifies the means. And both of our great parties have been guilty of such tactics in the past.

In recent years, however, the campaign excesses that have occurred on all sides have provided a sobering demonstration of how far this false doctrine can take us. The lesson is clear: America, in its political campaigns, must not again fall into the trap of letting the end, however great that end is, justify the means.

I urge the leaders of both political parties, I urge citizens, all of you, everywhere, to join in working towards a new set of standards, new rules and procedures – to ensure that future elections will be as nearly free of such abuses as they possibly can be made. This is my goal. I ask you to join in making it America's goal.

When I was inaugurated for a second term this past January 20, I gave each member of my Cabinet and each member of my senior White House staff a special four-year calendar, with each day marked to show the number of days remaining to the Administration. In the inscription of each calendar, I wrote these words: 'The Presidential term which begins today consists of 1,461 days – no more, no less. Each day can be a day of strengthening and renewal for America; each can add depth and dimension to the American experience. If we strive together, if we make the most of the challenge and the opportunity that these days offer us, they can stand out as great days for America, and great moments in the history of the world.'

I looked at my own calendar this morning up at Camp David as I was working on this speech. It showed exactly 1,361 days remaining in my term. I want these to be the best days in America's history, because I love America. I deeply believe that America is the hope of the world, and I know that in the quality and wisdom of the leadership America gives lies the only hope for millions of people all over the world, that they can live their lives in peace and freedom. We must be worthy of that hope, in every sense of the word.

Tonight, I ask for your prayers to help me in everything that I do through the days of my Presidency to be worthy of their hopes and of yours. God bless America and God bless each and every one of you.

•

Taking the lie-detector

JOHN DEAN

President Nixon's counsel was John Dean, the architect of the cover-up in the Watergate scandal, and, when it began to break, its scapegoat.

Here he describes a meeting at his home with his attorney, Charles Shaffer, after learning that he was being set up to take the rap.

I took Charlie step by step through my dealings with the President on the cover-up, from the first meeting, on September 15, 1972, through the last. Charlie's cigar went out somewhere along the line, but he didn't notice.

'What do you think?' I asked finally.

Charlie stood up and walked across the room. He stopped and turned. His head was shaking and his lips were tight, as if they were fighting to hold back the words: 'The President is a goddam criminal, that's what I think.'

I nodded.

Charlie began pacing. 'Now, listen, I want to go back over a couple of points. I want you to tell me again what he said about it being no problem to get a million bucks, and what you told him about laundering money. That's the damndest conversation I ever heard. The P. sounds like the Godfather, for Christ's sake.'

He sat back down in the easy chair beside our fireplace and listened as I repeated the conversation.

'Now tell me about the clemency offer again,' he said.

I repeated it.

'The P.'s in trouble. Big trouble,' he concluded and was off pacing again. Then, as he lit a cigar, 'The P. needs a lawyer and he better get himself a good one.'

'Well, now you can understand why I suggested that Silbert and Glanzer get that tape of my meeting with Nixon on April fifteenth,' I said.

'Yeah, I see.' Charlie sat down again with a sigh. He was quiet for a long time. When he finally spoke, his mood had changed. 'I don't think I ever told you this, but I voted for Nixon last time. Everybody, I guess, figures that an old Kennedy Democrat like me would love to nail Nixon, but I'd figured the bastard would make a better President than McGovern. You know,' he continued as he watched the smoke from his cigar swirl up toward the lamp beside him, 'it's damn depressing, what you just told me.' He was silent again.

'Would you like a drink?' Mo asked Charles as she came down the stairs to check on us.

'I'll have a little brandy if you've got some, thanks.' Charlie waited until she was out of the room and then spoke to me softly. 'I don't think you ought to tell McCandless about the P. I don't think this stuff should be leaked to the press. He'll learn about it in due time, but not now. Okay?'

'I agree.'

Charlie sighed again. 'You against the President. Shit. I can't believe it. I knew you were carrying a load around in your head, but I didn't realize it was a goddam atom bomb. I want to think about this for a while. We're going to take this one step at a time. It may be your word against Nixon's and the rest of them, and that doesn't make me very comfortable.'

'It doesn't make me very comfortable either.'

'Not that I don't believe you,' Charlie reassured me, and I knew he meant it.

He had said the same thing to me a few weeks earlier, at a time when he had had doubts. It had been an awkward situation for him and most uncomfortable for me. I had gone to his office to meet with him and found that something was bothering him. 'I had a talk today with Silbert and Ganzer,' he had said. 'John, they don't believe your story about Gray destroying documents, which makes them very leery of what else you told them.' Charlie's worried tone upset me. He always sounded confident, about everything. 'They say Petersen talked to Gray, and Gray has denied ever receiving any documents from you or Erlichman, let alone destroying them.' Charlie shifted in his chair. 'Now, I believe you,' he added hastily, 'but . . .' He was struggling for the right words. I knew my face must be registering my concern, and Charlie was trying to comfort me, but his words didn't offer solace, '. . . but I'm not the prosecutor in this case.'

'Charlie, I'm telling you the truth. Gray told me he'd destroyed those documents, I'd swear to it under oath,' I pleaded, looking for stronger assurance than the mere fact that my own lawyer believed me.

'Here's the problem. They say, "Why should we believe Dean?" You see, it's your word against his, and just because I tell them Gray's a damn liar doesn't help us a bit. We've got to convince them, and I've got an idea I'd like to run by you.' Charlie was more fidgety than I'd ever seen him. He spun a pencil with his hand as he spoke.

'Sure,' I said, but I felt desperate. I'd been trying to convince myself that if I said what had happened I'd be believed. Now even Charlie wants more, I thought.

'Here's what I'm thinking. You don't have to do this if you don't want to, but it might be a good idea if you took a lie-detector test. If the results don't come out right, we'll put the goddam report in the bottom drawer and bury it.' Charlie was testing me.

'Hell, Charlie, I'm ready. Gray's lying, and if that's what I've got to do to prove it, fine.'

'Terrific. That's terrific. I'll set it up for you as soon as we can do it. I've got the man.' He was smiling for the first time since I had arrived, which made me feel better.

Charlie called a private investigator and made the arrangements. The next day I would 'get on the box', as he called it.

Charlie's investigator friend and the lie-detector test were waiting for me in the uninviting back room of a sterile prefabricated office building in suburban Maryland. What if I fail, I kept thinking; then I'm going to be in really big trouble. I had nearly convinced myself that no machine could register anything about me because my central nervous system was carrying more voltage than it was built to handle. The tester tried to put me at ease. The purpose, he explained, was not to trick or surprise me. We reviewed the questions carefully.

There was no way to get comfortable in the hardwood chair, with terminals attached to my fingers, a blood-pressure tourniquet around one of my arms, and a rubber belt around my chest. Wires ran behind me to 'the box'. The tourniquet cut off the circulation in my arm. I felt a tingling feeling as my fingers fell asleep, then pain. This was normal, the tester said when I complained. He kept asking questions: 'Did you turn documents from Hunt's safe over to Pat Gray? . . . Did Mr Gray tell you he had destroyed the documents from Hunt's safe you had given him?'

'We're almost finished,' he said. 'But I want to do one more test. Please select a card.' He held out a fan of half a dozen playing cards. 'Now, remember the card you selected. I'm going to call off all the cards, and I want you to lie to me about which card you selected.' He read off the cards and I picked the wrong one. He peered at his instruments, laughing. 'That's a good sign. You damn near broke my machine when you lied.' I felt better as he unhooked me from the straps and wires.

Charlie called when he received the report the next day. He was riding high again. 'Son, from now on whenever there's any doubt about who's telling the truth, you're going to get on the box. I already called Silbert and told him to get Gray on the box, because my man passed with flying colours.' Gray, of course, never took a lie-detector test; he finally confessed that he had destroyed the documents.

The polygraph test was not wasted. It led us to an important decision: I would testify only to facts on which I was prepared to take a lie-detector test. Often when we were preparing testimony in sensitive areas, Charlie would lean over, smiling, and ask whether I was ready to go on the box about it. It would give us a boost as we squared off against the President.

On 25 June 1973 John Dean testified to the Senate Watergate Committee that Nixon had taken part in the cover-up for illegality for eight months. Nixon resigned from office the following year. Dean records his reaction to hearing Nixon's resignation speech on television: 'The cover-up had been a stupid error. Lying about it had been deadly for him. It was over now. He'd been caught in his lies, so why didn't he confess? Was he really far wiser and shrewder than most would give him credit for? Would history say he'd been unfairly forced from office? Was he planting seeds of doubt? Or did he fear prosecution and jail? I didn't know, but I found comfort in the fact that he himself had caused his demise. Not I.'

•

Placebos

SISSELA BOK

The common practice of prescribing placebos to unwitting patients illustrates the two miscalculations so common to minor forms of deceit: ignoring possible harm and failing to see how gestures assumed to be trivial build up into collectively undesirable practices. Placebos have been used since the beginning of medicine. They can be sugar pills, salt-water injections – in fact, any medical procedure which has no specific effect on a patient's condition, but which can have powerful psychological effects leading to relief from symptoms such as pain or depression.

Placebos are prescribed with great frequency. Exactly how often cannot be known, the less so as physicians do not ordinarily talk publicly about using them. At times, self-deception enters in on the part of physicians, so that they have unwarranted faith in the powers of what can work only as a placebo. As with salesmanship, medication often involves unjustified belief in the excellence of what is suggested to others. In the past, most remedies were of a kind that, unknown to the medical profession and their patients, could have only placebic benefits, if any.

The derivation of 'placebo', from the Latin for 'I shall please', gives the word a benevolent ring, somehow placing placebos beyond moral criticism and conjuring up images of hypochondriacs whose vague ailments are dispelled through adroit prescriptions of beneficent sugar pills. Physicians often give a humorous tinge to instructions for prescribing these substances, which helps to remove them from serious ethical concern. One authority wrote in a pharmacological journal that the placebo should be given a name previously unknown to the patient and preferably Latin and polysyllabic, and added:

> [I]t is wise if it be prescribed with some assurance and emphasis for psychotherapeutic effect. The older physicians each had his favourite placebic prescriptions – one chose tincture of Condurango, another the Fluidextract of *Cimicifuga nigra*.

After all, health professionals argue, are not placebos far less dangerous than some genuine drugs? And more likely to produce a cure than if nothing at all is prescribed? Such a view was expressed in a letter to the *Lancet*:

> Whenever pain can be relieved with a ml of saline, why should we inject an opiate? Do anxieties or discomforts that are allayed with starch capsules require administration of a barbiturate, diazepam, or propoxyphene?

Such a simplistic view conceals the real costs of placebos, both to individuals and to the practice of medicine. First, the resort to placebos may actually prevent the treatment of an underlying, undiagnosed problem. And even if the placebo 'works', the effect is often short-lived; the symptoms may recur, or crop up in other forms. Very often, the symptoms of which the patient complains are bound to go away by themselves, sometimes even from the mere contact with a health professional. In those cases, the placebo itself is unnecessary; having recourse to it merely reinforces a tendency to depend upon pills or treatments where none is needed.

In the aggregate, the costs of placebos are immense. Many millions of dollars are expended on drugs, diagnostic tests, and psychotherapies of a placebic nature. Even operations can be of this nature – a hysterectomy may thus be performed, not because the condition of the patient requires such surgery, but because she goes from one doctor to another seeking to have the surgery performed, or because she is judged to have a great fear of cancer which might be alleviated by the very fact of the operation.

Even apart from financial and emotional costs and the squandering of resources, the practice of giving placebos is wasteful of a very precious good: the trust on which so much in the medical relationship depends. The trust of those patients who find out they have been duped is lost, sometimes irretrievably. They may then lose confidence in physicians and even in bona fide medication which they may need in the future. They may obtain for themselves more harmful drugs or attach their hopes to debilitating fad cures.

The following description of a case where a placebo was prescribed reflects a common approach:

> A seventeen-year-old girl visited her pediatrician, who had been taking care of her since infancy. She went to his office without her parents, although her mother had made the appointment for her over the telephone. She told the pediatrician that she was very healthy, but that she thought she had some emotional problems. She stated that she was having trouble sleeping at night, that she was very nervous most of the day. She was a senior in high school and claimed she was doing quite poorly in most of her subjects. She was worried about what she was going to do next year. She was somewhat overweight. This, she felt, was part of her problem. She claimed she was not very attractive to the opposite sex and could not seem to 'get boys interested in me'. She had a few close friends of the same sex.
>
> Her life at home was quite chaotic and stressful. There were frequent battles with her younger brother, who was fourteen, and with her parents. She claimed her parents were always 'on my back'. She described her mother as extremely rigid and her father as a disciplinarian, who was quite old-fashioned in his values.
>
> In all, she spent about twenty minutes talking with her pediatrician. She told him that what she thought she really

needed was tranquilizers, and that that was the reason she came. She felt that this was an extremely difficult year for her, and if she could have something to calm her nerves until she got over her current crises, everything would go better.

The pediatrician told her that he did not really believe in giving tranquilizers to a girl of her age. He said he thought it would be a bad precedent for her to establish. She was very insistent, however, and claimed that if he did not give her tranquilizers, she would 'get them somehow'. Finally, he agreed to call her pharmacy and order medication for her nerves. She accepted graciously. He suggested that she call him in a few days to let him know how things were going. He also called her parents to say that he had a talk with her and he was giving her some medicine that might help her nerves.

Five days later, the girl called the pediatrician back to say that the pills were really working well. She claimed that she had calmed down a great deal, that she was working things out better with her parents, and had a new outlook on life. He suggested that she keep taking them twice a day for the rest of the school year. She agreed.

A month later, the girl ran out of pills and called her pediatrician for a refill. She found that he was away on vacation. She was quite distraught at not having any medication left, so she called her uncle who was a surgeon in the next town. He called the pharmacy to renew her pills and, in speaking to the druggist, found out that they were only vitamins. He told the girl that the pills were only vitamins and that she could get them over the counter and didn't really need him to refill them. The girl became very distraught, feeling that she had been deceived and betrayed by her pediatrician. Her parents, when they heard, commented that they thought the pediatrician was 'very clever'.

The patients who do *not* discover the deception and are left believing that a placebic remedy has worked may continue to rely on it under the wrong circumstances. This is especially true with drugs such as antibiotics, which are sometimes used as placebos and sometimes for their specific action. Many parents, for example, come to believe that they must ask for the prescription of antibiotics every time their child has a fever or a cold. The fact that so many doctors accede to such requests perpetuates the dependence of these families on medical care they do not need and weakens their ability to cope with health problems. Worst of all, those children who cannot tolerate antibiotics may have severe reactions, sometimes fatal, to such unnecessary medication.

Such deceptive practices, by their very nature, tend to escape the normal restraints of accountability and can therefore spread more easily than others. There are many instances in which an innocuous-seeming practice has grown to become a large-scale and more dangerous one. Although warnings against the 'entering wedge' are often rhetorical devices, they can at times express justifiable caution; especially when there are great pressures to move along the undesirable path and when the safeguards are insufficient.

In this perspective, there is much reason for concern about placebos. The safeguards against this practice are few or nonexistent – both because it is secretive in nature and because it is condoned but rarely carefully discussed in the medical literature. And the pressures are very great, and growing stronger, from drug companies, patients eager for cures, and busy physicians, for more medication, whether it is needed or not. Given this lack of safeguards and these strong pressures, the use of placebos can spread in a number of ways.

The clearest danger lies in the gradual shift from pharmacologically inert placebos to more active ones. It is not always easy to distinguish completely inert substances from somewhat active ones and these in turn from more active ones. It may be hard to distinguish between a quantity of an active substance so low that it has little or no effect and quantities that have some effect. It is not always clear to doctors whether patients require an inert placebo or possibly a more active one, and there can be the temptation to resort to an active one just in case it might also have a specific effect. It is also much easier to deceive a patient with a medication that is known to be 'real' and to have power. One recent textbook in medicine goes so far as to advocate the use of small doses of effective compounds as placebos rather than inert substances – because it is important for both the doctor and the patient to believe in the treatment! This shift is made easier because the dangers and side effects of active agents are not always known or considered important by the physician.

Meanwhile, the number of patients receiving placebos increases as more and more people seek and receive medical care and as their desire for instant, push-button alleviation of symptoms is stimulated by drug advertising and by rising expectations of what science can do. The use of placebos for children grows as well, and the temptations to manipulate the truth are less easily resisted once such great inroads have already been made.

Deception by placebo can also spread from therapy and diagnosis to experimentation. Much experimentation with placebos is honest and consented to by the experimental subjects, especially since the advent of strict rules governing such experimentation. But grievous abuses have taken place where placebos were given to unsuspecting subjects who believed they had received another substance. In 1971, for example, a number of Mexican-American women applied to a family-planning clinic for contraceptives. Some of them were given oral contraceptives and others were given placebos, or dummy pills that looked like the real thing. Without fully informed consent, the women were being used in an experiment to explore the side effects of various contraceptive pills. Some of those who were given placebos experienced a predictable side effect – they became pregnant. The investigators neither assumed financial responsibility for the babies nor indicated any concern about having bypassed the 'informed consent' that is required in ethical experiments with human beings. One contented himself with the observation that if only the law had permitted it, he could have aborted the pregnant women!

The failure to think about the ethical problems in such a case stems at least in part from the innocent-seeming white lies so often told in giving placebos. The spread from therapy to experimentation and from harmlessness to its opposite often goes unnoticed in part *because* of the triviality believed to be connected with placebos as white lies. This lack of foresight and concern is most frequent when the subjects in the experiment are least likely to object or defend themselves; as with the poor, the institutionalized, and the very young.

In view of all these ways in which placebo usage can spread, it is not enough to look at each incident of manipulation in isolation, no matter how benevolent it may be. When the costs and benefits are weighed, not only the individual consequences must be considered, but also the cumulative ones. Reports of deceptive practices inevitably leak out, and the resulting suspicion is heightened by the anxiety which threats to health always create. And so even the health professionals who do not mislead their patients are injured by those who do; the entire institution of medicine is threatened by practices lacking in candor, however harmless the results may appear in some individual cases.

This is not to say that all placebos must be ruled out; merely that they cannot be excused as innocuous. They should be prescribed but rarely, and only after a careful diagnosis and consideration of non-deceptive alternatives; they should be used in experimentation only after subjects have consented to their use.

•

The most important pun in the English language

CHRISTOPHER RICKS

As with *sense*, so with *lie* the importance of a pun must be in the first place a matter of the enduring and central matters which it encompasses. Lies are important irrespective of any pun that may visit them. For one thing, the telling of the truth is necessary to those social and cultural agreements without which there cannot be a society or a culture. Even the devils know this, for as Sir Thomas Browne said, 'so also in Moral verities, although they deceive us, they lie not unto each other; as well understanding that all community is continued by Truth, and that of Hell cannot exist without it.' For another thing, telling the truth is a necessary condition for the existence of a language at all. Which is why in the language – indeed, in most or all languages, one may guess – there is no truth verb that is the counterpart to the verb to lie. (And there are, from similar causes or with similar effects, no puns on *true* and *truth* that amount to anything.) You cannot truth, a fact which both makes the telling of the truth a less glib matter than lying ('the truth, the whole truth, and nothing but the truth'), and also brings out that speaking has to be posited on a presumption of the speaking of the truth. Even if it were not accepted that words *about* words all have a special force, though not necessarily a greater force than other words (for this claim might be merely a literary critic's professional predilection), it is nevertheless the case that *lie* has the special potency of immediately paradoxical properties, since it strikes at the roots of language and may strike, self-incriminatingly, at itself. The importance of lying therefore ranges from all those daily falsehoods in the ordinary world to such abstract but intense considerations of language, society, and philosophy. In 1970 there was published a book wholly devoted to the paradox of the liar.

Yet the importance of the phenomenon of lying is a necessary but not a sufficient condition of any claimed importance for the pun on *lie* and *lying*. Then there are the linguistic pressures on the word *lie* which themselves make the word a creator of pressure. There is, first, a depopulation around *lie* which gives it the potency of salience. For instance, *lie* calls up no manifest etymology for us; as a short and simple Old English word, it seems – as does the word *truth* – to be a root concept behind or below which we cannot penetrate. (The contrast would be with the words *veracity* and *mendacity* which send our thoughts abroad, in both senses.) Next, there is the fact that there are no profound or memorable proverbs about lies or truth, so that the words themselves have to muster all the energy of the phenomena. A comparable depopulation, lending prominence and salience to *lie* and *truth*, is that by which a great many lie and truth terms have fallen out of the language, as if by some evolutionary concentration upon the survival of the fittest words. Middle English *gab*, to lie, survives only in its weakened child, *gabble*; *leasing* has gone, as has the plural *lyings*; the adjective *lie* (from Old English *lyȝe*, lying); various transitive and quasi-transitive uses of to lie (*OED* 3 and 4); and 'to give the lie to' (accuse of lying). You can no longer 'make a lie', you can only tell it; you can now lie only *about*, not – as you once could – of, on, or upon (*OED* 1b).

Again, there is the salience given by the marked absence of synonyms for *lie*; all we have is either ephemeral or infantile slang (bounce, crammer, whopper, fib – to cite Roget's *Thesaurus*) or euphemisms: *falsehood* and *untruth*, neither of which strictly speaking means *lie* and both of which therefore can on occasions have the special offence of a euphemism.

... The final linguistic consideration is one of the many asymmetries between *lie* and *truth*, one which lends to *lie* (and to its pun) a range of suggestions which are denied to or disdained by *truth*. This is the fact that rhymes for *truth* are few, and only one of them* has much potentiality for discovering or urging insights ... This marked paucity of suggestive rhyming for *truth*, which lends it a lonely dignity and integrity, contrasts sharply with the manifest and manifold rhymes which crowd upon or from *lie*: *fly* (with its altruism or cowardice), *die* (with its moment of truth and its horizontality), *I* and *my* (with their sincerity or insincerity), *eye* (with its honesty or shiftiness), and so on.

... It is Shakespeare's work which provides the transition from those linguistic considerations which give salience to the *lie/lie* pun, to the more largely human considerations which give

*The word 'youth'. [Ed.]

importance to it. For there is a *prima facie* likelihood that a pun which is so ubiquitously necessary to the greatest writer in the language is a very important pun. Shakespeare, who needs and wants the words *lie*, *lies*, and *lying* hundreds of times in his work, has only three times the punless form *lied*. We should ask ourselves whether the fretfulness or impatience which we sometimes feel with these puns is to Shakespeare's discredit or to ours – have we lost, or become blinded to, the important considerations that presumably seemed to Shakespeare to raise above triviality such an insistence as this?

That, Lye, shall lie so heavy on my Sword,
That it shall render Vengeance, and Revenge,
Till thou the Lye-giver, and that Lye, do lye
In earth as quiet, as thy Father's Scull.
(*Richard II* IV.i)

. . . The importance of the *lie/lie* pun is that it concentrates an extraordinarily wide-ranging and profound network of truth-testing situations and postures. It brings mendacity up against those situations and postures which constitute the great moments or endurances of truth: the child-bed, the love-bed, the bed of sleep and dreams, the sick-bed, the death-bed, the grave . . . And even perhaps the modern secular counterpart to the confessional's kneeling: the psychiatrist's couch. It concentrates this network, or rather concentrated it, since historical and cultural circumstances are now disintegrating it.

•

Faking orgasms

SHERE HITE

The pressure on women to orgasm during intercourse is so great that an enormous number of women fake orgasms – some infrequently, most 'sometimes', but some women said they do it every single time.

Do you ever fake orgasms?

567	*Yes*
775	*No*
318	*Used to*
4	*'It's no use, it's not convincing'*
1,664	*Total*

'I used to fake orgasms all the time, and always with vaginal penetration. I came from the school of it's not right – you'll emasculate the man – if you don't let him think he's satisfied you. With the onset of the women's movement, and its personal effect on me, I've stopped faking them. My husband used to ask, "Did you come?" – and when the answer was "yes" – even if I was faking it – that was cool for him. Then when I started saying "no" a couple of times, he quit asking. Now, if I complain I didn't come, he's either asleep, or says he's sorry and turns over and goes to sleep.'

'I never fake orgasm. I am angry with other women who do, because then men can tell me that I am incapable sexually, because I do not have vaginal climaxes, and other women they have slept with do. Since I have never had a vaginal climax, I question their existence, or at least their general prevalence, and wonder if another woman's faking an orgasm has made it harder for me when I am honest.'

'I fake it during clitoral stimulation and during intercourse when I'm not in the mood. It's easier and faster than saying "no" and then worrying about my husband's ego and feelings for me, etc. He, like most other men, gets really frightened and hurt when I say "no" and I hear about it in passing a week later.'

'I have, and occasionally still do fake orgasms during intercourse, but not often. When I do it now it's because I know I'm not going to have an orgasm but my man is working really hard for me and really wants to give me one and would be very disappointed to know it's no use. As we live together longer it becomes less necessary because our sex is better and we know each other better. In the past I would do it to protect the man's ego and occasionally (with one man) because he would be mad if I didn't have one. I hate faking it, though, and I really hated it with that one man, but he was a typical dominant egocentric chauvinistic horse's ass.'

'During my marriage I was excellent at faking orgasms and so for maybe four years I never really had any satisfying sexual experiences. Unfortunately, I was totally faithful to my husband so I was pretty miserable physically. I masturbated a whole lot! After my separation I explored sex with a variety of partners and had a sexual awakening so to speak.'

'Yes, I used to, more to give a positive reinforcement for something I liked even though I didn't orgasm.'

'I used to, when my husband had a complex about sex and a marriage counselor told me I should build up his ego.'

'No, but I may act more excited than I really am.'

'I used to, because my partner was comparing me to another woman he was sleeping with. He made me feel terrible with descriptions of how she went into a screaming orgasm before he even entered her.'

'Yes, when I haven't had one for quite a while, I do it so my partner won't think he isn't pleasing me. I don't feel orgasms are all that important (he seems to) and I don't feel it's his fault if I don't come but . . . sometimes it is his fault, though, I guess.'

'I was afraid to appear "less of a woman" and emasculate my partner. So I did it, but he found me out.'

'Sometimes it builds a man's ego to let him think he's successful. Therefore if I really like a man and want him to think I enjoyed sex more than I did, I do it.'

'Only to get me or him "off the hook".'

'For fifteen years I was the world's best faker. Honestly – they should have a phallic trophy – mounted on a pedestal (like in art history books) for *all women* – I think they all fake it with men.'

•

Shamming

DONALD WOODS

As founder of the Black Consciousness Movement, Steve Biko was a natural target for the South African authorities. On 18 August 1977 he was arrested, interrogated and beaten. By 12 September he was dead. The inquest into his death began in Pretoria on 14 November, and among those who gave evidence was Colonel P. J. Goosen, the head of the Eastern Cape Security Police, in whose custody Biko had died. Donald Woods describes how Goosen contended that, at the time, he believed Biko to have been shamming the serious head injuries which resulted in his death, 'a contention,' says Woods, 'that should have been branded publicly as a lie, since Goosen's own telex message to Pretoria contradicted this contention'. Suffering from a serious brain injury, on Goosen's orders Biko was transported, naked in the back of a Land-Rover, from the Port Elizabeth prison where he had been held to a prison hospital in Pretoria, 1,200 kilometres away.

Mr Kentridge said that in his affidavit Colonel Goosen had said that Dr Lang had come to the conclusion that Mr Biko was shamming a slight paralysis.

COLONEL GOOSEN: Dr Hersch and Dr Lang told me they could find nothing physically wrong and strengthened my suspicion that he was shamming illness.

MR KENTRIDGE: In your affidavit you said that you were present on the evening when Dr Hersch examined Mr Biko. Dr Lang was also there. You say that when Drs Lang and Tucker examined him he pretended that his one arm was slightly weak but at the prison he indicated the other arm was slightly weaker, but that you couldn't remember which arm was shown.

Mr Kentridge said he could find no mention of this in Dr Lang's evidence, although this had certainly made an impression on Colonel Goosen.

COLONEL GOOSEN: I can't remember which arm it was but for me it was very noticeable that he showed another arm. It was just observation. I made no note of it.
MR KENTRIDGE: Surely that can't be true? If it made such an impression on you, you must have a picture of it in your mind? I find it strange that you cannot say which arm it was.

Mr Kentridge said Dr Tucker had also made an affidavit in which he said that Mr Biko, when asked to move his limbs, could not move his left limbs properly.

COLONEL GOOSEN: I wasn't present at Dr Tucker's examination.
MR KENTRIDGE: I will suggest that this evidence of yours is a complete invention. I'll show you why. In your affidavit you said: 'It was noticeable that during Dr Lang's and Dr Tucker's examination of the 7th and the 8th Mr Biko pretended that one arm was slightly weak.' Yesterday you told us you had not been present. So this statement must be a falsehood.
COLONEL GOOSEN: Drs Lang and Tucker came to my office and there was a discussion. I wanted to know what the diagnosis was. During the discussion I was told that he pretended that one arm was weak. Dr Lang again drew my attention to it at the prison.
MR KENTRIDGE: Why didn't Dr Lang mention this?

COLONEL GOOSEN: He will probably give evidence.
MR KENTRIDGE: Dr Lang said in his affidavit that Mr Biko had refused water and food and had displayed a weakness of all four limbs. Why should he tell you something different in his report?

Colonel Goosen said that this discussion took place immediately after the examination. He was present at the examination of Drs Hersch and Lang.

Mr Kentridge said that according to the report, when the reflexes were tested, different arms were shown as weak, but the doctors did not regard this as sinister. One could not pretend reflexes, he said. He put it to Colonel Goosen that this alleged discrepancy was an invention on his part.

MR KENTRIDGE: You said in your affidavit that at the time when you decided to send Mr Biko to Pretoria he had been examined by three doctors and you had been assured by them that there was nothing wrong and that it was the general view that he was shamming illness. Are you trying to tell us that Dr Hersch also could find nothing wrong?
COLONEL GOOSEN: I had a discussion with Dr Hersch. I was very eager to know his diagnosis. He said that he could find nothing physically wrong and he suggested that a lumbar puncture should be taken the next day.
MR KENTRIDGE: On what basis do you say that Dr Hersch was also of the opinion that there was nothing wrong with Mr Biko?
COLONEL GOOSEN: I did not say that this was a general view of the doctors. I was giving my own opinion. Dr Lang agreed with me to a large extent.

Mr Kentridge re-read the paragraph in the affidavit. Was that not intended to include Dr Hersch? he asked. Colonel Goosen replied that he meant that Dr Lang was of the opinion and other people may have been of the opinion. Dr Lang had told him that neither he, Dr Tucker, nor Dr Hersch could find anything wrong and that he could return Mr Biko to the Walmer police station.

MR KENTRIDGE: Did Dr Lang ever tell you that Dr Hersch thought that Mr Biko was shamming illness?
COLONEL GOOSEN: Not in those words.
MR KENTRIDGE: It did not happen, did it? I will suggest that you put the paragraph in your affidavit in order to deliberately mislead. Did not Dr Lang tell you that Dr Hersch had found red blood cells in the spinal fluid? What did he tell you?

Colonel Goosen said that he was told that a lumbar puncture had been done and that Dr Lang and Dr Hersch wanted to keep Mr Biko in the prison hospital for observation. He said he ordered Mr Biko to be sent to Pretoria because they had the facilities for a proper examination there.

MR KENTRIDGE: What was wrong with Port Elizabeth? There are very good hospitals in Port Elizabeth.
COLONEL GOOSEN: With Mr Biko's background there were good reasons why he could not be kept there.
MR KENTRIDGE: Often in hospitals, prisoners are kept under a twenty-four-hour guard? I know you made a lot of the fact that he studied yoga. Did you think he was a magician?
COLONEL GOOSEN: I still thought he was feigning. I thought it was possible that he could be assisted to escape and leave the country. I have often had prisoners under guard in hospitals who succeeded in escaping.
MR KENTRIDGE: Wasn't the real reason that you did not want anybody to see Mr Biko in that condition? You did not think he would die and until he recovered you wanted to keep him out of sight?
COLONEL GOOSEN: I had no reason to hide him. Neither I nor any of my colleagues, nor the doctors, saw any external injuries.

MR KENTRIDGE: Do you know that General Gericke, the officer commanding the Pretoria prison, said in an affidavit that if he had not the proper facilities in prison Biko would have been sent to a public hospital for treatment?
COLONEL GOOSEN: Had I known what his condition was I would have agreed to that but I thought he was feigning illness.

Colonel Goosen said that when he could not get a military plane he asked Dr Tucker if he could convey Mr Biko by road. Dr Tucker said that provided they allowed Mr Biko to lie on a soft mattress there was no reason why not.

MR KENTRIDGE: What facilities was Mr Biko to have?
COLONEL GOOSEN: A relatively luxurious Land-Rover was used. Seats were removed to put the mattress on the floor.
MR KENTRIDGE: We understand that the only facility available was a container of water.
COLONEL GOOSEN: We still thought he was shamming. The doctors did not prescribe anything.
MR KENTRIDGE: Do you know that Mr Biko went to Pretoria without even a medical history accompanying him?
COLONEL GOOSEN: I phoned Brigadier Dorfling of the Central Prison and asked who would treat Mr Biko. He told me it would be Dr Brandt. He told me to tell Dr Brandt to contact Drs Lang and Tucker in Port Elizabeth. Colonel Dorfling was phoned twice. I think everything possible was done to inform Pretoria.

. . . Colonel Goosen said that when Mr Biko died he realized that he had not been shamming at all. Mr Kentridge replied: 'Unluckily this realization came too late for Mr Biko.' Colonel Goosen said that this was a tragic occurrence for the police of South Africa because of the propaganda that could follow it. He had discussed Mr Biko's death with his colleagues but nobody put up any theories. He had no idea of what the cause of death could have been.

. . . The court found: 'That on the available evidence the death cannot be attributed to any act or omission amounting to a criminal offence on the part of any person.'

•

The lie in adultery

PENNY VINCENZI

Adultery is of course a lie in itself. It is a betrayal, a denial, a pretence, a deceit, and the only way to lend it any virtue whatsoever is to lie about it and keep lying even though trees may grow on your tongue or you are struck by lightning or any other of the well-known punishments for lying are meted out to you. (Indeed, if the tree did start to grow or you were struck by lightning, that could well be the best thing that could possibly happen to you, were you being confronted by your own infidelity by an outraged spouse, for it would provide a most splendid diversion; but alas it is unlikely, for like most of the folk-lore about lying it is entirely untrue.) It says in the Oxford Dictionary that adultery is voluntary sexual intercourse of a married person with one of the opposite sex other than his or her spouse. Presumably if it was involuntary that would be quite all right, and that might be one of the lies you could try if all the others failed; 'I really didn't notice it was happening,' has at least the charm of originality if not the ring of truth. 'It doesn't mean anything,' on the other hand gets no marks at all for trying, and neither does 'It's purely physical,' or 'It's you I love.'

I am not attempting here to defend or even to excuse adultery, I am merely treating it as a fact of life. But it can be made less painful, less destructive, less dangerous by the use of a few accomplished lies. I do not see that anything will be gained by one partner saying to another, 'I want to tell you that I've slept with Fred/Doris and it was most enjoyable'; a great deal less will be lost if nothing is said at all, and if anything has to be said then it should imply that even if Fred and Doris had been slept with, which is by no means established and indeed a most distasteful notion, it would have been an experience of very little pleasure.

I know a liar of some distinction; her suggestion for the faithless cornered *in flagrante* is novel but worth a try, 'You should say you were extremely cold and he was trying to keep you warm.'

Now few people were born yesterday (and the few that were are seldom married) and people born earlier are unlikely to believe that particular story. But the point is that it's something to say with more charm and kindness behind it than 'We haven't finished yet,' or 'John, this is Nigel,' or even 'Go away.' Anything's worth a try, because what you have to remember is that the adulteree wants to believe your lie. This is the first and greatest rule of lying in these circumstances, and the second is almost as important and is this: it is plain downright folly to Confess All when you could quite possibly get away with just a bit of the truth and a great big dollop of fabrication. Which bit is important too. Choose it with care, for it's not always obvious. One night at the sales conference might be less hurtful to hear about than a year of lascivious lunches; and by the same token a hotel bill for two makes less painful reading than a bundle of love letters. It's not the deed, it's the thought that counts, and if the thoughts are loving and poetic rather than merely lustful and prurient, then they are better kept hidden.

Back to the beginning though, and the start of the affair; and that is the time you're most tempted to tell, when it seems so harmless and charming and amusing and it is really so chilling and alarming and serious. For affairs are born of boredom, conceived in conceit, and you do wish it to be known that you are fancied, and fawned upon, and that you excite lust and lechery. But you must not talk, and you must not tell; or at any rate not the truth. This is the time to lie, remorselessly and resourcefully, by fair means and foul, by both word and implication, from Alpha to Omega, from beginning to end. Have alibis ready, not in ones and twos but sixes and sevens. Rehearse your stories, prepare your script; enlist conspirators and be ready with reinforcements.

Keep your lies elaborate; they're harder to check on. 'We all had to go to a meeting, and then we had drinks at the Wine Bar in Soho, you know the one, and then dinner at that frightfully expensive French restaurant we went to once – God it's gone off. Then Bill insisted we went to some club or other, and I found myself sitting at a table with some sales rep. and his dreadful girlfriend, who was very drunk, and they knew a pub in Fleet Street that's open all night and we ended up there,' is better than 'I had to work late.'

Alibis likewise: 'Jane's having the children tomorrow because I want to go to Harrods, I believe they've got some sort of sale on, although if they haven't I shall probably try and get my coat somewhere else, and I'm hoping to meet Margot for lunch, although she's not sure if she can make it, and if she can't I might ring Mummy, or possibly even get my hair done, God knows it needs it. And anyway, I want to look for your birthday present,' is better than 'I'm going to town tomorrow.' Most husbands and the majority of wives will drift into boredom only half-way through; gamble on that fact and it's odds-on you'll win.

Confronted by suspicion, deny, deny thrice and throw in some indignation for good measure. 'You must be mad' is a good phrase; so is 'I don't know how you can even think such a thing.' 'Well, I might one day but not with him/her,' is close to the wind but clever, and 'How dare you?' is excellent because you can turn the whole discussion into a thunderous row which will give you time to think. A hearty peal of laughter is a most disarming thing; and 'I'm very hurt,' and 'I thought you trusted me,' will turn the most outraged thoughts in on themselves. If you can keep your wife when all about you are losing theirs, then it's probably because you are a better liar than the rest.

It is as well to have some lies ready for emergencies; a moment's silence speaks volumes of guilt. But unless you are actually found tucked up in bed together, there are few situations so totally incriminating that they could not be explained away somehow. Confronted by the facts, lie staunchly on. People in cars can be neighbours, workmates, or your best friend's second cousin; people in restaurants can be employers, employees, or your second cousin's best friend. Curious telephone calls can be faults on the line, heavy breathers or the secretary of the badminton club. Letters are difficult, but you could try, 'I knew him at college and I've always kept the letter,' or 'It's terribly embarrassing but some girl in the typing pool's got a crush on me,' and throw in 'Now would I carry it about with me if it was serious?' for good measure.

There is one masterly phrase which the adulterer should keep by him when all else fails. It explains away all but the most advanced sexual behaviour and although it carries a sting in its tail, the poison is not deadly. It is, 'I'm sorry darling, but I was drunk.' Try it and see; it works, but only once.

Even when you are cornered, confronted and confounded, you should still not stoop to the truth. You owe your partner more than that. Say it was the very first time; say you were doing it because he or she had promised you a rise, or a cheap mortgage or a course of free driving lessons. Say that he (or she) was a sex therapist and you were seeking to improve your technique (and thence your marriage). Say you didn't want to; say you couldn't help it; say you can't remember how you got there. Say anything at all, so long as it's a lie. The truth may come to light; but then again it may not, and there's nothing to be gained by your flicking the switch. Adultery and those it hurts should be kept in the dark.

•

The Auschwitz lie

SIMON WIESENTHAL

In January 1988 Austrian television began broadcasting a series entitled *Zur Person* ('Personal Encounter'). I was invited as the first guest and was interviewed by the well-known Austrian journalist Franz Ferdinand Wolf. The interview was broadcast live from the Vienna Josefstadt Theatre.

Within minutes of the beginning of the transmission shouts were suddenly heard. 'Murderer!' someone called out. And 'You're a liar!' Three men leaned over the balustrade of the first tier and threw stacks of leaflets into the audience. The state police had observed them entering the theatre, but 'under the law' had not been allowed to intervene until the three had become 'active'. Their leader was an old acquaintance: Gerd Honsik, head of the Austrian 'Foreigners Halt' movement and editor of the periodical *Halt*.

As I write these lines the latest issue of that periodical is being distributed outside Vienna's schools. Austrian juveniles thus receive information such as, roughly, the following: 'Why was the Anschluss annulled? Stupidity? Spinelessness? Crime? The regime owes us an answer!' *Halt* even offers some poetry by printing the ballad 'War of Flowers', by an unknown poetess whose heart overbrimmed with these stanzas:

War das ein Jauchzen, als der Führer kam,
das Volk seinem Wege wuchs zum Strome,
wie eine Flut, die schier kein Ende nahm.
Und alle harrten, daß er komme, komme.

Und jeder wußte, was sein Kommen hieß:
(hat nie geschmeichelt und hat nichts verborgen)
das nicht zum Dulden – das zum Kämpfen wies,
sein Weg auf seiner Suche nach dem Morgen.

Im Beilfallstosen hören sie ihn nahen,
und sehen ihn im offenen Wagen kommen.
Es wächst der Urschrei brüllend zum Orkan,
und alle sind vor Seligkeit benommen.

So wie ein hunderttausenköpfig Tier
erhebt die Menge sich zu wildem Leben

und angestrampelt wie ein schneller Stier
*stampft die Begeisterung auf Hitlers Wegen.**

The ballad ends with the exclamation: 'Give generously! So we can hold out!'

Halt, of course, as it expressly points out in every issue (print run 30,000 copies), is 'more than a newspaper! *Halt* is struggle against the lie.' The lie it sets out to struggle against is essentially the lie of the gas chambers which, allegedly, never existed in the Third Reich. To support the lie, *Halt* quotes an alleged document dating from 1948, implying that there were no killings by poison gas in Mauthausen or certain other camps. That document is signed by one 'Müller, Major', and one 'Lachoud' testified 'to its correctness'. Both are said to have been members of the military police service with the Allied military command. According to information from the Austrian Ministry of the Interior, no such office ever existed. Nearly all other *Halt* articles dispense similar nonsense.

But should one fight against such journals? Should one sue them? Should one ban them? I believe one should. The youngsters who have these rags thrust into their hands are often very ignorant about the Third Reich. If they are served up such a concoction of lies and alleged evidence some of them, at least, may be impressed. What must impress them even more is that nobody is taking any action against these articles, from which they are bound to conclude that if these statements are not

*The jubilation when the Führer came, / the people along his road grew into a river, / like a flood which truly had no end. / And all were waiting for him to come. // And everyone knew what his coming meant: / (he never flattered and never concealed anything) / something pointing not to suffering but to struggle, / his road of search for a morrow. // Amidst the roar of cheers they hear him approach, / and see him coming in the open car. / The primal shout grows roaring into a hurricane, / and all are stunned by bliss. // Like to a hundred-thousand-headed beast / the crowd rises up to savage life / and stampeding like a swift bull / enthusiasm tramples along Hitler's paths.

stopped then they must probably be true. We should not allow this kind of conclusion.

I believe, moreover, that the state must observe its own laws, and these laws stipulate that neo-Nazi activity is punishable. The journal *Halt* constitutes the continuous offence of neo-Nazi activity. This is obvious to anyone reading it, even though the authors are forever using certain protective formulations designed to present their outpourings as a scholarly historical discussion.

I would, however, urge that the dissemination of such matter be made an offence in itself. My reason is that National Socialist activity in Austria carries a minimum punishment of five years' imprisonment, and because no jury would wish to put anyone behind bars for some idiotic scribbling, this kind of trial invariably ends in acquittal. If, on the other hand, the punishment were a matter of months then the offenders would be sentenced. Unlike many of my friends I do believe that there is a good case for making the allegations that 'Auschwitz is a lie' a punishable offence. It has never yet been made for scholarly reasons but has always served the exclusive aim of making Nazism seem harmless and/or agitating against 'the Jews' who are allegedly spreading that lie.

This is opposed by the view that the denial of the existence of gas chambers actually testifies to a relatively decent attitude: those concerned thereby admit that it would be a crime to gas Jews – and they don't wish to see Hitler accused of such a crime. This may be true of a few lunatics who actually regard the gas chambers as Allied constructions. In fact, however, one is dealing with people who may be insane but who are also cynical: they deny the gas chambers just as Hitler had denied his intention ever to wage war. I believe, moreover, that the survivors of the Holocaust, just like the members of any religious community, are entitled not to have their martyrdom mocked. The claim of the 'Auschwitz lie' is a slap in the face of all those who have gone through the martyrdom of Auschwitz, and indeed a slap in the face of their children. On the soil of Germany, which bears the responsibility for Auschwitz, it seems to me entirely legitimate to protect the survivors and their children against such slaps by penal legislation.

There is a difference between an American leaflet and a paper published in Austria or West Germany spreading the lie of the 'Auschwitz lie', and a difference between a mentally unbalanced American being responsible for it and a practising West German lawyer. For my part, I am certainly determined to make use of the facilities provided by the law against incorrigible people like that, even though this will sometimes assume the character of a grotesque mini-war which I would normally regard as beneath me. The fact is, I not only believe that the brochures of those people are less harmless than they are sometimes depicted, but that the people themselves, ridiculous as they are, could be dangerous. (I can think of no one more ridiculous than Adolf Hitler.)

A good illustration of my thesis is the attorney, Manfred Roeder from Bensheim in Hesse. He came to my attention as the author of the preface to the brochure *The Auschwitz Lie* by Thies Christophersen. Thies Christophersen had spent the war at Rajsko, an ancillary camp of Auschwitz, where Auschwitz inmates were used as forced labour: attempts were made then to grow plants at Rajsko from which rubber might be obtained for German industry. I don't know what induced Christophersen to dispute that there had been gas chambers in Auschwitz or that Jews had been murdered there: the Rajsko inmates were indeed not gassed, because they were needed. It is conceivable that Christophersen became so involved in his theses that subsequently he did not want to retract them. In view of the overwhelming evidence for mass murder at Auschwitz this would suggest mental derangement, but there will always be a few lunatics. The problem only arises from the fact that such balderdash has actually been published and that the preface by an attorney has stamped it as a serious contribution to the discussion.

I therefore wrote to the Chamber of Lawyers in Frankfurt and demanded that disciplinary proceedings be instituted against Roeder. Roeder's reaction was the publication, in his periodical *Bürgerinitiative (Citizens' Initiative)*, of a letter of vilification by a former Austrian Nazi called Munk, who was wanted by the provincial court in Innsbruck for fraud and had therefore fled to Argentina. In that letter, posted in Argentina, Munk asserted that I had not been in a concentration camp for a single day, that in reality I had no engineer's degree, and that during the war I had been an informer of the Security Service in Bucharest.

I sued, and the hearing was held in the court of Roeder's home town of Bensheim in Hesse. The walls of the courthouse were decorated with small swastika flags, and four policemen with dogs escorted me through a cordon of some two hundred 'citizens' whose 'initiative' in Roeder's sense of the word consisted of catcalls: 'There's a stench of garlic here . . . Down with international Jewry . . . Judah perish . . . Hitler hasn't gassed all the Jews . . .,' their scanned comments belying the 'Auschwitz lie'. The courtroom, too, was filled with Roeder's supporters and the judge explained how he saw the proceedings: 'We are not at the Nuremberg Tribunal here, which passed its sentence on the grounds of falsified documents.' Indeed we were not at the Nuremberg Tribunal: the judge, in no way up to the publicity of the case, adjourned the proceedings as soon as they had opened.

The newspapers were indignant at this open demonstration of neo-Nazism and the Minister President of Hesse apologized to me for the incidents. Whereupon Manfred Roeder instantly went on to the offensive again: he called West Germany a 'Zionist republic' and, regarding this as the peak of mockery, framed its sovereign eagle in a Star of David. However, he committed the mistake this time of personally insulting a number of German politicians also, who took out actions against him. These actions were combined into one, and in February 1976 new proceedings took place in Darmstadt. There Roeder was finally sentenced – bound over for seven months of good behaviour.

The good behaviour looked like this: in the spring of 1980 bombings took place in several German towns, for which a 'Deutsche Aktionsgruppe' ('German Action Group') claimed responsibility. In August there followed an act of arson against a refugee hostel, when two Vietnamese lost their lives. In their investigations of this the German police eventually succeeded in arresting six members of the German Action Group – their leader was Manfred Roeder. On 28 June 1982 he was sentenced to thirteen years' imprisonment for 'heading a terrorist association'.

Anyone thinking that only lunatics would have taken Roeder's verbal attacks on me seriously would be mistaken. In Austria not only the paper of former SS men, *Der Kamerad* (*The Comrade*), published the Hermann Munk letter, but even Federal Chancellor Bruno Kreisky referred to it when, as reported in an earlier chapter, he accused me in an interview with a foreign correspondent of having worked for the Gestapo.

When I sued *Kamerad* for the Munk letter, the SS old comrades' association submitted to the court two essential witnesses in support of the truth of Munk's allegation. One was the former SS leader Jan Verbelen, who had been sentenced to death in Belgium *in absentia* and in 1963 had been arrested in Austria at my instigation, though of course acquitted there. The other was Bruno Kreisky. A pity no one took a photograph: the Chancellor of the Republic and the ex-SS man and right-wing extremist on the same page.

Needless to say, neither witness knew anything to support Munk's allegations. Munk himself had already been questioned in Buenos Aires, by way of the legal assistance arrangement, at the time of my suit against Roeder, and had declared that what he had written was not based on personal knowledge but had been told him by a German, who unfortunately was no longer alive. *Kamerad* was convicted of slander because, as the judge stated, the journal had been unable to produce 'even a shadow of proof' of its accusations.

But being unable to produce even a shadow of proof of their allegations has never bothered the neo-Nazis – nor has it ever stopped them from denying the most crushing evidence against them.

•

A catalogue of inconsistencies: the sinking of the Belgrano

ARTHUR GAVSHON AND DESMOND RICE

On 2 April 1982, Argentinian military forces occupied the Falkland Islands. The British government dispatched a task force to recapture the Falklands, declared a 200-mile total exclusion zone round the islands, and warned that any Argentinian naval vessel found within that limit would be sunk. The Argentinian cruiser *General Belgrano* was among several vessels which put to sea around 15 April. On the afternoon of 2 May, while still some twenty miles outside the exclusion zone, she was sunk by the British submarine HMS *Conqueror* with the loss of 368 lives. The torpedoes had been launched with the full authority of the British Cabinet. The question was, why? What was the point of having an exclusion zone if ships outside it were to be attacked? John Nott, the British Defence Secretary, stated that 'this heavily armed surface attack group was close to the total exclusion zone and was closing on elements of our task force which was only hours away.' But the evidence seemed to indicate that the *Belgrano* had been following a course *away* from the task force and the exclusion zone when torpedoed. It was just one of a number of 'inconsistencies' surrounding the official version of the sinking.

OFFICIAL UK POSITION	*CONTRADICTIONS*
	On the use of force
First British attacks on Argentine positions on 1 May 1982 were intended to 'concentrate Argentinian minds' on the need for peace. 'No further military action is envisaged for the moment other than making the Total Exclusion Zone secure.' (Foreign Secretary Francis Pym, Press Conference, Washington, 1 May 1982)	A Northwood signal on 30 April 1982 told Commander Wreford-Brown that the government had decided to use 'more military force' and had ordered the 'destruction' of the Argentine carrier *25 de Mayo*. (30 April 1982 excerpt from diary of crew member of HMS *Conqueror*)
	When the Belgrano *was detected*
'The next day, 2 May, at 8 a.m. time, one of our submarines detected the Argentine cruiser *General Belgrano* escorted by two destroyers.' (John Nott, former UK Defence Minister, House of Commons, 4 May 1982. *Hansard*, cols. 29–30)	'We located her on our London passive sonar, and sighted her visually on the afternoon of May 1. We took up a position astern and followed the *General Belgrano* for over 30 hours. We reported that we were in contact with her.' (Wreford-Brown, *Our Falklands War*, Geoffrey Underwood, 1983, p. 16)
'I was informed of the *Conqueror*'s signal, that she was in contact with the *Belgrano*, at around 9 or 10 on the morning of Sunday, May 2nd.'	'HMS *Conqueror* . . . detected an Argentine oiler auxiliary which was accompanying the *Belgrano* on 30 April. She sighted the *Belgrano* for the first time on 1 May . . .' (Mrs Thatcher's letter to Denzil Davies, MP, 4 April 1984)

The Belgrano *as 'threat'*

'This heavily armed surface attack group was close to the Total Exclusion Zone and was closing on elements of our Task Force, which was only hours away.' (John Nott, ibid.)

'Continuing passage to an area where the threats are from the cruiser *Belgrano* – an ancient ex-US 2nd World War ship with no sonar or ASW capability, two Allen Summer Class destroyers – equally decrepit – and an oiler . . .' (30 April 1982 entry, *Conqueror* diarist)

'According to my recollection, that signal reported the *Belgrano* heading towards the Task Force.' (Lord Lewin, ibid.)

'When torpedoed, we were pointing straight at the Argentinian coast on a bearing we had been following for hours.' (Captain Bonzo, *Belgrano* commander, 4 April 1983)

'We were told that the *Belgrano* posed a threat, that it had the capacity within a time of about 6 hours of steaming towards our fleet, getting within range of it . . .' (Cecil Parkinson, MP, former War Cabinet member, 'Panorama', 16 April 1984)

'Absolute nonsense. The nearest British surface ship must have been 250 miles off. I'd have needed 14 hours to catch it at my top cruising speed of 18 knots, provided it stopped dead in its tracks.' (Captain Bonzo, 3 June 1983)

'They spent the night meticulously paralleling the Exclusion Zone about 18 miles to the south of it.' (*Conqueror* diarist, morning 2 May 1982)

'Six hours is a danger . . . We all changed the Rule of Engagement to enable a ship which was a danger to our Task Force to be sunk.' (Mrs Thatcher, 'Newsnight', 2 June 1983)

'She was not an absolutely immediate threat to our surface ships.' (Lord Lewin, 'Panorama', 16 April 1984)

Who pressed the button?

'The actual decision to launch a torpedo was clearly one taken by the submarine commander.' (John Nott, House of Commons, 5 May 1982. *Hansard*, Vol. 23, col. 156)

'I went straight to Chequers and called the War Cabinet into a side-room and told them the situation. I said we could not wait. Here was an opportunity to knock off a major unit of the Argentine fleet. The Cabinet said go ahead. [Mrs Thatcher] was superb ...' (Lord Lewin, *Sunday Mirror*, 11 September 1984)

•

Close encounters with the truth

HENRY PORTER

The popular press has always had a rather cavalier attitude towards the truth. Quite often it would seem that fiction and news are taken to be synonymous. The most egregious offenders in this respect have been the *Sun*, the *News of the World*, *Sunday Sport* and, in the United States, the *National Enquirer*. The following is an account of how the *News of the World* (or 'the Screws' as it is more affectionately known, for reasons relating to the most common subject-matter), under the editorship of Derek Jameson, decided that if fiction sold newspapers, science fiction would sell even more.

In June 1983, while the rest of us were absorbed by the General Election, the paper turned to extra-terrestrial matters. Under the headline CLOSE ENCOUNTER AT THE SHAMROCK CAFÉ, Keith Beabey and Pippa Sibley revealed that three women had been kidnapped by a UFO after they had spent a pleasant evening together near Wolverhampton. It started like this:

> Strange red and white lights hovered overhead as three women drove home from their weekly night out.
>
> Mysteriously their car came to a halt outside the Shamrock Café on the A5 in Shropshire, though the driver had her foot hard down on the accelerator.
>
> Then the lights suddenly vanished and the trio rushed excitedly to a nearby police station, where they reported a close encounter with a UFO.
>
> But that was when they noticed something even stranger happening. The drive to the police station should have taken five minutes. Instead it took twenty-five.
>
> Only now, with the help of hypnosis, under the strictest supervision, has an explanation been found for those twenty missing minutes. And it is amazing.
>
> Each of the women has independently told the same story that they did have a close encounter, far closer than they first imagined. For each says that she was taken aboard a spacecraft, examined by alien beings and then released.

The paper then reproduced the accounts of each of the three women, Rosemary Hawkins, Valerie Walters, and Viv Hayward. Here is Rosemary's:

> Bright lights. White tinged with yellow and red. So strange its three [sic]. No sound.
>
> We are frightened the lights are attached to a spacecraft of some kind.
>
> I am floating and I'm not in the car any more with Viv or Val, I feel big and bloated.
>
> It's a semi-circular room. I'm on a bed in the room like a long table on a stand.
>
> There's something coming. I can hear them. Something

> is in the room. It's metal. It doesn't walk, it sort of rolls on wheels.
>
> It's about four feet tall, round on the top with a round body and round legs.
>
> It's looking at me. There's more coming. It's the same noise. There are four. They are around me.
>
> They haven't got a face. Their heads move up and down. That's how I know they are talking to me.
>
> They don't seem to be nasty. They just want to have a look. I feel so relaxed and friendly. I like them.

By contrast Viv found the aliens rather frightening. They put their hands inside her legs and pulled her bones about a bit and then released her. She described them thus: 'They are four feet tall. They have no hair. They are ugly. They have strange-looking noses; thin arms, I can't see their legs. They are dressed in green cloaks.'

This entertaining scoop was accompanied by an equally entertaining drawing of one of the women being examined by those curious little beings from another world, who anyone who used to read *Eagle* would recognize. As far as I remember your average Martian is always made of metal, favours the colour green, never has a face, is unfailingly inquisitive and is always lacking in stature. Tempting though it was to entertain the idea that a flying saucer had landed near the Shamrock Café on the A5, everyone chose to ignore the *News of the World*'s revelations.

Undaunted, in October the paper announced: UFO LANDS IN SUFFOLK – AND THAT'S OFFICIAL. Mr Keith Beabey it was, again, who wrote:

> A UFO has landed in Britain – and that staggering fact has been officially confirmed.
>
> Despite a massive cover-up *News of the World* investigators have proof that the mysterious craft came to earth in a red ball of light at 3 a.m. on December 27, 1980.

> It happened in a pine forest called Tangham Wood just half a mile away from the United States Air Force base at RAF Woodbridge in Suffolk.
>
> An American airman who was there told us there were beings in silver space suits aboard the craft.
>
> Farm cattle and forest animals ran berserk as the spacecraft, a sloping silver dish about 20 ft across its base, silently glided to land in a blinding explosion of lights.
>
> About 200 military and civilian personnel, British and American, witnessed the event. The airman said the visitors appeared to be expected.

Can the *News of the World* believe that none of its readers have seen *Close Encounters of the Third Kind*? Obviously. The two main witnesses to the event are a man named 'Art Wallace', a junior airman whose identity is protected by the *News of the World* for 'security reasons' and Lt.-Colonel Charles Halt, deputy commander of the USAF 81st Tactical Fighter Wing stationed at Woodbridge. The latter filed a report to his superiors which went as follows:

> Early in the morning two USAF security police patrolmen saw unusual lights outside the back gate of Woodbridge.
>
> Thinking an aircraft might have crashed or been forced down they called for permission to go outside the gate to investigate.
>
> The on-duty flight chief allowed three patrolmen to proceed on foot.
>
> The individuals reported seeing a strange glowing object in the forest.
>
> The object was described as being metallic in appearance and triangular in shape, approximately two to three metres across the base and approximately two metres high. It illuminated the entire forest with a white light.
>
> The object itself had a pulsating red light on top and a

> bank of blue lights underneath. The object was hovering on legs. As the patrolmen approached the object it manoeuvred through the trees and disappeared.
>
> At the time the animals on a nearby farm went into a frenzy. The object was sighted approximately an hour later near the back gate.
>
> The next day three depressions one and a half inches deep and seven inches in diameter were found where the object had been sighted on the ground.
>
> Later during the night a red sunlike light was seen through the trees. It moved about and pulsated. At one point it appeared to throw off glowing particles and then broke into five separate white objects and disappeared.
>
> Immediately thereafter the red starlike objects were noted in the sky, two objects in the North and one in the South, all of which were about 10 degrees above the horizon. The objects moved rapidly and displayed green-blue lights. The objects in the North appeared elliptical through an 8–12 power lens.
>
> They turned full circle. The objects in the North remained in the sky for an hour or more. The objects in the South were visible for two or three hours and beamed down a storm of lights from time to time.

Inside, the paper carried a startling interview with 'Art Wallace' who said that he had seen a craft with a green light on top and that he understood from his fellow patrolmen that there were little men inside wearing silver suits.

This time the *News of the World* was not entirely ignored. Adrian Berry, the level-headed Science Editor of the *Daily Telegraph*, wrote that he too had found a UFO and produced a picture of it hovering over St Paul's Cathedral in London. He wrote: 'Our photographer Paul Armiger was standing beside St Paul's when this huge spacecraft came roaring over his head. He knew its occupant must have flown all the way from Alpha Centauri to kidnap the Dean . . .'

He went on to suggest that the *News of the World*'s 'evidence' was, if anything, less convincing. He continued:

> All that had happened was that a United States Air Force Colonel at RAF Woodbridge had seen an unexplained light in the surrounding woods. This could only have been the rotating beam of Orford Ness lighthouse. The only problem when one looks into these stories is that usually the town cannot be found on any map and never existed, and the scientists did not utter a word of what they are quoted as saying, their remarks having been invented by unscrupulous reporters . . . Would alien visitors really seek information about humanity from the dullest and least reliable of mankind? Would they really rush about in disc-shaped vehicles with abysmal aerodynamic qualities?

Derek Jameson wrote to the *Daily Telegraph* to defend his paper's exclusive story, drawing Berry's attention to the depression mentioned in the Colonel's report. Berry had an answer for this too, which he was kind enough to share with us through the Letters column of his own paper: 'Mr Thurkettle, a Forestry Commission official, who examined the site, has attributed the depressions to rabbits. The local police say that they were probably made by an animal.'

Berry had used the word 'impudence' to describe the *News of the World*'s report; it is hard to disagree. Here was a newspaper claiming that there had been official verification when there had been none, and that 200 people had been expecting the landing when only one could be found to talk about it – and even he wanted to remain anonymous.

The following Sunday the paper returned to the subject by revealing that there had been a SINISTER PLOT TO HUSH UP THE TRUTH. A section was devoted to our friend 'Art Wallace', who, it turns out, had tried to re-enlist with the air force but had been rejected because there was no record of his first term of service. He is quoted as saying that he may have been drugged and brainwashed.

With the country crawling with little silver men and the skies crowded with unidentified craft the *News of the World*'s sister paper, the *Sun*, eventually decided to ask the question that must have been at the back of many minds: IS YOUR NEIGHBOUR FROM OUTER SPACE? With the help of a UFO investigator named Brad Steiger and a theoretical biologist, Dr Thomas Easton, they gave eight telltale tip-offs that can give an alien away . . .

But perhaps one is being unjust in ridiculing this particular range of fiction from the Bouverie Street dream factory. The UFO articles were all commissioned in the belief that they would amuse the readership, which to an extent they must have. The only mistake seems to be for journalists like Derek Jameson to state in public that they believe their own stories.

•

Lies, damned lies, and statistics

DARRELL HUFF

'Figures often beguile me,' said Mark Twain, 'particularly when I have the arranging of them myself; in which case the remark attributed to Disraeli would often apply with justice and force: "There are three kinds of lies: lies, damned lies, and statistics."' Actually, it's unlikely that Disraeli did say this. Certainly there is nothing in *Hansard*, or any of the biographies, so if anyone knows the source of Disraeli's remark perhaps they would be kind enough to let me know. Incidentally, the phrase has also been attributed to Henry Labouchere, Abraham Hewitt and Commander Holloway R. Frost. Darrell Huff explains how to lie with 'the well-chosen average'.

You, I trust, are not a snob, and I certainly am not an estate agent. But let's say that you are and that I am and that you are looking for property to buy along a road I know well. Having sized you up, I take pains to tell you that the average income in this neighbourhood is some £10,000 a year. Maybe that clinches your interest in living here; anyway, you buy and that handsome figure sticks in your mind. More than likely, since we have agreed that for the purposes of the moment you are a bit of a snob, you toss it in casually when telling your friends about where you live.

A year or so later we meet again. As a member of some ratepayers' committee I am circulating a petition to keep the rates down or assessments down or bus fares down. My plea is that we cannot afford the increase: after all, the average income in this neighbourhood is only £2,000 a year. Perhaps you go along with me and my committee in this – you're not only a snob, you're stingy too – but you can't help being surprised to hear about that measly £2,000. Am I lying now, or was I lying last year?

You can't pin it on me either time. That is the essential beauty of doing your lying with statistics. Both those figures are legitimate averages, legally arrived at. Both represent the same data, the same people, the same incomes. All the same it is obvious that at least one of them must be so misleading as to rival an out-and-out lie.

My trick was to use a different kind of average each time, the word 'average' having a very loose meaning. It is a trick commonly used, sometimes in innocence but often in guilt, by fellows wishing to influence public opinion or sell advertising space. When you are told that something is an average you still don't know very much about it unless you can find out which of the common kinds of average it is – mean, median, or mode.

The £10,000 figure I used when I wanted a big one is a mean, the arithmetic average of the incomes of all the families in the neighbourhood. You get it by adding up all the incomes and dividing by the number there are. The smaller figure is a median, and so it tells you that half the families in question have more than £2,000 a year and half have less. I might also have used the mode, which is the most frequently met-with figure in a series. If in this neighbourhood there are more families with incomes of £3,000 a year than with any other amount, £3,000 a year is the modal income.

In this case, as is usually true with income figures, an unqualified 'average' is virtually meaningless. One factor that adds to the confusion is that with some kinds of information all the averages fall so close together that, for casual purposes, it may not be vital to distinguish among them.

If you read that the average height of the men of some primitive tribe is only five feet, you get a fairly good idea of the stature of these people. You don't have to ask whether that average is a mean, median, or mode; it would come out about the same . . .

The different averages come out close together when you deal with data, such as those having to do with many human characteristics, that have the grace to fall close to what is called the normal distribution. If you draw a curve to represent it you get something shaped like a bell, and mean, median, and mode fall at the same point.

Consequently one kind of average is as good as another for describing the heights of men, but for describing their pocketbooks it is not. If you should list the annual incomes of all the families in a given city you might find that they ranged from not much to perhaps £20,000 or so, and you might find a few very large ones. More than ninety-five per cent of the incomes would be under £5,000, putting them way over towards the left-hand side of the curve. Instead of being symmetrical, like a bell, it would be skewed. Its shape would be a little like that of a child's slide, the ladder rising sharply to a peak, the working part gradually sloping down. The mean would be quite a distance from the median. You can see what this would do to the validity of any comparison made between the 'average' (mean) of one year and the 'average' (median) of another.

In the neighbourhood where I sold you some property the

two averages are particularly far apart because the distribution is markedly skewed. It happens that most of your neighbours are small farmers or wage-earners employed in a near-by village or elderly retired people on pensions. But three of the inhabitants are millionaire week-enders and these three boost the total income, and therefore the arithmetical average, enormously. They boost it to a figure that practically everybody in the neighbourhood has a good deal less than. You have in reality the case that sounds like a joke or a figure of speech: nearly everybody is below average.

That's why when you read an announcement by a corporation executive or a business proprietor that the average pay of the people who work in his establishment is so much, the figure may mean something and it may not. If the average is a median, you can learn something significant from it: Half the employees make more than that; half make less. But if it is a mean (and believe me it may be that if its nature is unspecified) you may be getting nothing more revealing than the average of one £25,000 income – the proprietor's – and the salaries of a crew of underpaid workers. 'Average annual pay of £3,800' may conceal both the £1,400 salaries and the owner's profits taken in the form of a whopping salary.

How neatly this can be worked into a whipsaw device, in which the worse the story, the better it looks, is illustrated in some company statements. Let's try our hand at one in a small way.

You are one of three partners who own a small manufacturing business. It is now the end of a very good year. You have paid out £99,000 to the ninety employees who do the work of making and shipping the chairs or whatever it is that you manufacture. You and your partners have paid yourselves £5,500 each in salaries. You find there are profits for the year of £21,000 to be divided equally among you. How are you going to describe this? To make it easy to understand, you put it in the form of averages. Since all the employees are doing about the same kind of work for similar pay it won't make much difference whether you use a mean or a median. This is what you come out with

Average wage of employees	£1,100
Average salary and profit of owners	£12,500

This looks terrible, doesn't it? Let's try it another way. Take £15,000 of the profits and distribute it among the three partners as bonuses. And this time when you average up the wages, include yourself and your partners. And be sure to use a mean.

Average wage or salary	£1,403
Average profit of owners	£2,000

Ah. That looks better. Not as good as you could make it look, but good enough. Less than six per cent of the money available for wages and profits has gone into profits, and you can go further and show that too if you like. Anyway, you've got figures now that you can publish, post on a bulletin board, or use in bargaining.

This is pretty crude because the example is simplified, but it is nothing to what has been done in the name of accounting. Given a complex corporation with hierarchies of employees ranging all the way from beginning typist to president with a several hundred thousand dollar bonus, all sorts of things can be covered up in this manner.

So when you see an average-pay figure, first ask: Average of what? Who's included? The United States Steel Corporation once said that its employees' average weekly earnings went up 107 per cent in less than a decade. So they did – but some of the punch goes out of the magnificent increase when you note the earlier figure includes a much larger number of partially employed people. If you work half-time one year and full-time the next, your earnings will double, but that doesn't indicate anything at all about your wage rate.

You may have read in the paper that the income of the average American family was $6,490 in some specified year. You should not try to make too much out of that figure unless you also know what 'family' has been used to mean, as well as what kind of average this is. (And who says so and how he knows and how accurate the figure is.)

The figure you saw may have come from the Bureau of the Census. If you have the Bureau's full report you'll have no trouble finding right there the rest of the information you need: that this average is a median; that 'family' signifies 'two or more persons related to each other and living together'. You will also learn, if you turn back to the tables, that the figure is based on a sample of such size that there are nineteen chances out of twenty that the estimate is correct within a margin of, say, $71 plus or minus.

That probability and that margin add up to a pretty good estimate. The Census people have both skill enough and money enough to bring their sampling studies down to a fair degree of precision. Presumably they have no particular axes to grind. Not all the figures you see are born under such happy circumstances, nor are all of them accompanied by any information at all to show how precise or imprecise they may be . . .

Meanwhile you may want to try your scepticism on some items from 'A Letter from the Publisher' in *Time* magazine. Of new subscribers it said, 'Their median age is 34 years and their average family income is $7,270 a year.' An earlier survey of 'old *TIME*rs' had found that their 'median age was 41 years . . . Average income was $9,535 . . .' The natural question is why, when median is given for ages both times, the kind of average for incomes is carefully unspecified. Could it be that the mean was used instead because it is bigger, thus seeming to dangle a richer readership before advertisers?

•

Who uses the polygraph test?

PAUL EKMANN

As behaviourist Paul Ekmann explains, while it is correct that the polygraph is sometimes called the lie-detector, the term is misleading. 'The polygraph doesn't detect lies *per se* . . . All that the polygraph measures is autonomic nervous system signs of arousal – physiological changes generated primarily because a person is emotionally aroused.' Lying can be inferred from this behaviour. But, says Ekmann, feelings of nervous arousal might equally be felt by some innocent persons, and thus the system is vulnerable to error. The lie-catcher must always estimate the likelihood that a polygraph sign of emotional arousal indicates lying or truthfulness. But on the whole, while judgements based on behavioural clues alone were not much better than chance, judgements based on the polygraph, without contact with the suspects, were much better than chance. It's hardly surprising that the intelligence agencies should have frequent resort to the polygraph. But in America it's not just the CIA that uses the polygraph.

Use of the polygraph to detect some form of lying is widespread and growing. It is hard to be certain just how many polygraph tests are given in the United States; the best guess is over one million a year. The majority – about 300,000 a year – are given by private employers. These tests are given as part of pre-employment screening, to control internal crime, and as part of procedures used in recommending promotions. Pre-employment screening is 'heavily relied upon by members of the National Association of Drug Stores and the National Association of Convenience Stores, by Brinks Inc.' and Associated Grocers. Although it is illegal in eighteen states to ask employees to take the polygraph test, employers reportedly can find ways around those laws. 'Employers may tell the employee that they suspect them of theft, but that if the employee can find a way to demonstrate innocence, the employer will not discharge the employee.' In thirty-one states, employees can be asked to take a polygraph test. The private employers who make most use of the polygraph are banks and retail operations. About half of the 4,700 McDonald's fast food outlets, for example, give a polygraph test for pre-employment screening.

After business, the next most frequent use of the polygraph test is as part of criminal investigations. It is not only used on criminal suspects but sometimes also with witnesses or victims whose reports are doubted. The Justice Department, FBI, and most police departments follow the policy of using the polygraph only after investigations have narrowed down the list of suspects. Most states do not allow the results of the polygraph to be reported in a trial. Twenty-two states do allow the polygraph test as evidence if it has been stipulated in advance of the test and agreed to by both prosecution and defense. Defense attorneys usually make such an agreement in return for the prosecutor's agreement to drop the case if the polygraph shows the suspect was truthful. Usually . . . prosecutors don't make such an offer if they have strong evidence that they think would convince a jury of a suspect's guilt.

In New Mexico and Massachusetts, polygraph test results can be introduced over the objection of one of the parties. The results cannot be admitted unless stipulated in advance in most, but not all, Federal Judicial Circuit Courts of Appeal. No United States Circuit Court of Appeal has reversed a district court for denying the admission of polygraph evidence. According to Richard K. Willard, Deputy Assistant United States Attorney General, 'There has never been a Supreme Court ruling on the admissibility of polygraph evidence in federal court.'

The federal government is the third largest user of the polygraph test to detect lying. In 1982 22,597 tests were reported by various federal agencies.*

*The polygraph is currently used by: US Army Criminal Investigation Command; US Army Intelligence and Security Command; Naval Investigative Service; Air Force Office of Special Investigations; US Marine Corps Criminal Investigation Division; National Security Agency; Secret Service; FBI; Postal Inspection Service; Alcohol, Tobacco and Firearms Administration; Drug Enforcement Administration; CIA; US Marshalls; Customs Service; and the Department of Labor.

Economical with the truth: the Spycatcher *trial*

MALCOLM TURNBULL

In 1985, convinced that MI5 had been infiltrated by Russian agents, former agent Peter Wright signed a contract with William Heinemann to publish his dossier of facts. News of Wright's book, *Spycatcher*, leaked out, and the British Government sought to block its publication through the Australian courts. The result was one of the most celebrated trials in legal history – a trial that turned the case in favour of Wright and made his book an international bestseller. Perhaps the key event during the trial was the brilliant cross-examination by Wright's counsel, Malcolm Turnbull, of the British Cabinet Secretary, Sir Robert Armstrong. Much of the defence case rested on the fact that other books had been published which might be said to be no less revealing of the way that MI5 worked than *Spycatcher*: for example, *A Matter of Trust: MI5 1945–72* by Nigel West, a pseudonym for Tory MP Rupert Allason; and Chapman Pincher's *Their Trade is Treachery* and *Too Secret Too Long*. Before the trial, Turnbull had served interrogatories (questions relevant to disputed factual issues raised in the proceedings, the answers to which must be sworn as true) on the British Government regarding the Government's prior knowledge of the publication of these books. As Turnbull explains: 'The Government's case was that Wright owed an absolute duty of silence. It didn't matter whether he wanted to publish material which was out of date, common knowledge, evidence of crimes. He had to stay mum, no matter what. Our interrogatories of course were largely aimed at making out our defences that the book contained evidence of crimes and that in any event its contents had been previously published by other authors, in circumstances where the Government could have stopped those other authors but had failed to do so.' Turnbull began his cross-examination by handing Armstrong a copy of West's book, and referring to one of his defence interrogatories – No. 33: did he stand by the original answer that there was nothing in West's book which the author had obtained in breach of a duty of confidentiality owed to the Crown? Armstrong answered that it was true as a description of what the Attorney-General believed at the time. The cross-examination continued in this vein, with Armstrong starting to shift his ground, suggesting 'that the answer to the interrogatory spoke of an expectation that confidential information in *A Matter of Trust* would be removed, leaving open the possibility that not all of it had been'. Turnbull was on strong ground. He had a copy of West's original manuscript, and could see that it had been barely affected by the agreed edits. And before long Armstrong had retreated considerably from the original answer to interrogatory 33. 'It was not the case that "those matters obtained in breach of confidence" were removed from the text of *A Matter of Trust*, but rather only those matters which the Government and West's lawyers had agreed should be removed. I drove in hard on Armstrong, insisting that his sworn answer to Interrogatory 33 had been designed to mislead':

18 November 1986

A. I am sorry if I have misled His Honour and the court in this respect. But that was the intention of the interrogatory, it was that the answer should refer to those matters which had been the subject of negotiation and they were all matters which had been obtained by the defendant* in breach of a duty of confidentiality.
Q. You admit that answer was misleading, don't you?
A. I say that it did not say 'all'.
Q. It was misleading by omission, was it not?
A. It was not intended to be so.
Q. It was calculated to mislead.
A. It was not calculated to mislead.
Q. It was not intended by you to mislead, is that what you say?
A. That is what I have just said. If it misled, I regret that.
Q. Sir Robert, your whole life has been involved in writing

*Nigel West.

submissions, writing documents, writing memoranda, expressing yourself fully and clearly has it not?

A. That is certainly part of my training and my duty.

Q. And yet you are confronted with an answer which a court has ordered you to answer on oath and you answer it inadequately; why is that?

A. I have not agreed that it was inadequate. I regret it very much if the answer is interpreted in that way.

Q. It is not a matter of interpretation. How can it be a matter of interpretation? It is plain on its face. The answer states that the plaintiff believed that the matters in the book which were obtained in breach of confidence would be removed. It does not say 'some of the matters'; it does not say 'that matters we thought were too politically sensitive to let out of the bag'. It says 'the matters in the manuscript'.

A. It says 'those matters contained in the manuscript which the plaintiff* believed had been obtained by the defendant in breach of confidentiality owed to the Crown'. I cannot argue that that is an extensive covering of all the matters in the manuscript which were so obtained. I can only relate it to the matters which were removed as a result of agreement between the Crown and the publishers and the authors.

Q. Sir Robert, how high in your scale of values is telling the truth?

A. It reckons very high.

Q. Is it the highest?

A. There are a number of things which I would not wish to grade in order of priority.

Q. Would you tell an untruth to protect what you perceived as national security?

A. I would not wish to do so.

Q. You may not wish to do so. But can you tell us whether you would under no circumstances tell an untruth to protect national security as you saw it?

*The British Government.

A. I do not think I can answer a question like that. I have not been faced with such a situation.
Q. You have never, happily, been put in a position where you had to tell an untruth to protect national security?
A. We can all imagine situations in which somebody might be put in that situation. For instance, the situation which you are put into if you are about to devalue your currency.
Q. Yes, I understand that.
A. And you may be forced, as indeed people have been forced, to say something which is untrue. I have fortunately not been put into such a situation.
Q. A little while ago you said that you had not been. Now you are saying you cannot remember?
A. I do not distinguish between those.

Armstrong's answer was unfortunate, because I followed it up by showing him a letter he had written to Mr William Armstrong, the chairman of Sidgwick and Jackson, publishers of *Their Trade is Treachery*. He had written to his namesake on 23 March 1981 in these terms:

CONFIDENTIAL 23 March 1981

I have seen the extracts in the *Daily Mail* today from Mr Chapman Pincher's forthcoming book *Their Trade is Treachery*. The Prime Minister is in my judgement likely to come under pressure to make some statement on the matters with which Mr Pincher is dealing. I believe you will agree with me that, if she is to make a statement, it is in the public interest that she should be in a position to do so with the least possible delay. Clearly she cannot do so until she has seen, not just the extracts published in the *Daily Mail* but the book itself. I should like to be able to put her in a position where she could make a statement this Thursday [26 March] if she should wish to do so.

I should therefore be very grateful if you would be

willing to make one or (preferably) two copies of the book available to me as soon as possible today or tomorrow.

I can understand your need and wish to protect the confidentiality of the book until publication date, which is (I understand) 26th March. I can assure you that, if you are able to comply with my request, confidentiality will be strictly observed, that the copies will not go outside this office and the Prime Minister's office, and that until the book has been published there will be no disclosure to the Press or the broadcasting authorities of any part of the contents of the book.

I can also assure you that the only purpose of this request is to equip the Prime Minister to make a statement, if she should need or be minded to do so, with the least possible delay. The request is not made with a view to seeking to prevent or delay publication. And I can assure you that we shall not do so.

(signed)
Robert Armstrong

Q. That letter was calculated to mislead, was it not?

A. It was calculated to ask for a copy of the book on which we could take direct action.

Q. It was calculated to mislead Mr Armstrong to believe that the Government did not have a copy of the book. Correct?

A. It was calculated not to disclose to Mr Armstrong that the Government had a copy of the book in order to protect the confidentiality of the source from which it came.

Q. In fact a copy of the book had been stolen from the printers.

A. No.

Q. Where had it come from?

A. I don't know where it had come from, but it had not been obtained by those means.

Q. I am very assured by that, Sir Robert. Would you agree that

Mr William Armstrong on reading this letter would inescapably come to the conclusion that the Government did not have a copy of the book?

A. Mr William Armstrong had been taking strenuous steps to keep the book under very close cover and I was concerned to write a letter which did not disclose that we had a copy of the book.

Q. You intended that letter to cause Mr Armstrong – or is it Sir William Armstrong?

A. Mr Armstrong.

Q. To cause Mr Armstrong to continue in his belief that his security measures had been effective?

A. To continue in his belief that the Government did not have a copy of the book.

Q. And the Government did have a copy of the book?

A. The Government did have a copy of the book.

Q. It had the book at least a month before the letter was written?

A. I cannot answer for the exact period.

Q. You said in answer to interrogatories that the Government obtained a copy of the book in or about February?

A. That's right.

Q. So it would be . . .

A. . . . about a month.

Q. You said to His Honour a little while ago that you could not remember an occasion when you had been placed in the unhappy circumstance of having to misrepresent the facts or to lie in order to protect the sources of MI5 or national security?

A. I think I said that I had not been in a position where I had to tell an untruth. I think that was the nature of the question I answered.

Q. This letter is an untruth, is it not?

A. It is what I have said. It was designed to protect the confidentiality of the source and to avoid the disclosure that a copy of the book had been obtained.

Q. Sir Robert . . .
A. If that is misrepresenting, yes, it was.
Q. Do you understand the difference between a truth and an untruth?
A. I hope so.
Q. And a statement is true if it is an accurate representation of the facts, is it not?
A. I think that is certainly one definition of truth.
Q. And a statement is untrue if it misstates the facts, is it not?
A. If it misstates the facts. This does not misstate the facts. You say it misrepresents the facts.
Q. What is the distinction between misrepresenting and misstating the facts?
A. In this letter, as I have explained, it was designed, it was written so as not to disclose the fact that a copy of the book had been obtained.
Q. It misrepresented the facts.
A. If that was misrepresenting the facts, it was misrepresenting the facts.
Q. It did misrepresent the facts, did it not?
A. If it did so, if you say it did, if you say that is what this letter was doing, very well.
Q. Sir Robert, it is not what I say. I am asking what you say. Do you admit that the letter misrepresented the facts as they were?
A. It was designed, as I have said, not to disclose to Mr Armstrong that a copy of the book had been obtained beforehand, and that was in order to protect the confidentiality of the source from which it had been obtained.
Q. I will ask you that question again . . .
His Honour. Mr Turnbull, I am not sure if we are making any progress. We may have fallen into an exercise in semantics. As I understand it, Sir Robert says, according to my note, that he would not wish to tell an untruth to protect the national security. He has never been put in a position in which he has

been required to do so. However it is my impression – and I ask Sir Robert to assent or deny the accuracy of it – that he would not say that he would not be willing to mislead people if that were necessary in the national interest. Is that a correct assessment, Sir Robert?

A. I would not wish to do so. But in this case, as I said, I said what I did say not so much to protect the national security as to protect the confidentiality of the source from which the book came.

His Honour. It certainly would be with the intention to mislead?

A. Certainly with the intention that Mr Armstrong should not be aware that the Government had already seen a copy of the book.

Mr Turnbull. You said earlier that you had not been put in a position where you had to tell an untruth in order to protect the national security or a source of the security services. I put it to you that in this letter you did just that?

A. I have already said that the letter was not written to protect national security but to protect the source, the confidentiality of the source from which the book was obtained.

Q. I put it to you that this letter contains an untruth. That is the question.

A. It does not say that we have already got a copy of the book, that is quite true.

Q. So it contains an untruth?

A. Well, it does not contain that truth.

Q. See, you could have written to Mr Armstrong and said: Dear Mr Armstrong, I read in the *Mail* that Pincher is publishing another one of his books, could you shoot me over an advance copy, and don't worry, we won't do anything to stop it. You could have done that, could you not?

A. Isn't that what the letter does?

Q. No. Please answer the question.

A. I thought that is what the letter did.

Q. No it does not. It does more than that. If you had written to the publisher and said: Dear Mr Armstrong, I read in the *Daily Mail* that Pincher is writing a book. Don't worry, we are not going to do anything to stop it, can you shoot me over a couple of copies, I am sure Mr Armstrong would have been delighted, he could have taken his solicitors off standby and he probably would have brought the books around personally with a bunch of flowers.

A. He did not bring a bunch of flowers, but . . .

Q. Anyway, he was happy to bring the book around?

A. The book came around. I don't know whether he brought it himself.

Q. You went further than that. You went further than you needed to get a copy of the book. You conveyed to Armstrong, to William Armstrong, the clear impression that you did not already have a copy of the book, did you not?

A. Yes, I did, because I was wishing to protect the confidentiality of the source from which we had obtained it.

Q. And that impression was not a true impression, was it?

A. Well, we clearly had a copy of the book.

Q. So it contains a lie.

A. It was a misleading impression. It does not contain a lie, I don't think.

Q. What is the difference between a misleading impression and a lie?

A. A lie is a straight untruth.

Q. What is a misleading impression – a sort of bent untruth?

A. As one person said, it is perhaps being economical with the truth.

Armstrong's answer, intended as a little joke, brought a gasp of disbelief from the courtroom. How could he be so candid about his own cynicism? It was as though he had summed up the whole Whitehall tradition. He was rattled now. The press gallery were laughing at him and some were sneering too. The confidence had gone and it was now a rather frightened Robert Armstrong who faced the cross-examiner. His minders, only ten feet away in the well of the court, could have been in Antarctica for all the help they could give him. He was all alone now, and he knew it. And as we went on, his answers became even more disturbing.

•

Where power lies: the Westland affair

MAGNUS LINKLATER AND DAVID LEIGH

Perhaps the most bitter and sordid Cabinet row since the Second World War centred on the future of the Westland helicopter company. The Defence Secretary, Michael Heseltine, favoured selling Westland to a European consortium, whereas the Trade and Industry Secretary, Leon Brittan, favoured greater American participation. Following a 'leak' to the newspapers of a confidential letter to Heseltine from Sir Patrick Mayhew, a Government law officer, criticizing Heseltine's actions as Defence Secretary, Heseltine decided to make a statement in reply. However, he felt obliged to resign 'on a point of honour' when the Prime Minister, Margaret Thatcher, insisted that his public statements in the affair be cleared through her office. The controversy settled on the source of the leak. Copies of Mayhew's letter had been sent to two press secretaries – Bernard Ingham at the Prime Minister's office, and Colette Bowe at the DTI. It seems probable that while Brittan was keen that the letter, which did considerable damage to the European lobby, should be leaked, he did not really have the authority to make such a decision and decided to leave the matter to the Downing Street press secretary, Bernard Ingham. Ingham spoke to Bowe on the phone and gave her to understand that she should give the contents of Mayhew's letter to the press. Ingham was technically her boss, and so, despite considerable misgivings, she obeyed. Mayhew was appalled to see the contents of his letter in the evening papers, and suspicion settled on Leon Brittan. A confidential inquiry ensued, but this did little to satisfy the House of Commons, and pressure on Brittan grew stronger. Brittan continued to acquit himself well enough, but that was before Sir Robert Armstrong's confidential inquiry recommended that, with regard to the leak, the Prime Minister interview the Minister most directly concerned – Leon Brittan. On the afternoon of the day Brittan was 'interviewed', Tam Dalyell, a thorn in the increasingly tender flesh of the Government, named Colette Bowe as the source of the leak. For her part, Bowe told the posse of reporters who proceeded to besiege her, 'If you have any questions about leaks, you should refer them to Ten Downing Street.' Magnus Linklater and David Leigh, award-winning journalists at the *Observer* newspaper, describe how Mrs Thatcher prepared and made a statement to the House.

That evening Ten Downing Street stonewalled on questions and worked late. Mrs Thatcher's statement would not only have to be robust, it would need to tread the most delicate path through the damning evidence presented by Armstrong's report.

Brittan began from a simple position: he had been acting under the authority of his Prime Minister. In those circumstances, he was ready for her to reveal that he had sanctioned the leak, but he was insistent that she should acknowledge her own role.

One must infer that Mrs Thatcher could not do so – at least not quite in those terms. She could, however, claim that her officials had acted without her knowledge.

The fact that this involved doing what Brittan had been at pains to avoid in the course of the day – passing the blame on to officials – did not in the end weigh as heavily as the need to protect the office of the Prime Minister.

It was, by all accounts, a long and agonized discussion which carried on the following morning, right up to that day's Cabinet meeting. By the time she went in, Mrs Thatcher had her story straight. 'The truth must be told,' said her deputy, Lord Whitelaw, in the course of talks, 'and it must be told in full.'

But a different decision had already been taken. The whole truth was, in fact, to be delicately skirted.

As a result, perhaps, there was nothing noticeably robust about the statement Mrs Thatcher gave that afternoon in the House of Commons. MPs, used to varying degrees of Thatcher stridency, were taken aback by the low monotone she employed to race through her account of the leaking of the Mayhew letter.

It was heard in near silence until towards the end when it began to arouse a combination of hilarity and derision. Most of her backbenchers listened in embarrassed silence. The House, as the *Guardian* reported next day, was 'tossed on an ocean of sheer disbelief'.

The sequence of events as recounted by the Prime Minister was, indeed, incredible, for it required MPs to believe that she had never herself asked a single pertinent question about a scandalous action which directly affected her Government.

She claimed that she had been given the 'full facts' only on Wednesday, sixteen days after the leak and at the end of Armstrong's inquiry. She admitted that officials in her own office had been involved, but she herself had not been consulted. The urgency of the affair had been caused by the overriding necessity to get Mayhew's views publicized before Cuckney's* 4 p.m. press conference.

It was, she said, Brittan who had approved the leak, and officials at the DTI and Downing Street who had arranged it:

> They did not seek my agreement. They considered – and they were right – that I should agree with my Rt. Hon. friend the Secretary of State for Trade and Industry, that the [Mayhew letter] should become public knowledge as soon as possible and before Sir John Cuckney's press conference. It was accepted that the Department of Trade and

*Sir John Cuckney, Chairman of Westland, who supported the American bid.

> Industry should disclose that fact and that, in view of the urgency of the matter, the disclosure should be made by means of a telephone communication to the Press Association. I should have said that a different way must be found of making the relevant facts known . . .
>
> . . . insofar as what my office said to the Department was based on the belief that I should have taken that view [of the need for 'public knowledge' of the letter], had I been consulted, they were right.

To accept Mrs Thatcher's full explanation it was necessary to believe that both she and Bernard Ingham had behaved entirely out of character; that she had never thought to ask a man in her own office, and with whom she worked in conditions of great intimacy, how a leak of major political significance had been effected; and that he, who knew more about the art of leaking than any other man in the country, had never told her what happened.

It showed a Prime Minister apparently unable to control her own officials, but approving of the use of smear tactics against a fellow-Minister.

'What I minded most of all was the aura of seedy incompetence it exposed,' said one Tory backbencher. Another senior Tory was more outspoken. 'It was a pack of lies,' he said.

The statement brought Opposition Leader Neil Kinnock's most powerful assault on the integrity of the Prime Minister. Her explanation, he said, had been given, not through frankness but because of 'heavy and inerasable guilt': 'The stain will stay with you for as long as you endure in politics.'

But perhaps the most effective interjection came from one of her own backbenchers, Alexander Fletcher, a former Minister, who asked, 'Are you satisfied that the statement you have made this afternoon has enhanced the integrity of the Government?'

It was an unanswerable question, and Mrs Thatcher did not seek, directly, to answer it. Shortly afterwards, the Opposition claimed an emergency Commons debate to be held the following Monday.

Almost forgotten in the course of question and answer was the man who had been named as the instigator of the leak. Leon Brittan was now more exposed than he had ever been. Although he had approved the wording of Mrs Thatcher's statement beforehand, hearing it read out was different. The manner in which it was delivered, the tone of voice, the implication of guilty conduct, and the distancing of the Prime Minister from the act itself, all placed him, as a Minister, under acute pressure.*

•

Amphibology

JOHN CORNWELL

In late 1987, crime-writer John Cornwell was invited by the Vatican to conduct a new investigation into the true circumstances of the sudden death of Pope John Paul I after a reign of only thirty-three days. There was almost certainly evidence of mendacity in the circumstances surrounding John Paul I's death, if not of foul play. In this extract, Cornwell inquires of a priest as to current Catholic teaching on lying.

After dinner in the English College, I was sitting at 'recreation' in a circle of staff and students taking coffee; my neighbour was an earnest-looking young priest who described himself as a specialist in moral theology.

After a while I steered the subject of our conversation to the Roman Catholic Church's teaching on lying. I was recalling the heated nineteenth-century debate between John Henry Newman and Charles Kingsley, the Anglican author and clergyman, who alleged that the Roman clergy encouraged lying 'on a system'. It had occurred to me that some of my clerical witnesses might well

*Leon Brittan resigned from the Cabinet the next day.

believe that it was moral to tell a lie in order to avoid a scandal. If this were seen as legitimate behaviour, where did it end? Could I take the word of any one of my clerical informants who might have a motive to avoid scandalizing the faithful?

'Are there any circumstances,' I asked the young moral scholar, 'in which one can tell a lie?'

'Aha!' he began with a twinkle in his eye. 'Well, you might find some of the older generation, brought up on the old moral handbooks, who would give you some fairly involved answers to that question.' He wrung his hands and leaned forward. 'But even by the standards of the old scholastic textbooks a lie is *always* held to be intrinsically evil, and it can never be justified for any reason whatsoever.'

'But can there be such a thing as a subdivision of the lie?' I asked, groping in my memory for some of the lost formulae of my seminary training.

'Indeed. Lies can be *profitable*, as they say, or *harmful*, depending on whether they benefit the liar without harm to another, or whether they cause injury. A moral theologian of the old school would say that the first sort – you know, boasting and so forth – are venial sins, and the second sort are grievous sins. Under the heading of venial you can have lies that are merely jocose, or a type of insincerity, or a kind of hypocrisy – like if you pretend to be virtuous or holy when you're nothing of the kind.' He smiled at me self-consciously. 'But they're all wrong, because a lie is a voluntary utterance contrary to intellectual conviction.'

'But what about a white lie, or what I seem to remember we called "economy of the truth", or the good old Jesuit equivocation?'

'Ah, now! That's not exactly lying, you see. That comes under the heading of mental reservation and the principle of amphibology.'

'Amphibology?'

'That's it. It means a statement with several meanings. If I say, "Peter is *at home* this evening", I could mean either that he was giving a dinner party later on, or that he was literally physically present in his house right now. You're allowed to have recourse to broad mental restriction of this kind, where a prudent man could gather the intended meanings from the surrounding circumstances; but you couldn't engage in strict mental reservation, intending deliberately to mislead, because that's an odious lie. I mean, even Christ himself engaged in amphibology on occasion . . .'

'Let's take the example of the Vatican telling the world that Magee found the body of the Pope, when in fact it was the nun. They say they did this to avoid scandal.'

'Aha! That could be the principle of double effect. That's when an action has two results; one may be good and the other bad, like when an abortion would save the mother's life and you permit it for that reason, despite the other consequences. But I don't think it applies in this case. There are various forms of scandal: you have active scandal, passive scandal, formal or diabolical scandal. But the interesting one here is *passive* scandal. That's where scandal results not from an evil action, but from a good action which is accepted by another through ignorance or through malice as an occasion of sin. This would apply to an action that leads people to believe that the Pope slept with the nun if you announce that this nun woke him with coffee in the morning. There is no moral obligation to avoid the scandal that arises from pure maliciousness, although you must avoid it if you can when it arises through people's weakness or natural inclinations. But you shouldn't tell a lie to avoid it, anyway.'

'OK,' I said. 'Here's another question. Say the Church had got itself mixed up in fraudulent or criminal financial deals likely to cause grave scandal to both Catholics and non-Catholics. I suppose they can just keep quiet about it, but would it be permissible for the Vatican to tell a deliberate lie, or deliberately mislead through amphibology, or whatever you like to call it, in order to make people think that they were in no sense guilty?'

'There's only one answer to that,' said the moral theologian, 'and it's *no*!'

Plausible deniability: the patriotism of Colonel Oliver North

BEN BRADLEE, JNR.

In an effort to secure the release of Americans taken hostage by pro-Iranian Lebanese Shiites, the administration of President Ronald Reagan secretly sold arms to Tehran despite the fact that Reagan himself had placed Iran on an arms-embargo list. At the time the story broke, it was discovered (following the crash of 'the Hasenfus plane' in Nicaragua – a plane carrying CIA documentation) that millions of dollars from the profits of the Iran arms sales had been diverted to the Contras – rebels fighting against the Sandinistas in Nicaragua. But Congress had recently voted to stop the flow of arms to the Contras, and therefore the diversion of monies from Iran was illegal. One of the key personnel in these illegal White House operations was a Marine colonel, Oliver North, attached to the staff of the National Security Council. Much of his work was secret, although there was no doubt that he had been the driving force behind the whole covert operation involving Iran and the Contras. The question was: how far was the President himself involved? A congressional committee started an investigation into the whole affair and summoned Colonel North to give evidence. It was perhaps the most spectacular piece of congressional evidence ever given. His show of candour made him into an American hero. North was eventually indicted. But as Ben Bradlee says, 'his celebrity overwhelmed his transgressions. He proved once again that a great actor can save even a lousy script.' Here, Bradlee describes some of the key moments in Ollies act, which took place in the very Senate Caucus Room where the McCarthy and Watergate hearings had taken place.

Since the committees, in dividing up responsibilities for witnesses, had designated North as a House witness,* John Nields, the chief House counsel, began the questioning. He had no deposition to guide him. He would just have to start.

'Colonel North,' Nields said, 'were you involved in the use of the proceeds of sales of weapons to Iran for the purpose of assisting the Contras in Nicaragua?'

North took the Fifth.

There were a few gasps among the spectators at the mere thought that after seven months of silence, and before a nationally televised audience, he would plead the Fifth Amendment again. But Brendan Sullivan was just protecting the record. The committees were prepared for this ritual step. Inouye routinely reminded North that he was there pursuant to a committee subpoena, and under court order, he could not take the Fifth. He had been granted immunity from prosecution based on testimony he provided. Ollie would now finally talk.

To Nields, the most important issue raised by the Iran–Contra case was the abuse of secrecy, and the question of how the government could best balance the need occasionally to conduct covert operations with the principles of an open, democratic society. So he moved immediately to what for him was the heart of the matter. He asked North if the Iran initiative and the Contra resupply program were covert operations.

'Yes, they were,' said North.

'And covert operations are designed to keep secrets from our enemies?'

'That is correct.'

'But these operations were designed to be secret from the American people?'

'I think what is important, Mr Nields, is that we somehow arrive at some kind of understanding right here and now as to what a covert operation is,' North said. If Nields – whose thinning light brown hair worn over his ears and collar made him look as if he might have been a hippie in the sixties – didn't

*Senate and House of Representatives committees were present.

know what a covert op was, then, by God, Ollie would tell him. 'If we could find a way to insulate with a bubble over these hearings, that are being broadcast in Moscow, and talk about covert operations to the American people without it getting into the hands of our adversaries, I'm sure we would do that. But we haven't found the way to do it.'

'But you put it somewhat differently to the Iranians with whom you were negotiating on the eighth and ninth of October in Frankfurt, Germany, didn't you?' countered Nields. 'You said to them that Secretary of Defense Weinberger in his last session with the President said, "I don't think we should send one more screw . . . until we have our Americans back from Beirut, because when the American people find out that this has happened, they'll impeach you" – referring to the President.'

Sullivan objected, but North didn't mind answering. 'That is a bald-faced lie told to the Iranians,' he conceded, 'and I will tell you right now, I'd have offered the Iranians a free trip to Disneyland if we could have gotten Americans home for it.'

'And when the Hasenfus plane went down in Nicaragua, the United States government told the American people that the United States government had no connection whatsoever with that airplane,' continued Nields. 'Is that also true?'

'No, it was not true. I had an indirect connection with that flight . . .'

Now Nields would try and lecture North: 'In certain communist countries the government's activities are kept secret from the people. But that's not the way we do things in America, is it?'

. . . 'Counsel,' said North, 'I would like to go back to what I just said a few moments ago. I think it is very important for the American people to understand that this is a dangerous world; that we live at risk and that this nation is at risk in a dangerous world. And that they ought not to be led to believe, as a consequence of these hearings, that this nation cannot or should not conduct covert operations. By their very nature, covert operations . . . are a lie. There is a great deceit, deception practiced in the conduct of covert operations. They are at essence, a lie . . . The American people ought not to be led to believe by the way you're asking that question that we intentionally deceived the American people, or had that intent to begin with. The effort to conduct these operations was made in such a way that our adversaries would not have knowledge of them, or that we could deny American association with it, or the association of this government with those activities. And that is not wrong.'

Nields was not making the headway on the secrecy issue that he had hoped for, so he decided to drop that line of questioning.

. . . For someone who had told numerous colleagues that he would be the one who would inevitably 'take the fall' for the Iran–Contra affair, North's first day of testimony was notable for his decided reluctance to take that fall alone. By the end of the day he had accused several cabinet-level officials of conspiring to give false information to the President and to Congress, or of being aware of elements of the Iran or Contra operations.

Ollie spoke contemptuously of 'heroes' who had come forward in November of 1986 to blow the whistle on false cover stories that he and others were putting out. 'I didn't make a lot of the decisions I am accused of making,' he said, adding later that there had been 'a whole cadence of people' who had 'wittingly' participated in cover-ups. 'I didn't consider myself to be the lone wolf out here creating paper that nobody else knew about . . .'

'By putting out this false version of the facts, you were committing, were you not, the entire Administration to telling a false story?' asked Nields.

'Well . . . I'm not trying to pass the buck here, okay?' said a visibly irritated North. 'I did a lot of things, and I want to stand up and say that I'm proud of them. I don't want you to think, Counsel, that I went about this all on my own. I realize there's a lot of folks around that think there's a loose cannon on the gundeck of state at the NSC. That wasn't what I heard while I worked there. I've only heard it since I left. People used to walk up to me and tell me what a great job I was doing, and the fact is there were many, many people – to include the former assistant to the President for national security affairs, the current national security advisor, the attorney general of the United States of America, the director of central intelligence, all of whom knew that to be wrong.'

It had been MacFarlane,* North said, who had charged him with keeping the Contras together 'body and soul', and the job had expanded after funds dried up in 1984. 'I guess it just fell to me by default,' he said.

Without being prompted, North said that it was Casey,† who after the Iran–Contra operations began to unravel in the fall of 1986 told him to destroy documents. 'Director Casey and I had a lengthy discussion about the fact that this whole thing was coming unraveled, and that things ought to be cleaned up, and I started cleaning things up,' North said. He also named Assistant Secretary of State Elliott Abrams, Assistant Secretary of Defense Richard Armitage and the CIA's Alan Fiers and Dewey Clarridge as having been aware of some or all of his covert operations.

North tried to pass off his shredding as routine, but acknowledged that after learning of Meese's inquiry on November 21 he had been shredding with 'increased intensity'. That got a laugh.

But when he tried to be funny, North tended to bomb. 'My memory has been shredded,' he responded during one exchange about shredding documents. And when Nields asked him about the number of memos that he sent Poindexter‡ or President Reagan, North replied: 'Judging by the pile of paper you just gave me, I sent too many.'

*The former National Security Advisor.
†The former CIA Director.
‡Former National Security Advisor.

He made clear his disgust with Congress: 'There were other countries in the world and other people in this country who were more willing to help the Nicaraguan resistance survive and cause democracy to prosper in Central America than this body here.' And after acknowledging that he cut back on his memo-writing after Congress began showing an interest in his Central American activities, he said defiantly: 'I didn't want to show Congress a single word on this whole thing.'

But at the end of the day, though he had acknowledged a catalog of sins – including not telling the truth to Congress, destroying evidence and covering up to protect the President – North's dramatic sense of time and place had clearly succeeded in papering over his admissions, throwing the committees on the defensive and casting himself as the well-meaning patriotic prince.

. . . Where Nields had been uninterested in learning about North the man in preparing for his examination of the witness, [Arthur] Liman had devoted considerable time to learning as much as he could about the Marine's character and persona. Liman sought to understand what made North tick. He had approached Ollie's friends and asked them to tell him about Ollie. He had talked to Fawn Hall* informally about her impressions of her former boss. He had even tried to chat up Brendan Sullivan;† Sullivan did not bite. He did not want any kind of a relationship with Liman, formal or informal, that might have given the Senate counsel the opportunity to better know – and therefore best – North.

Liman was curious about the Annapolis connection that bound the key Iran–Contra players: North, MacFarlane and Poindexter. He wondered to what extent they would feel they had to go down with the ship rather than come clean. Was taking the fall a natural reflex for all of them?

*North's secretary.
†North's attorney.

And he wondered, too, about the effect of Vietnam on North – his frustration and anger at what had happened, and how that had motivated him: Congress and the press had lost the war. Now, perhaps, when Ollie's turn came to be in power, he would feel he had to rectify past wrongs and show the world how to fight a war right.

Finally there was North's unabashed zeal, his strong conviction – along with Secord – that he, rather than Congress, the press or anyone else, knew best what was in the national interest. Liman was a firm believer in Justice Brandeis' credo that the people who had done the most damage historically were people who thought they had discovered the truth and were prepared to pursue it at all costs.

'I think I understood Oliver North as well as a stranger can know another person,' Liman says. 'And I was not surprised at all. I knew that he was charismatic. I knew that he was an extraordinarily persuasive person.'

He said that until Nields finished with North, he didn't really know what he was going to ask. He had known generally what areas Nields was going to explore, but he had not known what North's answers were going to be. 'I don't know whether, when John finished, I was going to ask him any questions, questions for an hour or questions for a day. And also, I made it a practice, since I was counsel for the Senate committee, to get a sense of what the members want me to do, and I can't get that sense until the witness is finished testifying.

'I saw no reason to be confrontational with North. North got on the stand and said, "I lied, I cheated, I deceived and I did it all for my country and on orders." And to me, therefore, it became important to try and bring out the implications of what he was saying . . . He has a great sense of place and time, Oliver North . . . He saw himself as playing on the stage of the country. He understood that he would damage his credibility not just with the committee but with the nation if he minced words, and so he got up there and the first words out of his mouth were: "I lied, I deceived, I shredded, I altered, and how many times do you want to humiliate me by making me repeat it?" That's a very tough kind of testimony to deal with.'

. . . So on the afternoon of July 9 Liman began a sympathetic dissection of North, intending to tie together thematically what the witness had laid out in the raw to Nields. America's hearts were still no doubt with Ollie on view at the witness table. Liman was jowly, with a double chin, fettucine hair and a decided New York accent. 'It was apple pie versus bagels and cream cheese,' wrote the Los Angeles *Times*' Howard Rosenberg.

'Colonel,' asked Liman, 'is it fair to say that November 25, 1986,* was one of the worst days in your life?'

North, suspecting some kind of curve ball, conferred with Sullivan.

'I wasn't asking if it was one of the worst days in Mr Sullivan's life,' said Liman, drawing laughter from the audience.

North came back to the microphone and took the high road: 'I will tell you honestly, Counsel, that I have had many worse days than that. Most of those were days when young Marines died, and there have been days since then that are worse in some respects. I would not recount the last three days that I have been here as being particularly pleasant. It was a difficult day.'

Liman moved toward an exploration of the fall-guy plan, seemingly more than willing to buy North's belief that he was a scapegoat – that November 25 was a day when his life changed forever, and he became the subject of a criminal investigation.

North, at one point referring to his role as that of a 'Roman centurion', said that the fall-guy plan assumed that 'this was not going to be a matter of criminal behavior but rather one of deniability for the White House . . . for political purposes. And when I say "political purposes", I'm speaking not only of domestic, but international ramifications. That is one of the essences of plausible deniability in a covert operation.'

*The day the Iran–Contra affair obliged Reagan to relieve North of his duties on the NSC.

'Are you saying, Colonel, that you were prepared to take the rap for political purposes, but not for criminal purposes?'

'Precisely . . . There was probably not another person on the planet Earth as shocked as I was to hear that someone thought it was criminal,' North said. 'And I can tell you that that shock was compounded when I heard later that there was to be an independent counsel, and further compounded when I was the only name in the appointment order for that independent counsel – the only person on the planet Earth named in that appointment order, Counsel.'

North wanted to have it both ways on the fall-guy issue: he wanted the credit for being the one who was ready, willing and able to stand up and take the heat, yet he was also bringing just about everyone but the President into the soup with him. In seeking to make the distinction between taking a political hit and a criminal hit, he was attempting to create the impression that he was willing to be the fall guy, but not the patsy.

Whatever, Liman seemed sympathetic to North for having taken an unanticipated fall. But while presumably disarming North with this tactic, he was also drawing from the witness repeated acknowledgements that his behavior in lying and deceiving was in violation of the Naval Academy's values of honor and trustworthiness that he had sworn to uphold as a midshipman.

Where North had owned the morning, now Liman's silky, seemingly sympathetic line of questioning seemed to throw Ollie off balance.

Senator Lee Hamilton, Chairman of the House Intelligence Committee, gave his impression of Oliver North at the close of his testimony:

'What strikes me is that despite your very good intentions, you were a participant in actions which catapulted a president into the most serious crisis of his presidency, drove the Congress of the United States to launch an unprecedented investigation, and I think probably damaged the cause, or the causes that you sought to promote . . .

'In your opening statement you said that these hearings have caused serious damage to our national interests. But I wonder whether the damage has been caused by these hearings, or by the acts which prompted these hearings? I wonder whether you would have the Congress do nothing after it had been lied to, misled and ignored? . . .

'Now let me tell you what bothers me. I want to talk about two things: first policy and then process . . . I am very troubled by your defense of our secret arms sales to Iran . . . I am impressed that policy was driven by a series of lies – lies to the Iranians, lies to the Central Intelligence Agency, lies to the Attorney General, lies to our friends and allies, lies to Congress and lies to the American people.

. . . 'As I understand your testimony, you did what you did because those were your orders, and because you believed that it was for a good cause. I cannot agree that the end has justified these means . . . The means employed were a profound threat to the democratic process . . . Methods and means are what this country is all about.'

•

Liar's privilege

THE ECONOMIST

Lord, how this world is given to lying. Quite so, Falstaff, but there is lying and lying. Consider the cases of the two European heads of state who have just been rumbled. Kurt Waldheim deliberately obscured details of his career in the German army. What was he up to in the Second World War? Nothing creditable, according to the diggers-up of documents. But that is not the point. He lied and for that reason deserves punishment. The other villain is Nicolae Ceausescu. He said he was modestly surprised on his 70th birthday to receive greetings from, among others, Queen Elizabeth and the Kings of Spain and Sweden.

The monarchs must have been surprised too. The Romanian dictator is not on their birthday-card list. He, or perhaps his toadies, had been falsely dropping names. The Ceausescu lie, though, provoked a weary smile rather than a scowl.

The difference between the two liars, apart from the difference between war and a birthday party, is that Mr Waldheim breached the liars' code of privilege; Mr Ceausescu did not. The code permits the lie of flattery, particularly when the subject is a person of power. Sycophants are the breath of life to the boss. The code also acknowledges that diplomats lie for their country, that truth is the first casualty of war.

Politicians are not expected to lie, but may conceal the whole truth until they have been sacked and are writing their memoirs. The code has a special sub-section devoted to spying. A British civil servant, Sir Robert Armstrong, conceded that he was 'economical with the truth' when giving evidence in the *Spycatcher* case. Spies themselves are totally exempt from telling the truth; you could not be a double agent otherwise. Lovers are allowed beautiful lies. Divorce courts expect lies. Most greetings contain harmless lies. This is a nice surprise. Good to see you.

Privileged liars prefer not to be called liars. The code has its own vocabulary, with elegant words like hypocrisy, euphemism and insincerity, and jokey ones like whoppers and fibs. As a rough and ready guide to privileged lying, ask yourself: Is it reasonable to expect this person to be entirely frank, given his job, background and prejudices? If the answer is no, he qualifies for the liar's privilege.

A few years ago nobody doubted that Mr Waldheim was a man of integrity. Before he became President of Austria he was Secretary General of the United Nations, a kind of secular pope, regarded as infallible in his purpose, if not always in his judgements. It would, in other circumstances, be judged a small sin: he fudged his CV. But this act poisoned his whole reputation. Men of integrity are barred from the liar's code. His excuse of a 'frailty of memory' is not acceptable. Send him to the pillory. He has brought into disrepute the ordinary, everyday lying needed to get through the day without causing unnecessary offence. As Elizabeth Bowen, a novelist, observed, never to lie is to have no lock on your door. Lying, in its white and off-white forms, will survive. No problem. Take care. Have a nice day. You're welcome.

•

Rock bottom: the Gibraltar killings

PRIVATE EYE

It all started with a lie.

On Sunday 6 March, 1988, at 4.45 p.m., the Ministry of Defence issued the following statement: 'A suspected bomb has been found in Gibraltar and three suspects have been shot by civilian police.' At 9 p.m. the statement was expanded: 'Security forces were involved in the shootings and military personnel dealt with a suspect bomb.' The following morning, 7 March, Ian Stewart, then Armed Forces Minister, said on the *Today* programme that a large bomb had been defused.

The lie was heavily reported. All British national daily newspapers on 7 March reported that a car bomb had been placed by the IRA in Gibraltar. Eight out of the eleven reported that the bomb was 500 lbs; one plumped for 400 lbs, one 440 lbs and one (the *Sun*) a 'massive car bomb'. *The Times* printed a map of where the bomb had been parked. Responsible newspapers, including the *Guardian* and the *Telegraph*, and television news bulletins from ITN and the BBC, reported that the bomb had been defused. A number of papers also reported that the three people who had been shot were armed; and that there had been a 'shoot-out' before they were killed.

The shootings had taken place at 3.40 the previous afternoon, only an hour before the first Ministry of Defence bulletin. Many months later, when asked about the 'disinformation' from the MoD on the day of the shootings, Tom King, Secretary of State for Northern Ireland, gave journalists (on the usual confidence lobby basis) an ingenious explanation. He said the phone lines from Gibraltar were so few that no one could get through to the Ministry with the real facts. This rather curious admission of the weaknesses of British army signals (the army base at Gibraltar bristles with aerials) fails to explain why the story about the bomb was rushed out within the hour. The information which the newspapers printed, however, could not all have come from the MoD, which issued only two terse bulletins.

The information about the size of the bomb, for instance, came from unofficial sources, some of them in the Ministry, but chiefly from MI5. The security services, and MI5 in particular, keep a number of 'contacts' in newspapers and television and are very generous with information. With very few 'stringers' at work on the Rock of Gibraltar on a Sunday, the hacks in London were delighted to get such information and they readily passed it on.

The bomb in the car, however, was not of 500 lbs, nor of 440 lbs, nor 400 lbs. It could not properly be described as 'massive'. It was not there.

A faintly embarrassed Foreign Secretary, Sir Geoffrey Howe, told the House of Commons that afternoon: 'Shortly before 1 p.m. yesterday afternoon, one of those subsequently shot brought a white Renault car into Gibraltar and was seen to park it in the area where the band for the guard-mounting ceremony assembles. Before leaving the car, he was seen to spend some time making adjustments in the vehicle. An hour and a half later, the two others subsequently shot were seen to enter Gibraltar on foot, and shortly before 3 p.m. joined the third terrorist in the town. Their presence and actions near the parked Renault car gave rise to strong suspicion that it contained a bomb, which appeared to be corroborated by a rapid technical examination of the car.

'About 3.30 p.m., all three left the scene and started to walk back towards the border. On their way towards the border, they were challenged by the security forces. When challenged, they made movements which led the military personnel operating in support of the Gibraltar police to conclude that their own lives and the lives of others were under threat. In the light of this response, they were shot. Those killed were subsequently found not to be carrying arms. The parked Renault car was subsequently dealt with by the military bomb disposal team. It has now been established that it did not contain an explosive device.'

No arms. No bomb. No defusing. The fact that the Ministry of Defence and all Britain's media had been putting out entirely false information to the British people took a little while to sink in. Labour's foreign affairs spokesman, for instance, Mr George Robertson, was so persuaded by the lie that he didn't even listen to the Foreign Secretary's statement.

'The very fact,' he declared immediately after Sir Geoffrey had sat down, 'that this enormous potential bomb was placed opposite both an old folks' home and a school underlined the cynical hypocrisy of the IRA . . .' Poor Mr Robertson was putting an 'enormous car bomb' where the Foreign Secretary said it wasn't, but no one could blame him too much. By that time, whatever the Foreign Secretary said, the entire nation believed there was a car bomb placed in a public street in Gibraltar, since that was what they had been unanimously told by the British press and television.

The following day it was announced with audible sighs of relief that a huge quantity of explosive had been found in a car which had been parked in Spain, and which was connected to the three shot people: Sean Savage, Daniel McCann and Mairead Farrell. The IRA had been planning a car bomb after all; it just hadn't been taken to Gibraltar. Any slight irritation about the false stories told by the media and the Ministry quickly vanished.

Over the next few days a picture emerged of what had happened in Gibraltar. The three terrorists had been plotting to bomb the Gibraltar parade. Their plan had been known to British intelligence for five months. For all of that time, MI5 and British military intelligence had been in close contact with the Spanish security services.

A fourth IRA member, a woman, had been followed for weeks while she looked over the Gibraltar site. The three people who were later killed were followed into Spain. The white Renault car, which was driven by Sean Savage from Malaga to Gibraltar on 6 March, had, insisted all the newspapers, been followed all the way to the border by Spanish intelligence.

About this there was a unanimity which suggested a specific briefing from the Ministry of Defence.

. . . Once over the border, the story went on, the car was parked where a military parade was going to take place in the centre of Gibraltar on Tuesday (8 March). Sean Savage then met up with his two colleagues and they started to leave the Rock on foot. They were being followed by SAS sharpshooters and armed Gibraltar police, when suddenly they grew suspicious. They 'made movements' which suggested they might be drawing weapons or setting off the bomb, so they were shot.

This story was not questioned for several weeks. There were a few complaints (most surprisingly, perhaps, in the leader column of the *Daily Telegraph*) about the shooting in the streets of suspects, but most of these were laid to rest by the assurances that the terrorist trio were, after all, in the business of bomb-planting and that they had been challenged and eventually shot only in the assailants' clear belief that a lot of other people's lives were in danger.

This amiable attitude persisted until April, when Thames Television announced that it intended to broadcast on 28 April a programme asking one or two questions about the shootings. The effect on the Government was electric. Sir Geoffrey Howe aggressively requested that the programme be postponed until after the inquest into the deaths. Neither Thames nor the Independent Broadcasting Authority could agree. The programme, they claimed, was a responsible account and there was no reason why it should not be shown.

. . . Thames's programme, *Death on the Rock*, was broadcast on 28 April. The first part of it was devoted entirely to a ferocious attack on the IRA and its bombing campaign. In the second part, the programme produced witnesses who challenged Sir Geoffrey's view of the killings. A former army bomb-disposal expert, Lt.-Colonel George Styles, said it was perfectly possible just by looking at a car to tell whether it had a significant bomb in it.

Mrs Carmen Proetta, who lives in a flat overlooking the garage where the shootings took place, said the first two terrorists to be shot, McCann and Farrell, had their hands raised in the air at the time they were shot. She told Thames TV: 'They [security forces] didn't do anything, they just jumped with their guns in their hands, and they just went and shot these people. That's all. They didn't say anything, they didn't scream, they didn't shout, they didn't do anything. These people were turning their heads back to see what was happening, and when they saw these men had guns in their hands they put their hands up. It looked like the man was protecting the girl because he stood in front of her, but there was no chance. I mean they went to the floor immediately, they dropped.'

Mrs Proetta and another witness, Mrs Jose Celicia, said they saw the gunmen fire at the bodies on the ground. Stephen Bullock, a British lawyer, gave a graphic account of how close the gunmen were to their victims when they fired.

The programme also broadcast a statement by an anonymous witness who said that he had seen Sean Savage being shot at after he had fallen from the first shots, by a gunman who had put his foot on the terrorist's body.

. . . The 'popular' newspapers launched a hysterical and unanimous attack on Carmen Proetta, alleging that she had run an escort agency for rich Arabs. The *Sun* described her as 'The Tart of Gib' and titillated its readers with a front-page article introduced by the following: 'The *Sun* reveals sleazy truth about wife in SAS row.' The *Daily Mail* attacked the programme's producer, Roger Bolton, revealing that he had 'co-operated with terrorists', and 'had secret dealings with Irish republican groups'.

All these allegations were completely untrue. All of them ended up in the libel courts, with heavy damages and apologies from the newspapers to the injured parties.

. . . But *Death on the Rock* had had an even more profound impact on the Government than was reflected in the unanimous squawking of its newspapers. The programme's main witness, Carmen Proetta, had not been interviewed by the Gibraltar police, who were assisting the coroner in his inquiries for the inquest (which had started off as a routine, formal inquiry), suddenly became much more significant. Suddenly it became obvious that the gunmen themselves would have to tell their story at the inquest.

On 30 September 1988 a jury found that all three killings had been lawful, despite numerous evidentiary contradictions, not least from the Gibraltar police, and the SAS squad which carried out the executions. For anyone wondering whether the British Government did operate a 'shoot to kill' policy in Northern Ireland, the answer seemed clear.

•

Pseudologia phantastica

GRAHAM REED

This is . . . the fabrication by hysterical individuals of 'experiences' which are intrinsically improbable or readily disprovable. On subsequent retailing of such tall stories further details and elaborations are added, particularly if doubt has been expressed by earlier audiences. Each addition becomes progressively more fantastic, so that the implausibility of the original tale is reinforced. The motivation for this sort of behaviour is a need to attract respect, sympathy or merely attention, a need which is the characterizing feature of the hysterical personality.

The author* was once due to test a young lady who arrived at the clinic rather late, giving the impression of one who is distraught but bravely fighting back the tears. After sitting down, she requested time to compose herself because: 'I feel a bit shaken. You see, I'm afraid something has just happened that

*Chairman of the Department of Psychology, York University, Toronto.

rather upset me.' After a show of decent reluctance, she then explained that she had caught her bus to the clinic in good time. Her lateness was due to the fact that, as she was about to alight, the conductor had brutally ravished her. The author agreed that this was conduct unbecoming to a municipal employee, and remarked that it was particularly unusual in mid-afternoon, on a main road in the city centre and in the setting of a crowded bus. He inquired whether she had reported the outrage to the police, to which the young lady replied, with wide-eyed sincerity, that she had not done so because: 'That would have made me late for my appointment here.' The author's scepticism was confirmed after the session, when he took the young lady back to the waiting-room. For there was her mother, who had accompanied her to the clinic that afternoon and had noticed nothing untoward during the journey. The young lady was not at all disconcerted by her mother's amazed denials of her story. The rape, she explained, had taken place as she was about to follow her mother down the bus stairs. She had not mentioned the matter as they walked from the bus stop to the clinic, because the conductor had also tried to strangle her with his ticket-punch strap, so that she was temporarily unable to speak.

The rape tale above may reasonably be interpreted as a hastily invented excuse which got out of hand, coupled with a more general need to gain attention. The young lady in question was physically ill-favoured, and lacking in sparkle. It could be that if she had had enough wit to make up a better story she would not have required such attention-seeking devices in the first place. But this is not necessarily so, because the problem is one of self-evaluation. It is not uncommon for individuals who *are* attractive and (at least initially) interesting to others to regard themselves nevertheless as social nonentities.

The *direction* taken by such attention-seeking fabrications naturally also reflects individual wish-fulfilment. The male equivalent of our young lady is that man who haunts most clubs and 'locals'. According to him he is, to all intents and purposes, in hiding from a veritable legion of love-crazed women. Oddly enough, these are for the most part film stars, prima ballerinas, Italian countesses or the glamorous wives of eminent men. Every hint of doubt from the listener merely elicits more colourful details and additional persona. But the content of pseudologia phantastica is of course not restricted to sexual exploits. Heroism, martyrdom, distinguished origins, scientific invention, financial coups or social fame – all are grist to the mill. Very often the claimant becomes the butt of his fellows, who discover that in the face of scepticism or interrogation he is spurred to even giddier heights of implausibility.

In other instances, however, the fictional character of the 'reminiscences' may not be appreciated by the audience. It is ironic to realize that the term 'pseudologia phantastica' is applied generally to the behaviour of patients merely because their reports are demonstrably untrue. There must be many people who are not under psychiatric treatment because their reports have *not* been recognized as untrue. Hysterics are notorious for their histrionic talents and for their apparent sincerity. On superficial acquaintance they tend to be very convincing, so it is likely that for every patient under treatment there are many non-patients whose equally fantastic reminiscences are accepted as genuine. Presumably the successful confidence trickster comes from the same mould as the psychiatric patient, as do those who appear before the courts for masquerading as high-ranking officers or peers of the realm. Less mischievous but probably of the same ilk are the people who are triggered off by events appearing in newspaper headlines. Thus, reports of unsolved murders result in numbers of people who claim to be the murderer and are quite prepared to support their 'confession' with circumstantial but readily falsifiable details. Every time one person is reported as having seen a ghost or a flying saucer, a crowd of others suddenly 'remember' that they too witnessed the phenomenon.

When children engage in the sort of behaviour recounted above, adults regard them with amused tolerance. Most of us accept that in childhood the boundaries between fantasy and reality are blurred, and the concepts of 'truth' and 'falsehood' are slow to develop. In adults, however, such behaviour is judged in moral terms. The alternative term for pseudologia phantastica is 'pathological lying', which immediately suggests reprehensible behaviour rather than a symptom of personality disorder. Adults are presumed to know the difference between fact and fancy, truth and falsehood, and in our culture to mix the two during verbal report is to be guilty of lying. This is defined as the intentional making of false statements, usually with the purpose of misleading others. It is presupposed that the liar is fully aware of what is true and what is false, and that he is consciously imparting the latter with deliberate intention of deceiving. This is doubtless a fair description of much braggadocio and tall story-telling. We may invent stories to avoid reproach, to impress, to denigrate our enemies or to further our ambitions. More innocuously, we may do so merely to amuse our listeners or even to avoid hurting their feelings. We know what we are doing and, if required, can immediately disavow our stories or modify them in accordance with fact. But for many people the situation is not so simple. We all 'remember' by selective reconstruction. If the discrepancies between what we recall and what actually occurred can be brought to our notice, we do not then accuse others of having lied, but merely of having misremembered. Similarly, we do not regard the amnesic patient's confabulations as lies. We realize that he is filling in the gaps in his memory with fragments of earlier memories. It seems reasonable to suggest that hysterical confabulation involves the same process. In hysterical amnesia the patient's problems are solved at one level by the inaccessibility of much stored information, including that which has disturbed or threatened him. His experience may be interpreted as the reflection of a negative type of defence. Pseudologia phantastica may be regarded as the obverse of this, utilizing a similar process in the opposite direction. Instead of the under- employment of retrieval mechanisms, they are over-employed but in an unduly associative and flexible manner. In the first case, certain schemata are isolated; in the second they are too readily related.

•

The triumph of the lie

ANDREW HIGGINS

Peking, 13 June 1989 – The woman was clearly mad. She must have been mad, because only the mad dare show their grief in public any more.

Wailing and shaking her matted hair, she confronted me yesterday outside the Bank of China on a side street leading to Tiananmen Square. She had been there for hours, people said, pacing back and forth in front of a coil of barbed wire and a group of helmeted soldiers with guns.

In her hands she held a crumpled piece of paper scrawled with a message in blue ink – no doubt the answer to her torment, the name of a son, a husband or whoever else it was who had been killed in the massacre which, as everyone sane now pretends to know, never really took place.

Whatever she had to say, the People's Liberation Army quickly made sure it went unsaid. Barking an order to stop, one soldier trained his rifle on the woman's soiled pink jacket. A colleague leapt over the barbed wire to grab the message and lead her away. Another counter-revolutionary plot had been foiled.

Peking, they say, is back to normal. Unlike the woman with matted hair, the Chinese state has had no trouble projecting its own message, its own version of events.

If the lie is big enough and repeated often enough, people might actually start to believe it. And even if they don't, they will, like their children, at least be in no doubt about their lines. When a local party cadre comes to quiz them, when they attend political education classes at work, or when a reporter from state television or an official newspaper comes to ask their views on armed soldiers lolling outside their door, they will know what to say. 'The people's army loves the people, the people love the army.' Only the mad may forget their lines. Only a man deranged by the loss of his wife would dare, as one did, to unfurl the banner of protest. Or, as another did, scream abuse at the column of troops passing by on patrol.

The sane have gone all quiet, waiting for the storm to pass, waiting for an end to this terrible normality of mass arrests, incessant propaganda and silent, cowed obedience. Those lucky enough to have money and passports have fled. Others well-enough known have taken refuge in foreign embassies. Most, however, have no choice but to fall silent. With truth turned firmly on its head, everyone knows that soldiers, not the people they massacred, were the only true victims. Anyone who has watched television knows how one soldier was burned to death, how another was strung up from an overpass, how others were incinerated alive inside their tanks and armoured carriers. To be sure, such atrocities did occur. But what of the hundreds – thousands – of unarmed civilians who perished too? Not a word.

'Salute the People's Liberation Army of China' reads the banner on the Peking Hotel, from whose balcony I last week watched thirty or more people mowed down in a single volley of gunfire. 'Salute the public security forces, salute the police, salute the armed militia'.

•

Terminological inexactitudes

THE INDEPENDENT

It was the Prime Minister's former Cabinet secretary, Sir Robert (now Lord) Armstrong, who admitted to being 'economical with the truth'. It was only his little joke, made under pressure in a courtroom where he should never have found himself, and it would be wrong to hold it against him for ever. Yet in the Prime Minister's entourage the habit of economy with the truth sometimes contrasts with her personification of the antique virtues and Victorian values.

There was Sir Robert's attempt to explain why it was all right for Chapman Pincher, but not for Peter Wright, to publish secrets. Untrue statements were made about the sinking of the Argentine cruiser *Belgrano*. Absurd imputations were made against the bishops when the Church of England report, *Faith in the City*, was published. There were – to put it no higher – lamentable equivocations in the Westland affair, and grave doubts remain about the Government's response to the Colin Wallace allegations.

There has been no convincing explanation of the attempt to smear John Stalker by bringing unsustainable charges against his friend, Kevin Taylor, and the failure to make amends to Mr Stalker. Only just before Christmas there was the disconcerting revelation that Lord Young of Graffham, Secretary of State for Trade and Industry, had offered secret 'sweeteners' to induce British Aerospace to buy the Rover Group in what turned out to be one of the great sweetheart deals in the history of public finance. 'I can offer three possibilities,' Lord Young wrote to Professor Roland Smith, the BAe chairman, about one particular piece of 'creative accounting' on offer from Her Majesty's Government, 'in ascending order of risk that the deferment will be picked up by the European Commission'. The tone is less that one would expect from a minister of the Crown, and more that of a professional adviser marking a client's card about what he might induce the Revenue to 'wear'.

Then there has been the attempt to persuade the public first that the average poll tax would come to £278, when it is clear that it will come to at least 35 per cent more; and second that this was to be blamed on reckless spending by left-wing councils, which turns out not to be the case.

These were some of the celebrated instances of what might be called intellectual dishonesty in the inner circles of the Thatcher administration. But perhaps it is the small change of half-truth, cumulatively piling up over the weeks and months in the piggy banks of the public mind, that has done more than these few major furores to draw attention to the decline of respect for the truth under this Government.

Examples of the shifty suppression of the true, the deft suggestion of the half-true, have been so numerous, from the Government in the House of Commons and even more from its secret briefers and nod-and-wink artists, that every connoisseur will have a choice collection. But consider two of this week's items:

Only last Monday the Prime Minister herself bolstered her case for abandoning the prohibition on investments in South Africa by mentioning, after a strange phrase about investment of a 'compound nature within and without South Africa' that might or might not have applied to BMW, that BMW South Africa 'has just announced the latest £25m instalment in a five-year investment programme'. The impression is left that BMW was breaking sanctions, but the investment in question was made from profits retained within South Africa. On Tuesday the Foreign Secretary told the House of Commons that Mrs Thatcher had received a message from President Bush saying that only 'legal difficulties' prevented him from following her line on sanctions. Well, yes; but the legal difficulties in question were hardly trivial. They include the Anti-Apartheid Act of 1986 and the United States Constitution, which does not empower Mr Bush to lift sanctions without action by Congress.

Mrs Thatcher is a great admirer of the United States, and her favourite president, in eight hours of videotaped evidence under oath, is trying to remember what he knew about the Iran-Contra affair and when he knew it. More relevant to our situation, perhaps, are the words of another great Republican, Theodore Roosevelt. 'No people,' he once said, 'were ever yet benefited by riches if their prosperity corrupted their virtue. It is of more importance that we should show ourselves honest, brave, truthful and intelligent, than that we should own all the grain elevators and railroads in the world.'

•

Sources

Ambrose, Stephen E., *Eisenhower the President, Vol. 2: 1952–1969*, George Allen & Unwin

Anon. (page 254), 'Famous Irish Trials', in *Cases that Changed the Law*, n.d.

Anon. (page 44), in J. McNeill and H. Garner, *Medieval Handbooks of Penance*, Columbia Press, New York, 1938

Anon. (page 57), 'The Prester John Letter', trans. Sir Denison Ross, in *Travel and Travellers of the Middle Ages*, ed. A. P. Newton, 1926

Anon. (pages 155, 194 and 220), in *Sketches of Imposture and Credulity*, Thomas Tegg & Son, 1837

Aquinas, Thomas, *Summa Theologica*, trans. Fathers of the English Dominican Province, Burns Oates & Washburn, 1922

Aristotle, *The Nichomachean Ethics*, trans. J. A. K. Thomson, 1953; Penguin, 1976

Augustine, St (pages 33 and 35), 'On Lying', in *Treatises on Various Subjects*, ed. R. J. Deferrari, Fathers of the Church, Catholic University Press, New York, 1952

Bacon, Francis, *Essays*, Everyman edition, 1906

Barnum, Phineas T., *The Humbugs of the World*, 1866

Barron, John, *KGB*, Hodder & Stoughton, 1974

Bentham, Jeremy, 'Petition for Justice', in *The Works of Jeremy Bentham*, ed. Sir J. Bowring, 1838–43

Bible, The, King James version

Blake, Robert, *Disraeli*, Eyre and Spottiswoode, 1969

Bok, Sissela, *Lying: Moral Choice in Public and Private Life*, Pantheon, 1978

Bourienne, *Memoirs of Napoleon*, trans. Richard Bentley, 1836

Bradlee, Ben, Jnr., *Guts and Glory: The Rise and Fall of Oliver North*, Grafton Books, 1988

Brown, Dee, *Bury My Heart at Wounded Knee*, Barrie & Jenkins, 1971

Bryce Report, *On Alleged German Atrocities*, Wellington House Literature, 1914

Butler, Samuel (page 246), *Alps and Sanctuaries*, 1881; (page 248), 'Truth and Convenience', in *Notebooks*, 1912

Calvin, John, 'Advantages from an Inventory of Relics', in *Tracts Relating to the Reformation*, 1844

Cambrensis, Giraldus, 'The Itinerary of Wales', in *The Historical Works*, trans. Sir Richard Colt Hoare, 1863

Carlyle, Thomas (page 215), *Count Cagliostro*, 1883; (page 229), *History of Frederick the Great*, 1858; (page 231), *Latter-day Pamphlets*, 1850

Carr, Albert Z., 'Is Business Bluffing Ethical?', *Harvard Business Review*, January–February 1968

Casanova, *Memoirs*, trans. Arthur Machen, Putnam & Sons, New York, 1960

Cave-Brown, Anthony, *Bodyguard of Lies*, W. H. Allen, 1976
Cellini, Benvenuto, *Autobiography*, trans. George Bull, Penguin, 1956
Central Commission for Investigation of German Crimes in Poland, Report, 1947
Chadwick, Owen, *Mackenzie's Grave*, Hodder & Stoughton, 1959
Chatterton, Thomas, correspondence in E. W. Meyerstein, *Life of Thomas Chatterton*, 1930
Cicero (page 25), 'On Duties, III', in *Selected Works*, trans. Michael Grant, Penguin, 1960; (page 27), 'On Duties, II', in *Cicero and the Good Life*, trans. Michael Grant, Penguin, 1971
Clare, George, *Berlin Days 1946–47*, Macmillan, 1989
Coleridge, Samuel Taylor, *Table Talk*, 1812
Conquest, Robert, *The Harvest of Sorrow*, Hutchinson, 1986
Cornwell, John, *A Thief in the Night*, Viking, 1989
Curtis, Charles P., 'The Ethics of Advocacy', *Stanford Law Review*, No. 4, 1951
Dawson, Charles, and Woodward, A. S., 'On the Discovery of a Palaeolithic Human Skull and Mandible in a Flint-Bearing Gravel overlying the Wealden (Hastings Bed) at Piltdown, Fletching, Sussex', *Quarterly Journal of the London Geological Society*, No. 69, 1912
Dean, John, *Blind Ambition*, W. H. Allen, 1977
Dekker, Thomas, *The Seven Deadly Sins*, 1606
De Quincey, Thomas, *Uncollected Writings*, 1841
D'Israeli, Isaac (pages 140 and 190), *Curiosities of Literature*, 1791
Dr Giles, in Dorothy Whitelock, *English Historical Documents, Vol. 1: A.D. 500–1042*, Oxford University Press, 1953
Economist, The, 'Liar's Privilege', 5 March 1988
Ekmann, Paul (pages 405 and 492), *Telling Lies*, Penguin Books Canada Ltd, 1985
Epictetus, *The Encheiridion*, trans. George Long, George Bell, 1877
Farrar, J. A., *Literary Forgeries*, Longmans Green & Co., 1907
Florence of Worcester, in Dorothy Whitelock, *English Historical Documents, Vol. 1: A.D. 500–1042*, Oxford University Press, 1953
Freeman, E. A., *History of the Norman Conquest*, 1869
Freud, Sigmund (page 269), *The Complete Psychological Works*, trans. and ed. James Strachey, 1976; (page 289), *Collected Papers*, trans. and ed. James Strachey, 1950
Froissart, *Chronicles*, trans. Geoffrey Brereton, Penguin, 1968
Gairdner, J., *Life of Richard III*, 1898
Gavshon, Arthur, and Rice, Desmond, *The Sinking of the Belgrano*, Secker & Warburg, 1984
Al-Ghazali, 'The Deliverance of Error', in W. Montgomery Watt, *The Faith and Practice of Al-Ghazali*, Allen & Unwin, 1953
Gisevius, Hans Bernd, *To the Bitter End*, Jonathan Cape, 1948
Gosse, Edmund, *Father and Son*, 1907
Gregorius, Ferdinand, *Lucrezia Borgia*, trans. J. L. Garner, John Murray, 1904
Grotius, Hugo, *On the Law of War and Peace*, trans. Francis W. Kelsey, Bobbs-Merrill & Co., New York, 1925

Hansard (page 352), Debate on the Supply of British News Abroad, 16 February 1938; (page 410), Personal Statement by the Minister of Defence, Mr John Profumo, 22 March 1963

Hazlitt, William, 'On Patronage and Puffing', in *Table Talk*, 1821–2

Helvetius, in *Sketches of Imposture, Deception and Credulity* (anon.), Thomas Tegg & Son, 1837

Henry VIII, *Letters*, ed. M. St Claire Byrne, Cassell, 1968

Herodotus, *Histories*, trans. Aubrey de Sélincourt, Penguin, 1954

Higgins, Andrew, 'The Triumph of the Lie', *Independent*, 27 December 1989

Hite, Shere, *The Hite Report*, Macmillan, 1976

Hitler, Adolf (page 327), *Mein Kampf*, trans. Ralph Manheim, Hutchinson, 1969; (page 323), *Mein Kampf*, Hurst & Blackwell, 1933; (page 359), speeches from *My New Order*, ed. and trans. de Sales, 1942

Holmes, Oliver Wendell, *The Autocrat of the Breakfast Table*, 1832

Huff, Darrell, *How to Lie with Statistics*, 1954; Penguin 1981

Huxley, Aldous, *The Devils of Loudun*, Chatto & Windus, 1952

Independent, The (page 532), 24 February 1990

Ingannevole, Bartholomaeus, in Sixto V, Papa, *Index Librorum Prohibitorum, Confectus et Publicatus: at Vero a Successoribus ejus in Sede Romana Suppressus*, ed. Josepho Mendham, 1835; editor's translation

Irving, Washington (pages 73 and 75), *A History of the Life and Voyages of Christopher Columbus*, 1828

Jacobs, Louis, *Jewish Values*, Valentine Mitchell, 1960

Johnson, Paul, *The Intellectuals*, Weidenfeld & Nicolson, 1988

Johnson, Samuel (page 163), *The Adventurer*, No. 50, 28 April 1753; (page 209), *Sermons*, 1812

Kant, Immanuel, *Critique of Practical Reason and Other Writings*, trans. Lewis White Beck, University of Chicago Press, 1949

Kingsmill, Hugh, *Frank Harris*, 1932; Biografia, 1987

Kipling, Rudyard, *France at War*, Macmillan, 1917

Koestler, Arthur, *The Invisible Writing*, Hutchinson, 1969

Lawrence, T. E., *Seven Pillars of Wisdom*, 1935; Penguin, 1983

Leigh, David, *The Wilson Plot*, Heinemann, 1988

Levitt, Morton and Michael (pages 386 and 388), *Tissue of Lies*, McGraw-Hill, New York, 1979

Linklater, Magnus, and Leigh, David, *Not With Honour. The Inside Story of the Westland Scandal*, Sphere, 1986

Lloyd George, Earl, *Lloyd George*, Muller, Blond and White, 1960

Loyola, Ignatius, 'Spiritual Exercises', in *Documents of the Christian Church*, ed. Henry Bettenson, Oxford University Press, 1949

Luther, Martin, in *Table Talk*, n.d.

Macaulay, Lord, *The History of England*, ed. Hugh Trevor-Roper, Penguin, 1986

Machiavelli, Niccolò (page 79), *The Prince*, trans. George Bull, Penguin, 1961; (page 81), *The Discourses*, trans. Leslie J. Walker, Penguin, 1970

Mandeville, Sir John, *Travels*, trans. C. W. R. D. Moseley, Penguin, 1983

Mencken, H. L., *Prejudices*, Fourth Series, Jonathan Cape, 1925

Meyers, Jeffrey, *Ernest Hemingway*, Macmillan, 1985
Milton, John, 'Of Duties to Our Neighbour', in *A Treatise on the Christian Doctrine*, trans. Charles Sumner, 1861
Montaigne, Michel de, *Essays*, trans. J. M. Cohen, Penguin, 1958
Montgomery Hyde, H., *Norman Birkett*, Hamish Hamilton, 1965
Newman, Cardinal, *Apologia Pro Vita Sua*, Longmans, 1880
Nietzsche, Friedrich, *The Anti-Christ*, trans. R. J. Hollingdale, Penguin, 1968
Nixon, Richard, text of his televised statement, in *The Times*, 22 May 1973
Notker the Stammerer, *Life of Charlemagne*, trans. Lewis Thorpe, Penguin, 1969
O'Connell, Daniel, in W. F. Monypenny and G. E. Buckle, *Life of Disraeli*
Orwell, George, *Inside the Whale and Other Essays*, 1940; Penguin, 1982
Paley, William, *Principles of Moral and Political Philosophy*, 1785
Pascal, Blaise (pages 115 and 117), *Provincial Letters*, trans. George Pearce, Longmans, 1846
Pepys, Samuel, Diaries, in *The Shorter Pepys*, ed. Ronald Latham, Penguin, 1985
Philby, Kim, *My Silent War*, 1968; Grafton Books, 1989
Pinkerton, J., *Walpoliana*, n.d.
Plato (page 17), *The Republic*, trans. Sir Desmond Lee, 1955, Penguin, 1987; (page 19), *The Republic*, trans. Benjamin Jowett, 1871
Plutarch, *Fall of the Roman Republic*, trans. Rex Warner, Penguin, 1958
Pollock, John, *The Popish Plot*, Duckworth, 1903
Porter, Henry, *Lies, Damned Lies, and a few Exclusives*, Chatto & Windus, 1984
Potter, Jeremy, *Good King Richard*, Constable, 1983
Private Eye, 'Rock Bottom: The Gibraltar Killings', February 1989
Procopius (pages 41 and 42), *The Secret History*, trans. G. A. Williamson, Penguin, 1966
Psellus, Michael, 'Chronographia', in *Fourteen Byzantine Rulers*, trans. E. R. A. Sewter, Penguin, 1966
Quintilian, *The Institutes*, trans. H. E. Butler, Heinemann, 1921
Rawlinson, Peter, *A Price Too High*, Weidenfeld & Nicolson, 1989
Reed, Graham, *The Psychology of Anomalous Experience*, Prometheus Books, New York, 1988
Ricks, Christopher, 'Lies', in *The Force of Poetry*, Oxford University Press, 1984
Rousseau, Jean Jacques (page 158), *Confessions*, trans. J. M. Cohen, Penguin, 1953; (page 176), *Reveries of the Solitary Walker*, trans. Peter France, Penguin, 1979
Ruskin, John, *Modern Painters*, 1859–60
Shaw, George Bernard, *Everybody's Political What's What*, Constable, 1944
Shawcross, William, *Sideshow*, Andre Deutsch, 1979
Speer, Albert, *Inside the Third Reich*, Weidenfeld & Nicolson, 1970
Steele, Sir Richard, *The Spectator*, No. 352, 14 April 1712
Stevenson, Frances, *Lloyd George. A Diary*, Hutchinson, 1971
Stevenson, R. L., 'Truth of Intercourse', from *Virginibus Puerisque*, 1881
Sturmer, Der, 'Jewish Ritual Murder', trans. and ed. Eva Maria Hood, *Christian Vanguard*, USA, 1976
Swedenborg, Emanuel, *Earths in the Universe*, 1758
Swift, Jonathan, 'The Art of Political Lying', in *The Examiner*, No. 51, n.d.
Symons, A. J. A., *The Quest for Corvo*, 1934; Penguin, 1980

Tacitus (pages 29 and 30), in Michael Grant, *The Annals of Imperial Rome*, Penguin, 1956
Taylor, Jeremy (pages 121 and 124), 'The Rule of Conscience', in *The Whole Works*, ed. R. Heber, 1922
Times, The, 'German Corpse Factory', 17 April 1917
Toynbee, Paget, and Whibley, Leonard, *The Correspondence of Thomas Gray*, Clarendon Press, Oxford, 1935
Trelawny, Edward J., *Adventures of a Younger Son*, 1831
Trevor-Roper, Hugh, *The Hidden Life of Sir Edmund Backhouse*, Penguin, 1978
Turnbull, Malcolm, *The Spycatcher Trial*, Heinemann, 1988
Tusa, Ann and John (pages 375 and 378), *The Nuremberg Trial*, Macmillan, 1983
Twain, Mark (page 275), *Speeches*; (page 314), *Collected Works*, University of California Press, 1967
Vincenzi, Penny, *The Compleat Liar*, Cassell, 1977
Voltaire, *Philosophical Dictionary*, trans. Theodore Besterman, Penguin, 1972
Walton, Izaak, *The Lives of John Donne . . . Robert Sanderson*, World's Classics, 1956
Warren, W. L., *King John*, Eyre & Spottiswoode, 1961
Wat, Aleksander, *My Century*, trans. Richard Lourie, University of California Press, 1988
Watts, Sarah Miles, and Tebbel, John, *The Press and the Presidency*, Oxford University Press, 1985
Wesley, John, A Sermon to the People of Bethnal Green (12 November), in *Sermons*, 1775
West, W. J., *Truth Betrayed*, Duckworth, 1987
Wiesenthal, Simon, *Justice Not Vengeance*, Weidenfeld & Nicolson, 1989
Wilde, Oscar, 'The Decay of Lying', from *The Nineteenth Century*, 1889
William of Malmesbury, *The Chronicle*, trans. J. A. Giles, 1876
Woods, Donald, *Biko*, Penguin, 1979
Xenophon, *The Persian Expedition*, trans. Rex Warner, Penguin, 1979
Youssopov, Prince, *How I Killed Rasputin*, Jonathan Cape, 1927
Zola, Emile, *J'accuse*, 1888; editor's translation

Acknowledgements

W. H. Allen & Co. plc (and Harper & Row, Publisher, Inc.), for *Bodyguard of Lies* by Anthony Cave-Brown. Copyright © 1975 by Anthony Cave-Brown; (and Simon & Schuster, Inc.) *Blind Ambition* by John Dean, copyright © 1976 by John W. Dean;

Barrie & Jenkins and Henry Holt and Company, Inc. for *Bury My Heart at Wounded Knee* by Dee Brown. Copyright © 1970 by Dee Brown;

Basic Books, Inc., Publishers, New York, for *Collected Papers*, Volume II, by Sigmund Freud. Authorized translation under the supervision of Joan Riviere. Published by arrangement with the Hogarth Press and the Institute of Psycho-Analysis, London;

Burns & Oates Ltd for *Summa Theologica* by Thomas Aquinas, trans. the Fathers of the English Dominican Province, Burns, Oates & Washbourne, London 1922;

The Catholic University of America Press for *Treatises on Various Subjects* by St Augustine, edited by R. J. Deferrari, Fathers of the Church, New York 1952;

Century Hutchinson Publishing Group (and Curtis Brown Ltd) for *The Harvest of Sorrow* by Robert Conquest, copyright © 1986 by Robert Conquest; (and Houghton Mifflin Company) for *Mein Kampf* by Adolf Hitler. Copyright 1943 and copyright © renewed 1971 by Houghton Mifflin Co.;

Owen Chadwick for *Mackenzie's Grave* by Owen Chadwick, Hodder & Stoughton, 1959;

Chatto & Windus Ltd (and Rogers, Coleridge & White Ltd) for *Lies, Damned Lies and a Few Exclusives* by Henry Porter, copyright © Henry Porter, 1984; (and Mrs Laura Huxley) for *The Devils of Loudun* by Aldous Huxley (Chatto & Windus, 1952);

Columbia University Press for *Medieval Handbooks of Penance* by J. McNeill and H. Garner, copyright © 1938 Columbia University Press, New York;

Constable Publishers for *Good King Richard* by J. Potter, 1983;

Dorset Press, a division of Marboro Books Corporation, for article in *Der Stürmer*, quoted in *Julius Streicher* by Randall L. Bytwerk, Dorset Press, by arrangement with Stein & Day, 1988;

Doubleday for *Seven Pillars of Wisdom* by T. E. Lawrence, copyright 1926, 1935 by Doubleday, a division of Bantam, Doubleday, Dell Publishing Group, Inc.;

Gerald Duckworth & Co. Ltd for *Truth Betrayed* by W. J. West, 1987;

The Economist for 'Liar's Privilege', © *The Economist*, 1988;

Eyre & Spottiswoode for *Disraeli* by Robert Blake;

Sigmund Freud Copyrights, The Institute of Psychoanalysis and the Hogarth Press for the standard edition of *The Complete Psychological Works of Sigmund Freud*, trans. and ed. James Strachey;

A. Gavshon and D. Rice for *The Sinking of the Belgrano* by A. Gavshon and D. Rice (Martin Secker & Warburg, 1984);

Grafton Books, a division of the Collins Publishing Group, (and Sterling Lord Literistic, Inc.), for *The Rise and fall of Oliver North* by Ben Bradlee, copyright © 1988 by Ben Bradlee Jnr; *My Silent War* by Kim Philby;

Hamish Hamilton Ltd for *Norman Birkett* by H. Montgomery-Hyde, copyright © H. Montgomery-Hyde, 1965;

Harvard Business Review for excerpts from 'Is Business Bluffing Ethical?' by Albert Z. Carr, Jan.–Feb. 1968. Copyright © 1968 by the President and Fellows of Harvard College; all rights reserved;

A. M. Heath & Co. Ltd, the estate of the late Sonia Brownell Orwell, Secker & Warburg and Harcourt Brace Jovanovich, Inc. for *Inside the Whale and Other Essays* by George Orwell;

William Heinemann Ltd (and Pantheon Books, a division of Random House, Inc.) for *The Wilson Plot* by David Leigh, copyright © 1988 by David Leigh;

David Higham Associates Ltd and Hutchinson for *Lloyd George, A Diary* by Frances Stevenson, edited by A. J. P. Taylor; *Voltaire's Philosophical Dictionary*, translated by Theodore Besterman;

Hodder & Stoughton and the author for *The KGB* by John Barron (Hodder & Stoughton, 1974);

The *Independent* for 'Terminological Inexactitudes' and 'The Triumph of the Lie';

McGraw-Hill Publishing Co. for *Tissue of Lies* by Morton and Michael Levitt (1979);

Macmillan for *Berlin Days* by George Clare; (and Harper & Row, Publisher, Inc.) *Hemingway, A Biography* by Jeffrey Meyers, copyright © 1985 by Jeffrey Meyers; (and Atheneum, a division of Macmillan Publishing Company, Inc.) *The Nuremburg Trial* by Ann and John Tusa, copyright © 1983 by John Tusa and Ann Tusa;

Macmillan Publishing Company (and the author) for *The Hite Report on Female Sexuality* by Shere Hite. Copyright © 1976 by Shere Hite; *Critique of Practical Reason and Other Writings* by Immanuel Kant, translated by Lewis White Beck. Copyright 1956 by the Bobbs-Merrill Company, renewal copyright © 1984 by Lewis White Beck; (and the author) *The Complete Liar* by Penny Vincenzi, copyright © 1977;

Methuen for *King John* by W. L. Warren, Eyre & Spottiswoode, 1961; *English Historical Documents*, Vol. 1, ed. Dorothy Whitelock;

W. W. Norton & Company, Inc. and Abner Stein for *Telling Lies, Clues to Deceit in the Marketplace, Politics and Marriage*, copyright © 1985 by Paul Ekmann;

Octagon Books, A Division of Hippocrene Books, Inc., for *My New Order* by Adolf Hitler, edited and translated by de Sales, 1942;

Octopus Publishing Group Australia for *The Spycatcher Trial* by Malcolm Turnbull, Heinemann 1988;

Oxford University Press for *Documents of the Christian Church* edited by Henry Bettenson, 1949; *The Force of Poetry* by Christopher Ricks, © Christopher Ricks, 1984; *The Correspondence of Thomas Grey* edited by Paget Toynbee and L. Whibley, 1935;

Oxford University Press, Inc. for *The Press and the Presidency: From George Washington to Ronald Reagan* by John Tebbel and Sarah Miles Watts. Copyright © 1985 by John Tebbel and Sarah Miles Watts (excerpt slightly adapted);

Pantheon Books, a division of Random House, Inc. for *Lying: Moral Choice in Public and Private Life* by Sissela Bok, copyright © 1978 by Sissela Bok;

Penguin Books Ltd for *The Autobiography of Benvenuto Cellini*, translated by George Bull (Penguin Classics, 1956), copyright © George Bull, 1956; *Selected Works* by Cicero, translated by Michael Grant (Penguin Classics, Revised Edition, 1960), copyright © Michael Grant, 1960, 1965, 1971; *On the Good Life* by Cicero, translated by Michael Grant (Penguin Classics, 1971), translation copyright © Michael Grant Publications Ltd, 1971; (and John Cornwell): *A Thief in the Night* by John Cornwell (Viking, 1989), copyright © John Cornwell, 1989; *Essays* by Michel de Montaigne, translated by J. M. Cohen (Penguin Classics, 1958), copyright © J. M. Cohen, 1958; *Chronicles* by Froissart, translated and edited by Geoffrey Brereton (Penguin Classics, 1968), copyright © Geoffrey Brereton, 1968; *The Histories* by Herodotus, translated by Aubrey de Sélincourt (Penguin Classics, 1954), copyright © the Estate of Aubrey de Sélincourt, 1954; *The Prince* by Niccolò Machiavelli, translated by George Bull (Penguin Classics, Revised Edition, 1981), copyright © George Bull, 1961, 1975, 1981; *The Discourses* by Niccolò Machiavelli, translated by Leslie J. Walker, S. J. (Penguin Classics, 1970), translation copyright © Leslie J. Walker, S. J., 1970; *The Travels of Sir John Mandeville* translated by C. W. R. D. Moseley (Penguin Classics, 1983), translation copyright © C. W. R. D. Moseley, 1983; *The Anti-Christ* by Friedrich Nietzsche, translated by R. J. Hollingdale (Penguin Classics, 1968), translation copyright © R. J. Hollingdale, 1968; *Two Lives of Charlemagne by Einhard and Notker the Stammerer*, translated by Lewis Thorpe (Penguin Classics, 1969), copyright © Lewis Thorpe, 1969; *The Republic* by Plato, translated by Desmond Lee (Penguin Classics, Second Edition, 1974), copyright © Desmond Lee, 1955, 1974; *Fall of the Roman Republic* by Plutarch, translated by Rex Warner (Penguin Classics, 1958), copyright © Rex Warner, 1958; *The Secret History* by Procopius, translated by G. A. Williamson (Penguin Classics, 1966), copyright © G. A. Williamson, 1966; *Fourteen Byzantine Rulers* by Michael Psellus, translated by E. R. A. Sewter (Penguin Classics, 1966), copyright © the Estate of E. R. A. Sewter, 1966; *The Confessions* by Jean-Jacques Rousseau, translated by J. M. Cohen (Penguin Classics, 1954), copyright © J. M. Cohen, 1954; *Reveries of the Solitary Walker* by Jean-Jacques Rousseau, translated by Peter France (Penguin Classics, 1979), copyright © Peter France, 1979; *The Annals of Imperial Rome* by Tacitus, translated by Michael Grant (Penguin Classics, Revised Edition, 1971), copyright © Michael Grant Publications Ltd, 1956, 1959, 1971; (and Henry Holt and Company, Inc.) *Biko* by Donald Woods (Penguin Books, Revised Edition, 1987), copyright © Donald Woods, 1978, 1987; *The Persian Expedition* by Xenophon, translated by Rex Warner (Penguin Classics, 1949), copyright © Rex Warner, 1949; *The Quest for Corvo: An Experiment in Biography* by A. J. A. Symons (Penguin Books, 1940), copyright © A. J. A. Symons, 1934;

The Peters Fraser & Dunlop Group Ltd for *The Invisible Writing* by Arthur Koestler; *A Hidden Life; The Life of Sir Edmund Backhouse* by Hugh Trevor-Roper;

Laurence Pollinger Ltd and the Watkins/Loomis Agency, Inc. for *How to Lie with Statistics* by Darrell Huff, Victor Gollancz Ltd and W. W. Norton, Inc., 1954;

Private Eye for 'Rock Bottom: The Gibraltar Killings';

Prometheus Books, Buffalo, N. Y. for *The Psychology of Anomalous Experience; A Cognitive Approach* (revised edition) by Graham Reed. Copyright © 1988 by Graham Reed;

Charles Scribner's Sons, an imprint of Macmillan Publishing Company, for *By-Line* by Ernest Hemingway, edited by William White. Copyright 1938 by Ken, Inc. and Ernest Hemingway; renewal copyright © 1966 by Mary Hemingway;

Simon & Schuster, Inc. and Elaine Greene Ltd for *Sideshow* by William Shawcross; copyright © William Shawcross 1979, 1981, 1986, 1987;

Society of Authors for *Everybody's Political What's What* by George Bernard Shaw (Constable, 1944);

Sphere Books for *Not With Honour. The Inside Story of the Westland Scandal* by M. Linklater and D. Leigh, 1986;

Unwin Hyman Ltd (and the John A. Ware Literary Agency) for *Eisenhower the President*, Vol. 2 1952–1969 by S. E. Ambrose; copyright © 1984 by Stephen E. Ambrose, published by Simon & Schuster 1984, Touchstone Books 1985; *The Nichomachean Ethics* by Aristotle, translated by J. A. K. Thomson; *The Faith and Practice of Al-Ghazali* by W. Montgomery Watt, Allen & Unwin 1953;

The University of California Press for *My Century: Memoirs of a Polish Revolutionist* by Aleksander Wat, trans. and ed. by Richard Lourie, copyright © 1988 The Regents of the University of California;

Vallentine Mitchell & Co. Ltd for *The Book of Jewish Values* by Louis Jacobs, 1960;

George Weidenfeld and Nicolson Ltd for *The Intellectuals* by Paul Johnson; *A Price Too High* by Sir Peter Rawlinson; *Justice not Vengeance* by Simon Weisenthal.

Every effort has been made to trace copyright holders. The publishers would be interested to hear from any copyright holders not here acknowledged.